John W. Sul

3 3 3 7 E. 45 St.

Tulsa, OK. 74135

August 5, 1989

Feminism and Freedom

Feminism and Freedom

Michael Levin

Transaction Books
New Brunswick (USA) and Oxford (UK)

Second Printing, 1988
Copyright (c) 1987 by Transaction Publishers, New Brunswick, New Jersey
08903

Library of Congress Catalog Number: 87-5955
ISBN 0-88738-125-1 (cloth); 0-88738-670-9 (paper)
Printed in the United States of America

Library of Congress Cataloging in Publication Data

Levin, Michael E.
    Feminism and freedom.

    Bibliography: p.
    Includes index.
    1. Feminism—United States. 2. Sex differences (Psychology). 3. Liberty.
I. Title.
HQ1426.L477 1987 305.4'2 87-5955
ISBN 0-88738-125-1
ISBN 0-88738-670-9 (pbk.)

For Mark and Eric . . .

Agesilaus was exceedingly fond of his children; and it is to him that the story belongs, that when they were little ones, he used to make a horse of a stick, and ride with them; and being caught at this sport by a friend, he desired him not to mention it till he himself were the father of children.

—Plutarch, *Life of Agesilaus*

Contents

Preface ix
Acknowledgments xi

1. Overview 1
2. What is Feminism? 16
3. Innateness 55
4. Sex Differences 70
5. Affirmative Action 98
6. Comparable Worth 131
7. Education: The Lower Grades 156
8. Education: The Universities 173
9. Feminism, Education, and the State 192
10. Sports 208
11. The Forces of Order 222
12. Language 250
13. Sex, the Family, and the Liberal Order 264
14. Feminism and the Future 297

Bibliography 307
Index 324

Preface

The reader should bear in mind that there is always a stretch of time between the completion of a manuscript and its appearance as a book. Any book dealing with public policy and the prevalence of ideas in society is inevitably a snapshot of the culture as it was, say, a year before. For instance, by the time the reader has this book in his hands, many of the legal questions treated as open will have been resolved by the courts. (Thus, in late February the Supreme Court ruled that pornography is not discrimination against women.) Public policy may have mutated. By the same token, some of the scientific studies cited may have been superseded or—very occasionally, when they hinge on statistical inference—called into question. However, I do not expect my major conclusions to be invalidated or the larger issues dealt with to go away.

The reader may be put off by the relentlessness of my argument. Surely no body of ideas is wrong about *everything,* as I imply feminism is. Yet while feminism may have accomplished some good *per accidens,* I would no more pander to the reader by straining to praise rape crisis centers than I would strain to praise the punctuality of trains under Mussolini were I discussing fascism. Any theory whose basic assumption about human nature is completely erroneous—as I argue is the case with feminism—is indeed bound to be wrong about everything else. I have felt compelled by my conscience to present feminism as I see it.

Steven Goldberg wrote *The Inevitability of Patriarchy* (a book which also defends the social determinativeness of innate sex differences) with one type of unsympathetic reader in mind, the reader who is credulous toward environmentalism and hypercritical toward nativism. I have written this book with a different type of unsympathetic reader in mind, the one who concedes the absurdity of pure environmentalism but is sure that only "radical" feminists are pure environmentalists and that, in addition, nobody listens to these "radicals." Since it is a principal thesis of this book that feminism in all its forms and through all its doctrinal mutations is essentially environmentalistic and that it is precisely this environmentalism that has influenced public policy and public orthodoxy, I have had to assemble a large group of citations to document the persistence and influence of environmentalism. I regret having had to deform my exposition to accommodate my unsympathetic reader.

I should also add that, where Goldberg and others speak of innate "drives" and "emotions," I generally talk of innate *preferences*. I trust that this usage will help to break down a false opposition between liberal values and "biological determinism." Man is never freer than when he is acting on his biologically determined preferences. Construed behaviorally, an organism prefers one alternative to another if it tries harder to get the one than the other. In addition to construing preference as essentially pairwise, I assume as well that an organism's preferences tend to be instantaneously transitive (if it prefers A to B and B to C, it prefers A to C) and roughly asymmetrical over time (if at one time it prefers A to B, it will not soon after prefer B to A). Transitivity is needed for defining rational preference orderings for individuals, and asymmetry may be needed to generate stable social institutions from individual preference orderings.

The reader may be puzzled, as I myself have sometimes been, that a philosopher should devote several years of his finite existence to feminism, when he could be thinking about the problem of induction or a hundred other intrinsically more interesting topics. I could plead a sense of obligation: *Somebody* had to say the things I say in this book. I could mention that what made me a philosopher in the first place was impatience with ignorance and irrationality, salient traits of feminist writing. But these explanations would be post hoc. I do not think anybody really knows the sources of his own deepest concerns; that is a task for biography, not autobiography. In the end, authors do not choose their topics; they choose him.

New York City
May 1986

Acknowledgments

Parts of some previous essays appear in the present book: "Feminism and Thought Control," *Commentary* (June 1982); "Comparable Worth: The Feminist Road to Socialism," *Commentary* (September 1984); "Feminism, Stage Three," *Commentary* (August 1986); "Women in the Military: The Record So Far," *Public Interest* (Summer 1984); and "Women's Studies: Ersatz Scholarship," *New Perspectives* (Summer 1985).

The encouragement, advice, and (sometimes without their knowing it) ideas of many people contributed to this book. My thanks to Scott Kuehl, George Gilder, Steven Goldberg, Phyllis Schlafly, Mary Jo Bohr, Diane Ravitch, Midge Decter, Robert Gordon, Linda Gottfredson, Onalee McGraw, Geoffrey Partington, Neal Kozodoy, Mack Owen, Howard Dickman, Leslie Lenkowski, Angelo Aiosa, Tom Main, William Hammett, Gabriel Möens, Todd Lindberg, Theron Raines, Duncan Anderson, Diane McGuiness, Morris Silver, Joan Taylor, Paul Vitz, Jackie Butler, Pat Williams, David Asman, and Michael Aronson. I also wish to thank the members of the military, police, and intelligence communities who aided me with the understanding that their names would not be used. Special thanks to Babette Francis for deepening my understanding of the issues I discuss.

My deepest debt by far is to my wife Margarita, with whom I discussed every idea in this book. The balance and clarity of her judgement were a necessary counterweight to my own enthusiasms. Having in the past taught me much about philosophy and the foundations of mathematics, she taught me detachment toward an emotionally charged subject—no easy tutelage, with two small sons and her own dissertation in progress to worry about.

The general level of rigor at which I aim owes much to the prodding of Chris Boorse, whose stern criticism showed me the inadequacy of previous drafts.

1

Overview

When the eighty-eight women who took the New York City Fire Department's entrance examination in 1977 failed its physical strength component, they filed a class-action sex discrimination lawsuit in federal court. The court found for the plaintiffs, agreeing in *Berkman v. NYFD* that the strength test was not job-related and therefore in violation of Title VII of the Civil Rights Act.[1] The court thereupon ordered the city to hire forty-five female firefighters and to construct a special, less demanding physical examination for female candidates, with males still to be held to the extant, more difficult—and ostensibly inappropriate—standard. In addition, the court ordered the city to provide special training to the eighty-eight female plaintiffs—but none for the 54 percent of the males who also failed the test—on the grounds that certain "tricks of the trade" available to all male candidates were not available to them.

New York declined to appeal *Berkman* and instructed its regular firemen to maintain public silence. Since *Berkman,* 38 of the original group of 145 women given special training by the NYFD have entered service as firefighters, and almost all personnel actions taken by the NYFD have required the approval of the presiding judge, Charles Sifton. Continuing litigation has resulted in further easing of the physical standards applied to female firefighting applicants.

The use of statistics in *Berkman* is particularly instructive. According to the guidelines of the Equal Employment Opportunity Commission, which are controlling in cases like *Berkman,* a test for a job is presumed to be discriminatory if the passing rate for women is less than 80 percent of that rate for men. The wider the gap, the less defeasible is the presumption. The court accordingly asked how likely it would be, in the absence of discrimination, that none of the eighty-eight women passed while 46 percent of the men did. As the court correctly noted, "the pass rates were separated by more than eight standard deviations" (1982 at 205), and the probability that this could happen is so small—less than one in 10 trillion—as to amount to virtual impossibility. The court's conclusion that discrimination must have occurred is entirely cogent, *if strength is assumed to be uncorrelated with sex.* A difference in failure rates on a strength test is consistent with the

1

absence of bias if it is allowed that men are on average stronger than women. The court found an outcome of fewer than thirty-seven passes unacceptably improbable because it adopted the hypothesis that gender and strength are independent variables. Rejecting the hypothesis that gender and strength are in any way connected, the court construed an observed correlation between gender and strength as an artifact to be eliminated by special treatment for one sex. Since women are the same as men, the EEOC and the court reasoned, special steps must be taken to compensate for their manifest differences.

Public reaction to *Berkman* varied. The local tabloids treated it as a joke ("Firebelles!" headlined one), while the more serious press took it, in the words of one slick magazine, as a matter of "opening the doors for women." Other commentators drew attention to the decision's conflict with common sense, public safety, the judgement of the public officials closest to the matter at hand, and the undoubted preferences of the majority. It remained for the Special Counsel for the New York City Commission on the Status of Women to draw the most appropriate connection: The NYFD's latest employees "would never have had the chance to show what [they] could do . . . were it not for the efforts of the feminists and 'women's libbers.' "[2] That is so: Were it not for the ascendancy of feminist ideas, the hypothesis that strength varies randomly with sex would have been unthinkable as the basis for a finding of fact and a guide for policy.

Berkman illustrates as well the extent to which feminism has achieved its effects through the state, particularly unelected officials of the courts and the regulatory agencies, and those elected officials most remote from their constituencies. Gender quotas, limitations on free speech to combat "psychological damage to women" (to cite EEOC guidelines once again), among many other feminist innovations, are all state actions. What is more, the vagueness of such feminist-inspired initiatives as have been passed by elected officials—chiefly civil rights legislation governing gender, and the Equal Rights Amendments of various states—require that they be constantly interpreted, usually by unelected officials.

This, in short, is the thesis of the present book: It is not by accident that feminism has had its major impact through the necessarily coercive machinery of the state rather than through the private decisions of individuals. Although feminism speaks the language of liberation, self-fulfillment, options, and the removal of barriers, these phrases invariably mean their opposites and disguise an agenda at variance with the ideals of a free society. Feminism has been presented and widely received as a liberating force, a new view of the relations between the sexes emphasizing openness and freedom from oppressive stereotypes. The burden of the present book is to show in broad theoretical perspective and factual detail that this conventional wisdom is mistaken. Feminism is an antidemocratic, if not totalitarian, ideology.

Feminism is a program for making different beings—men and women—turn out alike, and like that other egalitarian, Procrustes, it must do a good deal of chopping to fit the real world into its ideal. More precisely, feminism is the thesis that males and females are already innately alike, with the current order of things—in which males and females appear to differ and occupy quite different social roles—being a harmful distortion of this fundamental similarity. Recognizing no innate gender differences that might explain observed gender differences and the broad structure of society, feminists are compelled to interpret these manifest differences as artifacts, judged by feminists to benefit men unfairly. Believing that overtly uncoerced behavior is the product of oppression, feminists must devise ever subtler theories about the social pressures "keeping women in their place"—pressures to be detected and cancelled.

The reader may feel an impulse to object that I am talking about radical feminism while ignoring moderate feminism, a more responsible position which concedes innate sex differences and wishes only to correct wrongs undeniably done to women. For now I refer the reader to the review of feminist literature in the following chapter, which shows, I believe definitively, that complete environmentalism—the denial that innate sex differences have anything to do with the broad structure of society—is central to feminism, and that moderate feminism is a chimera. But even the reader wishing to distinguish moderate from radical feminism must concede that *Berkman* is radical by any standards, and that if radical feminism is sufficiently influential to sway the federal judiciary, its credentials and implications deserve close scrutiny.

The second major contention of this book complements the first. If, as I argue in chapters 3 and 4, those broad features of society attributed by feminism to discriminatory socialization are in fact produced by innate gender differences, efforts to eradicate those features must be futile and neverending. Reforms designed to end when sexism disappears will have to be retained indefinitely, imposing increasingly heavy costs on their nonmalleable subjects. Since innate gender differences express themselves as differences in the typical preferences of men and women, so that people will never freely act in ways which produce a world devoid of sexism, the equalization of the sexes in personal behavior and in the work world demands implacable surveillance and interference. In the end it is impossible to overcome the biological inevitability of sex roles, but it is possible to try—and to violate liberal values in the process. A good summary of my main thesis might run: equality of outcome entails inequality of opportunity.

Akin to the idea that radical feminism exaggerates a more tenable moderate position is the idea that, whatever its exaggerations, the radical feminism that emerged in the 1960s was a response to genuine injustices. This claim collapses under the demand for a specification of these injustices. The denial of the vote to women and long-void laws against the possession of property by women are patently irrelevant, since the issue raised here is the character of *contemporary* society. Indeed, it is a serious distortion of history to view the suffragettes of a century ago as forerunners of today's feminists. In addition to being concerned with well-defined legal reforms, nineteenth-century feminists were if anything more convinced than anyone is today not only of innate sex differences, but of the innate superiority of women. The old feminists hoped that greater female participation in public life would raise the moral tone of society, and, in particular, by reducing drunkenness and allowing a woman to be more confident of a sober husband's income, make it easier for her to stay home and raise her children. (The suffragettes were a major force behind the prohibition movement.) Contemporary feminism, by contrast, is best viewed as an extension of the racial civil rights movement, which emphasizes the similarity of populations.

Feminists themselves are strikingly ready to dismiss as superficial the reforms won by their nineteenth-century predecessors. Kate Millett admits that "the male's *de jure* property has recently been modified through the granting of divorce, protection, citizenship, and property to women. [However,] their chattel status continues."[3] She goes on to chide early feminist "concentration on suffrage" for "its failure to challenge patriarchal ideology at a sufficiently deep and radical level." Despite the propensity of feminists and their commentators to frame issues in terms of the "politics" of women's status, legal reform is of interest to most feminists mainly as an instrument for working wholesale changes on society. Indifference to legal reform is in any case forced on feminists by the absence of anything to reform. Private discrimination against women has been illegal since 1964, and public discrimination at the state and municipal levels has been illegal since 1972. When at the behest of President Ronald Reagan the State of Georgia reviewed its statutes for possible discrimination, it reported that the most serious inequity in the state code was the occurrence of 10,000 "he's" as against 150 "she's." Popular discourse continues to allude to "much outright sex discrimination,"[4] but the examples of discrimination cited invariably concern the use of criteria in various activities that men are more likely to meet. Without some showing that these criteria are deployed *for the purpose* of excluding women, or that the discrepant effects of these criteria are *caused by* arbitrary socialization, these effects are not "discriminatory." The actual state of affairs is well illustrated by *Berkman:* extensive institutionalized preference favoring women over men. Feminists who explain their grievance in terms of laws against women driving buses may have a legitimate case, but it is one against Edwardian England, not a society in which female bus drivers are promoted over males with greater seniority.

To be sure, the claim that women do not yet enjoy equal opportunity is most frequently made not in connection with legal barriers but in terms of the tendency of people to think sex-stereotypically and to communicate sex-typed norms to the young. This claim will be considered in due course, but it suffices for now to reflect that, if the formation of stereotypic beliefs is a spontaneous response to perceptions of the world, altering these possibly oppressive beliefs will require manipulation of both the average person's spontaneous tendency to form beliefs and the social environment which prompts them. If the social environment is itself a spontaneous expression of innate sex differences, attempting (and inevitably failing) to alter this environment will require yet further intrusion.

Shifting the locus of unfairness from the realm of law to that of sex role stereotyping involves a shift from what can reasonably be called "political" to the entire range of extra-political institutions and behavior. Most of society's institutions emerge from the myriad uncoordinated decisions of individuals; to call these practices and institutions "political" suggests a disregard for the distinction between public and private and disdain for the private realm itself. It is not surprising that feminists who use the word "political" so expansively also speak as if they believe in an actual world-wide conspiracy against women.[5] Once this usage is adopted, everything from office flirtation to children's horseplay becomes assessable for its tendency to abet the political decision about women's condition. Erstwhile private matters become questions of socially determined rights, and are pulled within the authority of the state.

To deny that women are victims of systematic discrimination is not to assert that contemporary Western civilization is perfect. Like every society it has its problems, some of them affecting women in distinctive ways. Yet feminism cannot be seen as a response to these problems, for its perspective distorts even legitimate concerns beyond recognition. Feminists object to pornography, for instance, but not on the grounds that it coarsens relations between the sexes, but because it is alleged to be one more patriarchal mechanism for controlling women:

> Pornography is the holy corpus of men who would rather die than change. Dachau brought into the bedroom and celebrated, every vile prison or dungeon brought into the bedroom and celebrated, police torture and thug mentality brought into the bedroom and celebrated—men reveal themselves and all that matters to them in these depictions of real history, plasticized and

rarefied, represented as the common erotic stuff of male desire. . . . Pornography reveals that male pleasure is inextricably tied to victimizing. . . . It is in the male experience of pleasure that one finds the meaning of male history.[6]

If pornography is a tool of oppression, it cannot be protected speech: "The First Amendment protects only those who can exercise the rights it protects [and pornography is] trade in a class of persons who have been systematically denied the rights protected by the First Amendment."[7] Catherine MacKinnon argues in a similar vein that since "silence . . . has been women's sexuality under conditions of subordination by and to men,"[8] the First Amendment itself is no more than a tool of the ruling sex.

Rape, another legitimate concern, is diagnosed similarly as, in Susan Brownmiller's words, "a conscious process of fear and intimidation by which *all men* keep *all women* in a state of fear."[9] For Catherine MacKinnon, "it is difficult to avoid the conclusion that penetration itself is known to be a violation."[10] Robin Morgan is only one of a great many feminists who define rape as any act of intercourse not initiated by a woman.[11]

These contentions do not so much analyze rape and pornography, or emphasize previously unrecognized aspects of these phenomena, as caricature them to fit them into a general case against the "patriarchal" dominance of men in society. The assumption that it is partriarchy in this sense that offends feminists, rather than any specific social ill, also explains their conflation of the position of women in Western democracies with that of women elsewhere, and the proneness of feminists to trivialize the sometimes brutal treatment of women in parts of the non-Western world on the infrequent occasions when it is mentioned at all.[12] One finds equal indifference to the special difficulties facing women in the Eastern Bloc. During the 1970s, American feminists initially paid a measure of attention to Club Maria, a small group of Soviet women who called themselves feminists. This attention declined as Club Maria made clear that it sought to restore respect for motherhood in the Soviet Union and to relieve women from the burden of doing men's work. Western feminists lodged few protests when Maria's founder was sentenced to four years at hard labor for "slandering the Soviet State."

In trying to discern those legitimate grievances said to be responsible for feminism, it is useful to ask what empirical evidence of widespread female unhappiness was offered in the initial feminist works. Benjamin Barber has said that by the end of the post–World War II period the situation of "real women" had become "painful, frustrating, inequitable, unfair."[13] Why?

> It is a problem of injustice, discrimination and inequality at a level of mundanity. . . . Housewives are committing suicide. That is the problem. Educated women cannot find jobs. That is the problem. The physical and psychological demands of having babies can no longer occupy a lifetime. That is the

problem. Marriages that once had to survive only (say) twenty years in a stable society are now supposed to last (say) fifty in an unstable society.[14]

Again, I do not deny that Barber is pointing to some real problems, particularly the failure of evolution to prepare human beings for the boredom of a life in which material needs are easily met. Still, while longevity and low infant mortality rates may in this sense be misfortunes, they cannot be called inequities (unless women find long-lasting marriages less satisfying than men do). Barber's one substantial claim, his reference to suicide, is without foundation. For the last several decades, the suicide rate among American males has been more than three times that for American females.[15] Indeed, women in Western society are better off than men by every objective measure of well-being. Women live longer, enjoy better health, are less prone to insanity, alcoholism, drug abuse, and crime. The female felony rate is about 5 percent of the male rate. Perhaps these variables do not really indicate well-being, but it is by such indices that racial minorities—to which women are so frequently compared—are judged to lead less satisfying lives than Whites.

In *The Feminine Mystique*,[16] the book to which contemporary feminism is usually traced, Betty Friedan offered two pieces of factual evidence to sustain her discovery of "the disease with no name," the malaise of the suburban housewife. One was the increased female enrollment in night school courses offered by colleges. Friedan supplied no statistics to support the existence of this trend, which is in any case susceptible of numerous interpretations besides female discontent. Her second datum was the high consumption of tranquilizers by American women. Again Friedan offered no figures, nor could she have, since pharmaceutical companies kept no aggregated statistics for the production of psychotherapeutic drugs in the late 1950s, the period about which she was writing. There were 27.7 million prescriptions written for Diazepam in 1982,[17] none containing more than the sixty pills permitted by FDA regulations. Since females over the age of nineteen account for just under 50 percent of drug usage in the United States,[18] adult American women may be assumed to have taken at most 800 million tranquilizers in 1982. I do not know whether this constitues an epidemic, but since drug usage has generally followed population growth,[19] and the U.S. population grew by more than 15 percent between the late 1950s and 1982, the figure of billions—widely used by Friedan and her contemporaries for yearly tranquilizer consumption by American females during the 1950s—is almost certainly imaginary. The sweeping claims Friedan built on her supposed data—claims which themselves became the factual basis for yet more sweeping indictments of American society—were baseless.

If Friedan's facts are best compared to phony war-time atrocity stories, further psychological data completely dispel the notion that contemporary American females are psychologically disordered. Little girls are clear on sex differences—like little boys, little girls agree that girls cry more and that boys fight and throw things[20]—and by early elementary school boys and girls have sex-typed jobs similarly.[21] However, each sex thinks its own kind is superior: Boys think boys are smarter, quieter, braver, kinder, and have more fun, which is precisely what girls think of girls.[22] Kohlberg reports studies showing that children from ages five to fourteen believe their own sex to be best.[23] Most research on preferences and sex stereo-types suggests that both males and females support these stereotypes.[24] Such support may be deemed morally undesirable, but in point of firm pos-session of a sense of gender, little girls are as psychologically healthy as boys and not at all submissively resigned to second-class citizenship and lower status.

The reader may be anxious to inform me of cases known to him of a competent woman being denied a desirable position just because she is a woman. I do not deny that such cases exist, but I ask the reader to remember three points. First, no accumulation of anecdotes can demon-strate an intrinsic societal bias against women. Second, a social arrange-ment can do no more than treat people better than other possible arrange-ments; perfect justice is unattainable. Third, the wrongs with which the reader is acquainted must be kept in perspective. Can being denied a mer-ited promotion honestly be compared to being beaten for drinking from a Whites-only fountain, the sort of treatment Blacks experienced two genera-tions ago?

A sense of history is too often absent from discussions of the relative positions of men and women in contemporary society. Women in past eras suffered indignities that would be considered intolerable today, but so did most men. If women did not vote until the twentieth century, it must be recalled that *nobody* voted prior to the eighteenth. Far older than the fran-chise and the notion of universal rights is the idea that men must protect women, a duty in whose service men have endured enormous hardships. If sex roles are to be regarded as the outcome of bargaining in which men received dominance in exchange for the risk of violent death, it is hardly clear that they got the better deal.

As groundless as the idea that feminism is a movement of liberal reform is the idea that it is passé. The immoderate language of twenty years ago is encountered less frequently today, but no doctrine is more influential in shaping institutional and public life than feminism. Under current federal law, a prospective employer is forbidden to ask a female job applicant if she plans to have children. The Supreme Court has outlawed pension plans that use the greater longevity of women as a factor in computing premiums.[25] Public speakers can no longer use "he" or "man" comfortably. Critics reflexively apologize before praising books, movies, or ideas that might displease feminists. Newspaper reports on menstrual disorders note that feminists do not like the idea that there are such things, as if nature were obliged not to mark sex distinctions, or as if citing facts at odds with feminism were intrinsically presumptuous. The navy retains the present design for the cockpits of its combat aircraft because women have difficulty fitting into the new, more efficient designs—even though women are presently barred from flying such aircraft.

Political leaders of every persuasion reflexively employ gender quotas. The liberal governor of New York State reprimanded a selection committee for not including a female among its candidates for the state's Supreme Court while simultaneously praising all the candidates as "first-rate." A conservative president highly critical of quotas as a private citizen decided that his first Supreme Court appointment had to be a woman. As we will see in chapter 5, the quota mentality now dominates all phases of employment.

We will also see, in considerable detail, the extent of feminist censorship of schoolbooks and judicial control of private association. The courts have involved themselves in university tenure decisions involving women, and have heavily penalized organizations for failing to pay women what the courts deem they deserve. I have confirmed in correspondence with the responsible executives that the national television networks instruct their writers to include nontraditional women in every script. (That they do so is in any case evident from the casting of network television programs.) The advertising industry has plainly adopted similar protocols: An advertisement for New York Life Insurance shows the "1981 woman," attaché case in hand, boarding a helicopter while her children are left "to the sharing concern of her husband." The director of the Project on the Status and Education of Women, funded by the Ford Foundation and Carnegie Corporation, boasts that "the most comprehensive national policy in the world regarding discrimination against women and girls in the schoolroom is now in place. . . . [I]t is unlikely that Congress would ever overturn the legislation."[26] The National Education Association advocates the pursuit of "psychological androgyny" as far as is "consistent with democracy."

The popular press continues to suggest that wanting to marry and raise children is a curious goal for a woman. It is becoming somewhat more acceptable for a woman to find parenting important, but it is still unacceptable to assert that it is more important for a woman than for a man. Typical of this genre is an article entitled "What Does a Woman Need? Not to Depend on a Man," which appeared in *People*,[27] a periodical widely thought to be devoid of ideological content. In this article, a psychologist advises that 95 percent of all women are "desperately dependent" on men and that a too-devoted wife is apt to lose her husband to a mistress. *Parents,* another ostensibly conventional publication, runs a bulletin entitled "Are Parents Sexist?" They are, it turns out, especially fathers and *Parents* instructs working women consciously to emulate the "ruthlessness" of men.[28]

The support given by the Ford Foundation to the Project on the Status and Education of Women is not an isolated phenomenon. The major philanthropic foundations are guided by, and in turn help to finance, feminist ideas. Between December 1983 and February 1984, the Ford Foundation announced grants totaling $900,000 for "women's rights," including $330,000 to the Women's Equity Action League to "focus more attention on the access of women to jobs and promotion opportunities in the military," $45,000 to the National Committee on Pay Equity, $200,000 to the Ms Foundation for Women, and $150,000 to the Feminist Press.[29] Between October and December 1985, the Ford Foundation contributed $750,000 toward "women's rights," including $15,000 in travel funds for "the Third Latin American and Caribbean Feminist Encounter in Brazil."[30]

Looking beyond the United States, feminists in other Western countries have advocated and in some cases realized proposals more extreme than any advanced by their American counterparts. In France, the Mitterrand government passed a law forbidding the proportion of male candidates in local elections to exceed 70 percent.[31] A report by Canada's governmentally chartered Institute for Research on Public Policy recommends the legal imposition of female employment quotas on any firm which installs a computer, on the gounds that computers will generate an economy which prizes technical skills more likely to be developed by men.[32] Eileen Byrne, current occupant of the Chair of Policy Studies at the University of Queensland and a regular consultant to the Australian government, suggests halting the development of computer technology altogether until "social reconstruction" gives women an access to technology equal to men's.[33] (To the charge of Ludditism, Byrne relies: "The Luddites are a much misunderstood phenomenon."[34])

Anyone doubting the influence of feminism might recall that over 400 delegates to the 1984 National Convention of the Democratic Party belonged to the National Organization for Women, perhaps the paradigm feminist organization.[35] He might also recall the feminist domination, in terms of participants and agenda, of the 1985 Nairobi Conference marking the end of the United Nations Decade for Women.[36] Should feminism seem passé, this is almost certainly because it has attained presuppositional status. That women have been and remain systematically mistreated; that gender differences should be minimized to the very exaggerated extent to which they exist at all; that women need work outside the home; that, more generally, the elements of a satisfying life are essentially the same for men and women; that, above all, it is a very bad thing for any activity to be identified as distinctively masculine—these are items of intellectual baggage everyone now carries around, too commonplace to warrant explicit statement. The decline of utopian fantasy is a tribute to Peguy's aphorism that everything begins in feeling and ends in politics.

If not conviction, then at least assent is expected for feminist pieties. Ronald Reagan caused an uproar by casually remarking that if it were not for women, "men would still be in skin suits." Since he was praising women, the scandal must have been his implicit differentiation of the natural impulses of men and women. To cite an incident witnessed by this author, I happened not long ago to be present when a department store salesman was demonstrating an appliance called Ice Cream Boy. A woman in the crowd asked why it was not called Ice Cream *Girl.* As a murmur of disapproval at the choice of the word *boy* ran through the crowd, the salesman apologetically suggested that Ice Cream Girl might imply, unsuitably, that females should be in the kitchen. Well, suggested a third party with a third nervous chuckle, why not Ice Cream Child? A murmur of satisfaction from the crowd closed the topic. Wishing to probe further, I remarked to the woman who had initiated the exchange that feminism can impel one to unusual behavior. "It certainly can," she agreed, "but it doesn't have to if you don't let it." Nobody in that crowd cared what the ice cream maker was called, but each thought that the others cared and feared being found wanting in zeal.

Gender differences will emerge in any human social organization. Since every human activity is either the province of one sex or a joint endeavor of both in which these differences manifest themselves, it is possible to find sexism everywhere. While in that sense feminism conflicts with every human activity, the present book concentrates on the conflict between feminism and those institutions central to a free society. Among the most important are the free market and education. The only way to stifle, or try to stifle, the manifestation of gender differences in people's working lives is through a rigid program of job quotas and pay scales, matters considered in chapters 5 and 6. The only way to stifle, or try to stifle, the manifestation of gender differences in children's perceptions of each other is through a rigid program of exhorting them to disregard their senses, matters considered in chapters 7 through 9.

Free societies like all others must use force to preserve order; the primary institutions by which they do so are the police and the military. The maintenance of order has always been a male function, as have similar functions with similar requirements of strength and audacity, like firefighting. Chapter 11 examines the effects of feminist ideas of equality on these institutions. The remaining chapters concern institutions whose connection with democracy is less direct, but which illustrate the dialectic of feminism in unusually pure form. In the final chapter I speculate, somewhat tentatively, about the psychological origins of feminism, the mutations feminist ideology is likely to undergo in the foreseeable future, and the reasons for the receptiveness of contemporary culture to feminism.

Because feminism is regularly called the "women's movement," any criticism of feminism is apt to be viewed as an attack on women. It is a measure of the ability of slogans to paralyze thought that any writer should have to explicitly disavow the patent absurdity that men are better than women, but I shall enter one such disavowal here.[37] Men are not better than women and women are not better than men; men and women differ. Feminists may describe their opponents as those who think that "men are better than women," but it is not clear who in Western society holds such a view or what it might mean. "Better" is ill-defined in isolation—one thing being better than another only in some specific respect. To say, as the evidence suggests, that men are better than women at mathematics while women are better than men at caring for children is not to say that mathematics is more important than caring for children or vice versa. Anyone who insists that merely asserting these facts amounts to insulting women must himself believe that male talents are self-evidently more important than female talents. It is this sort of advocate of the cause of women who believes women to be inferior.

Nor do I embrace the view that men are morally better than women. No one has ever dreamed of claiming that men are kinder, more generous, and less prone to aggression. To the contrary, the received stereotype is that women are incapable of the satanic excesses which men have reached. Yet, while the moral superiority of males is a straw man not worth attacking, feminists often put themselves in the perverse position of *defending* this straw man. Feminists characteristically explain the greater person-orientedness of women in environmentalist terms extremely unflattering to women themselves.[38] More recently, the discovery of rivalry among certain primate females has encouraged speculation that human females may happily prove to be as nasty as human males. (Rivalry among primate females generally concerns resources for offspring, while male primate rivalry concerns group dominance; nothing in recent primatology challenges standard views about sex differences.)

It should go without saying that innate sex differences are statistical. Some women are better at mathematics than most men. Neither sex monopolizes any nonanatomical trait. It should also go without saying that the within-sex variance for nonanatomical traits exceeds mean sex differences; the gap in mathematical ability between Gauss and Casey Stengel doubtless exceeds that between the average man and the average woman. I have been unable to find anyone who denies these triusms, which are irrelevant to the existence and consequences of mean gender differences.

I am willing to endorse the treatment of people as "individuals," but it is pointless to expect society to ignore inescapably obvious inductive generalizations which are, on the evidence, rooted in biology. Women with unusual traits have had to face extra difficulties just because they were women (as have men with unusual traits), and these difficulties are due to the currency of expectations based on the majority of cases. But such instances do not show that the broad structure of society inherently thwarts the desires of the great majority of women.

Notes

1. *Berkman v. NYFD,* 536 FSupp 177 (1982); 580 FSupp 226 (1983).
2. Lynn Hecht Schafran, letter, *New York* (January 31, 1983): 5.
3. Kate Millett, *Sexual Politics* (New York: Doubleday, 1970), p. 34.
4. Lori Andrews, "Learning the Rules of the Game," *Parents* (January 1982): 34.
5. "The political nature of woman's condition has rarely been recognized. . . . [*W*]oman's condition, here and now, is the result of a slowly formed, deeply entrenched, extraordinarily pervasive cultural and therefore political decision." Vivian Gornick and Barbara Moran, "Introduction," in *Woman in Sexist Society,* ed. idem (New York: Mentor, 1971), p. xv.
6. Andrea Dworkin, *Men Possessing Women* (New York: Putnam, 1981), pp. 13–14. Dworkin offers the same analysis of pornographic material that does not involve men doing anything to women. In homosexual pornography produced by men "the lesbian is colonized," while the male homosexual is "the symbolic female" (pp. 47, 128). Men find child pornography arousing "because a youth is not fully disassociated from women" (p. 57). Feminist writing on pornography ignores its essentially masturbatory purpose, which distinguishes devotees of pornography from the vast majority of men who prefer intercourse.
7. Ibid., p. 9.
8. Catherine MacKinnon, "Feminism, Marxism, Method, and the State: An Agenda for Theory," *Signs* 7 (1982): 526.
9. Susan Brownmiller, *Against Our Will* (New York: Simon & Schuster, 1975), p. 15. Miss Brownmiller has subsequently characterized her statement as "imprecise."
10. She continues: "Perhaps the wrong of rape has proven so difficult to articulate because the unquestionable starting point has been that rape is definable as distinct from intercourse, when for women it is difficult to distinguish them under conditions of male dominance." MacKinnon, pp. 646–48.
11. Robin Morgan, *Going Too Far* (New York: Random House, 1977). The most complete discussion of feminist writing on rape, pornography, and the Constitution is David Bryden, "Between Two Constitutions: Feminism and Pornography," *Constitutional Commentary* 2 (Winter 1985): 147–89.

12. "There exists a planetary caste system, essentially the same in Saudi Arabia and in New York, differing only in degree." Mary Daly, "The Qualitative Leap beyond Patriarchal Religion," in *Women and Values: Readings in Recent Feminist Philosophy,* ed. Marilyn Pearsall (Belmont, Cal.: Wadsworth, 1986), p. 198.
13. Benjamin Barber, *Liberating Feminism* (New York: Delta, 1976), p. 97.
14. Ibid., p. 83.
15. In 1981 the male suicide rate was 315 percent that of the female rate; in 1982 it was 336 percent. See *Advance Report on Final Mortality Statistics,* National Center for Health Statistics Report 33, 3, Supplement (June 22, 1984), p. 6, table D; and Report 33, 9, Supplement (December 20, 1984), p. 5, table D.
16. Betty Friedan, *The Feminist Mystique* (New York: W.W. Norton, 1963).
17. Carlene Baum et al., "Drug Use and Expenditures in 1982," *Journal of the American Medical Association* 253 (January 18, 1985): 382–86.
18. Ibid., p. 384, table 1.
19. Ibid., p. 383, figure 1.
20. L.S. Tibbetts, "Sex Role Stereotyping in the Lower Grades: Part of the Solution," *Jounral of Vocational Behavior* 6 (1975): 255–61.
21. See Tibbetts; also Nancy Schlossberg and Jane Goodman, "A Woman's Place: Children's Sex Stereotyping of Occupations," *Vocational Guidance Quarterly* 20 (1972): 266–270.
22. See Tibbetts.
23. Lawrence Kohlberg, "A Cognitive-Developmental Analysis of Children's Sex-Role Concepts and Attitudes," in *The Development of Sex Differences,* ed. Eleanor Maccoby (Palo Alto: Stanford University Press, 1966).
24. See Donald Broverman et al., "Sex Role Stereotypes: A Current Appraisal," *Jounral of Social Issues* 28 (1972): 59–78.
25. *Manhart v. Los Angeles,* 403 US 702 (1978). See also "Equal Rights Ruling for Auto Insurance Expected to Spread," *New York Times* (October 23, 1984): A18.
26. Bernice Sandler, *On Campus with Women* 26 (Spring 1980): 3.
27. "What Does a Woman Need? Not to Depend on a Man," *People* (September 13, 1982): 75–79.
28. See Andrews.
29. *Ford Foundation Newsletter* 15, 1 (February 1, 1984): 5.
30. Ibid., 16, 6 (December 1, 1985): 9.
31. "Gazette," *Ms* (May 1983): 32.
32. Heather Menzies, *Women and the Chip* (Montreal: Institute on Public Policy, 1981).
33. Eileen Byrne, *Women and Social Reconstruction: The Twenty-Ninth Tate Memorial Lecture* (Brisbane: University of Queensland Press, 1982).
34. Ibid., p. 8.
35. I refer to groups advocating feminist policies as "feminist groups," irrespective of the presence of women in their names. Whether feminists speak for women in general should not be pre-judged by terminology. The membership of NOW has never exceeded one quarter of 1 percent of the adult female population of the United States.
36. For a fuller description of the Nairobi Conference, see Michael Levin, "What Nairobi Wrought," *Commentary* 80 (October 1985): 48–52.
37. Not that such disavowels are effective. A recent book asserts that the present author disapproves of affirmative action because of the "inferiority" of women (Anne Fausto-Sterling, *Myths of Gender* [New York: Basic Books, 1986], p. 6). No doubt this book will be similarly misread.

38. Doris Gold explains that women volunteer for charitable activities as a result of "powerful social disapproval, coupled with their own psychological conditioning of self-negation and ambivalent self-recognition." Doris Gold, "Women and Volunteerism," in Gornick and Moran, p. 534.

2

What is Feminism?

Characterizing Feminism

An adequate characterization of feminism should meet four conditions. First, it should be acceptable to those who call themselves feminists and consistent with the understanding of feminism held by sympathetic outsiders. Second, it should construe feminism, which presents itself as a critique of some of the broadest features of society, as comprehensive and systematic. Third, it should construe feminism as more than a platitude which no reasonable person would dispute but which has no practical consequences. Fourth, it should construe feminism as a view that is taken seriously by a significant number of people.

The third and fourth conditions present certain difficulties. The ban on triviality rules out the most commonly offered definitions of feminism, such as "justice for women" and "opposition to sexism," insofar as the crucial term *sexism* is in turn defined as "failure to give equal consideration on the basis of sex alone."[1] Consider "justice for women." The pure principle of justice, that similar cases are to be treated similarly, is empty and tautological, its meaning entirely dependent on the criterion used to determine the similarity among cases and the evidence considered relevant to whether men and women satisfy the criterion chosen. Thus, to determine whether history textbooks emphasizing male statesmen are just, it must first be decided whether justice is the distribution of equal shares to all, to the equally needy, to those faring equally well in laissez-faire competition, or perhaps some other standard altogether. It must then be determined empirically whether men and women are equal in the sense specified, and if they are, whether androcentric history textbooks fail to provide shares equal in the sense specified. To demand just treatment for women is to demand nothing in particular about how women should be treated; this platitudinous demand therefore cannot be what anyone has in mind by "feminism." For similar reasons it is unavailing to characterize feminists and their critics as agreeing about ends—the equitable treatment of women—and disagreeing (only) about means. Equity is too vacuous to be anybody's goal; it is a goal given substance by the means chosen to it. Disagreement about such matters

16

as quotas, textbook censorship, and comparable worth are disagreements about the feminist conception of equity itself, hence disagreeing about ends.

The fourth condition creates difficulties inasmuch as it seems to imply that feminism cannot be absurd, for much that feminists say seems too absurd for anyone to take seriously. Thus Richard Wasserstrom endorses an "assimilationist ideal" for society in which sex "would be the functional equivalent of the eye color of individuals in our society today":

> Just as the normal, typical adult is virtually oblivious to the eye color of other persons for all major interpersonal relations, so the normal, typical adult in this kind of non-sexist society would be indifferent to the sexual, physiological differences of other persons for all interpersonal relationships.[2]

One is reluctant to attribute to a distinguished legal philosopher the view that in an ideal society many people would not know the sex of their spouses, but if what Wasserstrom is saying does not imply this, what is he saying? When considering feminism, it is useful to balance the charitable maxim that no one should be saddled with a belief that is too silly, with Hobbes's observation that "men believeth many times impossibilities." Satisfying the third and fourth conditions simultaneously presents further problems since, as we will see, any substantial criticism of sex roles risks commitment to unviable empirical assumptions.

Mindful of these difficulties, let us begin with selections from the full range of feminist thought: two texts historically central to anything deserving to be called feminism, a more contemporary classic source, a radical feminist, aphorisms from two mainstream activists, documents of the U.S. government and the United Nations, and the work of seven academic feminists writing for serious publishers.[3]

> What is now called the nature of women is an eminently artificial thing—the result of forced repression in some directions, unnatural stimulation in others. . . . [N]o class of dependents have had their character so entirely distorted from its natural proportions by the relation with their masters.
>
> —John Stuart Mill, 1869

> The great danger which threatens the infant in our
> culture lies in the fact that the mother to whom it is
> confided in all its helplessness is almost always a
> discontented woman: sexually she is frigid or
> unsatisfied; socially she feels herself inferior to men;
> she has no independent grasp on the world or on the
> future. . . . [In a world] where men and women would
> be equal, [a girl] will be brought up
> from the first with the same demands
> and rewards, the same severity and the same

freedom, as her brothers, taking part in the same
studies, the same games, promised the same future,
surrounded with women and men who seemed her undoubted
equals.

—Simone de Beauvoir, 1948

[T]he standards of femininity, however suitable they may
have been in the past, may now be dysfunctional. They are
not standards of good mental health.

—Jessie Bernard, 1971

The sexes are inherently in everything alike, save
reproductive systems, secondary sexual characteristics,
orgasmic capacity, and genetic and morphological
structure.

—Kate Millett, 1970

If there were another word more all-embracing than
revolution, I would use it.

—Shulamith Firestone, 1970

We're talking about a revolution, not just reform. It's
the deepest possible change there is.

—Gloria Steinem, circa 1972

I want to have a part in creating a new society. . . .
I have never reached my potential because of social
conditions. I'm not going to get the rewards. I've been
crippled.

—Member of NOW, 1974

When we ask why girls and women come to choose courses of
study and occupations that lead them to a segregated and
disadvantaged role in later life, part of the answer is
"socialization." Somehow, the social environment
conveys the message that some activities are appropriate
and some inappropriate, that girls and women possess
certain capabilities and lack others.

—U.S. Department of Health, Education, and
Welfare, 1980

The States Parties to the present Convention, *Aware*
that a change in the traditional role of men as well
as women in society and in the family is needed to
achieve full equality between men and women, *have
agreed* to adopt appropriate legislative and other
measures, including sanctions where appropriate, to

modify the social and cultural patterns of conduct of men
and women, with a view to achieving the elimination of
prejudices and customary and all other practices which
are based on the idea of the inferiority or the
superiority of either of the sexes or on stereotyped
roles for men and women.

—United Nations Convention on the Elimination of All
Forms of Discrimination Against Women
(signed by the United States 1978).

A sexually egalitarian society is one in which virtually
no public recognition is given to the fact that there is
a physiological sex difference between persons. This is
not to say that the different reproductive functions of
each sex should be unacknowledged in such a society nor
that there should be no physicians specializing in male
and female complaints, etc. But it is to say that, except
in this sort of context, the question whether someone is
male or female should have no significance.

—Alison Jagger, 1974

Change in women's roles means change in every aspect of
society.

—Judith Long Laws, 1979

Feminism is in its nature radical. . . . It is the
social institutions of which we complain primarily. . . .
If you consider the past there is no doubt at all that
the whole structure of society was designed *to keep
women entirely in the power of men.* This no doubt
sounds like pure feminist rant, but it is not.

—Janet Richards, 1980

Whatever sex differences in behavior now exist and
whatever their origins we have no reason to assume that
they would be barriers to any egalitarian society we may
want to build.

—Marian Lowe, 1983

[B]ecause the sexual division of labor around
childbearing prevails and defines women's position,
a policy emphasizing material benefits and services to
encourage childbearing may ease the material burdens of
motherhood; but it may operate to perpetuate the existing
sexual division of labor and women's social
subordination. . . . A feminist and socialist
transformation of the existing conditions of reproduction

would seek . . . a new set of social relations. . . .
The changes we require are total.

—Rosalind Petchesky, 1984

If we could imagine a culture free of values and
constraints concerning sexuality, human beings would
probably express their sexuality, physicality,
friendship, and loving emotions in a variety of ways that
would not be necessarily influenced by others' biological
sex. . . . In particular, the institutions and
ideologies of heterosexuality (i.e. heterosexism) are the
primary force in the maintenance of patriarchal rule and
the social, economic and political subordination of women.

—Ruth Bleier, 1984

The Lowe and Bleier citations are particularly noteworthy for being
taken from works in Pergamon's Athene Series, "An International Collection of Feminist Books," described as follows by the publisher: "The
ATHENE SERIES assumes that all those who are concerned with formulat-
ing explanations of the way the world works need to know and appreciate
the significance of basic feminist principles." Anyone who dismisses Lowe
or Bleier as typical of feminism must deny that the editors of the Athene
Series know what feminism is.

As it emerges from these sources, feminism in its contemporary form has
four central tenets:

1. Anatomical differences apart, men and women are the same. Infant boys
   and girls are born with virtually the same capacities to acquire skills and
   motives, and if raised identically would develop identically.
2. Men unfairly occupy positions of dominance because the myth that men
   are more aggressive than women has been perpetuated by the practice of
   raising boys to be oriented toward mastery and girls to be oriented
   toward people. If this stereotyping ceased, leadership would be equally
   divided between the sexes. Sexist socialization harms boys as well as
   girls by denying both the full range of possible aspirations, but on the
   whole boys get the better of the deal because they grow up to run everything.
3. True human individuality and fulfillment will come about only when
   people view themselves as *human* repositories of talents and traits, and
   deny that sex has any significant effect on one's individual nature.
   Traditional femininity is a suffocating and pathological response to
   women's heretofore restricted lives, and will have to be abandoned.
4. These desirable changes will require the complete transformation of
   society.

Clause (1) may appear too sweeping, in light of the verbal assent to innate nonanatomical sex differences given by a number of writers who call themselves feminists. These writers say merely that any differences which may exist are irrelevant to extant rigid sex roles, which are produced by conditioning as per clause (2). Some of the passages cited above are consistent with this seemingly less extreme environmentalism, as is "stage two" feminism to be considered presently. It might seem that a view of this sort could be accommodated by replacing clause (1) by (1a): *None of the observed traits of human beings can be explained as manifestations of innate sex differences. These differences, while perhaps real, are irrelevant to the nature of society and the possibilities of social change.*

In fact, however, (1) and (1a) are equivalent. Clause (1) obviously entails (1a)—non-existent differences cannot explain anything—and, together with the principle of parsimony used elsewhere in science, (1a) implies (1). If innate sex differences do not affect the individual and group behavior of human beings, they do not affect the only phenomena they are likely to affect, and positing such differences is pointless. Nothing distinguishes a world with an inefficacious cause from a world without it. Thus, whether someone genuinely accepts innate sex differences depends entirely on whether he believes they help to explain general features of society. Anyone who says he grants innate sex differences but goes on to deny that they are explanatory is merely giving lip service to them. We will have occasion later to catalogue the protean forms this lip service can take; for now we may continue to identify feminism with the original four tenets.

This account of feminism is explicit in the writings of feminists themselves and informed observers. One figure who has had participant observer status is Alice Rossi, at one time a feminist and also a past president of the American Sociological Association. She may be presumed to speak with authority. In 1964 she wrote:

It will be an assumption of this essay that by far the majority of the differences between the sexes which have been noted in social science research are socially rather than physiologically determined. . . . It will be a major thesis of this essay that we need to reassert the claim to sex equality. . . . By sex equality I mean a socially androgynous conception of the roles of mean and women, in which they are equal and similar in such spheres as intellectual, artistic, political and occupational interests and participation, complementary only in those spheres dictated by physiological differences between the sexes. [It includes] equivalence and substitutability [as] part of the general definition of the parental role. . . . [The liberated woman's] intellectual aggressiveness as well as her brother's tender sentiments will be welcomed and accepted as *human* characteristics, without the self-questioning doubt of latent homosexuality that troubles many college-age men and women in our era when these qualities are sex-linked. . . . If a social movement rests content with legal changes without making as strong an effort to change the social institutions through which they are expressed, it will remain a hollow victory.[4]

Note that Rossi took the social causation theory to be an "assumption" not worth questioning, and the sex differences themselves to be findings of "social science research" rather than part of the lore of every culture. By 1977 Rossi had developed serious doubts about her proposals, and with considerable intellectual courage published a partial recantation in which she described feminism in more objective language as "an egalitarian ideology that denies any innate sex differences and assumes that a 'unisex' socialization will produce men and women that are free of the traditional culturally induced sex differences" and which shares with much social science "an extreme emphasis on cultural determinism."[5]

Muriel Carden, a sociologist commissioned by the Ford and Russell Sage foundations to study feminism, summarized it similarly:

> Far too much has been made of the biological differences between men and women. Different socialization processes account for a larger part of the observed differences in men's and women's behavior, while biology plays only a minor part. Thus their [feminists'] argument for equality is based upon the belief that the biologically derived differences between the sexes are relatively minor and that a most inequitable system has been built upon the assumption that such differences are basic and major. . . . [A]lmost everyone co-operates in this "oppressive" socialization or conditioning. Parents, teachers, toy manufacturers, and writers of children's books encourage girls to be "feminine."[6]

The claim that feminism functions as an ideological belief system has been empirically tested by Claire Fulenwider.[7] Following standard social scientific usage, she defines an ideology as a system of beliefs (as opposed to a set of attitudes) which "describe present reality . . . explain present reality—that is, show how it has developed historically [and prescribe] in what ways it is good or bad [and] posit a plan for changing present reality."[8] Minimizing the differences between radical, socialist, and reform feminism, Fulenwider finds all feminist writers agreeing that

> women are unjustly treated, that they are maintained in subordinate roles and positions, and that they are consistently removed from most vital decision-making opportunities of society. Furthermore, this discrimination against and exploitation and oppression of women are seen by feminists as rationally justified by a dominant sexist ideology. . . . Overall, however, [despite differences in emphasis by reform, socialist, and radical feminists], values and goals of the women's movement show fairly widespread agreement. The eradication of sexism—in practice and in attitude—is probably the most basic goal. Commitment to expanding options for women in all spheres of society is another shared aim, as is freedom from oppression and from gender-role

stereotyping. . . . Feminists concur that major social structural changes—in the economy, in politics, and in social practices and expectations—are essential.[9]

To test this hypothesis, Fulenwider first asked over 2,000 respondents to score their agreement with eleven statements, including: "Women should have an equal role with men in running business, industry, and government"; "Our society, not nature, teaches women to prefer homemaking"; "Men have more of the top jobs because society discriminates against women [rather than because] men have more drive"; and "Women must work together to change laws and customs that are unfair to all women"— essentially tenets (1) through (4). A panel of judges concurred that strong agreement with these statements is a criterion of commitment to feminism. Fulenwider then predicted that if feminism is an ideological framework for interpreting social reality, a high combined score on the criterion should constrain views about other political issues, a high score on one criterion statement should predict high scores on the others, and finally, that scores on the criterion should depend on a single underlying variable. Fulenwider's data bore out these predictions and, especially for women, scores on the criterion variable correlated highly with self-positioning along the single "abstract ordering dimension" of "role equality."[10] The "overriding conclusion" was that feminism "gives clear evidence of centrality, rationality, and constraint," and serves as a "political ideology."[11]

Once all nonanatomical sex differences are taken to be social in origin, an analogy between women and racial minorities is inevitable. The supposed powerlessness, confinement, and poverty of women, and the prevalence of stereotypic beliefs about them, must be caused in much the way that the similarly inferior social position of American Blacks is caused. That the condition of women is universal while that of American Blacks is temporary and local—Blacks run everything in Black African countries—is taken to show the very pervasiveness of sexist conditioning. To forestall further verbal disputation, I will use this analogy in an operational definition of "feminist": A feminist is anyone who takes seriously the analogy between Blacks and women. Anyone who compares the present status of women to that of Blacks in the antebellum South, and the outlook of nonfeminist women to the slave mentality, is a feminist. So too is anyone who thinks that raising children to disregard gender is as easy and important as raising children to disregard skin color. Here are three feminists, one self-described, one a legal scholar engaged in popular debate, and one a philosopher writing for his peers in a professional periodical:

> The kind of feminine self-image which lowers aspiration and permits the acceptance of a dependent status [is] similar to the defeatist attitude of other minority groups.

Not so many years ago, black probationary firemen were looked on with disdain and fear. And when Jews, some with college degrees, turned to firefighting during the Depression, their value in action was seriously questioned. . . . Are women really in such a different position?

The treatment of our western European ancestors accorded North American Indians, blacks, and the native people of Mexico remains the barbarous deed that it always was. The systematic exploitation of women in our (and other) societies is not any less wrong.[12]

The dissent in *Frontiero v. Richardson* written by Justice William Brennan and joined by three other justices is feminist in this operational sense: "The position of women in our society was, in many respects, comparable to that of blacks under the pre–Civil War slave codes."[13] Four of nine positive scores from the Supreme Court indicates an operational test sensitive to an important social phenomenon.

Refinements

The four central tenets of feminism must be expanded in a number of ways. First, it must be emphasized that the inequity of the sexual division of labor is said to be two-fold. The horizontal division of tasks into male and female, overlap notwithstanding, largely confines women to domestic tasks while allowing males to do everything else. The vertical division of tasks into subordinate and superordinate reserves for men the topmost positions of prestige and authority in all spheres, including those in which men and women participate jointly. In the United States, men are chief executives and women secretaries; in the Kalahari desert, men do the high-status hunting while women do the low-status gathering. A specific task may be considered male in one society and female in another, but it always enjoys higher status when it is male.

A second refinement, or perhaps gap that needs filling, concerns the process by which sex roles have come to be assigned. Many feminists treat the present order as a male conspiracy. Others, who recognize the unlikelihood of a universal conspiracy, argue that sex stereotypes perpetuate themselves: Each generation, having been raised to accept conventional sex roles, raises its own children to those same roles. But this more sophisticated theory merely postpones the problem, which reemerges in the following form: If women originally wanted power just as badly as men, how did sex stereotyping *begin?* Did patriarchy emerge independently many times, or did it radiate to all societies from a single central sources?[14] However often it happened, how did prehistoric women as well as men come to be convinced that women do not want power as much as men do, and how did power come to be monopolized by men? As we will see, any noncircular version of feminist environmentalism must posit a historical moment at which men used their superior physical strength to wrest control.

The third salient feature of feminism is its attention to the family. The attribution of inequalities to socialization naturally generates suspicion about the chief instrument of socialization, the family, and its accompanying emotions. Juliet Mitchell and Nancy Chodorow reject love between men and women "enculturated in patriarchal society" as an inauthentic product of "social ideology."[15] For Mill, the family was "a school of despotism" (a judgement that may reflect Mill's own unhappy upbringing by a tyrannical father). Chodorow again:

> The social organization of parenting produces sexual inequality, not simply role differentiation. It is politically and socially important to confront this organization. Even though it is an arrangement that seems universal, directly rooted in biology, and inevitable, it can be changed. . . . The elimination of the present organization of parenting [so that] children could be dependent at the outset on people of both genders . . . depends on the conscious organization and activity of all women and men who recognize that their interests lie in transforming the social organization of gender and eliminating sexual inequality.[16]

Simone de Beauvoir yokes the family with private property as the two chiefs sources of human misery:

> Since the oppression of women has its cause in the will to perpetuate the family and to keep patrimony intact, woman escapes complete dependence to the degree to which she escapes from the family; if a society that forbids private property also rejects the family, the lot of women in it is found to be considerably ameliorated.[17]

Letty Pogrebin urges "action on all fronts" from "the first millisecond of birth" on:

> everything we do with, to, for and around children—our speaking habits, living styles, adult relationships, chores, academic standards and our way of dealing with punishment, privilege, religion, television, sex, money and love . . . words, actions, reactions, gestures, attitudes and patterns of behavior—your own, your children's, and everyone else's—until you become, almost without trying, proudly and irresistibly antisexist.[18]

The allusion to speaking habits is prompted by research indicating that parents address male and female babies differently. Pogrebin advises parents to cancel this effect by practicing their full vocal ranges in talking to infants of either sex, "to learn to *hear* sexism before it rises in our throats."[19]

Simone de Beauvoir, like the vast majority of feminists, regards the radical alteration of parenting as more than a utopian fantasy. She finds it "easy to visualize" a world "where men and women would be equal,"

> for that is precisely what the Soviet Union promised: women trained and raised exactly like men. . . . [M]arriage was to be based on a free agreement that the spouses could break at will; maternity was to be voluntary; pregnancy leaves were to be paid for by the State, which would assume charge of the children, signifying not that they would be *taken away* from their parents, but that they would not be *abandoned* to them.[20]

De Beauvoir is so far from alone among feminists in admiring Marxist-Leninism that this admiration, together with hostility to "capitalism," can be considered virtually a further distinguishing mark of feminism. The main criticism offered of the Soviet Union is that it has not gone far enough. Kate Millett sides with Trotsky against Lenin because "there was no realization [on Lenin's part] that while every practical effort should be made to implement a sexual revolution, the real test would be in changing attitudes."[21] To be sure, feminists are attracted primarily to the ideas that the Soviet state proclaims itself as embodying, rather than to the Soviet regime itself, but with that understood, a great many well-known feminists, including de Beauvoir, Millett, Firestone, Bleier, Mitchell, Chodorow, MacKinnon, Steinem, Sheila Rowbotham, Margaret Benston, Angela Davis, Eli Zaretsky, Evelyn Reed, Barbara Ehrenreich, Vivian Howe, and Rayna Rapp identify themselves as socialists or Marxists of some sort. According to Germaine Greer, "the forcing-house of most of the younger women's liberation groups was the university left wing."[22] Catherine MacKinnon explains the link between feminism and Marxism in more general terms:

> As the organized expropriation of the work of some for the benefit of others defines a class—workers—the organized expropriation of the sexuality of some for the use of others defines the sex, woman. Heterosexuality is its structure, gender and family its congealed forms, sex roles its qualities generalized to social persona, reproduction a consequence, and control its issue. [Marxism and feminism] argue, respectively, that the relations in which many work and few gain, in which some fuck and others get fucked, are the prime moments of politics.[23]

There is no doubt that the founders of Marxism were feminists. In *The Origin of the Family,* Engels wrote:

> It will be plain that the first condition for the liberation of the wife is to bring the whole female sex into public industry and that this in turn demands the abolition of the monogamous family as the economic unit of society. Monogamous marriage comes on the scene as the subjugation of the one sex by the

other. . . . The emancipation of woman will be possible only when . . . domestic work no longer claims anything but an insignificant portion of her time.

Now, there is nothing in Marxist *moral* theory that demands identical treatment of the sexes. If each is entitled to what he needs and owes what he can produce, men and women have different entitlements and obligations if they differ biologically in their needs and abilities.[24] At the same time, the Marxist axiom that economic factors are the sole cause of social and personal relations, by precluding any biological factor, does lead immediately to the factual assumptions of feminism. Marxists must, in logical consistency, be feminists.

Feminism and Freedom

The claim by feminists to be proponents of liberation, together with widespread feminist sympathy for a tradition hostile to individual liberty, raises the question of just what feminists mean by freedom. The notion of freedom assumed in everyday expressions like "a free afternoon" and "freedom of speech" is noninterference: Speaking freely is saying what one wants to without constraint. This is also the idea of freedom behind everyday ascriptions of responsibility. It has been developed by a long philosophical tradition, and seems to me correct. More pertinently, it is also the idea of freedom implicit in the feminist demand that women be given power and control over their lives. Like all demands for power and control, this one is directed against forces thought to prevent women from doing what they want. Women are unfree under patriarchy because patriarchy prevents them from doing what they want.

One may wonder how women can be said to be unfree in this sense when so much characteristically female behavior is, as it seems to be, quite voluntary. In reply, some feminists straightforwardly deny that women like doing most of what they do, and claim that women do it because they are made to. Ruth Bleier maintains that in the past "for many (most?) heterosexual women sex was either to be neutrally endured or painful or forced and obligatory."[25] Female compliance with male demands is extorted by the threat of rape, wife-beating, and other forms of violence.

An answer somewhat more faithful to the realities of experience (but still a radical answer) is that, while women under patriarchy may be doing what they want, the conditions under which their wants were formed were constrained. Women have had no chance to acquire different wants. Now, that women have not chosen their wants is insufficient reason to deny that women are free, since no one, male or female, chooses his wants. Everyone's wants would have been somewhat different had he been raised differently. If a woman doing what she wishes to do is nevertheless unfree because her wishes were influenced by factors beyond her control, then no one is free. (Some philosophers have drawn precisely this conclusion, but the conclusion that free will is completely illusory is obviously irrelevant to whether women *alone* are unfree, or less free than men.) Still, there are cases in which, because of the nature and origin of the motivating want, doing what one wants is nonetheless unfree, and it is to these cases that the ostensibly free actions of women are compared. A brainwashed prisoner does not sign a confession freely, although he may have come to believe in his country's guilt and wish to expose it, because his willingness to sign was forced on him. An Epsilon docilely carrying out his duties in Huxley's *Brave New World* is unfree because someone engineered his personality. Women are said to be similarly unfree when they "voluntarily" subordinate themselves to their husbands: They have been brainwashed to want to.

> In a review of the mechanisms for constructing a "difference" and dominance relations between males and females, it becomes clear that such an effort can be effective only if an entire society, particularly the parents, is in agreement with the ultimate goals. Whether there are or are not biological, psychological, or genetic differences, as defined by the "average" male versus the "average" female, is really irrelevant to the task of rearing specific individuals to serve specific functions. A society has the infinite capacity for flexibility, and the socialization of its members can maximize or minimize any differences that might exist. One is reminded of Huxley's *Brave New World,* in which differential treatment is carried to any extreme: where individuals are born and bred to specific tasks and are isolated from any alternative life style. They have no option to choose. Value systems can be designed to promote acceptance of the difference and roles. Value systems can isolate individuals of different groups from one another. We are not approaching a brave new world. We have been living in it, although it is not quite as efficient as Huxley's nor as complex in its groups and role projections.[26]

Before the brainwashing hypothesis can be examined directly, its empirical and conceptual presuppositions must be extracted. Several factors distinguish a victim of brainwashing from ordinary people, whose preferences have also ultimately been caused by external forces. The most salient factor is the contrast between his posttreatment personality and his considerably richer original personality which, but for the treatment, he would still have. Had things been different, the prisoner would not be confessing, zombie-like, to imaginary crimes. The zombie-like manner is itself a major element in the popular idea of brainwashing. Huxley's Epsilons are less than autonomous not primarily because someone limited their preferences by impoverishing their prenatal environment, but because their range of activities is abnormally narrow. If the prisoner emerges clear-eyed and responsive from the brainwashing session, *a new personality* has been created, and the uncoerced acts of this new personality are fully free.[27] Even metaphorically calling the average woman brainwashed, therefore, attributes to her an underlying personality far richer than the one she displays under patriarchy, and assumes that she, along with the average man, could have developed a range of preferences far wider than those she actually exhibits. Both attributions assume, in turn, that the human personalities currently on view are not significantly determined by biological factors, an assumption inconsistent with Mintz's dismissal of biological factors as irrelevant. (It should anyway be apparent that Mintz is making strong environmentalist assumptions when she speaks of society as infinitely flexible and capable of minimizing sex differences to any extent.)

The idea that voluntary sex-typed behavior is inauthentic explains the readiness to call for state action that is prominent in the feminist political agenda. The inauthentic preferences now enslaving people will change when, but only when, people stop acting in ways which perpetuate them. Reform therefore requires that people temporarily act against their own preferences and those of others until everyone's new behavior generates more authentic preferences. The problem is starting the process, since no one will wish to adopt the meritorious but unorthodox practices before they are adopted by everyone else. In the language of economics, feminist reform presents a coordination problem: how to get people to adopt a practice that benefits all when all follow it, but disadvantages anyone who follows it when others do not.[28] The first children raised nonsexistly will be subject to environmental countercues like their playmates' ridicule; as few pioneers will subject their children to ridicule in the name of an ideal, nonsexist childrearing will not work unless everyone does it. Worse, freeloaders can take advantage of local antisexist behavior. An employer who continues to hire on merit and pay market wages will outcompete any business rival who hires female role models without regard to merit and pays them their "comparable worth" without demanding increased productivity. An employer who establishes in-house day-care to accommodate female employees may suffer if his competitors choose to attract the cheapest labor force without regard to the convenience of females.

The accepted solution for coordination problems is to have the state *make* everyone act in the individually adverse but collectively beneficial way. Everyone wants a lighthouse, but private parties cannot finance one by renting its light to seafarers, since freeloaders need only sail near a lessor to catch the free spillover light. Everyone is waiting for everyone else to subscribe to the lighthouse fund, and to everyone's regret, the lighthouse is not built. At this point the government, able to exact payment from everyone, steps in to build the lighthouse with taxes or user's fees. There is no longer room to try to outmaneuver suckers, and all the would-be maneuverers are better off.

The various antisexism scenarios we will examine suggest a parallel resolution: avert the adverse consequences of antisexism by denying people the liberty to refuse to go along with antisexist reforms. Feminists are prone to look to the government not because they like to see other people pushed around, but because their plans require a coordinating mechanism. As this is being written,[29] for instance, Congress has before it a proposal to require all employers to grant four months' maternity leave to pregnant employees, on the grounds that many employers now replace women who leave their jobs to have children. Such a law is needed, if it is, precisely because employers who do not automatically grant maternity leave enjoy a competitive advantage over those who do, and will act to gain that advantage if not forbidden by law.

There is of course no *logical* link between feminism and advocacy of state intervention. Just as a libertarian can consistently regret the failure of private action to secure the advantages of a lighthouse, all the while insisting that construction of a lighthouse exceeds the bounds of permissible state action, so a libertarian feminist can consistently hold sex roles to be unjust artifacts while insisting that the co-ordinating mechanisms needed to eliminate sex roles—such as mandatory maternity leave—exceed the bounds of permissible state action. Still, the libertarian feminist remains committed to the same empirical theory about society that actuates her more statist sisters, and the ranks of libertarian feminism are bound in any event to remain thin, since it is psychologically difficult to regard a situation as extremely unjust without wishing to deploy the power of the state against it. In point of logic feminists aims cannot be achieved without state coercion, and in point of fact those who subscribe to feminist theory will tend to endorse state action.

The need to start anew with a clean slate also explains the readiness to misrepresent reality. Like a concern with every facet of life and the conviction that expressed preferences are inauthentic, the impulse to suppress discordant empirical facts is a trait common to all totalitarian ideologies. This impulse is rooted in two fears. One is the fear that persisting memories of the old ways may prove attractive to those embarked on the initially difficult new ways. The second is the fear that reality itself amounts to a validation of sorts; the old ways cannot be all that bad if people are demonstrably getting along while following them. Legitimation by reality is best opposed not by an outright denial of the facts—which only calls them to people's attention—but by the pretense that they never existed. A major goal of totalitarian education thus becomes the creation of a new order by making it seem already in place. In 1964 Alice Rossi advocated ending "class excursions into the community . . . to introduce American children to building, construction, airports or zoos," because "going out into the community this way, youngsters would observe men and women in their present occupational roles." She recommended instead "having children see and hear a woman scientist or doctor; a man dancer or artist; both men and women who are business executives, writers and architects."[30] While Rossi has developed second thoughts about the feasibility of these ideas, they remain central to the thinking of other feminists.

Innate Sex Differences Again

The average person familiar with the public debate would unquestionably include complete environmentalism in any definition of feminism, and feminists themselves have repeatedly proclaimed this tenet.[31] This inclusion is correct on logical as well as textual grounds. So far as feminist plans go, it is pointless to aspire toward an ideal of sexual equality that biology renders impossible. The goal of releasing personalities far richer than those people now possess is likewise pointless if people have their present personalities courtesy of biology and lack any underlying personalities to be released. But it is in its evaluative role that feminism depends most crucially on environmentalism. If the broad features of human society flow from innately programmed preferences of men and women, these features are not products of oppression, and the feminist indictment of them as such is in error. Whether the assignment of sex roles is a device to keep women in thrall depends on how this assignment came about and how it is sustained. It is not an oppressive device if it came about because men and women for the most part innately prefer things the way they are, or as an unintended consequence of preferences. (Compare: The bridge of the nose is not a device *for* keeping eyeglasses in place unless the bridge of the nose came into existence because it supports eyeglasses and continues to exist because it supports eyeglasses.) Like any finding of wrong, the feminist critique of society rests on a prior theory of fact, in this case a factual theory about the causes of the relations between the sexes. Legal verdicts are based on factual findings; after instructing the jury as to what sort of act counts as a crime, the judge asks them to decide whether an act of that sort was committed. A charge of theft is rebuttable by the factual showing that the accused robber received the wallet as a gift. By the same token, a charge of discrimination is rebuttable by showing (for instance) that the numerical preponderance of men in positions of power came about through individual choices.

It is precisely because the legitimacy of the position of men depends on the way in which men got their position that feminists argue that men have gotten where they are because women have been prevented from reaching (or aspiring to) those same positions, i.e. that women *would have gotten* those positions but for being interdicted. It is not a desire for rhetorical effect but the logic of the argument that leads Janet Richards to say that "all social arrangements . . . *were designed to ensure that women should be in the power and service of men,*"[32] and Kate Millett to describe sex as "an arrangement whereby one group of persons is controlled by another."[33] The case against patriarchy cannot allow that men run things because men are more interested than women in running things. The case hinges on a question of fact, and we must heed the injunction of Mao Zedong: "No investigation, no right to speak!"

However, because it is possible to *say* that one recognizes innate sex differences without really doing so, this investigation must await a survey of common evasions—a survey also intended to verify that environmentalism is indeed the *nervus probandi* of feminism in all its forms.

Perfunctory Acknowledgement Followed by Silence

For instance, while the HEW document cited above seems to admit the possibility of non-social causes of sex segregation ("part of the answer is 'socialization'"), this possibility is not mentioned thereafter in the document, or in any of the dozens of references it cites. At other times, the concession that there are *some* innate nonanatomical sex differences is followed, inconsistently, by denial of the innateness of any specific sex difference that is brought up in context.

A variant form of pseudoconcession is covered by tenet (1a) and illustrated by the citation from Marian Lowe: Sex differences exist but are irrelevant to any actual or possible society. It is sometimes difficult to see that this is what an author is up to, since one way to treat a factor as *ir*relevant is simply to fail to treat it as relevant. Thus Jessie Bernard begins *Women, Wives, Mothers* with the statement: "Men and women are different. A highly sophisticated corpus of research documents biological, psychological, social and cultural differences between them."[34] However, after a review of the evidence documenting the "inferior status of women" (in which the corpus of research cited at the outset is heavily criticized), Bernard concludes that a "new society" based on an "information net" will soon coalesce around "the values characterizing women up to now." Since Bernard neglects to consider the possibility that the sex differences conceded initially might bear on the possibility of this new order, she has in effect withdrawn her concession. Once again, a difference assumed to make no difference is assumed to be no difference.

Describing Innate Sex Differences as Small

This tactic figures prominently in discussions of the difference between male and female mean scores on mathematics aptitude tests, which Ruth Bleier (along with a great many others) dismisses as "small" and "almost trivial."[35] Calling this or any other sex difference small carries the implication that it is *too* small to explain any socially observed sex difference, and perhaps that the innate difference is too small to *deserve* to play a significant causal role.

The trouble with this idea is the absence of any standard for the size of a sex difference apart from the extent of its influence on the structure of society. One cannot first decide that a sex difference is small and conclude therefrom that it cannot be responsible for some given social phenomenon; one must first determine what phenomena can be explained by the difference in question and from that determination decide whether the difference is large or small. It is easy to see in the physical sciences that the importance of a factor cannot be assessed a priori. Even though the difference between the two natural isotopes of uranium is "only" three neutrons (about 1 percent of the atomic weight of uranium), those three neutrons determine whether an explosive chain reaction can be sustained—a large difference indeed. The same holds in the biosocial world. A small mean difference in mathematical aptitude also means small discrepancies at the extremes of the bell curve—it means, for instance, that 99.9 percent of the population above a certain percentile will be male. If mathematical creativity should turn out to require an aptitude drawn from that percentile, then virtually all important mathematical discoveries will be made by males, the general population will perceive mathematics as a male activity, relatively able girls will not aspire to success in mathematics—and the "small" mean difference will have had a major social effect.

It might seem doubtful to someone unfamiliar with automobiles that the twenty gallons of gasoline an automobile carries in its fuel tank is a big enough part of the automobile to be what makes it go. And no doubt the gasoline could not make the car go without the intervening mechanisms of combustion chamber, drive shaft, and axles. Still, it is the combustion of gasoline that makes cars go; no further causal variable is required. There is no way to estimate the importance of gasoline a priori; you have to determine its role in the system to which it belongs. Nor can you decide in advance that a sex difference is small. To do so is to assume that it is causally irrelevant to the system to which it belongs, and hence, in effect, nonexistent.

Appeal to the Fact/Value Gap

This is probably the most frequently cited reason for waving aside the question of sex differences. It begins from the truism that the way people *are* does not dictate how they *should* be. In particular, it is argued, the appropriate attitude to take toward sex differences, whatever they may be, is that they are raw material to be shaped in accordance with our values. It is the values that should be the object of primary concern. Maccoby and Jacklin conclude their survey of sex differences on this note:

> We suggest that societies have the option of minimizing rather than maximizing sex differences through their socialization practices. A society could, for example, devote its energies more toward moderating male aggression than toward preparing women to submit to male aggression. . . . It is up to human beings to select those [institutions] that foster the life styles they most value.[36]

Christine Pierce holds that nothing follows if men are instinctively more aggressive than women: "Perhaps women are needed to rescue men from being caught up in their own anatomical destiny."[37] Janet Richards compares male dominance to rape:

> Even if men are naturally inclined to dominance it does not follow that they ought to be allowed to run everything. Their being naturally dominant might be an excellent reason for imposing special restrictions to keep their nature under control. We do not think that men whose nature inclines them to rape ought to be given free rein to go around raping, so why should the naturally dominant be allowed to go around dominating? . . . If women are weak and need protection, it should have been the men who were controlled.[38]

This argument is often supplemented with a dilemma constructed by Mill: If sex roles are biologically unalterable, feminist reforms will not change them; and if sex roles *are* alterable, feminist reforms must be judged on their merits. Either way, there is no need to worry about what is biologically inevitable.

But the question of innate sex differences is not so easily evaded. Once again, since it is irrational to try to do what is known to be impossible, it is irrational not to try to determine whether biology precludes some envisioned reform. What is more, "impossibility" has a somewhat different meaning when applied to physical systems than when applied to homeostatic social systems. The internal state variables of homeostatic systems tend to converge to a relatively small number of values which can persist stably over time. There are states through which a society can temporarily pass which are nonetheless impossible in the sense of being unstable; they are states that no society can occupy permanently. By contrast, a mechanical system like a galaxy cannot even temporarily occupy a mechanically impossible state. It must not be assumed, therefore, that a social innovation possible in the sense that it can be instituted in the short run is also possible in the sense of corresponding to a condition that a society could stably occupy. Indeed, homeostatic systems like societies can occupy physically possible states beyond their elastic limits. These are not unstable states from which the system must rebound, but states from which the system cannot evolve back into stability, and which lead to the system's disintegration. It is obviously possible for all fertile women in a society to refuse to bear children, so that a childless society is possible for one generation, but after that the society will cease to exist.

To put the latter point in different but equivalent terms, "necessary" is meant conditionally in assertions like "sex roles are biologically necessary." To say that sex roles are biologically necessary is to say that there will be sex roles in any existing society. However, no law says that there must be sex roles no matter what—as there is a law that says that any two bodies will attract each other no matter what—since no law says that there must be any societies. It hardly follows, as Mill assumes, that feminist reforms will change nothing if sex roles are biologically necessary. Feminist reforms could not, by hypothesis, bring about a society with no sex roles, but the effort to destroy sex roles could in principle destroy society. (It is impossible to drive a car through a brick wall; does this mean that it is all the same whether one tries to drive through a brick wall or not?) I am not here sounding the alarm about any damage that feminism might or might not do; I am simply observing that Mill's argument does presuppose that sex roles are not biologically necessary features of a stable society.

Once it is granted that the mechanism that propels society toward and maintains it in stable states is individual preferences, the question naturally arises as to the *point* of manipulating sex differences in accordance with values. Let it be agreed for a moment that there might be arrangements consistent with biological laws that produce more sexually equal outcomes. Why are those arrangements preferable to the present one, if the present one arose under conditions of equal opportunity? While there is a tradition in social theory which finds equality valuable in itself, most egalitarians value equality because of a presumed causal connection between equality and other valued factors. Thus, when the question is pressed as to what is wrong with the present inequality of results, the reply almost inevitably is that *this inequality could not have come about under conditions of equal opportunity for men and women.* In other words, the wish to see sex differences manipulated toward more equal outcomes is virtually always (if not always clearly) premised on the denial that the present order really is the product of innate preferences. This denial amounts to an empirical theory about the origins of the present order. We may thus expect the ostensibly prospective citation of the fact/value gap to yield sooner or later to the theory that present reality involves the subjugation of women. Richards so yields when she talks of men being "allowed to dominate" under things as they are. Appeal to the fact/value gap as an argument for radical change assumes environmentalism after all.

The final lacuna in feminist appeal to the fact/value gasp is obliviousness to the question of who is to select and control the institutions to be fostered if it is decided that male impulses need more controlling than they currently receive. If males really are naturally more dominant, it will always be males who are in charge. The only agency that can prevent males in a human group from dominating it is a more powerful human group. However, one group's intervention in the affairs of another to strip its males of power does not transfer power to the females of the subject group; the real power goes to the dominant members of the dominant group—who will be males if males are more interested in dominance than females. (In forcing a private firm to hire more females managers, the government does not transfer power to the women in the firm; it transfers power to the males running the government.) Talk of controlling male aggression and imposing values on facts is incoherent without the assumption that women are innately as prone to seek power as men.

It is possible to miss this point if individual and collective choice are conflated. Human beings are undeniably capable of making reflective decisions, but this capacity is almost always exercised by individuals in individual circumstances. Institutions are not chosen by anybody; they emerge unintended from those individual decisions. No child is socialized by society. Every child is individually socialized by his parents, and from these private practices evolve shared norms which are logically and causally derivative. Collective decisions can be made by governments—"collective decision making" is no more than a grandiose name for state action—but governments generally concern themselves with sharply defined goals rather than overall social structure. Totalitarian governments have not been able to change social structure appreciably, and democratically enacted social reforms generally codify antecedent unwilled changes in mores.

That societies may differ in their emphasis on "masculine" or "feminine" traits, the status accorded women, and similar variables does not suggest that the character of a society is up to its members. The Swiss did not decide to acquire a reputation for precision. Nor does the variance that has existed in the assignment of sex roles show that significantly greater variation awaits only the will to create it. The variation that is possible is, once again, an empirical question that must be answered before one even begins to ask which variants are desirable.

Appeal to the fact/value gap is often more confusing than clarifying. Once the question of innate sex differences is recast as the question of the best collective response to innate sex differences, the option of letting private individuals do as they please tends to sink from sight. Maccoby and Jacklin take up the significance of sex differences in visual-spatial ability by asking: "If girls are, on the average, less skilled in visual-spatial tasks, does this mean that fewer of them should be admitted to graduate schools in engineering, architecture, and art?"[39] Maccoby and Jacklin cite no advocate of such a proposal, and I have been unable to find any; they frame the issue in this needlessly contentious way because they have fused the question of what sex differences mean for society with the quite different question of what people should do about them.[40] Maccoby and Jacklin fail to consider the possibility that people "should" do nothing beyond allowing students to choose subjects on the basis of their own interests and aptitudes, recognizing that in all likelihood fewer girls than boys will choose architecture if indeed a difference in visual-spatial ability does exist.

The tendency to see every fact as grist for evaluation also fosters misunderstanding about the implications of evolution. It is very frequently argued that, because drives once adaptive may no longer be so, these drives should no longer count. Thus Nancy Chodorow concedes that a hunter-gatherer past selected for aggressiveness in human males and nurturance in human females, but replies that "the [evolutionary] argument is allowed to stand for industrial societies like ours which do not need the division of labor for physical reproduction."[41] Chodorow does not see that the point of the evolutionary argument is not to *justify* sexual dimorphism, but to *establish its existence*. This dimorphism may prompt behavior that is maladaptive in our present environment, but it is silly to criticize evolution as if it were a purposive agent that had slipped. If the question is whether women feel responsible for child care because of conditioning or because of drives which were selected as mankind evolved (and this is the question Chodorow is concerned to answer), it does not matter whether those drives have since become maladaptive if they, not socialization, explain the institution of motherhood.

The Treatment of Innate Drives as Obstacles

Thus Betty Friedan:

> Even if it were true that all societies so far have been patriarchal and dominated by men, and even if that dominance is based on biological differences, it is irrelevant to the situation forcing women to demand equal opportunity in America and Britain today. Even if they are sorely handicapped by lack of testosterone it is inescapably necessary for women at this stage in human evolution to move to equality in society.[42]

This is less a denial of innate sex differences than sheer muddle. Since a handicap is anything that prevents someone from getting what he wants, it is logically impossible for not wanting something to be a handicap to its pursuit. A would-be competitor in a race may be handicapped by external factors like a muddy track or weak hamstrings, but he cannot be handicapped by his own indifference to winning. To treat a person's lack of desire as something that gets in his way is to draw an unreal distinction between *him* and his preferences and personality. If a woman's preferences and personality interfere with her, who is the *she* they interfere with? This abstract self must be conceived as a characterless monad, devoid of desires but nevertheless capable of autonomy. Such a view makes no literal sense, but it makes a kind of emotional sense for those who see so much value in male pursuits and so little value in female pursuits that they cannot believe that women do not want what men do.

"Women Are Better Than Men"

A familiar theme in feminist writing, particularly in the second stage said to have emerged after 1980, is that the world would be a better place if women were leaders because women are less belligerent than men.[43] Whatever its other merits, this idea would seem to involve a strong commitment to innate sex differences.

That commitment, however, is most equivocal because the critical point is left unclear: Is the greater cooperativeness of females innate, or is it the product of female socialization? The overall idea faces difficulty on either interpretation. If female cooperativeness is innate, how are women to reach positions of leadership whose attainment requires competitiveness? If female cooperativeness is learned, how did oppression produce moral superiority? And if oppression does produce morally superior beings, using female cooperativeness to ensure peace requires the perpetuation of the oppressive apparatus that produces it—a requirement at odds with the goal of liberation. The more popular second-stage writers, like Ehrenreich and Dowling, never explicitly contest environmentalism and so far as I can tell would be loath to attribute the female's superior moral nature to an innate program. But the ambivalence of the second stage surfaces very clearly in Carol Gilligan's work on sex differences in moral thinking. Gilligan received much attention for arguing that female moral judgement is distinguished by "an overriding concern with relationships and responsibilities . . . a world composed of relations rather than of people standing alone, a world that coheres through human connection rather than through systems of rules."[44]

This finding would seem to amount to no more than the common sense of the matter, which would have been derided as sexist stereotyping had it not been published by a woman. It certainly would not have surprised Freud, who held that the male superego must impose stricter, more impersonal rules to control the male's greater aggressiveness. The only interesting question raised by the cognitive-affective sex differences Gilligan identifies is their origin, and Gilligan firmly distances herself from any nativist interpretation: "No claims are being made about the origins of the differences described. . . . Clearly, these differences arise in a social context in which factors of socialization and power combine with reproductive biology."[45] Gilligan stresses the cooperative character of the games girls play as a contributor to the female moral style—without asking why girls choose cooperative games in the first place—and she leaves the overall impression that the female moral style is inculcated through early training. Separated from a nativist interpretation, Gilligan's conclusions come to little more than the triviality that groups raised in different environments, as boys and girls are said to be, develop different norms. It is not, after all, surprising that nomadic Arabs living on a harsh desert should value death in combat more than do contemporary Chicagoans. There is no distinctive female moral voice if men would have spoken in the same tones had they been raised as women are.

As it emerges, Giligan's ultimate aim is less to explain the female voice than to chide society for ignoring it: "Sex differences in aggression are usually interpreted by taking the male response as the norm, so that the absence of aggression in women is identified as the problem to be explained."[46] She cites no-one who regards female lack of aggression as a problem (Betty Friedan and Germaine Greer[47] come to mind), but Gilligan's use of sex differences is perhaps the distinguishing trait of "second-stage" feminism. To the very uncertain extent that innate sex differences are recognized, they become vehicles for expressing dissatisfaction at society's failure to accommodate the female nature—now described as complementary or superior to men's. The diabolization of men continues, with men now being blamed for the mistakes of first-stage feminism. If first-stage feminists imposed an impossible "superwoman" ideal on women, the tensions experienced by women trying to "'have it all" are laid to their copying male standards.[48] Men are blamed for a high divorce rate. Taking a position indistinguishable from the first stage, Barbara Ehrenreich explains that a marriage in which the woman depends on a man to earn a living is inherently unstable. The existence of female nurturance, regarded as a new discovery, is seen as opening new possibilities for rapprochement between men and women, the tapping of long-ignored nonmasculine thoughts and feelings, a new appreciation for the female world view, a new emphasis on the feminine in men, and dismay at what has been lost through the universal dominance by men of extrafamilial pursuits and female domination of childrearing.

Dissatisfaction with the present social order, moreover, leads second-stage feminists to the same practical recommendations as were advocated by first-stage feminists on environmentalist grounds. In *The Second Stage* Betty Friedan develops the view of testosterone as a handicap into a call for the total reorganization of society around women's "beta consciousness." Friedan remains adamant about quotas, an expanding female presence in the military, public funding for abortion, comparable worth, and along with Benjamin Barber, the "unfinished business" of the Equal Rights Amendment.[49] Other second-stage feminists continue to call for special preferences for women and for a statistical equality of outcome which, one would have thought, made sense only on environmentalist grounds. Elizabeth Wolgast begins *Equality and the Rights of Women* by stating: "We need an alternative to egalitarian reasoning" because "society does not create all the differences" between men and women.[50] It is better, she says, to "allow for various differences between the sexes,"[51] but the provisions she suggests are oddly atavistic:

> Such a bivalent view provides a justification for affirmative action policies because it rejects a neutral perspective from which the concerns of both sexes can be seen "objectively." [Society] should not adopt linear scales for distinguishing all individuals regardless of sex. It suggests that men and women of talent, for example, will not generally match on the same set of parameters, and therefore, if a single standard is assumed and if that should be drawn from a sample of males, the comparison with a sample of women may be invidious. Without awareness of the possible range of differences between the sexes, this linear approach to merit must be treated with suspicion.[52]

Does the use of innate sex differences as a stick for continuing to beat society and demand special treatment at least imply recognition of innate sex differences? Not at all, for, so far as I can tell, second-stage feminists agree with first-stage feminists that the organization of sex roles is to no significant extent the result of innate sex differences. To say that marriage must be changed to accommodate female needs is precisely to assume that female needs have nothing to do with the shape of marriage as it presently exists. It is this refusal to see social institutions as connected to the innate sex differences they say they recognize that accounts for the felt propriety of the term *feminist* to describe the authors I have cited.

It will not do to pretend that second-stage feminism is entirely coherent. While many one-time feminists are no longer able to deny altogether the existence of biologically based sex differences, they are at the same time unwilling to admit that women *lack* any of the traits that men have. Naturally, no social institution can accommodate creatures who are amalgams of men and women, so much social reconstruction remains to be done:

> Justice in social relations preserves (or creates) political and economic equality in the face of different roles, distinctive gender needs. . . . [T]he challenge of third stage feminism is how to make "different but equal" a reality, not because differences are ineluctable, but because equality is valuable only when it encourages rather than destroys them.[53]

Moderate Feminism

That some feminists, lesbian separatists among them,[54] are more radical and strident than others should not be taken to imply that there is a moderate feminist *position.* Society is either the residue of arbitrary conditioning—a radical position—or it is not. The radical analogy between Blacks and women is to be taken seriously, or it is not. There is no intermediate view about the basic structure of society.

This may be less obvious than it should be, in part, for purely verbal reasons. People convinced a priori that feminism is good, will often shop around for something inoffensive for "feminism" to denote. This is no doubt how "feminism" remains attached to platitudes and positions granted decades ago, like "equal pay for equal work." Willful misuse of words is bad manners, but harmless so long as its practitioners do not confuse what they are calling "feminism" with what other people call "feminism."

A more serious obstacle to seeing the impossibility of moderate feminism is the tendency to see feminism as an application of the liberal precept that people should be judged as individuals. When applied to relations between the sexes, this precept has no meaning that is both moderate and fixed. As advice about institutions like the law, this precept is radical, requiring for instance the legal recognition of homosexual marriage—a welcome reform, perhaps, but still a radical one. As advice about private conduct, the precept is either empty or based on adventurous factual assumptions. The precept "Don't make any assumptions about a woman on the basis of her sex" is not a belief system about the origin of society or a canon for evaluating it. It contains no implicit critique of extant sex roles or the victimization of women. It attaches to no program of action involving quotas, censorship, unisex actuarial tables, comparable worth, abortion, or homosexual rights—many of which liberals would deplore. It finds nothing objectionable in a woman seeking paid labor if she wishes it, but it sees nothing especially desirable about careers for women. It says nothing whatever about personal relations or emotions. Moderate feminism as liberal tolerance is at best a caution for dealing with career women.

The liberal precept that everyone deserves a fair go is so nearly vacuous because it is not specifically about women at all. It involves nothing about such obstacles as may exist to treating women as individuals, and nothing about the reliability of stereotypes. If liberalism is given content by being conjoined to the empirical contention that sex stereotypes are false (and that is why one must keep an open mind) and that men and women are really alike, the resolve to be scrupulously fair suddenly becomes radical. What makes liberalism far less applicable to relations between the sexes than it is to, say, relations between races, is that it assumes away any innate differences that might control people's responses to members of their own and opposite sex. If for instance men cannot help feeling more protective than competitive toward woman and more competitive than protective toward other men, the question of how men *should* act in new encounters is taken out of their hands. They will feel and act as they cannot help feeling and acting.

It is impossible to say at this point how many responses to new situations are learned projections from the lessons of old situations, but no doubt much of our behavior toward men and women *is* learned. This does not mean, however, that these acquired responses can be unlearned. People are bound to base their behavior and expectations on past experience, and if someone has always observed men and women to act differently, his subsequent attitudes are bound to reflect the belief that these regularities will continue. Probability assessments coalesce too unconsciously and impressionistically to be altered by formula—by just how much should one reduce one's estimate of the chances that the next woman he meets will want children?—and anyway belief is not subject to the will. The reader might try as an exercise to will himself to believe that Jews make terrible lawyers. Conversely, there is little point to urging people to change their stereotypes, because stereotypes change unprompted when the world does. After 1948 people stopped believing that Jews could not fight. If women cease being more interested in children than men, that stereotype too will vanish.

Many thoughtful persons continue to apply the liberal ideal to women out of concern that the persistence of stereotypes unfairly penalizes unusual women. To the extent that this concern denies the influence of biology and experience on attitudes, it is not a *moral* qualm, but it might be mentioned in passing that the right of unusual people to be treated as such is almost certainly imaginary. On what could such a right be based? Kantian considerations of reciprocity impose an omnilateral obligation to refrain from inflicting harm, but not an obligation to appreciate. Moreover, while a woman with atypical abilities may, thanks to stereotyping, face difficulties that a man with those same but more typically male abilities will escape, these difficulties must be balanced against the benefits conferred by stereotyping on the majority of typical men and women, who are told via stereotypes that their preferences are normal and desireable. While the one woman in fifty who does not want children may be made uncomfortable by the message that there is something wrong with her, the same message is reinforcing the other forty-nine women.

Whether the discomfort of the atypical few is too high a price for the comfort of the many is not a question that concerns me here, and I trust it will not deflect attention from my main point: The formation of stereotypes, like the formation of other generalizations, is a direct expression of individual spontaneity, and any attempt to interfere with it requires interference with processes whose variations between persons are important marks of individuality. Liberal open-mindedness risks runing athwart individual liberty just as surely as does "radical" egalitarianism.

It is not hard to see why there *seems* to be a middle ground between feminism and the platitude of open-mindedness. One may begin with the platitude, edge toward the social oppression theory under pressure to be specific, and hasten back to the platitude as the oppression theory becomes implausible. Shuttle back and forth quickly enough, and the resultant blur can be taken for a position. That some such self-deception is at work is suggested by the difficulty experienced by self-described moderate feminists in detailing what they are *for*. Benjamin Barber writes:

Once feminism is liberated from the narrow perspectives that put it at odds with the femininity its name ennobles, it can begin its true struggle to rescue the polity in which our humanity resides from its myriad enemies, and thereby to rescue women from the precarious perch somewhere between animality and divinity where their search for liberation has left them.[55]

Who, then, are "the real foes of liberation" that enlightened feminism will oppose? They are "the materialists and bureaucrats and interest-mongers and technocrats and behaviorists and ideologues and hedonists and bigots who together conspire to annihilate our human identity."[56] This miscellany cannot be called a helpful guide to what positive views moderate feminism might advocate.

Against the pious hope that one keep an open mind about women there stands a coherent theory about the nature of women issuing in an extensive program of action. I will *give* the word *feminism* to anyone who wishes to use it out of pious hope, and return to examining the coherent theory under any name anyone prefers for it.[57]

Feminism and Public Policy

At some risk of repetition, it is important to verify that feminism as defined here is a working assumption of public policy. Satisfaction on this point will presumably motivate the examination of that theory, whatever it is called.

Environmentalism implies that any significant statistical disparity in outcomes for men and women is due to outright discrimination or more subtly inequitable social forces. This interpretation of statistical data has been accepted by the U.S. Equal Employment Opportunity Commission, the Commission on Civil Rights, the departments of Health and Human Services, Labor, and Education, and Congress. It is also, very nearly, the opinion of the Supreme Court. The EEOC states: "Absent discrimination, it is to be expected that work forces will be more or less representative of the population in the community from which employees are hired."[58] The federal Uniform Guidelines on Employee Selection procedures presumes a ranking system for a job to be illegal if it statistically "underrepresents" women.[59] In 1980 the CCR argued that "a steady flow of data" shows "ongoing discriminatory attitudes and processes [on the part of] white males [toward] the rest of the population."[60] The data in question are abstracted from the commission's 1978 statistical report, *Social Indicators of Equality for Minorities and Women,* and is given as follows:

> Women and minorities are more likely to be unemployed, to have less presti-
> gious occupations than white males. . . . [W]omen are less likely to have
> completed as many years of high school than white males. . . . Majority
> female college graduates have average earnings less than majority males with
> a high school education. This indicator reflects a bleak picture for black
> young men and women and for majority women.[61]

The Commission sometimes explicitly endorses the assumption that equal outcomes are to be expected absent discrimination, as when it considers the lower overqualification rate of white males relative to Blacks and females: "In a labor market where the match between people's qualifications and their jobs is not influenced by minority or gender status, it would be expected that the different groups would have equal degrees of overqualification."[62] At other times the inference from statistical inequality to inequality of opportunity is tacit:

> women . . . have not achieved equal status with majority males on a series of
> 21 measures of equality in the areas of education, income, employment, occu-
> pations, poverty, and housing. Despite some absolute improvements in many
> of the areas . . . majority males have continued to enjoy broader opportunities
> and to reap disproportionate benefits while women . . . have in many
> instances fallen even further behind.[63]

There is a call for government action, but action not based on knowledge of the causes of the statistical inequalities in question:

> While the indicators alone will not decipher the causes of social trends, their
> clear delineation of trends should be sufficient to stimulate more intensive
> scrutiny of programs or to suggest adjustments to them. Through these indi-
> cators, attention is focussed on the limited effect of recent Federal efforts to
> enhance the conditions of women and minority men relative to majority
> males, indicating the need for more effective policy and program formation.[64]

The commission recommends the collection of further data, but again, none addressed to determining causes.

Many commentators have detected a shift in recent decades from equality of opportunity to equality of outcome as the governing criterion of equality. These passages suggest that no such shift has occurred. Rather, the empirical assumption that the sexes are equal in all relevant respects has forced the conclusion that opportunities equal in the traditional sense would result in equal outcomes. Equality is not being identified with equal outcomes; instead, unequal outcomes are being used as unrebuttable evidence that opportunities were unequal.

The Supreme Court has also concerned itself with undoing the supposed artificialities of sex stereotyping. It has not at this writing subjected sex-based legal classifications to "strict scrutiny," the standard it applies to racial classifications, but it did hold in *Craig v. Boren*[65] that a sex-based classification must be "substantially related" to "an important government objective," and it added in *Mississippi v. Hogan*[66] that an "extremely persuasive justification" is need to meet the *Craig* test. *Frontiero* raised the question of extending strict scrutiny to sex-based classifications, and four justices did vote to affirm this extension.

The Supreme Court, then, is quasi-feminist: It takes the conditions of Blacks and women to be substantially analogous, but has so far refused to treat them as legally equivalent. It would certainly be wrong to view the court as biased toward women; the court has been interested primarily in making the sexes come out alike. In some cases, this has meant permitting preferential treatment for women, and in other cases overthrowing privileges previously accorded women. Attributing such an intent to the court renders consistent such an otherwise incongruous pair of rulings as *Schlesinger* and *Orr*.[67] In *Schlesinger* the court upheld the navy's policy of making promotion easier for women than for men, while in *Orr* the court struck down an Alabama law stipulating that only husbands could pay alimony. *Orr* is consistent with the doctrine of rigid sex blindness, but *Schlesinger* is not; *Schlesinger* is consistent with favoritism for women, but *Orr* is not. However, both decisions are consistent with the doctrine that gender differences should not be allowed to have consequences. *Schlesinger* has the clear intent of helping to "integrate" the armed forces,[68] and indeed *Orr* had a similar intent: in the words of Justice Brennan, the Alabama statute impermissibly risked "reinforcing stereotypes about the 'proper place' of women and their need for special protection."[69]

This same tendency on the part of the courts is at work in the recent series of decisions affecting insurance. In addition to *Manhart*, the 1982 *Norris* decision held that a sex-based actuarial table "discriminates against women because it looks at them as a class instead of individuals"[70]—rather curious reasoning from a judiciary which regularly holds women to have been damaged as a class and to deserve compensation as a class, regardless of the histories of the specific women who benefit from court-ordered remedies. *Norris* was supplemented by a consent decree before a Pennsylvania court under which women will no longer have to pay higher disability rates despite their greater proneness to injury.[71] In 1984 the Pennsylvania Supreme Court ruled that the state's Equal Rights Amendment barred automobile insurance companies from basing insurance premiums on differences between male and female accident rates.[72] Parallel rulings have been made about pensions. In the past, retired men have normally received more per month than retired women who have paid identical amounts into the same pension fund, since the male's shorter life expectancy means that he must get his net return in a shorter time. In many jurisdictions women must now be given monthly payments equal to those given to men. It is doubtful that such judicial actions can be made fully rational by any interpretation (their net effect has been to require careful female drivers to subsidize reckless male drivers, and to require short-lived men to subsidize longer-lived women), but their overall intent would seem to be to prevent action based on information about sex differences.

The analogy between women and Blacks informs the passages cited from EEOC and CCR documents, and it is ubiquitous in civil rights legislation. Race and sex are jointly forbidden as bases for the treatment of individuals in the 1964 Civil Rights Act, the 1968 Civil Rights Act (barring discrimination in housing), Executive Order 11063 (barring discrimination in federally assisted housing), EO 11375 (mandating affirmative action for government contractors), EO 11478 (mandating affirmative action in the federal civil service), and twenty-two more specific federal civil rights laws covering matters from discrimination in disaster relief to affirmative action on the Alaska Pipeline.[73] Several laws protect women but not racial minorities; only the Food Stamp Act and the Public Work Employment Act of 1977 contain language which protects Blacks but not women. Many of these laws extend earlier laws which protected Blacks only. The history of this legislation involves little extended deliberation on the Black/female analogy; indeed, Blacks and women have marched so firmly in lockstep in the law that it is difficult to extract from it any distinctive views whatever about women. The advice given on these matters by government advisory bodies is often couched in language which suggests that its authors believe women to *be* a racial minority. The 1980 report of the President's Advisory Committee describes "the problem of sexism" as one of

> a multitude of other conditions which inhibit [women's] capacity to fully develop as productive human beings. Continued advancement will require vigorous enforcement of laws prohibiting inequitable treatment of women, and a national commitment to the elimination of sex discrimination, sex bias, sex stereotyping, racial stereotyping, and any form of differential treatment that abridges the rights of women.[74]

The proposed federal Equal Rights Amendment deserves mention as the chief legislative goal of contemporary feminism.[75] The preamble to Senate Judiciary Resolution 10, its present legislative embodiment, asserts that "being born female still constitutes a clear and present danger to the full attainment and the full development of the individual's character." The operative wording of the ERA is:

> Equality of rights under the law shall not be denied or abridged by the United States or by any State on account of sex. The Congress shall have the power to enforce by appropriate legislation the provisions of this article.

ERA supporters divide into those who cannot say what these words mean,[76] and those who see the ERA as ending the recognition of gender in society. Its proponents clearly intend it to make sex a suspect (and in practice impermissible) legal classification:

> Although opponents of the ERA maintain that the 14th Amendment provides adequate protection against sex discrimination, the Supreme Court of the United States has stopped short of applying the same 14th Amendment standards to sex discrimination that it does to race discrimination.[77]

The full implications of the ERA go considerably further. The legal claim of homosexuals to marriage licenses "would almost certainly be vindicated under the proposed ERA,"[78] as would broad state powers to impose "benign discrimination" favoring women.[79] Before they came to be regarded as liabilities, the conscription of women and public funding for abortion were cited by proponents of the ERA as two of its desirable consequences.[80] I know of no legal scholar who disputes the inference that all-male conscription denies to men the right not to join the armed services on the basis of sex, and would be illegal under the ERA.[81] As for the second hypothetical consequence, several state supreme courts have ruled that denial of public funds for abortion is discriminatory, since pregnancy is a condition unique to women, and it is not clear how a federal ERA could fail to support a similar interpretation.

A demand supposedly distinctive of "radical" feminism is numerical equality of outcomes in all activities—and feminists have urged that the Supreme Court's "disparate impact" test for discrimination, which since *Griggs v. Duke*[82] and *Dothard v. Rawlinson*[83] has forbidden facially sex-neutral laws that affect men and women differently, be applied to ERA. Judith Wegner argued before the Senate Judiciary Committee that

> interpretation of the Equal Rights Amendment to include a disparate impact, rather than discriminatory intent standard would provide additional protection against gender-based discrimination without unduly compromising competing

government interests. Based on this analysis, I strongly recommend that the
Committee go on record as supporting such an interpretation.[84]

Whatever may be the intrinsic meaning of the words of the ERA, its advocates clearly wish to see it applied with numerical literalness whenever
there is a government presence.[85]

The most open-ended feature of the ERA is the difference in language
between "rights under the law" and the Fourteenth Amendment guarantee
of "equal protection of the law." The equal protection clause speaks only of
state treatment of individuals; it requires the same enforcement of all laws
for all citizens, without reference to any further, nonlegal rights. But a right
"under" the law can be understood to cover not only rights created by statute, but, in addition, any prerogative in any private activity merely permitted by the law. Deployed with the disparate impact test, any activity whatever which affects the sexes differently would be construable as an abridge-
ment of "equality of rights under the law." And, while it is impossible to
predict judicial construction, pressure to interpret "right under the law" as
pretermitted action would be placed on the courts by the axiom that legislatures do nothing in vain. The courts can hardly be unaware that ERA was
proposed while the Fourteenth Amendment and the Civil Rights Act, which
bars private discrimination, were in effect. Thus, the ERA either redun-
dantly reiterates these two statutes—an interpretation which would put the
courts at swords' points with the axiom—or it goes beyond them, and there
is little way for the ERA to go beyond them other than by reconstruing
private action as action pretermitted by the law. There is a precedent for
this wide understanding of "right under the law" in *Pennsylvania v. Board
of Trustees*,[86] in which the Supreme Court held that a school established
with a private endowment for "poor White male orphans" could not
exclude Blacks because of the role of the courts in administering trustees.

Lawyers representing NOW were not being hyperbolic when they
claimed that ERA would remove the "legacy of the past, which leaves the
athletic prowess of males and females at different levels right now."[87] Athletic prowess like everything else falls within its ambit. In the rueful words
of an ERA supporter reflecting on its loss of public support, "under ERA
everything will become ERA's business."[88]

Later chapters will look more deeply into the impact of feminism on public policy. This overview is merely meant to suggest the extent of this
impact. Not that such exercises still the objection that I am talking about a
fringe phenomenon. Quoting people who call themselves feminists is commonly regarded as bad form, while critical examination of feminism is
equated with misogyny, the wish to disenfranchise women, and incipient
Nazism. These misunderstandings resist the most dogged efforts at

rectification. I do not know why otherwise reasonable people find it necessary to mishear any criticism of feminism as something idiotic (and therefore not needing consideration). Here is a research project for some curious psychologist.

Notes

1. Peter Singer, "Ten Years of Animal Liberation," *New York Review of Books* (January 17, 1985): 52.
2. Richard Wasserstrom, "On Racism and Sexism," in *Today's Moral Problems,* 2nd ed., ed. Richard Wasserstrom (New York: Macmillan, 1981), pp. 96–97.
3. John Stuart Mill, *The Subjection of Women* (1869), ch. 1; Simone de Beauvoir, *The Second Sex,* trans. H.M. Parshley (New York: Knopf, 1953), p. 513; Millett, *Sexual Politics,* ch. 1, sex. 2, p. 2; Shulamith Firestone, *The Dialectic of Sex* (New York: Morrow, 1970), p. 1; Steinem (cited by Carol Felsenthal), "How Feminists Failed," *Chicago* (June 1982): 139; member of NOW, cited in Muriel Carden, *The New Feminist Movement* (New York: Russell Sage, 1974), p. 12; Jessie Bernard, "The Paradox of the Happy Marriage," in Gornick and Moran, *Woman in Sexist Society,* p. 159; National Institute of Education Request for Proposal RFP-NIE-R-80-0018, Department of Health, Education, and Welfare, National Institute of Education (Washington, D.C.: April 30, 1980), p. 1; Allison Jagger, "On Sexual Equality," *Ethics* 84 (July 1984): 276; Judith Long Laws, *The Second X* (New York: Elsevier, 1979), p. 372; Janet Richards, *The Sceptical Feminist* (Boston: Routledge & Kegan Paul, 1980), pp. 273–84; Marion Lowe, "The Dialectics of Biology and Culture," in *Women's Nature,* ed. Marian Lowe and Ruth Hubbard (New York: Pergamon, 1983), p. 56; Rosalind Petchesky, *Abortion and Women's Choice* (New York: Pergamon, 1984), pp. 176–82; Ruth Bleier, *Science and Gender* (New York: Pergamon, 1984), pp. 176–82.
4. Alice Rossi, "Equality between the Sexes: An Immodest Proposal," *Daedalus* 93 (1964): 608–10.
5. Alice Rossi, "A Biosocial Perspective on Parenting," *Daedalus* 106 (1977): 1–2.
6. Carden, p. 11. The parochial reference to toy manufacturers and authors of children's books—factors irrelevant to the vast majority of societies—illustrates the difficulty of interpreting feminism charitably.
7. Claire Fulenwider, *Feminism in American Politics* (New York: Praeger, 1980), p. 56.
8. Ibid., p. 23.
9. Ibid., pp. 30–35.
10. Ibid., p. 47.
11. Ibid., p. 56.
12. Helen Hacker, "Women as a Minority Group," in *Who Discriminates against Women?* ed. Florence Denmark (Beverly Hills, Ca.: Sage, 1974), p. 134; Ralph Stern, letter, *New York* (January 31, 1983): 5; Christopher W. Morris, "Existential Limits to the Rectification of Past Wrongs," *American Philosophical Quarterly* 21 (April 1984): 177.
13. *Frontiero v. Richardson,* 411 US 677 (1973).
14. Anne Fausto-Sterling considers this possibility in *Myths of Gender.*

15. Nancy Chodorow, *The Reproduction of Mothering* (Berkeley, Ca.: University of California Press, 1978), p. 81; Juliet Mitchell, *Psychoanalysis and Feminism* (New York: Pantheon, 1974), cited in Chodorow, p. 81.
16. Ibid., pp. 214–19.
17. *The Second Sex*, p. 89.
18. Letty Pogrebin, *Growing Up Free* (New York: McGraw-Hill, 1980), pp. 516–17. Miss Pogrebin describes herself as a "moderate" situated midway between "traditionalists" and "radicals."
19. Ibid., p. 130.
20. *The Second Sex*, pp. 724–26.
21. *Sexual Politics*, p. 85.
22. See Germaine Greer, *The Female Eunuch* (New York: McGraw-Hill, 1970), pp. 313–29.
23. Catherine MacKinnon, "Feminism, Marxism, Method, and the State: An Agenda for Theory," *Signs* 7 (1982): 516–17.
24. The Soviet government for its part continues to move away from unisex equality. In 1981 it barred women from 460 jobs, apparently in response to health problems caused by women working under the same conditions as men. See Alexandra Biryukova, *Soviet Women: Their Role in Society, the Economy, the Trade Unions* (Moscow: Profizdat Publishers, 1981), pp. 31–41.
25. *Science and Gender*, p. 180.
26. Ellen Mintz, "The Prejudice of Parents," in Denmark, pp. 21–22.
27. But what became of the old personality? Has murder been done? These questions are obscure, but only because the suppositions that raise them are so contrary to fact. It is seldom helpful to assimilate ordinary behavior to abnormal behavior understood by its contrast with the normal. The position I defend in *Metaphysics and the Mind-Body Problem* (Oxford: Oxford University Press, 1979), is that free action is based on preferences one at least tacitly approves of. Thus, brainwashing victims do not act freely because nobody wants to have his preferences produced by brainwashing.
28. See R. Duncan Luce and Howard Raiffa, *Games and Decisions* (New York: Wiley, 1957), ch. 5.
29. May 1986.
30. "Immodest Proposal," p. 643.
31. "Biology is not enough to answer the question: Why is woman the *Other*?" (de Beauvoir). Elizabeth Janeway finds "little need to believe that men and women are born with psychological differences built into their brains because the workings of society and culture, by themselves, are perfectly capable of producing all the differences we know so well" (*Man's World, Woman's Place* [New York: Morrow, 1971], p. 10); Letty Pogrebin's list of the "*real* differences between the sexes" comprises "voice, appearance, size and feel" (*Growing Up Free*, p. 315). Anne Oakley has her doubts about Kate Millett's "difference in orgasmic capacity"; she takes anatomical research to show that "the ultimate sexual response, the orgasm, is physiologically identical in male and female, except for the minor difference of organ and secretion" (*Sex, Gender, and Society* [New York: Harper & Row, 1972], p. 128). Feminists with impeccable scientific credentials say the same things. Here is Estelle Ramey: "As an endocrinologist, I think virtually all the differences in male and female behavior are culturally, not hormonally, determined. . . . It is said, for instance, that men are innately more aggressive than women. But conditioning, not sex hormones, makes them

that way. Anyone seeing women at a bargain-basement sale—where aggression is viewed as appropriate—sees aggression that would make Atilla the Hun turn pale."

32. Richards, p. 138.
33. Miss Millett contends that there were prehistoric societies in which men did not "control" women, but admits (p. 27ff.) that there is no evidence for them.
34. Chicago: Aldine, 1975.
35. *Science and Gender*, p. 109.
36. Eleanor Maccoby and Carol Jacklin, *The Psychology of Sex Differences* (Stanford: Stanford University Press, 1974), p. 374.
37. "Natural Law Language and Women," in Gornick and Moran, p. 255.
38. *The Sceptical Feminist*, p. 44. Maccoby and Jacklin observe that the one message communicated to children more than all others combined is that boys should not fight. Their unawareness of how much socialization is devoted to controlling male aggression suggests that feminists like Pierce and Richards are unfamiliar with raising children.
39. *The Psychology of Sex Differences*, p. 366.
40. Maccoby and Jacklin attribute to Steven Goldberg the view that "where a biological basis exists, it behooves societies to socialize their children in such ways as to emphasize and exaggerate the difference" (ibid., p. 373). Goldberg argues only that societies *will* end up emphasizing sex differences, and he explicitly disavows the view Maccoby and Jacklin attribute to him: "I suspect that I shall also be criticized as having suggested that society *should* emphasize sex differences in its socialization. What society *should* do is a question that cannot be answered on scientific grounds and it is one that I do not concern myself with here" (*The Inevitability of Patriarchy,* 2nd ed. [London: Temple-Smith, 1977], p. 107).
41. *The Reproduction of Motherhood*, p. 21.
42. Betty Friedan, review of Goldberg, *New Statesman* (September 23, 1977): 44.
43. See e.g. Gloria Steinem, "What Would it be Like if Women Win," in *The American Sisterhood,* ed. Wendy Martin (New York: Harper & Row, 1970), pp. 184–88. On the "second stage," see Betty Friedan, *The Second Stage* (New York: Simon & Schuster, 1981); Susan MacMillan, *Women, Reason, and Nature* (Princeton, N.J.: Princeton University Press, 1983); Janet Sayers, *Biological Politics* (New York: Methuen, 1982); Elizabeth Wolgast, *Equality and the Rights of Women* (Cornell: Cornell University Press, 1981); Barbara Ehrenreich, *The Hearts of Men* (New York: Doubleday, 1983); Colette Dowling, *The Cinderella Complex* (New York: Summit, 1981); Carol Gilligan, *In a Different Voice* (Cambridge, Mass.: Harvard University Press, 1983); Jean Bethke Elshtain, "Feminism, Family, and Community," *Dissent* (November 1982): 442–49.
44. *In a Different Voice,* p. 29.
45. Ibid., p. 2.
46. Ibid., p. 43.
47. Thus Greer in *The Female Eunuch:* "What happens to the Jewish boy who never manages to escape the tyranny of his mother is exactly what happens to every girl whose upbringing is 'normal.' She is a female faggot. Like the male faggots she lives her life in a pet about guest lists and sauce bernaise, except when she is exercising by divine maternal right the same process that destroyed her lusts and desires upon the lusts and desires of her children. . . . She is a vain, demanding, servile bore."

48. See Suzanne Gordon, "The New Corporate Feminism," *The Nation* (February 5, 1983): 143–47.
49. Benjamin Barber, "Beyond the Feminist Mystique," *The New Republic* (July 11, 1983): 26–32.
50. *Equality and the Rights of Women,* pp. 16, 126.
51. Ibid., p. 126.
52. Ibid., p. 127.
53. "Beyond the Feminist Mystique," p. 32. "Not ineluctable" betrays the lingering tendency to deny sex differences in the crunch. In cataloguing evasions of innate sex differences, I have omitted simple inconsistency, as practiced for instance by Mill. At various junctures in *The Subjection of Women* he says: "There will never prove to be any natural tendencies common to women, and distinguishing their genius from men," "no-one is thus far entitled to any positive opinion on the subject," and "in accordance with the best general conclusions which the world's imperfect experience seems as yet to suggest, the general bent of their talents is toward the practical." It is ironic that contemporary feminists should disdain the reforms Mill argued for and helped win, while embracing his confused arguments.
54. See Charlotte Brunch, "Lesbians in Revolt," in *Women and Values,* ed. Marily Pearsall (Belmont, Ca.: Wadsworth, 1986), 128–31; Marily Frye, "Some Reflections on Separatism and Power," in Pearsall: 132–38.
55. *Liberating Feminism,* p. 131.
56. Ibid., p. 176.
57. Feminists are aware of the advantages of the language of reform. In their review of the political fortunes of feminist movement, Joyce Gelb and Marion Paley note:

> When an issue is perceived as one affecting *role equity* rather than *role change,* success is more likely. Role equity issues are those policies which extend rights now enjoyed by other groups (men, minorities) to women, and which appear to be relatively delineated or narrow in their implications, permitting policymakers to seek advantage with feminist groups and voters with little cost or controversy. In contrast, role change issues appear to produce change in the dependent role of wife, mother, and homemaker, holding out the potential of greater sexual freedom and independence in a variety of contexts. . . . In order to appear legitimate, [feminist] groups will find it necessary to focus on incremental issues. In this regard, role equity issues are less threatening than role change issues [Joyce Gelb and Marion Paley, *Women and Public Policy* Princeton, N.J.: Princeton University Press, 1982), pp. 7–10].

The authors conclude:

> Even guaranteeing equal employment practices may have no impact on family roles, which often mirror in microcosm women's subordinate societal roles. Hence key problems for the future remain in the policy areas we have described as *role change* issues, which clearly redistribute power and resources to women, often in a highly politicized, conflict-laden political setting [ibid., pp. 177–78].

58. *Statement on Affirmative Action for Women and Minorities,* EEOC, October 1977, Clearinghouse Publication S4.

59. 29 CFR, sec. 1607 (1979).
60. *Affirmative Action in the 1980's: Dismantling the Process of Discrimination,* USCCR, 1980, p. 4.
61. Ibid., pp. 4–5.
62. *Social Indicators,* p. 17.
63. Ibid., p. 91.
64. Ibid., pp. 88–89.
65. *Craig v. Boren,* 429 US 190, 197 (1976).
66. *Mississippi v. Hogan,* 458 US 718 (1982).
67. *Schlesinger v. Ballard,* 419 US 498 (1975); *Orr v. Orr,* 440 US 268 (1979).
68. At 577. The court argued that, since women are not eligible for combat, affording them easier promotion recreates a situation of "equal opportunity."
69. At 1113. A law that "gender classifies . . . carries with it the baggage of sexual stereotypes" (at 1114).
70. *Norris v. Arizona,* 671 F2d 330 (1982).
71. "Sex Discrimination Suit May Force Big Changes in Retirement Benefits," *Wall Street Journal* (January 10, 1983); sex. 2, p. 1.
72. "Equal Rights Ruling for Auto Insurance Expected to Spread."
73. See *Federal Civil Rights: A Sourcebook,* Subcommittee on the Constitution, Senate Judiciary Committee (November 1980).
74. *Voices of Women* (Washington, D.C.: U.S. Government Printing Office, 1980), p. 25.
75. The ERA seems unlikely to be ratified in the near future. Ten states ratified the ERA within a few hours of its clearing Congress on March 22, 1972, and another twenty states ratified it within the next few months. However, no state ratified it after 1977 and five states subsequently rescinded, suggesting an initial outburst of uncritical enthusiasm for ERA unlikely to be repeated.
76. In testimony before the Subcommittee on the Constitution of the Senate Judiciary Committee on May 23, 1983, the chief Congressional sponsor of the ERA, Senator Paul Tsongas, was unable to answer the chair's questions about the implications of the ERA for veteran's preferences, tax exemption for churches that do not ordain women, single-sex schools, and a variety of other issues. See *Hearings before the Subcommittee on the Constitution of the Committee on the Judiciary* on S.J. Res. 10, part 1 (U.S. Government Printing Office, 1985), pp. 21–24.
77. Mary Berry of the USCCR, testimony before the House Judiciary Committee, July 13, 1983.
78. Samuel Perkins and Arthur Silverstein, "The Legality of Homosexual Marriage," *Yale Law Review* 82 (January 1973): 573–89.
79. See Thomas Emerson et al., "The Equal Rights Amendment: A Constitutional Basis for Equal Rights," *Yale Law Review* 80 (April 1971): 872–985.
80. "Both sides [of the ERA debate] did agree that, under the Amendment, women would have to be drafted if men were, but the advocates of the Amendment said that women were ready to accept this obligation." "Comment on Passage of Equal Rights Constitutional Amendment," *New York Times* (March 26, 1972): 6. "The ERA would repeal 'laws that affect a woman's right to decide her own reproductive and sexual life,' according to the Women's National Political Caucus." "Goals Set by Women's Political Caucus," *New York Times* (July 13, 1971): 37.
81. See the Testimony of Antonia Chayes, *Hearings on S.J. Res. 10,* pp. 289–303.

82. *Griggs v. Duke Power Co.*, 401 US 424 (1971).
83. *Dothard v. Rawlinson*, 433 US 321 (1977).
84. Testimony of Judith Wegner, *Hearings on S.J. Res. 10, part 1*, p. 892.
85. On the basis of such an interpretation, Diane Eisler urges in *The Equal Rights Handbook* (New York: Avon, 1978)—a book endorsed by the League of Women Voters—that ERA would warrant court action to insure a 50 percent representation of women in administrative and judicial positions at all levels of government and in female characters on television (pp. 193–97). (Broadcasters who failed to comply would lose their licenses.) She adds that ERA would mandate changes in "the education programs of all schools, universities, vocational colleges, and apprenticeship programs" (p. 193).
86. *Pennsylvania v. Board of Trustees*, 353 US 230 (1957).
87. Cited in Daniel Seligman, "Moving South on ERA," *Fortune* (January 11, 1982): 31.
88. Felsenthal, p. 157.

3

Innateness

Chapter 4 will review the empirical evidence concerning sex differences in behavior. The present chapter is concerned with clarifying the concept of innateness. I approach these tasks with limited enthusiasm. Most people find the existence of innate sex differences self-evident. While the females of a few species behave in ways typical of the males of most other species, there are no highly evolved species whose males and females behave identically. Nor is the innateness of a wide range of sex differences in humans particularly controversial within the scientific community. Defending the existence of innate sex differences thus risks belaboring the extremely obvious. At the same time, those who doubt the existence of innate differences are unlikely to change their minds no matter what evidence is presented. Any veteran of adolescence and parenthood still able to believe that boys and girls are born alike has already withstood more evidence than any laboratory can provide.

It is always possible to posit unknown environmental variables to explain any behavior. Nativism can no more be established with mathematical certainty than can any other scientific hypothesis, and scientists do not normally demand certainty before accepting an hypothesis. However, the moral qualms many scientists feel about nativism have allowed and encouraged environmentalists to dig into a wholly defensive position. Instead of devising rigorous, testable environmental hypotheses to explain in detail a wide range of sex-typed behaviors, feminist scientific method amounts to little more than readiness to criticize the design of experiments already done and scrutinize any data for possible environmentalist reinterpretation. This reactive stance makes feminist discussion of science extremely argumentative and, unfortunately, induces a similar argumentativeness in discussions of those discussions. In consequence, the debate over nativism is less like normal scientific controversy than trench warfare, in which environmentalists grudgingly yield terrain reluctantly occupied by nativists. One hesitates to enter the crossfire.

My final reason for reluctance is that the definitive case for the existence and determinativeness of sex differences, particularly in aggression, has already been made by Steven Goldberg in *The Inevitability of Patriarchy*. My discussion differs from his in only two respects. One is my more explicit concern with the implications of nativism for evaluating the charge that social structure is biassed, and for the practical implications of this charge as it concerns individual liberty. The second is a relative difference in emphasis on evolutionary biology. Whereas Goldberg confines himself to the direct physiological and behavioral evidence for gender dimorphism and consciously distances himself from behavioral genetics, the reader will find in the next chapter that I take behavioral genetics to offer considerable reinforcement to the conclusions suggested by the direct evidence. Goldberg adheres to the perfectly sound maxim that the conclusion of a strong argument cannot be strengthened by a weaker argument. I, by contrast, emphasize that the case for an empirical regularity (like gender dimorphism) is strengthened when the regularity is shown to be a consequence of a deep theory, in this case the theory of evolution. This difference corresponds to no difference in substance. I have little to add to Goldberg's analysis of the facts of the case, particularly of the relation of innate sex differences to social institutions. Like Goldberg, I see the socialization that helps produce observed sex differences as following grooves etched by pre-existent dispositions. The perception of innate sex differences creates expectations about the behavior of males and females. These expectations are transmitted to children, who themselves tend to perceive the expected as the proper—a tendency familiar to any parent who has incurred his children's displeasure by putting a toy in the "wrong" place. Children growing into adults conform to these stereotypic norms, confirming the original perception that the sexes differ and thereby triggering another round of the cycle. This feedback effect produces different gender differentiations in different environments, but it always produces differentiation of some sort, the variance being limited by the basic biological sex differences.

Consider the amply documented tendency of five-year-olds to play with members of their own sex,[1] which for the sake of illustration we may assume to be innate. This tendency will manifest itself differently in different cultures. In the United States, where five-year-olds attend kindergarten, "they search everywhere for clues, hoping to create separate and final images" of boyness and girlness,[2] a search which builds on the already clear difference that boys fight while girls play quietly. When their teacher asks them to decorate a dragon for Chinese New Year, the boys and girls split up to work on their own dragons. The girls decorate theirs with flowers, the boys decorate theirs with spaceships. The girls hang their dragon in the doll corner and the boys hang theirs in the superhero corner. The teacher could dismantle these sex-typed dragons and make the children work together on a single dragon using uniform decorative motifs, but few teachers are prepared to force major tasks on unwilling children, and any teacher who does try finds it almost impossible to get children to do what they do not want to do. In all likelihood the two dragons will remain aloft as signals that boys like spaceships and girls like flowers, making it that much more likely that future classroom projects will be sex typed.

Goldberg and Barash call the manifest features of society "exaggerations" caused by socialization,[3] but if these features are causal consequences of sex differences via the feedback mechanism, they no more exaggerate sex differences than a meteor crater exaggerates the energy of the meteor that caused it. Meteor craters and sex roles are simply consequences of an independent variable acting in a given environment. It is clearer to say with Diane McGuiness that "society, by and large, reinforces traits that are already present,"[4] dropping talk of exaggeration.

In a feedback loop, the output of a system is a function of the state of its environment at a previous time, and the state of the environment is a function of the output of the system at a previous time. The loop is positive when the compound function increases monotonically within some range of stability, so that the output variable constantly grows. A positive feedback system may be made to pass through "impossible" states which may *seem* to be stable solutions of its equations. An outside force can push the output of the system back to what it was at some earlier time—possibly by returning the environment to an earlier state—but the system will immediately spring back. The output will immediately start to grow, and will, by the end of an easily calculable period, be what it would have been had no outside force interfered. Reversal of the growth of the output variable can be only be temporary. This effect is illustrated by the reemergence of sex roles in the Israeli kibbutzim.[5] Less than three decades after concentrated efforts were made by kibbutzniks to achieve unisex equality, traditional sex roles had reemerged. Female kibbutzniks had placed their babies in creches, but found themselves wanting to be near their babies and arranged for jobs near them. These jobs involved the physical maintenance of the kibbutz dormitories, the preparation of food, and other traditionally female tasks. Environmentalists explain the failure of the Israeli experiment in terms of the exposure of the original kibbutz generation to prior sexist conditioning, but it is simpler to see in it the elasticity of positive feedback loops.

Innateness

Were there no presumption in so many minds against nativism, a detailed discussion of the concept of innateness would be superfluous. Nobody doubts that there is an innate drive to eat. Innate sex differences have been denied on the grounds that some people struggle against sex differences, that sex differences have occasionally been altogether absent (some women display no maternal instincts), that there is no known neural mechanism that produces sexual differentiation in behavior, and that no known gene encodes for such behavior. Yet the same can be said, mutatis mutandis, about hunger. There are people who fast periodically, there are people who have starved themselves to death, no one has identified the mechanism that transforms changes in blood chemistry into food-seeking behavior, and no one has isolated a gene for getting hungry. And, just as it is impossible to specify precisely how innate sex differences might have produced social institutions like doffing one's hat in the presence of females, it is impossible to specify precisely how hunger has produced the myriad social institutions that surround food—yet no one doubts the social determinativeness of hunger. Hunger is *obviously* the independent variable behind these institutions and *obviously* constrains the shape of all possible societies. Any stable society must make provision for meals. It would invite ridicule to argue that because some cultures develop harvest festivals and others develop four-star restaurants, or because pork is a delicacy in some societies and an abomination in others, eating is learned behavior mindlessly reproduced in each generation, trapping cookbook authors, farmers, and consumers in a network of conditioning. It would verge on the idiotic to argue that eating must be learned because parents frequently tell their children to stop playing with their food.

Perhaps despite its seeming clarity, the idea of innateness really is hopelessly confused. Let us see.

The sort of thing that would be innate, if anything is, is a *disposition*. It is essential before going any further to be clear about the inherent conditionality of all dispositions, innate or acquired. An organism disposed to sneeze (whether innately or by training) will sneeze *if* stimulated by certain environmental triggers, like pepper. An unstimulated and unsneezing organism may be disposed to sneeze anyway. The "fixed action patterns" discussed by ethologists[6]—stereotyped patterns of behavior which go to completion with little need for sensory feedback—are, for all their inflexibility, also dispositional. The greylag goose executes its egg-retrieval program *if* it sees an egg near its nest. Most dispositions manifest themselves in a variety of ways depending on the trigger. Organisms sneeze with different intensities in response to different irritants. Finally, an organism's overt behavior may be the concerted action of several dispositions. A liking for sports cars may dispose a man to talk about them in the presence of other sports car buffs, and he may also be disposed to use sign language with those who do not speak English. The net result, in the presence of French sports car enthusiasts, is sign language about sports cars. It is a mistake to suppose that an innate behavioral program must manifest itself independently of environmental stimuli, and that only behavior which goes to completion without benefit of environmental feedback is programmable. Sequences of muscle movements released on cue are a rare and degenerate form of disposition.

Dispositions are not literally things inside organisms, but they need not be reified to be taken seriously: All talk of dispositions can be translated into talk of what organisms are disposed to do. At the same time, it is a working assumption of science that all dispositions—of living things or inanimate matter—are consequences of microstructure. Salt is soluble because of the crystal structure of salt molecules, and physiological psychology seeks to explain egg-retrieval programs and liking for sports cars in terms of neural mechanisms. There is nothing in the concept of behavioral dispositions to rule out their being traced to the soul, but the nervous system would have to remain the intermediary between the soul and behavior, and for this reason the soul is scientifically superfluous.

So much for dispositions generally. An *innate* disposition is an *unlearned* tendency to emit a (variety of) response(s) in an (a variety of) environment(s). In other words, innate behavior is to be understood by contrast with learned behavior, which can be defined as follows. The disposition of an organism O to emit reponse R in environment E at time t is *learned,* or *acquired,* if O is so disposed because the emission of R by O in E was reinforced before t. A response R is *reinforced,* in turn, if R is followed by something that generally increases the probability of (or *strengthens*) any behavior it is associated with. To grasp this alphabet soup more intuitively, picture an organism testing a number of behaviors in a given environment and eventually settling on a behavior that gets it as least as much of what it wants as any other. That is a learning history. Innate behavior is behavior *lacking* a learning history. The greylag's egg-rolling program is innate because the greylag did not first experiment with that response. Innateness construed as here also covers behavior emitted with different intensities in the same environment as the organism ages. Human males seek female company more avidly at age twenty than at ten or eighty; this variation is innate if not caused by a learning history. Thus, the display of the same age-dependent variation in behavior by all conspecifics is probably the unfolding of an innate program, since it would be too great a coincidence for all the conspecifics to have been subjected to the same reinforcement schedule.[7] Again: To call a disposition "innate" implies nothing positive about the causes of the behavior which manifests it; it is to say where the behavior did not come from.

Just this much conceptual clarity shows the way out of a problem posed repeatedly in the popular and scientific environmentalist literature: If sex differences are innate, why are they reinforced? (Compare: If eating is natural, why are children nagged to eat?)[8] Obviously, putting the question in normative terms by asking whether it is *rational* to reinforce an innate disposition, assumes, rather dubiously, that people reinforce innate dispositions with some purpose in mind. In fact, people act in ways which *have the effect* of strengthening sex-typed behavior, but they do not plan to.[9] And to understand why people might inadvertently reinforce sex-typed behavior, let us look at another case in which children are praised for doing what comes naturally, namely parental reinforcement of the child's innate disposition to acquire language by mimicry. To some extent, parental reinforcement of mimicry is probably itself innate,[10] just as some parental reinforcement of sex-appropriate behavior may well be innate, but let us ignore this factor. The fact is, the child's predisposition to learn language does not manifest itself in every possible environment, and some environments trigger more adaptive manifestations of this disposition than others. (Remember, innate dispositions can be multitrack and context-sensitive.) Since a group is more apt to survive the more fluent its members are, a society whose norms include the encouragement of children's first efforts at speech is more apt to survive, and transmit its norms, than a society which tolerates indifference to children's first efforts at speech. It does not matter why parents who encourage their children *think* they should do so. Any practice that strengthens the group will be selected in by the process of social evolution.[11]

The same filter screens the norms governing sex-typed behavior. Suppose women find nurturant behavior more rewarding than men do, whereas men are more apt than women to compete in most environments. Norms encouraging women to shun nurturance and compete with men will steer women away from environments in which they do what they enjoy, and toward environments in which they do not. More traditional norms, which encourage women to do what they enjoy, are more adaptive and will be selected over time. Since a group is more apt to survive the happier its members are, a society whose norms encourage women to seek opportunities for nurturance is more likely to survive, and transmit its norms, than a society indifferent or hostile to female enjoyment of nurturance. It does not matter why people *think* they should encourage girls to be feminine; such norms survive because they reinforce the most socially adaptive manifestations of innate dispositions.

Turning to more serious misgivings about innateness, it has been argued in various ways that the dependence of innate dispositions on environmental triggers erases the line between innate and acquired behavior. Consider a puzzle posed by Bock and Vandenberg about the male advantage in gross motor behavior. Suppose a slight male predisposition to use the large muscles stimulates those parts of the nervous system which control the large muscles, which in turn prompts young males to use those muscles more. If the gross motor behavior of males is a product of a positive feedback loop between male musculature and the nervous system—Is it innate, or acquired through the use of the muscles?[12] To be sure, there is little *practical* point in distinguishing what is innate from what is acquired once the initial disposition is triggered, assuming that the feedback cycle cannot be broken. However, nothing in the interaction itself prevents measurement of either the initial male advantage in the use of the large muscles or of differences in male and female responses to identical proprioceptive signals from the large muscles. Determining stress-induced changes in the disposition of a system to respond to further applied stresses is known in physics as a hysteresis problem, and physicists encounter no in-principle difficulties in calculating elastic and magnetic hysteresis. The retentivity, coercivity, and hysteresis loop of a magnetic sample are all measures of "innate" properties. There is no reason to regard the interaction of living organism and environment as any less analyzable. Even if the interaction between organism and environment proves unanalyzable, it by no means follows that innate traits of the human organism impose no constraints on possible societies. Just because (let us grant) no one can figure out precisely what elements in observed behavior are caused by innate factors, we are not thereby free to assume that, for any desired social structure, there exists some environment such that human beings placed in it will produce the indicated social structure.

A number of writers assume that, if a factor is genuinely innate, it should be possible to isolate its contribution to behavior *independently of environment*. Thus, after noting that the physical development of the brain in utero involves the interaction of genetic influences with "a range of particular environmental influences"—the fetal brain will obviously not develop if the umbilical cord is cut—Ruth Bleier concludes that science should "discard the concepts of instinct, innateness, or biological predispositions in human beings."[13] I doubt that any working scientist, including Bleier,[14] takes this argument seriously, but it does provide an occasion for further clarifying the environmental independence of innate factors. What makes a spider's web-spinning innate is not that the spider spins his web in no environment at all, or in intergalatic space—the closest approximation to the absence of an environment—but that, under certain specifiable conditions, he will spin a web without having spun one before. Similarly, to say that boys have greater innate spatial-visual ability than girls is not to say that this difference will manifest itself if boys and girls are *nowhere*, but that, given the *same* upbringing and the *same* environment, boys will on average outperform girls at visualizing the rotation of solids, reading upside-down maps, and other indicators of spatial ability.

So long as environmental variables can be controlled, detailed knowledge of an organism's learning history is unnecessary for there to be reasonable conjectures about which of its dispositions are innate. I have already mentioned the dependence of strength of emission with age across a biologically well-defined population and the presence of a response in all conspecifics as two tests of innateness. A third test is early appearance. The earlier a response appears, the less likely it is to have been learned, since the organism that emits it has had less time to learn it and the organism's capacity to learn may itself be incompletely developed. All three tests involve controls for environmental variables that do not require identification of the variables themselves. Finally, ethologists take a developmental sequence to be innate if it cannot be rearranged or made to appear earlier, and can be suppressed, if at all, only in environments that were not likely to have been encountered when the behavior was evolving.

John Locke threw the concept of innateness into confusion by insisting that anything innate must be manifest at birth.[15] Locke should have realized that innate factors often appear long after birth. Human males do not display facial hair on the delivery table, but all human males begin to display facial hair at about fifteen years of age in a wide range of environments, and it is impossible to make a male's beard start out bristly at the onset of puberty and lighten thereafter. Locke did not realize that human males are born with a facial hair program.[16]

Innate Schemata: Motivation and Cognition

It may be easy to grant the programmability of specific sequences of muscle contractions in response to fixed stimuli, but most human behavior is context-sensitive. A Masai warrior "gains status" by killing a lion while an American businessman "gains status" by winning a promotion. It is harder to see how something as abstract as status seeking might be programmable.

Many critics of sociobiology assume that only fixed action patterns are programmable. Lewontin, Rose, and Kamin appear to reject the greater innate dominance-aggression of males on the grounds that no single neuron controls all the different specific behaviors necessary for political dominance in different societies.[17] Ruth Bleier has no trouble disposing of behavioral genetics once she has attributed to it the assumption that specific human behaviors are programmed:

> There is simply no evidence whatsoever that patterns of behavior are inherited in simple and predictable ways as the theories of sociobiologists and other biological determinists would require. . . . Genes could not, as sociobiologists imply, encode the brain for all the behaviors required of a species that inhabits every possible terrestrial environmental niche. . . . Since behavior is an expression of brain function, the concept of instinctive behaviors and characteristics constituting a human *nature* assumes a genetic programming in the brain of evolved behavior patterns. . . . [W]hat exactly do genes "encode" when they encode hypergamy in females? Do they [i.e. sociobiologists] really mean that all females inherit a gene or a cluster of genes that drive them to look for and, of course, scheme to marry a rich man?[18]

Not only do behavioral geneticists reject the genetic coding of specific behavior patterns, it is a central tenet of contemporary behavioral genetics that learning and flexibility are themselves programmable. There is overwhelming empirical evidence that complex organisms are born with *schemata* whose details are left to be supplied by experience, each schema telling the organism what experiences to look for and when to look for them. Goslings imprint on virtually any middle-sized object that happens to be in their vicinity. The gosling's genes do not tell him to follow his mommy or Konrad Lorenz or any other particular object, but to follow *whatever* is salient during his first few days of life. This general schema was selected in because it was apt to get goslings to follow their mothers in the environments in which geese evolved, a gosling's mother being in most cases the most prominent object during the "critical period" for imprinting. To take another example, the ground squirrel's tendency to bury food is clearly innate, but the squirrel must learn which nearby substances are worth burying for later consumption, how hard to scratch his local soil, and other environmental contingencies. His program is a flowchart with learning subroutines: begin burrowing, determine intensity of digging needed to form trench, dig accordingly, find out what tastes good in the neighborhood, bring some to the trench. The perceptual cues which halt the subroutines are themselves innate ("Stop digging when the trench is an inch deep"). James Gould, who unabashedly speaks of "programmed learning" and "programmed memorization," describes learning as "one of the standard, off-the-shelf programming tricks available to evolution—and despite the usual dichotomy, this kind of learning is the epitome of instinct."[19]

Programmed learning does nothing to smudge and in fact presupposes the distinction between conditioned and unconditioned behavior. Environmental contingencies dictate the means an organism chooses to pursue unlearned ends. The squirrel stores breadcrumbs because breadcrumbs taste good, but he has not *learned* to store what tastes good. Nor, for that matter, has he learned to like breadcrumbs, although an encounter with them is obviously necessary to trigger his innate preference for things that taste like breadcrumbs. The intensity of the squirrel's breadcrumb-eating behavior is independent of its association with other rewards. (That girls must encounter dolls before they can want to play with them does not show that girls' interest in dolls is learned. It is an empirical question whether doll play is caused by association with reinforcers like parental approval, or is unlearned love at first sight.) All conditioning rests on a foundation of unlearned preferences. Unless an organism likes some things more than others prior to conditioning, there will be nothing with which to pair behaviors to be learned, and learning cannot begin. Conditioning also presupposes an unlearned sense of similarity. To reap again the rewards that a given response once won for him in a given environment, the organism must wait until a similar environment recurs before emitting the response. If no environment strikes the organism as similar to any other, the organism will do nothing, and never learn to emit the given response.

The presence of innate schemata in animals does not prove their presence in humans. It does not prove that specific male protective behaviors or specific female hypergamic behaviors are determinations of innate schemata. It does show, however, that such hypotheses cannot be dismissed on methodological grounds, and indeed these hypotheses do provide a natural model for much human behavior. To say that men instinctively protect their families is to say that men are programmed to learn what in their environment counts as a threat and what means are available in their environment to counter these threats, and then to employ the latter against the former. An Eskimo father storing blubber and an American father buying life insurance may both be acting from the identical unlearned motive. Kindergarten children may be following an innate program that tells them to learn what distinguishes boys from girls in their environment and then to heed those distinctions, whatever they happen to be. An innate component for sex role identification need not involve a gene for wearing Darth Vader masks.

Like programmed learning, the closely related phenomenon of "sensitive periods" during which certain kinds of learning are possible,[20] does not prove a significant innate component in human behavior, but it does show that such an interpretation cannot be dismissed a priori, and it provides a natural model for much otherwise puzzling human behavior. Many sex differences, such as a discrepancy in mathematical aptitude, appear or become heightened at puberty. To explain these effects environmentally requires that the same environmental contingencies affect nearly all boys and girls at nearly the same time. This is not impossible, but it is unlikely. If however, differentiation in mathematical ability is part of a maturational program, no such coincidence need be postulated.

Structure and Function

Acceptance by ethologists of innate programs has been helped by a smudging of the traditional distinction between structure and function. The development of tissues and organs in accordance with programs coded in the DNA is now beyond reasonable doubt. As the details of protein synthesis are uncovered, understanding of the transmission of organic structures is nearing completion. But sequences of actions are not protein structures and it is harder to imagine how much sequences could be encoded. What is more, the structure of an organ does not uniquely determine its use.[21] Opposable thumbs can pick up pens or swords.

From an evolutionary point of view, however, no line can realistically be drawn between the organs constructed for an organism by its genes and the uses to which its genes incline an organism to put its organs. An organism has an organ because the use of that organ for a specific range of actions, from among all those actions of which the organ is physically capable, was adaptive when the organism's ancestors were evolving. Wings, thumbs, and brains were selected in because certain of the uses of these structures increased the inclusive fitness of owners of these structures who used them in those ways.[22] It is therefore natural to suppose that, along with instructions for organ building, the DNA encodes dispositions to use organs in ways that once enhanced inclusive fitness. This conjecture is confirmed by the absence in nature of creatures with strong leg muscles but no leg-moving programs and creatures with opposable thumbs but no program for picking up small objects. And, while there is more emotional resistance to applying the same point to the brain, it is hard to see how the human brain could have been selected in as an all-purpose problem solver with no hard-wired program.

Drives

Self-reinforcement is one of evolution's techniques for getting creatures to act adaptively. Some behaviors cause organisms to lapse into reinforcing internal states, which are ordinarily called "feelings of pleasure." Genes that produced organisms whose adaptive behavior was self-reinforcing tended to survive, and we are their descendants. As David Barash puts it, behaviors which enhance inclusive fitness "taste sweet," just as behaviors which decrease inclusive fitness taste sour. Together with schematic programs, self-reinforcement gives empirical sense to *drives,* an idea which figures prominently in discussions of mating behavior and captures the subjective urgency of a number of innate dispositions.

Some adaptive behaviors, like eating and mating, are beyond the organism's full control. An organism can wiggle its tail by itself, but it cannot mate by itself. A *drive* is a disposition, evovled through adaption, to try to bring about a highly self-reinforcing end-state in virtually all environments. The strong affective component of the disposition evolved along with the disposition itself because this component was highly adaptive. An organism prompted by a drive senses that the goal-state will be self-reinforcing, or—equivalently—experiences absence of the end-state as punishing. It is the affective component of goal-directed behavior in organisms, a factor absent from purely cybernetic analyses of goal-directedness,[23] that sustains the hydraulic metaphor of drives as pressures. Organisms will do anything to eat or mate. Highly evolved animals certainly act *as if* they enjoy copulation and dislike losing prey, and presumably experience these occurrences with analogues of human pleasure and displeasure.

A drive may appear late in an organism's life, vanish seasonally, and be subverted by environments unlike those in which the drive evolved. Drive-powered behavior may be shaped by environmental input. As we have seen, none of these qualifications affect the innateness of drives, which are as nearly independent of environment as behavior can be. Some ethologists report "vacuum behavior," such as hole-digging paw motions dogs are apt to emit when impelled to dig imaginary holes, so strong and context-free is the pressure to dig. And while the expression of a drive may be extinguished by punishment, it of course does not follow that the drive itself was created by reward. That a lion given an electric shock every time he takes a bite of meat will eventually stop eating meat does not mean that his taste for meat was originally acquired through a learned association of meat with the absence of electric shocks. Nor does the absence of drive-expressive behavior in "abnormal" environments show that this behavior is significantly flexible, in the sense that its extinction carries no costs for the organism. The lion put off meat by electric shocks is caught between his drive to eat meat and his desire to avoid pain. Animals subjected to such treatment show symptoms of stress and the animal equivalent of neurosis. These experiments are a useful counterweight to glib assertions about the painless suppression of basic human drives in the service of "values."

Creationism

Mention of instincts in animals invites the charge of over-hasty generalization to man. One must indeed be careful not to treat superficial similarities between animal and human behavior as necessarily homologies. But there is the opposite danger of underestimating the analogy between animals and man. Neither the flexibility of the human brain nor the transcendence of the individual by culture remove man from the natural order. To doubt that man was shaped by the forces that shaped his predecessors is to doubt that man is the product of natural selection.

One usually thinks of creationism as a doctrine for religious fundamentalists, but from a methodological point of view, belief in the special creation of the human species is entailed by *any refusal to apply evolutionary theory to man*. It is irrelevant whether this refusal is sustained by a literalistic reading of scripture or commitment to a secular ideology. Indeed, a case can be made that religious critics of Darwin display a stronger sense of the unity of nature than do scientific critics of innateness in man. This is most especially true of scientists like Richard Lewontin and Stephen Jay Gould, who take a wholly naturalistic stance toward all living creatures apart from man (and are prepared to use the theory of evolution polemically in ideological debate), yet reject all but the most trivial comparisons of other living creatures to man.[24]

The underlying issue is the need to minimize explanatory principles. If A causes B, and a B-like phenomenon b is observed in a situation in which an A-like mechanism a is known to operate, parsimony dictates that a be presumed to be the cause of b. Refusal to make this presumption creates two mysteries: What did cause b, if not a? And what became of the causal powers of a? Newton expressed the point succinctly: "More is vain when less will serve. . . . Nature is pleased with simplicity, and affects not the pomp of superfluous causes." In particular, if the mating behavior of large animals was shaped by selectional pressures, and human beings exhibit similar mating behavior, *and* human beings were exposed to similar selectional pressures, to deny that these pressures shaped human mating behavior is to posit a superfluous cause. Whether we call it "God" or "culture," we are inventing a cause to do work already done by factors already known. (Environmentalism shares many of the intellectually stultifying traits of classical theology. It posits society as a cause which itself has no cause, for instance.)

Newton's principle has influenced my selection from the scientific literature on sex differences discussed in the following chapter. Applied to sex differences in childhood, it requires that an adult sex difference resembling an apparently innate sex difference found in children is to be attributed to the same innate factor. It would be too great a coincidence for an innate factor accounting for a difference in children to become inert at precisely the moment conditioning begins to produce a similar result in adults. Applied to the explanation of social institutions, Newton's principle decrees that what produces eating in individuals must constrain the social institutions that surround eating. If hunger did not produce these institutions, what did? And where else would individual hunger manifest itself socially, if not in these institutions? By parallel reasoning, Newton's principle leads us to attribute male domination of large-scale organizations to the innate tendency of individual males to seek dominance in small groups, should such an individual tendency be discovered.

Notes

1. See Vivian Gussin Paley, "Superheroes in the Doll Corner," *Natural History* (March 1985): 20–25.
2. Ibid., p. 20.
3. David Barash, *The Whisperings Within* (New York: Penguin, 1981), p. 72.
4. Diane McGuiness, "How Schools Discriminate against Boys," *Human Nature* 2 (February 1979): 82–88.
5. See Lionel Tiger and Joseph Sheper, *Women in the Kibbutz* (New York: Harcourt, Brace, Jovanovich, 1975).

6. See James Gould, *Ethology* (New York: Harper & Row, 1982), p. 37ff.

7. The degree of innateness, or "heritability," of a trait *T* in a population *P* is usually explicated as the ratio of the genetic variance of *P* to the phenotypic variance of *T* in *P*. This explication has the counterintuitive consequence that the heritability of having two ears is 0, since all the variation in the number of ears people possess is environmentally caused. (Vincent van Gogh's genotype resembled that of other van Goghs.) It might be preferable to relativize innateness to environment, speaking of the *E*-heritability of *T* in *P* as the ratio of the genotypic variance of *P* to the phenotypic variance of *T* in *P* in *E*—the overall heritability of *T* becoming a (not necessarily significant) set of *E*-heritabilities for a family of environments. The heritability of ear number is properly high for both environments free of demented impressionists with razors (everyone keeps his ears: phenotypic variance low) and in environments containing such threats (people lose their ears: phenotypic variance again low).

8. Elizabeth Janeway asks: "Why should anyone be praised for being what she is supposed to be by nature?" *Man's World, Woman's Place* (New York: Morrow, 1971), p. 52.

9. Letty Pogrebin (*Growing Up Free* [New York: McGraw-Hill, 1980]) calls the reinforcement of sex differences "the craziest contradiction of sexism," which assumes that society was designed. It would indeed be absurd to attribute to an omnicompetent social engineer the clumsy expedient of getting his creatures to act in ways he wishes by making them encourage each other to do so.

10. Gould suggests in *Ethology* that children learn to crawl because certain sorts of arm-leg coordination feel innately rewarding, which is why organisms may sometimes *struggle* to do what they are programmed to do. One is reminded of Justice Holmes's observation that "effort is the mode by which the inevitable comes to pass."

11. For a general discussion of the generate-and-test strategy, see Herbert Simon, *The Sciences of the Artificial,* 2nd ed. (Cambridge, Mass.: MIT Press, 1981), pp. 52–56, 149–50.

12. Darrell Bock and Steven Vandenberg, "Components of Heritable Variation in Mental Test Scores," in *Progress in Genetics,* ed. Steven Vandenberg (Baltimore, Md.: Johns Hopkins University Press, 1968), p. 400.

13. Ruth Bleier, *Science and Gender* (New York: Pergamon, 1984), p. 76. Bleier claims these concepts "obscure the social and political origins of inequality" and "undermine change."

14. Bleier subsequently asserts, with regard to male and female performance on tests of mathematical ability, that "the enormous differences in socialization are more than adequate to explain the almost trivial differences in mean score" (*Science and Gender,* p. 109), an assertion that is ill-formed if the contrast between nativist and environmentalists explanations is ill-drawn.

15. See Locke's *Essay Concerning Human Understanding,* I, 1, 5.

16. Locke's oversight is especially surprising, given that he was a physician. It is probably due to the strong distinction drawn by philosophers of his period between bodily processes and ideation.

17. Richard Lewontin, Steven Rose, and Leon Kamin, *Not in Our Genes* (New York: Pantheon, 1984).

18. *Science and Gender,* pp. 26–27, 42, 67, 70–71.

19. *Ethology,* p. 275.

20. See Gould, ch. 3. Time-dependent dispositions are common in nature. An elastic band will snap back if stretched for a while; after that it loses elasticity.

21. "[W]hat is really at issue in sociobiological theory is not the physical capacity for behavior that biology provides but rather the genetic encoding of the entire range of complex human behaviors" (Bleier, p. 17).

22. A trait enhances inclusive fitness as it increases the number of full or partial copies in the next generation of the genotype of an organism possessing that trait.

23. See e.g. G. Sommerhof, *Analytic Biology* (London: Oxford University Press, 1950). Such analyses have also been offered by Ernest Nagel and R.B. Braithwaite.

24. "[T]he canonical form for the biologistic view of human social and individual differences [includes] the citation of evidence from animals as corroboration. After all, people *are* animals, aren't they? Yes, indeed, and they have certain properties in common with other animals, like being made of cells. But the further one gets from the immediate properties of cells, the greater the diversity of causal patterns among species. . . . To understand human beings, I am afraid there is no substitute for understanding Homo sapiens" (Richard Lewontin, "Reply to Sandra Witelson," *New York Review of Books* [October 24, 1985]: 54). The abysmal level of argumentation in Lewontin's reply to Witelson, and even more its nasty tone, go far toward explaining why few scientists are willing to publicly defend nativism.

4

Sex Differences

Methodological Preliminaries

The present chapter reviews some of the literature on innate sex differences drawn from evolutionary biology, neurology, the controlled observation of children, and social anthropology. Each line of evidence is individually persuasive, and, taken jointly, they establish beyond rational doubt the existence of socially determinative innate sex differences. It is impossible to do more here than sketch in the most cursory way the extent of current research on sex differences; most of the studies I cite refer to dozens of further studies, whose pursuit quickly leads the interested reader to the frontiers. I make absolutely no claims to scientific originality, and no doubt many readers would be willing to stipulate that sex differences exist so that the discussion of their larger significance can proceed. Indeed, the accessibility of the immense volume of material on sex differences makes the continued respectability of feminism no less than a scandal. To the extent that this respectability is rationally based, it may rest on some misunderstandings about scientific method.

Stereotypes

Quite apart from the question of their social desirability, the universality of sex stereotypes strongly confirms their truth. Sex stereotypes are beliefs about important practical matters, and errors about important practical matters tend to die out along with the people who hold them. Nothing will go seriously wrong if everyone believes that the king descended from the sun god, but things *will* go seriously wrong if everyone starts making mistakes about what substances are poisonous. Mistakes about the best way to treat a mate and raise the next generation also make things go wrong. If stereotypes were capricious, they would be dysfunctional, and if they were dysfunctional we would not be here. Nor are stereotypes merely records of observations of social behavior which might still be explained environmentally, since many enduring stereotypes concern "the way boys and girls are" from birth.

70

Scientific Revolutions

Science, including social science, is not inherently debunking. The aim of science is to explain observation, not to show that observation is unreliable; if on the whole science were inconsistent with observation, it would destroy its own evidential foundation. The small number of celebrated cases in which science actually did overturn the evidence of the senses, such as the discovery that the Earth moves, are highly atypical and do not warrant the relativistic conclusions that some historians of science have drawn from them.[1] In particular, there is no reason to expect science to explain away observed sex differences as artifacts. To be sure, science has sometimes overturned *theories* that common sense constructed from a too narrow range of observations, as when Einstein showed that simultaneity is non-transitive. (Most other "counterintuitive" results of modern science, such as the reduction of acceleration to inertial motion along non-Euclidean geodesics, concern matters about which the man in the street has no antecedent opinion.) But even the most abstruse theory must be consistent with observations however narrowly circumscribed—and the question of the causation of sex differences does not turn on the basic properties of matter, the domain in which science is most free to flout preconceptions.

Null Results

A test for sex differences yields a *positive* result when it discriminates between men and women, a negative or *null* result when it fails to discriminate. It is sometimes alleged that null results about sex differences receive insufficient attention. If in fact the scientific community does take negative results about sex differences less seriously than it does positive results— there is reason to believe that the popular press overemphasizes negative results[2]—that is because negative results do in general provide less information. A replicable difference in the response of a test instrument to different subjects demonstrates that the subjects differ in some respect, while an undifferentiated response may show either the sameness of the subjects or the insensitivity of the instrument. Two individuals found equal in height by a ruler graduated in inches may actually differ in height by nearly an inch, whereas the individual consistently measured taller by such a ruler must really be taller. This asymmetry also explains why null results do not cancel positive results. If two individuals judged equal in height by a ruler graduated in inches are judged unequal in height by a more finely graduated ruler, the subjects are unequal in height and the null finding may be discarded.

Moreover, tests for sex differences with respect to a given trait must often specify the trait in narrow operational terms, so that a null result proves at most the indistinguishability of the sexes with respect to the operational criterion. The sexes may still differ on the underlying trait. Operationalization enhances clarity, but its limitations should be understood. For instance, there have been studies of cooperativeness in which questionnaires were administered to college students before and again after a co-ed group discussion of a campus issue. These questionnaires, answered in isolation, revealed no sex difference in tendency to conform to group consensus. Since this experiment does not test for tendency to consensus in the presence of others in a social setting, a variable central to the basic idea of cooperativeness, its bearing on sex differences is questionable.

Environmentalist Caveats of Scientists

Every student of sex differences acknowledges the role of socialization; many such scientists pronounce their findings consistent with feminism, and a number support its most sweeping demands. Yet it by no means follows that deploying scientific studies of gender differences against the empirical basis of feminism necessarily distorts these studies. A scientist's interpretation of his own results is distinct from the results themselves and does not automatically inherit their validity. A scientist investigating a problem is generally most conversant with the background hypotheses against which his results are to be understood, but these hypotheses are publicly known and may legitimately be brought to bear by outside observers. Consider two cases which anticipate some of the discussion to follow.

First, Benbow and Stanley suggest that sex differences in mathematical ability may be due to nonenvironmental "endogenous variables," but they remark that these endogenous variables need not be physiological. One is entitled to observe that a nonphysiological endogenous variable is quite unconstruable, unless it is the soul. And if the soul is scientifically suspect, it is no distortion to interpret the Benbow-Stanley data physiologically, thereby ignoring a possibility that its authors themselves may be willing to countenance.

Second, Goldberg and Lewis report that by the age of one boys more than girls are drawn to unusual objects, but the authors themselves appear to attribute this difference to "learning these sex-role behaviors independently of any internal motive" in response to parental reinforcement. However, Goldberg and Lewis supply no evidence that girls exposed to a "boy" reinforcement schedule would display a similar interest in unusual objects, and other studies indicate that this difference begins before the infant's attention can be controlled by reward. It is therefore permissible to impose on the Goldberg-Lewis data an interpretation contrary to their own.

It should also be emphasized that while socialization plays a central role in transforming innate sex differences into observed behavior, it remains a separate and open question whether socialization is an independent cause working in tandem with the DNA or whether, as Steven Goldberg and the present author maintain, socialization is itself determined by innate differences. If socialization is a dependent variable, it can loom large in the shaping of behavior without disconfirming a strong form of nativism.

While some environmentalist caveats express normal scientific caution, others are almost certainly responses to extrascientific pressures. Articles reporting nativist findings provoke uncommonly acrimonious correspondence to the scientific journals that publish them, and the journals themselves frequently invite environmentalist critics to reply to such articles, publishing these replies as instant rebuttals in the same issue. Scientists contemplating the publication of nativist findings know they are buying into an emotionally draining controversy. At least two sociologists have reported that criticizing environmentalism is likely to prove costly in terms of tenure, promotion, and financing for future research.[3] Influential philosophers have called for the suspension of certain lines of research inconsistent with environmentalism:

> What we are saying is that at this time, in this country, in this political climate, individual scientists should voluntarily refrain from the investigation of genotypical racial differences in IQ tests.[4]

The authors say they "do not approve" of violence against scientists who persist, but they nowhere express active disapproval of such violence and they expressly "accept full responsibility" for such violence as their essay may incite.[5] In such a climate, verbal concessions to environmentalism must in some cases (quite understandably) represent fear rather than scientific caution.

The Failure To Ask Why

Environmentalist explanations of sex role differentiation are often adequate in their own terms: Boys and girls *do* receive different cues from their parents and society. This adequacy tends to obscure the failure of all environmentalist explanations to explain why every society socializes boys and girls differently in the first place. If males and females have equal predispositions for aggression and nurturance, why have not half of all human societies encouraged women to be aggressive and men to be nurturant?[6] If socialization is autonomous, why has it always worked one way? Environmentalism must treat this regularity as a coincidence, or fall back on male conspiracies. Using culture as the all-purpose explanation of human behavior ignores the fact that culture itself is just one more natural phenomenon, a product of what is innate in man responding to the environments in which man has found himself. If culture always encourages people to raise boys and girls differently, then people are innately disposed to develop cultures which so encourage them.

The Burden of Proof

While part of the reason for the scientific sterility of feminism is its failure to ask why, a further cause of this sterility is the widespread impression that it is up to the nativist to prove the existence of innate sex differences, and that, if he cannot, sex differences may be presumed to be learned.[7] The environmentalist, vindicated until refuted, need only show by devices however ad hoc that nativism *might* be false. This reactive methodology violates the maxim that a hypothesis loses no credibility simply because it can be imagined to be false. Newton again:

> In experimental philosophy we are to look upon propositions inferred by general induction from phenomena as accurately or very nearly true, notwithstanding any contrary hypothesis that may be imagined, till such time as other phenomena occur, by which they may either be made more accurate, or liable to exceptions. This rule we must follow, that the argument of induction may not be evaded by hypotheses.

Anyone so minded can continue indefinitely to evade induction by hypothesis, even up to rejecting scientific method itself. In her review of Maccoby and Jacklin, who do conclude that the sexes differ with respect to aggression, mathematical ability, spatial-visualizing ability, and verbal ability, Judith Long Laws writes: "Among feminist scholars there is some consensus that we have exhausted what normal science has to offer and that the time has come to seek new paradigms."[8] (Some of these new paradigms are discussed in chapter 8.)

There is in fact no reason to place the burden of proof on the nativist. To be rationally acceptable, nativism need only be more plausible than its rivals, the various forms of environmentalism. The question to ask is not whether the relevant data proves the existence of innate factors beyond all possible doubt, but whether an innatist interpretation of the data is more plausible than an environmentalist one. Boys' outscoring girls on a test of mathematical ability *might* be due to the kinds of toys children play with, or the influence of the Moon. The serious question is one of probabilities.

The reactive strategy of attacking nativist studies piecemeal assumes— and this is sometimes explicitly stated—that if no single experiment establishes an innate component in behavior, the rejected experiments cannot support such a component if taken jointly. This precept is demonstrably false. If each of a set of disjoint hypotheses has a probability only moderately greater than .5, the probability that one of them is true rapidly approaches certainty.[9] A group of experimental results each of which makes an innate component of behavior more likely than not comes as close as reason can demand to proving the existence of an innate component.

The Evolution of Sex Differences[10]

Behavioral geneticists have proposed a general model for the emergence of gender dimorphism as an optimally adaptive strategy. According to this "parental investment" theory, populations whose females fit the feminist theory of what women are, would have been selected out long ago; therefore the women that exist do not fit the feminist theory. Behavioral genetics is not criticizing the woman feminists imagine human females to be; it is merely observing that her traits wold have been so maladaptive that extant human females (and of course human males) could not have descended from females of this sort.

Parental investment theory is based on the physical capacity of mammalian males to reproduce thousands of times more frequently than mammalian females. Females produce a few large, metabolically expensive eggs, while males produce hundreds of millions of cheap sperm. The several years required by gestation and postnatal care for her offspring means a further investment of metabolic resources by the female. She invests more of herself than the male in each of her offspring, and risks more in each act of copulation. Imagine, then, two hominid strains. The genes of one produce females who innately desire to reproduce in early adulthood, tend to bond with their offspring, find childrearing uniquely reinforcing, are patient and gentle, and are very choosy about the males they mate with. The genes of the second strain, on the other hand, produce females who are differently prewired. A female of the second strain

> will learn to take pleasure in her own body and a man's body and to view sex as a good and wonderful experience, but not as an exclusive basis for an ultimate commitment to another person. . . . She will have few children if she does have them, and view her pregnancies, childbirth and early months of motherhood as one among many equally important highlights of her life.[11]

The second strain will be overwhelmed by the first in almost any imaginable environment. Females of the first strain will be more interested in having babies and caring for them, and more careful about who gets to fertilize their precious eggs—so first-strain females will produce more reproducing descendants. The real edge for nurturance in females lies in its inclusive fitness, its tendency to favor the survival of near relations containing partial genotypic copies. A gene which tells the female that houses it to sacrifice herself for her young will outlast rival genes that urge their hosts to greater selfishness, since each sacrificed-for offspring of an altruistic host will contain a half-copy of the gene that encodes altruism.

Complementary reasoning explains male behavior. A gene housed in a man need not make its host quite so emotionally involved with its offspring, since a male can produce half-copies of his genes daily. Male genes that program a desire for intercourse with as many females as possible and a readiness to battle like-minded males for access to the females, are more likely to survive. These tendencies are strengthened and refined by a dialectic between the sexes that Darwin called sexual selection. A female does best by choosing a male who demonstrates the willingness and ability to protect her and her offspring by victory in those battles with other males. A tendency to withhold her sexual favors as a reward for the daring and attentive male is selected for in females, while enjoyment of shining before females and vanquishing other males is selected for in males. Males enjoy courting, and women enjoy being courted; each sex desires what the opposite sex wants it to desire. The preferences associated with mating are always congruent, there being no other adaptive solution.

Some anthropologists supplement this picture by reference to the harsh conditions of early hominid existence, which forced the physically stronger male to hunt protein concentrated on the hoof while the female cared for the home and gathered grains. This division of labor is thought to have selected for aggressiveness in men and nurturance in women (as well as male hand-eye coordination and male bonding), but the human hunter-gatherer past could only have accelerated a process already long at work thanks to mammalian biology. Marvin Harris cites the hunter-gatherer hypothesis as an explanation of universal male dominance which does not appeal to innate sex differences,[12] but the hunter role would almost certainly not have devolved on men had they not already been on average stronger and more daring than women, and in any case, the hunter role would have selected for aggressiveness in men once men had adopted it.

Although sociobiological hypotheses have been accused of being tailored to fit the known behaviors of animals, these hypotheses do unify previously disparate phenomena and yield testable predictions. The parental investment theory predicts that males who brood fertilized eggs, like the male seahorse, will be atypically selective in mating, and this has been observed.[13] It predicts second-order effects due to discontinuities in male fertility following ejaculation, such as female competition for access to fertile males, and these have been observed.[14] Mathematically elaborated, the theory predicts unanticipated aspects of the social behavior of "K-selected" animals—large animals in stable environments, like lions in prides. For example, it predicts that since K-selected females respond to observable correlates of fitness like victory in battle, males with nothing to fight about—no breeding sites, say—will evolve intrinsically maladaptive traits just to signal fitness by sheer survival under a handicap. The theory thus elegantly explains the peacock's unwieldy plumage and other seemingly pointless male displays. Such displays had been observed prior to the formulation of the parental investment theory, but were not built into the theory, and in that sense were *new* phenomena. This sort of *retrodiction* confirms a theory just as strongly as the successful *pre*diction of an event that does not actually occur until after the theory has been articulated.

All the animal evidence for the parental investment theory is evidence for the application of that theory to man. Speaking generally, whenever a theory predicts a phenomenon for which there is no direct evidence (as, let us momentarily allow, there is no direct evidence for gender dimorphism), all the direct evidence accumulated elsewhere for the theory is transmitted by the theory to the mooted phenomena. If the parental investment theory is true, then (probably) human males are innately more competitive than human females. If various observations about animals are reliable, then (probably) so is the parental investment theory. So, if those observations are reliable, then (somewhat less probably) human males are innately more competitive than human females.

Not that it would necessarily be circular to use the parental investment theory to validate stereotypes about gender differences and then use these stereotypes to confirm the parental investment theory, all without reference to animal evidence. The positioning of theory and observation for mutual support is common in science. The theory of relativity predicts the bending of light around the sun, but the measurements which seemed to indicate this displacement when the theory was first tested might also have been observational errors. Scientists were forced to choose between two conjunctions: "Einstein is right and light was observed to bend" versus "Einstein was wrong and the observation was spurious." The first conjunction was deemed more plausible on the basis of overall simplicity and coherence with the rest of science. Sociobiology forces a similar choice between two conjunctions: (1) The observation that men and women are inherently different is reliable and the parental investment theory is true; (2) The observation is unreliable and the theory is false. On its face, (1) unifies data far more effectively than (2). The way men and women seem to behave is *just* the way the parental investment theory predicts that they would behave.[15]

Curiously, many behavioral geneticists profess to find their results consistent with feminism. David Barash is almost apologetic:

> This [discussion of sex differences] is in many ways a troublesome chapter. I hope, of course, that it will not incur the wrath of feminists, but more than

that, I worry that it will be misinterpreted and used as support for the continued oppression of women.[16]

Unfortunately, Barash does not specify who will misuse his work or how,
nor does he consider the possibility that, if the parental investment theory is
correct, the oppression he worries about may be chimerical. (His book
incurred feminist wrath anyway.) Melvin Konner is equally circumspect:

> What then are we to make of these extraordinary facts? For the immediate
> future, at least as far as I am concerned, nothing. . . . If not now, then, my
> guess is, in the very near future, it will be extremely difficult for an informed,
> objective observer to discard the hypothesis that the genders differ in their
> degree of violent behavior for reasons that are in part physiological. . . . If
> the community of scientists whose work and knowledge are relevant should
> come to agree on this point, then it seems to me that one policy implication is
> plausible: Serious disarmament may ultimately necessitate an increase in the
> proportion of women in government. . . . [W]e would all be safer if the
> world's weapons systems were controlled by average women instead of aver-
> age men.[17]

As I mentioned in chapter 3, all proposals of this sort fail to explain who
will keep men from seizing positions of power from "average women,"
unless it is a supervenient group of exceptionally aggressive men, who will
then run things.

E.O. Wilson is more rigorous. He outlines three societal responses to
gender dimorphism, which he takes to be established: exaggeration of sex
differences, provision of equal opportunity, and "training to eliminate all
sexual differences in behavior."[18] He worries that under the first regimen
"some amount of injustice would be inevitable, and it could easily expand
to disastrous proportions." (He does not specify the nature of this disaster,
which must already be with us since sex differences are exaggerated in all
societies.) He finds the second option incongenial to personal liberty, since
"men are likely to maintain disproportionate representation in political life,
business and science. . . . The result might be legitimately viewed as restrictive to the complete emotional development of individuals." Wilson
seems to favor the third course, requiring "quotas and sex-biased education," although he does recognize that "the amount of regulation required
would place some personal freedom in jeopardy."[19] Whether the gains of a
"more harmonious and productive society" outweigh the individual liberty
to be lost cannot be decided on scientific grounds. However, the very
gender difference that Wilson wants to nullify, ironically enough, guarantees that men will monopolize the positions from which the attempted elimination of sex differences will be controlled.

Antenatal Effects of Hormones on the Brain

The principal direct evidence for innate gender differentiation comes from research on the developmental effects of hormones. It is common knowledge that hormones influence much sex-typed behavior. A baby's cry, for instance, release oxytocin in a woman, inclining her to attend to it.[20] But in addition to affecting postnatal behavior, hormones play a critical role in shaping the nervous system before birth.[21] The male XY chromosomal pair in a newly formed zygote signals the embryonic gonads to produce testosterone, which in turn "virilizes" the developing brain. The mammalian fetal brain unexposed to male hormones remains that of the homogametic sex, which in humans is the female. Precise measurements have been made of the differential effects of male sex hormones on animal brains. The locations of these effects have been mapped and the effects themselves photographed.[22]

There are two reasons for implicating these anatomical effects in sexually dimorphic behavior. First, those regions of the brain differentiated by prenatal hormones are involved in characteristically sex-linked behavior. Raisman and Field have demonstrated that testosterone at birth thickens the synaptic connections among local neurons in the hypothalamus of the male rat.[23] The hypothalamus mediates sex-linked behavior through regulating the production of gonadal hormones which trigger courtship and fighting. Toran-Allerand has photographed parallel effects of testosterone on the brains of newborn mice: Neurites grow more thickly and quickly in the hypothalamus of a mouse brain exposed to androgens, a thickening generally thought by neurologists to be critical to neuronal interactions. Toran-Allerand conjectures

> that steroid-induced variations in both the timing and extent of afferent axonal development could so influence dendritic differentiation and synaptic distribution of target neurons as to result in fundamentally different, gender specific, patterns of neural organization.[24]

(Roger Gorski presented full-color slides taken by Toran-Allerand at a lecture entitled "Sex and the Brain" at the American Museum of Natural History in April 1986; the neuronal thickening was dramatically evident even to the nonspecialist.) These effects have so far been observed only in animals, and neurologists are cautious about extrapolating them to man. At the same time, it is widely recognized that the subcortical regions of the human brain resemble their mammalian counterparts, and the overall similarity of human and mammalian fetal development makes it unlikely that the human fetus is exempt from similar hormonal influence.

Second, in natural experiments in which fetal hormonalization fails to match the subject's central nervous system to his sexual appearance (a mismatch that sometimes ends at puberty, the second wave of changes caused by a programmed release of hormones), the emotions and behaviors of the affected subjects have been found to conform to the prenatally determined sex of the brain rather than to the sex of socialization provoked by appearance. The best known of these studies have been conducted by John Money and his associates.[25] One study followed female congenital adrenal hyperplasiacs, whose brains had released male sex hormones in utero. The prenatal androgens had virilized both the brains and the genitals of these hyperplasiacs, but immediate postnatal surgery corrected their genital disfigurement, and they were raised as girls. A related study followed genetic females whose brains had been virilized in utero as a result of their mothers' exposure to medically administered progestogens.[26] The girls in both studies became tomboys, less inclined than most girls to play with dolls and fantasize about childrearing, more inclined to engage in strenuous outdoor play. They exhibited preferences "for utilitarian and functional rather than traditional feminine clothing, for toy cars and guns rather than dolls, and for career rather than being a mother."[27] These tomboys are reported not to have displayed an unusual readiness to initiate fighting,[28] but they preferred male peers and tended to dominate the female groups they joined. In a third study, Erhardt, Money, and Mascia followed genetic males whose gonads produced normal amounts of prenatal male hormones but whose tissues were insensitive to these hormones.[29] These genetic males with feminine nervous systems, and also feminine appearance, developed characteristically female habits.

There may be a question of how effectively the studies of the Money group controlled for environmental variables. Erhardt and her associates report that in almost every case a program of medication allowed close control of postnatal hormones, with the girls' parents either indifferent to their daughters' condition or concerned to make their daughters conventionally feminine. The Erhardt-Money-Mascia study did not control for appearance, however, and it might be argued that the sheer knowledge of the female hyperplasiacs' condition somehow led their parents to encourage tomboyism. Two further studies indicate these factors are irrelevant. Reinisch and Karow followed girls who were prenatally exposed to progestins, but were not born with virilized genitals and were not exposed to any special postnatal treatment.[30] The Reinisch-Karow females exhibited the same personality traits as the females in the Erhardt-Money-Mascia sample. Imperato-McGinley and her associates have studied the mirror-image situation, male pseudohermaphroditism, in the Dominican Republic.[31] A genetic deficiency in thirty-three genetic males prevented sufficient embryonic formation of dihydrotestosterone, the hormone which differentiates the genital tubercle in males. These males, whose nervous system had received the usual amount of antenatal testosterone, appeared female at birth. Of twenty-five who were postpubertal at the time of the study, nineteen had been raised as girls (the others had been raised equivocally); of the eighteen about whom information was available, seventeen thought of themselves as men, sixteen were living as men, and fifteen were or had been cohabiting with women. A lifetime of female socialization had failed to impede the emergence of psychosexual masculinity at sexual maturation. It seems unlikely that the girlish appearance of the pseudohermaphrodites could have planted the seeds of their psychosexual masculinity. Imperato-McGinley observes that since sex roles in rural Dominica are relatively rigid, her subjects, whose unusual-looking genitals were frequently seen at communal baths, had great incentive to conform themselves to their early socialization. To judge by their photographs, the pseudohermaphrodites looked like quite typical little girls during childhood, and muscular, virile men after puberty.

Much of the criticism directed against these studies, particularly those of Money, has concerned the alleged difficulty of defining the sort of stereotypically male behavior displayed by humans with virilized brains. Goldberg calls it "aggression" and "dominance tendency," and Money calls it "dominance-aggression." I think these words and the phenomenon they denote are clear enough, but it might help to think of masculine dominance-aggression in terms of Clausewitz's definition of war as "an act of violence intended to compel our opponent to fulfil our will." Dominance-aggression is the desire that others do what you want them to do rather than what they want to do. Women have preferences just as firm as men about how other people should behave, but a woman proverbially seeks to shape the behavior of others by indirection, getting them to want to do of their own accord what she wants them to do. Dominance-aggression is willingness to *make* others do what one wants them to do. It is dimorphism with respect to this trait that the Money studies indicate is physiologically determined.

Money, like Wilson, is personally sympathetic to feminism. He notes, correctly, that the male's physiologically-based dominance advantage "does not totally preordain the course of postnatal dimorphism of behavior differentiation," and he emphasizes the "sequential interaction" of nature and environment. He takes the elimination of gender roles to be not only feasible but desirable, apparently on the grounds that stereotyping is unfair to unusual individuals, and calls for a "consensual revolution [in] childrearing during the infantile and early childhood years when basic gender identity/role is differentiated."[32] As "there is a limit to how much can be changed by slow evolution instead of abrupt revolution," he believes that gender-differentiation must be eliminated all at once throughout society by government measures and "edicts": "If as a society we shall decide to commit ourselves to change everyone, then the program must, of necessity, begin with childrearing." Money explicitly compares this project to getting everyone to drive on the same side of the road, a paradigm coordination problem solved by state action.

Again, the desirability of the program Money envisions is beyond scientific assessment, but again, its coherence is undermined by the empirical data Money himself supplies. To whatever extent it is possible to change *gender* identity—an individual's idea of his sex and his conformity to (possibly arbitrary) social expectations based on sex—nothing will change *sexual* identity, which includes the male tendency to dominance-aggression. On Money's own showing, that tendency is biologically unalterable.

Sex Differences in Cognition and Neural Organization

There is widespread agreement among cognitive scientists that males excel at spatial and mathematical skills while females excel at verbal skills. These differences appear in childhood, increase during puberty, and stabilize thereafter, consistently with causation by a timed-released innate program.

Girls begin to speak earlier than boys, and when boys and girls start to vocalize to the same extent between the ages of three and five, female vocalization tends more to be speech and male vocalization tends more to be noise.[33] (This finding will surprise few parents.) Females are better at hearing high frequencies, a difference which increases with age and involves a capacity associated with the perception of inflection and spoken language.[34] Maccoby and Jacklin[35] report dozens of reading and vocabulary tests on which women consistently outperform men.

On the other hand, Bock and Kolakowski claim to have verified a "pronounced difference in favor of males" in spatial visualization, the ability to imagine the appearance of three-dimensional objects when rotated.[36] They estimate this difference to be 46 percent genetic in origin. In particular, they argue from their own experiments and a statistical analysis of the literature that this ability occurs in humans in a pattern associated with a sex-linked recessive gene, a high correlation for the presence of the trait between sons and mothers, and fathers and daughters.[37] Hartlage, Corah, and Stafford have found the correlation between mothers and sons to be (the statistically significant) .39, and that between fathers and daughters to range from .34 to .41.[38] These correlations both support sex linkage and disconfirm the primary environmental explanation of the male advantage in spatial ability, the transmission of this ability from father to son via instruction in tool handling and ball tossing. This hypothesis predicts, falsely, that spatial visualizing ability will be most highly correlated between father and son. The sex difference in spatial skills is probably more systematic than many of these studies indicate, for, as Harris and others have noted, women tend to solve spatial problems by coding them verbally whereas men tend to solve them directly.[39] A female asked to orient herself on an upside-down map is more likely than a male to say to herself, "First you turn left, and then you walk straight, . . ." whereas a man is more likely to "see" how to go.

Closely correlated with the male's spatial-visualizing advantage is the male advantage at mathematical abstraction, which is found to be greatest on tests involving geometrical reasoning. There are virtually no sex differences on the computational parts of mathematics taught in elementary school, but this null finding lends little weight to the hypothesis of equal innate mathematical ability (with girls becoming discouraged as they discover that mathematics is stereotypically male). The essence of mathematical reasoning is insight into abstract structure, which is unrelated to computation skills and the rote memorization often sufficient for their mastery.[40]

The Hier-Crowley study of nineteen male idiopathic hypogonadics supplies further physiological evidence of the innateness of spatial ability in males.[41] The subjects of this natural experiment were males who were masculinized normally in utero, developed normally until puberty, but did not mature sexually because of a pituitary malfunction at puberty. Hier and Crowley report that their subjects had abnormally small testes and female levels of serum testosterone. Their condition contrasts with that of acquired hypogonadics, who characteristically undergo normal puberties and suffer as adults from hypogonadism and female levels of serum testosterone as the result of some external cause. The Hier-Crowley idiopathic gonadics scored as well on verbal tests as five acquired hypogonadics and nineteen normal male controls, but less well than either group on tests of spatial ability. The acquired hypogonadics performed as well as the controls on the spatial tests. Hormone-replacement therapy did not improve the performance of the idiopathic hypogonadics, and idiopathic testicular volume showed a significant positive correlation with spatial ability. In light of their findings, Hier and Crowley propose that male cognitive development proceeds in two stages, the groundplan being laid by fetal androgens, with the release of a second wave of gonadic androgens at puberty being necessary for the achievement of normal levels of functioning.

Camilla Benbow and Julian Stanley have studied, at this writing, about 40,000 mathematically gifted youths.[42] Their initial sample contained 9,227 gifted junior high school students, 43 percent female and 57 percent male, in which the boys scored no better than the girls on age-appropriate mathematical aptitude tests, but consistently outscored the girls on the mathematical part of the Scholastic Aptitude Test, a more difficult test normed on high school juniors and seniors. The greatest discrepancies appeared in the upper ranges of mathematical reasoning ability, and this effect was consistently observed in later samples.[43] In one typical series of tests, 27 percent of the males scored over 600 on the SAT-M while no female did. The ratio of boys to girls increased at cutoffs of 420, 500, 600, and 700. Of the 280 children thirteen years of age or younger who scored 700 or better on the SAT-M, 260 were male.

These results are what one would expect if innate mathematical reasoning ability—described by Benbow and Stanley as an "endogenous variable"—is randomly distributed among boys and among girls, with the male mean lying above the female mean (and the variance among males being somewhat greater than among females). It is *not* what one would expect on a social-conditioning hypothesis, for no such hypothesis could explain the particular statistical contours of the Benbow-Stanley result. In any case, the Benbow-Stanley study controlled for the most obvious environmental variables. Since the girls outperformed the boys on the verbal part of the SAT, the girls may be presumed not to have suffered from a general fear of tests. The boys and girls in the sample had taken the same amount of mathematics, and afterward showed no difference in attitude toward mathematics attributable to sex. The boys and girls took courses in a similar pattern up to their high school SATs, so that any adverse socialization would have to be assumed, ad hoc, to affect aptitude test performance but not course selection. In fact, the girls received slightly better grades in high-school mathematics and sciences courses, although the boys did better on achievement and aptitude tests in mathematics and the mathematical sciences at the end of high school. Mathematical ability was a better predictor of other variables than was sex.

Lest the reader suspect I am presenting a one-sided case by ignoring criticism of these studies, I will mention all the environmentalist criticisms of these studies known to me. The intrinsic interest of these criticism is minute, but they convey something of the flavor of "feminist science."

There Is No Difference

Richard Lewontin, a geneticist, calls the question of male analytical ability "the garbage can of barroom speculation presented as science."[44] Ruth Bleier offers a novel argument for a similar conclusion: "The 'sex difference' investigated is a small *statistical* difference between entire groups when it exists and it does not distinguish between the two groups. That is, the two sexes are not different."[45] Bleier arrives at this absurd conclusion—absurd, because *some* unequally distributed factor must be causing the difference in the aggregated responses of boys and girls to the

SAT-M—by first interpreting a "sex difference" to be a trait possessed by all boys and no girls, and then attributing this straw-man to Benbow and Stanley. According to Bleier, Benbow and Stanley "try ostensibly to establish clear-cut mutually exclusive biological differences between the sexes,"[46] an attribution that the most cursory reading of Benbow and Stanley will show to be preposterous.

The popular objection that the SAT-M does not test a "fixed capacity" but only a "developed ability"[47] also denies that the Benbow-Stanley study is indicative of anything. A "developed ability" is, one gathers, an ability a child has at a time as the result of his experiences, and if no factor fixed independently of learning is involved, then girls with the same learning history as boys would develop the same ability as measured by the SAT-M. Critics observe, correctly, that the SAT-M does not predict mathematical creativity; the latter is so rare that even most students who score well on the SAT-M never make mathematical discoveries. But the SAT-M does validly predict subsequent class performance, and mathematical creativity *does* predict high SAT-M scores.

Hidden Variables

Jerome Kagan has suggested with regard to the Hier-Crowley study that idiopathic hypogonadics "try less hard" to think spatially because "they have unvirilized body builds during most of their adolescence, [and] are likely to question their ability to perform with excellence on tests they believe are solved most efficiently by more masculine males."[48] This hypothesis faces the clear difficulty that hypogonadics unfamiliar with the psychometric literature have no reason to think that doing well on tests of spatial visualization is part of being masculine. It also fails to explain why test performance correlates with testicular volume. It is difficult to imagine how hypogonadics could calibrate their expectations to the relative size of their gonads.

Psychologists Julia Sherman and Elizabeth Fennema are reported to be investigating the toys with which the Stanley-Benbow females played during childhood.[49] This line of inquiry again ignores the need to explain the particular contours of the data. Toys which in some general way might suppress mathematical reasoning will not explain the Benbow-Stanley results; what are required are toys which selectively inhibit mathematical reasoning on age-inappropriate tests only.

It has been suggested, finally, that gifted boys are more likely to volunteer for tests than gifted girls. This may well be true, but it would not explain why these girls in the top five percentiles of mathematical ability for their age who *could* keep up with the boys on the SAT-M did not volunteer for the Benbow-Stanley study, while those girls in the same rank who could not keep up with the boys did volunteer. Tomizuka and Tobias write: "Although it isn't *likely* that the most talented girls refused to enter the talent search, it is possible that, having other options, they did not."[50] It is easy to evade induction by inventing hidden variable hypothesis, much more difficult to fit them to the data.

No hidden variable hypothesis can come to grips with the fundamental *why* question: If boys are steered to mathematics by the stereotype of mathematics as masculine, where did the stereotype come from? It cannot have gained currency because men once arbitrarily appropriated mathematics for themselves, since that hypothesis assumes that mathematics was a going concern which the human race *found* and which, for obscure reasons, men decided to monopolize. There was no such thing as mathematics until people started doing it, and when they first started doing it there was nothing intrinsically masculine about it. It is simpler to explain the perceived masculinity of mathematics as a product of male mathematical aptitude, and then seek to explain this aptitude in more fundamental terms, than to explain the aptitude in terms of the perception while leaving the perception itself a mystery.

The Difference Is Small[51]

The effect observed by Benbow and Stanley is statistically large, in some phases of the study amounting to half a standard deviation. Boys' reaching the highest levels of mathematical aptitude thirteen times as frequently as girls would be a miracle on the null hypothesis. More crucially, as I stressed earlier, a big difference is what makes a big difference. Whatever the male mathematical advantage may look like in terms of raw score data, it is large if it explains why men make all the mathematical discoveries, why mathematics is perceived as a masculine skill, why women experience higher levels of anxiety when faced with mathematical problems, and allied phenomena. Innateness plus feedback—the Goldberg effect—is a plausible start toward explaining these "big" societal phenomena, whereas a well-defined environmentalist rival to show the innate difference irrelevant has yet to be fielded.

The formulaic, sometimes desperate responses to the Benbow-Stanley study all share a remarkable obliviousness to the phenomenon they are supposed to be addressing. No one familiar with mathematics takes seriously the idea that high levels of mathematical achievement can be significantly affected by encouragement or its opposite. Mathematical ability appears quite early—the great mathematicians have displayed scarcely believable precocity—and is almost eerily detached from experience. In the words of David Hilbert:

The first and oldest problems in every branch of mathematics stem from experience and are suggested by the world of external phenomena. . . . But, in the further development of a branch of mathematics, the human mind, encouraged by the success of its solutions, becomes conscious of its independence. By means of logical combination, generalization and specialization, by separating and collecting ideas in fortunate ways—often without appreciable influence from without—it evolves from itself alone new and fruitful problems, and appears then itself as the real questioner.[52]

Cerebral Lateralization and Morphology

The patterning of sex differences in mathematical and verbal ability leads naturally to a search for a basis in cerebral functioning, and much speculation has centered on cerebral lateralization.[53] Clinical studies of brain injury have shown that, in humans, the right cerebral hemisphere controls spatial visualizing and the left cerebral hemisphere controls speech. It is also known that the hemispheres control perception and behavior on the side of the body opposite to them. After it was found that removal of parts of the temporal lobe impairs visual-spatial and verbal performance more seriously in men than women,[54] it was conjectured that sex differences in cognition may be related to differences in interhemispheric communication. Some of the best-known tests of this hypothesis have been conducted by Sandra Witelson. She asked 200 children to hold objects with meaningless shapes in their right and left hands simultaneously, and, having screened the shapes and their hands from the children, Witelson had the children identify shapes in their hands from among six displayed visually. Boys were significantly better at describing the shapes they held in their left hands, while the girls showed no hand bias. Male brain function is apparently more lateralized, with the right (spatial) hemisphere dominant.[55]

One attractive explanation of the greater lateralization of function in the male brain is the later sexual maturation of males. The hemispheres are known to grow apart in the years preceding maturity, and this might be expected to attenuate the physical bridge between the hemispheres, the corpus callosum, in the male. Utamsing and Holloway have recently found evidence of just this morphological differentiation of the male and female brain,[56] the first observation of a physical difference in brain structure between the sexes. Not intending to investigate sex differences at all, Utamsing and Holloway obtained nine male brains and five female brains for an autopsy, and, performing all measurements "without any information on the sex, age, brain weight, and so forth of individual," inadvertently discovered "a sex difference in the shape of the caudal or posterior portion of the corpus callosum." They continue:

> The female splenium is more bulbous and larger than the male counterpart. . . . Partial correlations of maximal splenial width with sex by brain weight, body weight, height and age accounted for very little of the variance.

Since the nerves passing through the splenium are involved in interhemispheric information transfer,

> our results are congruent with a recent neurophysiological hypothesis that the female brain is less well lateralized—that is, manifests less hemispheric specialization—than the male brain for visuospatial functions.

Utamsing and Holloway emphasize the need for "quantitative ultrastructural information" about the number of fibers in the splenium. Also, the Utamsing-Holloway finding does not clarify why greater lateralization should favor the functions of the *right* hemisphere rather than the left. Nevertheless, Newton's strictures against positing needless causes makes this difference in brain morphology, should it be corroborated, a likely cause of some of the observed sex differences in behavior. As I argued in chapter 3, structural features of organs are normally expected to correspond to some special adaptive function; it would be very surprising if difference in brain structure did not also imply some difference in adaptive function.

Motivation and Molar Behavior

A superior male readiness to manipulate physical objects, akin to a superior readiness to manipulate visual forms in the imagination, has been found in studies of behavior. McGuiness and Pribram conclude that even as infants, males "tend to be more interested in objects than people, and are more skilled at gross motor movements," while female infants "respond more readily to the human voice than do male infants." In summary, "the male is biased to express his intention in action, and the female in communication."

This difference manifests itself early in life and in a variety of ways. By the age of one, boys are more drawn to unusual toys and more inclined to play with toys in novel ways.[57] Females are "particularly attentive to certain types of auditory cues, and they appear to attend to the emotional and meaningful properties of sounds," while "boys appear responsive to novel stimuli when it is non-social in character."[58] Maccoby and Jacklin had concluded from their survey of the research literature that boys and girls are equally sociable,[59] but McGuiness and Pribram point out that boys and girls differ in the kind of sociality they exhibit. Boys' interest in other people is functional—"Can they play games or build a tree house?"—whereas girls "seek out more intimate personal relationships." In game situations, males are more likely to form coalitions for purposes of winning, whereas women are more likely to form coalitions on the basis of emotional attachments.[60] In addition, "males excel in speed of gross motor outflow, while females excel in speed of discrete and finely controlled motor response. . . . [W]hen the response required demands attention to detail, females are superior."[61] Boys are superior at solving problems involving the manipulation of objects,[62] and become fascinated with objects at four to six months of age, before attention can be shaped by reinforcement.

Again heeding Newton's maxim of simplicity, it is plausible to see in these differences between the "sensitive" female and the "manipulative" male (differences familiar to every parent) the basis of observed sex differences and social institutions. Science and technology are naturally viewed as extensions of the male desire to take things apart and see how they work. Female sensitivity to auditory cues helps make sense of "women's intuition" about matters of feeling, an ability clearly adaptive for rearing young and inarticulate children. Female sensitivity and person-oriented sociality explain Carol Gilligan's observations about female moral thinking, if these observations are anything more than the reiteration of commonplaces of the social scientific literature and common sense.

The Universality of Male Dominance and Sex-Role Differentiation

No student of human behavior denies the male advantage in dominance-aggression and its universal correlate, preparedness to use force. After a determinedly sceptical review of the literature, Maccoby and Jacklin conclude that "the male's greater aggression has a biological component,"[63] as evidenced by boys' greater indulgence in mock fighting and "aggressive fantasies," and the greater aggressiveness of male primates. A number of even more determined feminists have attempted to refute Maccoby and Jacklin, but it should be stressed that the latter confined their attention to sex differences manifest before adolescence. The evidence they cite of the male advantage in aggression is therefore extremely fragmentary, omitting all anthropological data about war, violence, and political authority.

From the beginning of the historical and archaeological record, males have devoted an astonishing measure of their energy and ingenuity to killing each other. Violent crime is a male pursuit in every society. Konner reports cross-cultural studies which consistently find women dreaming of children and crying and men dreaming of coitus and weapons. Odysseus tricks Achilles into revealing himself by showing him a dagger. The heroes of Norse mythology spend their time in Valhalla fighting and carousing.

Every society that has ever existed has associated familial authority with the male and conferred the overwhelming majority of positions of power on males.[64] Efforts to eliminate these features in Israel, Sweden, and the Soviet Union have failed. Male dominance and the sexual division of labor are observed among such reputedly uncorrupted people as the !Kung.[65] !Kung juvenile playgroups are single-sex; boys spend far more time than girls in exploring technology (e.g. digging up termite mounds with arrows) and play rough-and-tumble play. !Kung men hunt and !Kung women gather; although what the women gather accounts for most of the tribe's calories and protein, hunting enjoys greater prestige. Margaret Mead remarked in *Male and Female:* "In every known human society, the male's need for achievement can be recognized."

I will not tax the reader's patience with a discussion of feminist attempts to prove the existence of matriarchies or equiarchies. These are generally pastiches of inscriptions, marriage contracts and Earth-mother myths; by reasoning equally cogent, Three Stooges movies prove that Americans normally poke each other's eyes. Of more interest are the two nonbiological explanations of patriarchy which at least recognize that a phenomenon observed in every society must be explained by the operation of some unitary factor. One explanation posits a universal male desire to keep track of offspring. I consider this idea elsewhere, but it suffices to observe here that this explanation assumes knowledge on the part of prehistoric man of the connection of intercourse to childbirth, and it fails to explain either the superior language abilities of females (loquacity is not usually encouraged in subject populations) or the male's greater proneness to show aggression against other men. Nancy Chodorow has offered a second explanation. She posits a male need to separate from the mother, which leads the male to demean his mother and later neglect his wife, whose overinvestment in her daughter cripples the daughter psychologically and triggers the next cycle of oppression. This explanation tacitly appeals to an unexplained sex difference: Why do girls not feel the same need for separation from the mother that boys do? Not surprisingly, this account quickly becomes circular. According to Chodorow, the typical mother instills her daughter with fear of men because of "her probable heterosexuality [and] her conscious acceptance of the ideology, meanings and expectations that go into being a gendered member of our society."[66] Instead of explaining where sexist ideology comes from, Chodorow ends by explaining sexist ideology in terms of itself.

Even if nothing were known of fetal hormonalization, cerebral lateralization, natural selection, or the behavior of infants, the failure of environmental explanations of patriarchy would force the conclusion that male dominance is biologically based.

Male Dominance and Democracy

The male's greater innate aggressiveness explains features of society that are easily overlooked when the emphasis is on "the status of women" but patent enough on a wider view. Any stable society must have found ways to socialize males away from aggression. This is why the principal message given to children by parents is that boys should not fight, and why social institutions always evolve toward channelling male energies, which produce chaos in a wide variety of environments, in constructive directions. Most of the rules of every society punish behavior to which men are distinctively drawn. What created and sustains most social rules is not that they keep women in the power of men but that they keep men from attacking each other. The basic function of law is to prevent the use of force; every moral code condemns aggression (at least against members of the immediate group) and praises cooperation.

The male advantage in dominance-aggression makes patriarchy inevitable because men will always strive harder than women to reach the top of hierarchies they encounter, and create hierarchies to reach the top of if none exist. Just as the social structure of a gorilla band does not exist apart from the tendencies of individual gorillas to react to each other in various ways, hierarchies exist because of the relational dispositions of individual human beings. That men monopolize leadership positions because they try harder to get them does not mean that men deserve these positions or that men do a better job in them than women would do if they became leaders. The only sense in which male dominance is "right" is that it expresses the free choices of individual men to strive for positions of power and the free choices of individual women to do other things.

The prediction that attempts to eliminate patriarchy within a group must sharply limit the freedom of the group's members, and can only be undertaken from without by a stronger group of men, corresponds closely to the current situation in Eastern Europe. It being part of orthodox Marxism that the Communist revolution will bring about sexual equality, women have been given an increasing share of offices in Communist governments. For instance, the proportion of women in the Czech national assembly rose from 7.1 percent in 1948 to 28.6 percent in 1973.[67] However, these women hold no real power:

> Given the limited role which the national legislatures play in the formation of policy in most of these countries, women's representation in these largely symbolic bodies is not a true measure of their actual influence at the national level. If we look at women's representation among the effective, or Communist party elites, a very different picture emerges. . . . As the importance of the office increases, the number of women declines. Thus, women are better represented in the symbolic, or governmental, elites than in the effective, or Communist party elites at all levels.[68]

In 1978, women accounted for only 8 of 199 positions in all Communist politburos. From 1948 to 1976 the proportion of females in the Central Committee of the Communist Party of the USSR grew insignificantly, from 2.5 percent to 3.3 percent.[69] Moreover, the women in these bodies

> are chosen for symbolic . . . and ideological reasons. . . . [M]any women did
> not actively seek their positions, but rather were asked by [male] party
> leaders to serve. . . . [These women] have not achieved their central commit-
> tee positions by virtue of long party work.[70]

Those women invited in "tend to be responsible for matters traditionally
viewed as women's concerns and seldom rise to positions of leadership."[71]
Despite its desire to appear to occupy the vanguard of social change, the
leadership of the Soviet Union puts its female ministers in charge of education and cultural affairs. Female deputies have little say about foreign policy
or economic planning. Women have become more visible in these non-
democratic governments because those in authority have wished to increase
female visibility, not because women have seized a greater share of the
power:

> The best explanation for the variation in the number of women in East Euro-
> pean elites is elite-determined demand, as expressed in recruitment policies.
> Sex appears to be one of the centrally determined norms which govern the
> selection of candidates for government and party offices in these countries.
> The recent increase in women's representation among top party as well as
> government elites in several of these countries coincides with explicit efforts
> by top party leaders to increase the visibility of women in public life and
> illustrates the ability of Communist leaders to influence the extent of women's
> representation.[72]

The strain between democratic liberties and the placement of proportional
numbers of women in political hierarchies is also beginning to be felt in the
West. I noted earlier an effort by the Mitterrand government in France to
limit the number of male candidates legally permitted to run for office.
Similar suggestions have been repeatedly broached by the West German
government.[73] In the United States, the Democratic Party has imposed strict
50/50 gender quotas on its internal workings. Nobody has to vote for
Democratic candidates, of course, but there have also been an increasing
number of calls to replace elective by appointive office precisely because
not enough women are chosen by election. A study done for the Fund for
Modern Courts observed that women, Blacks, and Hispanics are more often
chosen for the bench when judgeships are filled by appointment rather than
election, and concluded: "If the courts of the United States are to reflect the
citizens they serve, then qualified women and minority group members
must come to the bench in increasing numbers."[74] Applied to political institutions, this argument should be particularly worrisome to champions of a
republican form of government.

Notes

1. See Michael Levin, "Theory Change and Meaning Change," *Philosophy of Science* 46 (October 1979): 407–23. The most responsible statement of scientific relativism is T.S. Kuhn, *The Structure of Scientific Revolutions*, 2nd ed. (Chicago: University of Chicago Press, 1970).
2. Stanley Rothman has informed me that he plans to study the media's treatment of the scientific debate about sex differences.
3. Frederick Lynch, "Totem and Taboo in Sociology: The Politics of Affirmative Action Research," *Sociological Inquiry* 54 (Spring 1984): 124–41; Robert Gordon, "Taboo or Not Taboo: Research on IQ, Race, and Delinquency," in *Taboos in Criminology*, ed. Edward Sagarin (Beverly Hills, Ca.: Sage, 1980), pp. 37–67.
4. Ned Block and Gerald Dworkin, "Heritability and Inequality," in *The IQ Controversy*, ed. Ned Block and Gerald Dworkin (New York: Pantheon, 1976), p. 520.
5. Ibid., p. 521.
6. This point has been made by Goldberg, Barash, and Mary Midgley (*Beast and Man* [New York: Meridian, 1978], p. 56). The trenchant phrase "the failure to ask why" is Goldberg's.
7. I have extensively cited Ruth Bleier's *Science and Gender* not because it is especially challenging, but because several academic feminists referred me to it as the definitive statement of the feminist scientific case. Anne Fausto-Sterling's more recent *Myths of Gender* is somewhat less shrill, but quite similar in its argumentative techniques: evasion of induction by hypothesis (according to Fausto-Sterling, the Benbow-Stanley results might be due to girls' restrictive clothing), heavy weather over the definition of words like *aggression,* scepticism about the behavioral implications of brain differences, and hole-poking in a few of the many studies of hormonal effects on the brain.
8. *American Journal of Sociology* 83 (September 1977): 512.
9. The probability of a disjunction of hypotheses is the sum of their individual probabilities, less the sum of their pairwise products, plus their product. The probability of a disjunction of three hypotheses with individual probabilities of .8, .7, and .6 is .976. The disjunctive probability of independent hypotheses increases more rapidly.
10. See David Barash, *The Whisperings Within* (New York: Penguin, 1981); James Gould, *Ethology* (New York: Harper & Row, 1982); E.O. Wilson, *On Human Nature* (Cambridge, Mass.: Harvard University Press, 1978); E.O. Wilson, *Sociobiology* (Cambridge, Mass.: Harvard University Press, 1975); Richard Dawkins, *The Selfish Gene* (Oxford: Oxford University Press, 1976); John Maynard Smith, *The Theory of Evolution,* 3rd ed., (New York: Penguin, 1976); John Maynard Smith, *The Evolution of Sex* (Cambridge: Cambridge University Press, 1978); Donald Symons, *The Evolution of Human Sexuality* (New York: Oxford University Press, 1979); R.L. Trivers, "Parental Investment and Sexual Selection," in *Sexual Selection and the Descent of Man,* ed. B. Campbell (Chicago: Aldine, 1972), pp. 136–79; William Hamilton, "The Genetical Theory of Social Behavior: I and II," *Journal of Theoretical Biology* 7, 1 (1964): 1–52.
11. This is the liberated woman as described in Rossi, "Immodest Proposal," 648–56.
12. Marvin Harris, *Cannibals and Kings* (New York: Random House, 1977).

13. Symons, p. 24.
14. See Ken Nakatsuru and Donald L. Kramer, "Is Sperm Cheap? Limited Male Fertility and Female Choice in Lemon Tetra (Pisces, Characidae)," *Science* 216 (May 14, 1982): 753–55.
15. Sarah Hrdy (*The Woman that Never Evolved* [Cambridge, Mass.: Harvard University Press, 1981]) has suggested an alternative model in accordance with which women evolved to be competitive and sexually aggressive. It is not clear that there are any empirical observations for this model to explain, but let us take it to be offered as an account of the continual sexual receptivity of human females. This receptivity is usually explained as serving to cement human mating bonds. Hrdy argues that it was "evolved by women" to confuse men about paternity and thereby induce all the men with whom a woman has sex to help her and her offspring. This theory requires, somewhat implausibly, that hominid males understood the relation between intercourse and childbirth. More crucially, it ignores the more efficient strategies that males could evolve for dealing with children of doubtful paternity, such as infanticide as practiced by male lions upon assuming pride leadership. Had females developed the Hrdy strategy, paternal investment would have become maladaptive and surviving males would have developed "love-'em-and-leave-'em" strategy. Conceptually, Hrdy's theory treats males and females as ordinary competitors, since the female strategy would be "successful" to the extent that males misappropriate their resources to offspring not their own and lessen their own chances of survival. The existence of distinctive female/female competition raises no problem for the parental investment theory, which predicts that females will compete over resources for their offspring (rather than dominance, as males do). The "ruthlessness" of female/female competition among primates can easily be viewed as prototypical of the "cattiness" said to characterize feuds between human females.
16. *The Whispering Within*, p. 89.
17. Melvin Konner, *The Tangled Wing* (New York: Harper, 1982), p. 126.
18. *On Human Nature*, p. 133.
19. Ibid.
20. For more on the effects of female hormones on adult females, see H. Perskey, "Reproductive Hormones, Moods, and the Menstrual Cycle," in *Sex Differences in Behavior,* ed. R.C. Friedman et al. (New York: Wiley, 1974), pp. 455–66.
21. See N. MacLusky and F. Naftolin, "Sexual Differentiation of the Central Nervous System," *Science* 211 (March 20, 1981): 1294–1303.
22. MacLusky and Naftolin; also C. Dominique Toran-Allerand, "Sex Steroids and the Development of the Newborn Mouse Hypothalamus and Preoptic Area *in vitro:* Implications for Sexual Differentiation," *Brain Research* 106 (1976): 407–12. For the neuronal effect of testosterone on adult rats, see K.M. Kendrick and R.F. Drewett, "Testosterone Reduces Refractory Period of Stria Terminalis Neurons in the Rat Brain," *Science* 204 (1979): 877–79.
23. G. Raisman and P. Field, "Sexual Dimorphism in the Neuropil of the Preoptic Area of the Rat and Its Dependence on Neonatal Androgen," *Brain Research* 54 (1973): 1–29. Rat brains are most sensitive to hormones at birth rather than *in utero.*
24. "Sex Steroids," p. 411; also see Kendrick and Drewett.
25. John Money and Anke Erhardt, *Man and Woman, Boy and Girl* (Baltimore: Johns Hopkins University Press, 1972); John Money, *Sex Errors of the Body*

(Baltimore: Johns Hopkins University Press, 1968); John Money, "Prenatal Hormones and Postnatal Sexualization in Gender Identity Differentiation," in *Nebraska Symposium on Motivation,* ed. J. Cole and R. Dienstieber (Lincoln: University of Nebraska Press, 1973), pp. 221–95; Erhardt and Susan Baker, "Fetal Androgens, Human Central Nervous System Differentiation, and Behavior Sex Differences," in Friedman, pp. 33–50.

26. Androgen may first have to be converted into estrogen before it can affect cell nuclei, which may be why exogenous progestogen—and estrogen—can masculinize fetal brains.

27. Anke Erhardt and Heino Meyer-Blauberg, "Effects of Prenatal Hormones on Gender-Related Behavior, *Science* 211 (March 1984): 1312–18; see also Erhardt and Baker.

28. This raises the possibility of a threshold effect.

29. Daniel Mascia, John Money, and Anke Erhardt, "Fetal Feminization and Female Gender Identity in the Testicular Feminizing Syndrome of Androgen Insensitivity," *Archives for Sexual Behavior* 1 (1971): 131–42; John Money, Anke Erhardt, and Daniel Mascia, "Fetal Feminization Induced by Androgen Insensitivity in the Testicular Feminizing Syndrome," *Johns Hopkins Medical Journal* 123 (1968): 105–14.

30. June Reinisch and William Karow, "Prenatal Exposure to Synthetic Progestins and Estrogens: Effects on Human Development," *Archives for Sexual Behavior* 6 (1977): 257–88.

31. Julianne Imperato-McGinley, Luis Guerrero, Teofilo Gaultier, and R.E. Peterson, "Steroid 5α-Reductase Deficiency in Man: An Inherited Form of Male Pseudohermaphroditism," *Science* 186 (December 27, 1974): 1213–15; Imperato and Peterson, "Male Pseudohermaphroditism: The Complexities of Male Phenotypic Development," *American Journal of Medicine* 61 (August 1976): 251–72; Imperato-McGinley, Gaultier, and Erasmo Strula, "Androgens and the Evolution of Male Gender Identity among Pseudohermaphrodites with 5α-Reductase Deficiency," *New England Journal of Medicine* 300, 22 (May 31, 1979): 1233–37.

32. John Money, "Origins and Options: Male/Female Stereotypes," presented to the American Association for the Advancement of Science, 1975.

33. Peter K. Smith and Kevin Connolly, "Patterns of Play and Social Interaction in Pre-School Children," in *Ethological Studies in Child Behavior,* ed. N. Blurton-Jones (Cambridge: Cambridge University Press, 1972), pp. 65–95.

34. See Diane McGuiness and Karl Pribram, "The Origins of Sensory Bias in the Development of Gender Differences in Perception and Cognition," in *Cognitive Growth and Development,* ed. M. Bortner (New York: Brunner/Mazel, 1978), pp. 3–56.

35. Eleanor Maccoby and Carol Jacklin, *Psychology of Sex Differences* (Stanford: Stanford University Press, 1974), pp. 75–85.

36. R.D. Bock and D. Kolakowski, "Further Evidence of Sex-Linked Major-Gene Influence on Human Spatial Visualizing Ability," *American Journal of Genetics* 25 (January 1973): 1–14.

37. For an explanation of why sex-linked recessive traits have this character, see L.J. Harris, "Sex Differences in Spatial Ability: Possible Environmental, Genetic, and Neurological Factors," in *Asymmetrical Functions of the Brain,* ed. M. Kinsbourne (Cambridge: Cambridge University Press, 1978): 405–552.

38. L.C. Hartlage, "Sex-Linked Inheritance of Spatial Ability," *Perceptual and Motor Skills* 31 (October 1970): 610; N.L. Corah, "Differentiation in Children

and Their Parents," *Journal of Perception* 33 (1965): 300–308; R.E. Stafford, "Sex Differences in Spatial Visualization as Evidence of Sex-Linked Inheritance," *Perceptual and Motor Skills* 13 (July–December 1961): 428.

39. "Sex Differences in Spatial Ability."
40. See e.g. M.K. Barakat, "A Factorial Study of Mathematical Ability," *British Journal of Psychology, Statistical Section* 4 (1951): 137–56; L.G. Saad and W.O. Storer, *Understanding in Mathematics* (Edinburgh: Oliver & Boyd, 1960); I.M. Smith, "The Validity of Tests of Spatial Ability as Predictors of Success in Technical Courses," *British Journal of Educational Psychology* 30 (1969): 138–45.
41. D.B. Hier and W.F. Crowley, "Spatial Ability in Androgen-Deficient Men," *New England Journal of Medicine* 306, 20 (May 20, 1982): 1202–5. This study may shed light on Turner's Syndrome, which casts some doubt on the sex linkage of mathematical ability.
42. Camilla Benbow and Julian Stanley, " Sex Differences in Mathematical Ability: Fact or Artifact?" *Science* 210 (December 1980): 1262–64; "Consequences in High School and College of Sex Differences in Mathematical Reasoning: A Longitudinal Perspective," *American Educational Research* 19 (Winter 1982): 598–622; "Sex Differences in Mathematical Reasoning Ability: More Facts," *Science* 222 (December 2, 1983): 1029–31; "Gender and the Science Major: A Study of Mathematically Precocious Youth," *Advances in Motivation and Achievement* 2 (1984): 165–95; for correspondence, see *Science* 212 (April 10, 1981): 114–19.
43. This effect had been observed previously; see G. Kolata, "Math and Sex: Are Girls Born with Less Ability?" *Science* 210: 1234–35.
44. Quoted in "How the Sexes Differ," *Newsweek* (May 18, 1981): 18.
45. Ruth Bleier, *Science and Gender* (New York: Pergamon, 1984), p. 94.
46. Ibid., p. 109.
47. Alice Shaefer and Mary Gray, "Sex and Mathematics," *Science* 211 (January 16, 1981): 231; also see correspondence of Carl Tomizuka, Sheila Tobias, Elizabeth Stage, and Robert Karplus in *Science* 211.
48. Jerome Kagan, "The Idea of Spatial Ability," *New England Journal of Medicine* 306: 1225–7
49. Reported by Kolata.
50. Tomizuka and Tobias, p. 114.
51. Bleier, p. 102ff.; Jacqueline Eccles, "Bringing Women to Science," *The Research News* (September 1982): 3; Edward Burns, "Math Games," *Graduate Women* (January 1982): 13.
52. Hilbert made these remarks in "Mathematical Problems," his celebrated 1900 address to the Second International Congress of Mathematicians in Paris. The mathematical Intuitionist Brouwer, in many ways Hilbert's philosophical arch-foe, also saw mathematics as a free creation of the mind. The Platonist Kurt Goedel saw human mathematics as guided by the perception of transcendental entities, but again in a way wholly divorced from experience of empirical reality.
53. Jerre Levy, "Lateral Differences in the Human Brain in Cognition and Behavior Control," in *Cerebral Correlates of Conscious Experience,* ed. P. Buser and Rougel Buser (New York: North Holland, 1979), pp. 1–31; Jerre Levy, "Sex and the Brain," *Sciences* (March 1981): 20–28.
54. Herbert Landsdell, "A Sex Difference in Effect of Temporal Lobe Neurosurgery on Design Preference," *Nature* 1994 (1962): 852–54.

55. "Sex and the Single Hemisphere: Specialization of the Right Hemisphere for Spatial Processing," *Science* 193 (1976): 425–27.
56. Christine de Lacoste-Utamsing and Ralph Holloway: "Sexual Dimorphism in the Human Corpus Collosum," *Science* 216 (June 25, 1982): 1431–32.
57. See S. Goldberg and M. Lewis, "Play Behavior in the Year-Old Infant: Early Sex Differences," *Child Development* 40 (1969): 21–31.
58. McGuiness and Pribram, p. 20.
59. See Maccoby and Jacklin, p. 349.
60. Frans de Waal, interview, *Success* (January 1985), p. 29.
61. McGuiness and Pribram, p. 17.
62. S. Kreitler, H. Kreitler, and E. Ziegler, "Cognitive Orientation and Curiosity," *British Journal of Psychology* 65 (1974): 43–52.
63. Maccoby and Jacklin, p. 360.
64. See Steven Goldberg, *The Inevitability of Patriarchy* (London: Temple Smith, 1977) for extensive documentation.
65. The attempted homicide rate among the !Kung is about that of a major American city. For data on the !Kung see Gould, pp. 503–6.
66. *The Reproduction of Mothering*, p. 98.
67. Sharon Wolchik, *Women and Politics: The Eastern European Experience* (Institute for Sino-Soviet Studies, 1982), p. 258, table 12.2.
68. Ibid., pp. 258–59.
69. Ibid., p. 260, table 12.3.
70. Ibid., pp. 264–65, p. 272.
71. See Gail Lapidus, *Women in Soviet Society* (Berkeley: University of California Press, 1975), pp. 100–101.
72. Wolchik, p. 270
73. See *Women in the Federal Republic of Germany* (Bonn: Federal Ministry for Youth, Family Affairs, and Health, 1984), p. 44. "A number of women's organizations are demanding that quotas, i.e. certain percentages, be established for the inclusion of women in public bodies. Many women are against a mechanism of this kind because they fail to see why a majority group in society needs to employ measures normally used to protect minority interests." *Women in Society* (Bonn: Press and Information Office of the Government of the Federal Republic of Germany, n.d.)
74. See "Group Examines Selection of Minority Judges," *New York Times* (December 23, 1985): B7.

5

Affirmative Action

The Free Market and Feminism

Judged historically, the free market is the most successful economic arrangement. Permitting people to trade and associate freely for productive purposes has created unparalleled prosperity, along with support for the democratic institutions on which other forms of individual liberty have been found to depend. It is inevitable that feminists reject the free market, however, because they must interpret the expressions of sex differences facilitated by the freedom of the market as products of adverse socialization and discrimination.

Certainly, the observed differences between male and female labor market behavior are not in dispute; men and women do different sorts of work, and women earn lower average wages. It is also widely agreed that the immediate cause of these differences are differences in the motives which lead men and women into the labor market. Most married working women work to supplement their husband's income, which is regarded as the mainstay of the family budget.[1] Working mothers are expected to care for their children as well, or at any rate to supervise the arrangements for their care, an expectation that does not fall nearly so heavily upon fathers. Unmarried women often see work as an interregnum between school and marriage. For these reasons, women gravitate to jobs permitting easy entry, exit and re-entry to and from the workforce. Nor, finally, is it seriously questioned that men tend to seek (although of course not always find) more prestigious jobs and to try to "get ahead" more than women do. In short, men and women invest their human capital differently.[2]

As always, the question is why these things are so. Feminist theory takes them to be consequences of oppression. In the words of the Committee on Women's Employment and Related Social Issues of the National Research Council of the National Science Foundation:

> to the extent that sex segregation in the workplace connotes the inferiority of women or contributes to maintaining women as men's inferiors, it has great symbolic significance. To this extent, we believe it is fundamentally at odds

with the established goals of equal opportunity and equality under the law in American society.[3]

This theory is contradicted by the close match between many of the major differences in skills brought by men and women to the workplace and a number of the innate differences discussed in the preceding chapter. Together with the greater innate dominance-aggression of men, which manifests itself economically as greater competitiveness, this match strongly suggests that differences in workplace behavior are not best explained as products of the denial of equal opportunity. While it is somewhat artificial to divide the effects of gender on job-seeking behavior from its effects on wage-seeking behavior, I focus on workplace segregation in the present chapter, deferring wage disparities to the next.

In 1980, the National Opinion Research Center administered the Armed Services Vocational Aptitude Battery of ten tests to 12,000 randomly selected males and females between the ages of eighteen and twenty-three.[4] The ASVAB was then factored into four composite tests for "mechanical," "electronic," "administrative," and "general" aptitudes.[5] It was found that men scored considerably higher than women in mechanical and electronic aptitude, and slightly higher in general aptitude, while women exhibited greater administrative aptitude.[6] (On the individual tests, men for instance did considerably better on mechanical comprehension and women did considerably better on coding speed.[7]) These differences in aptitude were constant at all educational levels. Since the average female has 11.9 years of schooling to the average male's 11.8, these differences do not represent an educational deficit.[8] One might still wish to explain these aptitude differences in terms of socialization, but however they are explained they show that occupational segregation is not wholly the result of employer discrimination working on a homogeneous population of men and women.

Some innate sex differences correlate closely with aptitude for specific occupations, many of them prestigious, remunerative, and important in industrial society. Spatial ability is requisite for pipe fitting, technical drawing, and wood working,[9] and is the most important component of mechanical ability.[10] Only about 20 percent of girls in the elementary grades reach the average level of male performance on tests of spatial ability, and, according to the U.S. Employment Service, all classes of engineering and drafting as well as a high proportion of scientific and technical occupations require spatial ability in the top 10 percent of the U.S. population.[11] While one should normally be chary of explaining any social phenomenon *directly* in terms of some innate gender dimorphism, male domination of the technical and engineering professions is almost certainly due to the male's innate cognitive advantage rather than to a culturally induced female disadvantage.[12] Proportionally fewer women enter the technical fields than there are women in the population with the requisite raw skills, to be sure, but this is most plausibly attributed to the Goldberg feedback effect which selectively discourages women with marginal levels of skill—an injustice, perhaps, but one also borne by men with atypical skills. In any case, the sex segregation of the workforce is essentially the result of innate sex differences and unmanipulated expectations.

However, if one assumes that women would, given the opportunity, be as interested in and as suited for virtually the same work as men, one is compelled to interpret the continuing statistical segregation of the work force as evidencing discrimination. And, as the 1964 Civil Rights Act outlawed sex discrimination in all phases of employment, the claim that discrimination not only persists but is so pervasive as to demand extraordinary remedies must involve an unusual construction of "discrimination." One such construction prominent in government research on the question, an idea discussed in Chapter 2, is that women's own preferences obstruct equality of opportunity. A study by the Labor Department, *Women in Traditionally Male Jobs,* cites "the lack of female interest in many blue-collar jobs" as a "ubiquitous problem" in achieving "equal opportunity goals."[13] The Congressional Office of Technology Assessment cites "sex discrimination and sex stereotyping" as the barriers to women entering science and engineering:

> As long as women expect to assume the major role in housekeeping and childrearing, and to sacrifice their professional interests to those of their husbands, they will be less likely than men to select occupations like science and engineering that require major educational and labor force commitment.[14]

While this construal of "discrimination" may be unusually tortured, all studies which infer inequality of opportunities from a statistical disproportion in the number of women in a field must in some way warp the concept of discrimination. Since whatever causes the disproportionality is ipso facto discriminatory, intent as central to discrimination is displaced by unintended or "structural" discrimination. This shift in the operational test for discrimination immediately yields equality of outcome as the operational test for equality of opportunity. The view of the Equal Employment Opportunity Commission that "employment systems . . . however neutral and benign in intent [may] produce highly discriminatory effects" is reflected in the 1972 Equal Employment Opportunity Act, *Griggs* and *Dothard,* all of which prohibit "unintended discrimination."[15] *Griggs* found the requirement of a high school diploma to be racially discriminatory unless it can be shown to be a "business necessity." *Dothard* found height and weight requirements to be prima facie discriminatory against women. The EEOC forbids any hiring criterion with a differential effect on women which cannot be shown to be "job related," a showing which in practice has proven almost impossible to make to the courts' satisfaction. The courts have tended to regard any criterion that women cannot meet as a subterfuge for discrimination, although this backhand appeal to intent may also betray a continuing judicial discomfort with a purely consequential idea of discrimination.

This discomfort is natural, since "unintended discrimination" is a contradiction in terms. Sickle-cell anemia, a disease which strikes only Blacks, can hardly be called discriminatory, yet there is no difference in logic between sickle-cell anemia and a landlord who asks capriciously high rents in total ignorance of the inability of most Blacks to afford those rents. (To say, "But surely the landlord must know that most Blacks cannot afford his rents" reintroduces intent as a test for discrimination.) So far as Blacks are concerned, both are amoral natural phenomena which happen to respond differentially to Blacks.[16]

The case for "institutional" discrimination is often traced back to Robert K. Merton's essay "Discrimination and the American Creed,"[17] in which Merton is said to have identified discrimination without intent. In fact, Merton identified no such phenomenon. He was, rather, concerned with what he called the "unprejudiced discriminator," and he gave as his example the restaurant owner who excludes Blacks not because he dislikes them but because his customers do. It is obvious that while the restaurant owner's *motive* for excluding Blacks is relatively benign, his exclusion is still *intentional*. His purpose in acting is to exclude Blacks because they are Black. To the considerable extent to which it rests on Merton's work, the case for unintended discrimination does not exist.

Quotas

Once discrimination is separated from intent, and it is assumed that there should be as many women as men in some position, it becomes natural to seek to replace previously used criteria, including merit (or what employers have regarded as merit) with quotas. By "quotas" I understand the policy of favoring women (and minorities) in situations in which merit had formerly been the ideal criterion, on the basis of past discrimination women and Blacks are thought to have suffered. Quotas have nothing to do with giving someone a job he was discriminatorily denied; they involve, rather, the hiring, promotion, admission, or training of a given number of Blacks, Hispanics, or women regardless of whether these particular individuals have been wronged and regardless of the qualifications or culpability of competing White males, because of the wrongs alleged to have been done to other Blacks, Hispanics, and women in the past.

I understand "reverse discrimination" more broadly, to cover any measure designed to increase the likelihood that a female or member of a racial minority will get a position. Included are set-asides for women and minorities in contract allocation, studies of the "underutilization" of female employees not balanced by studies of the underutilization of male employees, training reserved for females, advertisements for openings placed in outlets thought to be especially accessible to women not balanced by special advertising directed at men, and so on. Reverse discrimination (or "inclusive discrimination," "benign discrimination," "positive discrimination," or "affirmative action") differs from ordinary discrimination only in its motives and its target (White males). IBM reserves scholarships for women intending to study engineering.[18] So long as IBM permits women to apply for all its other scholarships, IBM is denying men a chance to compete for certain goods just because they are men. However admirable IBM's policy may be, it is discrimination based on sex. Quotas are thought to be a particularly egregious form of reverse discrimination because they preclude White males from jobs, whereas the other measures I have mentioned merely reduce the chances of White males for jobs. For this reason quotas are less commonly defended than other forms of affirmative action, although in point of moral logic all are equivalent.

Goals and timetables inhabit a shadow zone between quotas and the less drastic forms of preferential treatment. A goal might be an increase in the number or proportion of women in a job, to be achieved through either the attrition of men or the creation of new positions. All entail a decrease in the number or proportion of men who hold the job, so all are discriminatory. To see this, imagine a contractor who employs ninety male bricklayers and five female bricklayers to have adopted the goal that 10 percent of his bricklayers should be female. Suppose ten new positions open up, committing him to the more specific goal of placing women in six of them. Suppose, finally, that women are to be allowed to compete for the other four new positions, and that the first four positions go to men on merit. What is the contractor to do if a man is the best-qualified applicant for the fifth position? A presumption exists against hiring the man that would not exist against hiring an identically qualified woman, and would not have existed against him had one of the first four jobs gone to a woman. The man's sex is by itself a factor working against him, and that is sex discrimination. If the goal has the force of law, hiring the man creates a prima facie liability for the employer that would not have been created by his hiring an identically qualified woman in the identical situation and would not have been created had he hired at least one woman for one of the first four positions. Abstracting for now from the legal question, the contractor faces a dilemma. If he hires the man he flouts the goal, turning it into an empty formula. If he hires a woman anyway, he flouts merit and the goal has become indistinguishable from a quota. Should it be suggested that his adopting the goal merely commits the employer to reexamining the credentials of the apparently best-qualified male to be sure he has not overlooked a better-qualified female, the goal is still discriminatory, for it would not commit the employer to reexamining the credentials of an identically qualified female in the identical circumstances, had she been the best available candidate, to ensure that a better qualified male had not been overlooked. Many scholars regard the distinction between goals and quotas as chimerical,[19] and certainly anyone who professes to understand it is obligated to explain what the contractor should do in the case outlined.

Gender quotas are at this writing the most pervasive influence of feminism on the American economy, although comparable worth has the potential to supersede them. Decisions about employment, union contracts, apprenticeships, admission to professional schools, and the casting and directing of motion pictures are made with an eye toward sex (and skin color). Nor is the question any other than preference. The official affirmative action policy of Time, Inc. runs as follows:

> [T]he company's policy on EEO and its supporting EEO Program . . . continue to be at the top of our list of priorities. . . . When making decisions concerning hiring, firing, promotion, transfer, training, compensation and benefits, there shall be no discrimination on the basis of race, religion, color, sex. . . . To make the commitment to our EEO policy even more meaningful, our Affirmative Action Program is designed to ensure that all employees participate fully in all areas, activities and levels of the company. . . . Managers share responsibility for implementing the Affirmative Action Program, including setting employment objectives to correct inequities that may exist in any area of employment. How we succeed in achieving these goals is reported semi-annually to the Board of Directors. Further, evaluation of the performance of Time Inc. managers takes into account their equal opportunity efforts and results.

As its warning to lower-level management makes clear, Time (despite its initial disclaimer) seeks to displace White men by women and members of racial minorities in its workforce.

Given the tenacity of the *clausus numerus* mindset, and given too that its chief beneficiaries are women—who constitute half the population, in contrast to Black and Hispanic males who together constitute about 10 percent of the population—one would expect to find powerful arguments for discriminating in favor of women, and especially powerful arguments for governmental support of such discrimination. Yet no case for gender quotas has ever been made. Gender quotas were simply grafted onto racial quotas

without any extended consideration given to whether the situation of women
and Blacks are really analogous:

> Title VII's prohibition against sex discrimination was added as a floor amend-
> ment. . . . As such there is no committee report and very little legislative his-
> tory to define the scope of that term.
>
> The dearth of legislative history accompanying the insertion of sex as a pro-
> tected class in Title VII has required that the courts rely heavily on legislative
> history supporting prohibition against race discrimination to determine the
> scope of protection from sex discrimination afforded employees and appli-
> cants for employment.[20]

The full floor debate, much of it frivolous, on the addition of sex to Title
VII, occupies 22 of the 350 pages of Congressional debate on Title VII.[21]

One suspects that the responsible officials conflated sex and race less
because of the force of the analogy between them than because of worry
that objections to gender quotas would raise difficult questions about racial
quotas. This fusion of gender with race has protected gender quotas, for
unlike the case for racial quotas, which is merely unsound, the case for
gender quotas is an intellectual scandal.

The Case for Quotas

There are three basic arguments for quotas, yielding as corollaries the
three basic arguments for gender quotas. I cannot demonstrate that every
argument that anyone might offer for quotas falls under one of these three,
but if these three fail, it seems extremely unlikely that any entirely new
argument is going to be successful.

Quotas Create Role Models

"Role models" are needed in unusual jobs to let women know that their
options are wider than prevalent sex stereotypes now permit them to realize. A self-sustaining influx of women into nontraditional jobs will be triggered once enough women—a number never specified—are in place. The
VERA Institute of justice argues that the lower felony arrest rate for female
officers shows the need for more female officers to create an atmosphere in
which females feel comfortable enough to do a better job.[22] Janet Richards
puts the argument clearly:

> What we want to achieve is . . . *an improvement of the position of women
> until society is fair to them,* and as a matter of fact probably the best way to
> achieve this is to appoint to positions of importance women who are rather
> less good at the work than the men who are in competition with them. As
> long as they are not such hopeless failures as to confirm everyone's ideas that
> women are not capable of any serious work, their holding those positions will

be enough to make others set their sights higher, and make people in general more used to seeing women in former male preserves and expecting more of them.[23]

A variant of this argument in the NOW amicus brief in *Goldberg v. Rostker*[24] claimed that registering and conscripting women would improve their image and decrease the incidence of rape.

Advocates of gender quotas have not pressed this argument with great enthusiasm. It rather conspicuously ignores the possible consequences of inserting less-than-the-best candidates into positions on which lives depend (like surgery or piloting commercial airliners). It seems to assume that the differences between incompetence, competence, and excellence are for the most part trivial, and that most people could do most things pretty well if given the chance.

Properly understood, furthermore, this argument has nothing to do with equality of opportunity. The creation of role models is not intended to guarantee women freedom equal to men's to pursue the occupations they wish, which is how equality of opportunity is usually understood, but to induce women to want to pursue occupations they do not want (and whose pursuit would allegedly make them happier than they are now). Not that there is any evidence for a role model effect of the appropriate sort; psychologists coined "role model" to refer to the function performed by parents in influencing the ego ideals of very young children, and ego ideals are formed before the age of five.

But the most serious difficulty with the role model argument is this: Even if there were a demonstrable role model effect, and women would be happier (if not freer) attempting nontraditional pursuits, *and* the damage done by placing incompetent women in important jobs was tolerable, the question would remain whether quotas were fair to the individual males bypassed in the process, males not themselves responsible for women's currently constricted aspirations. If quotas do men an injustice, the role model defense is unpersuasive.

Quotas as Preventive Measures

This argument maintains that discrimination is, while illegal, so subtle, pervasive, and vicious that it must be stopped in advance:

> Another depressing topic at [the Congressional Black Caucus] was the Administration's late-August announcement that it would sharply decrease the enforcement of federal affirmative-action regulations designed to prevent discrimination against women and against blacks and other minorities—a curtailment Representative Charles Rangel . . . charged would be a signal to those in the private sector that they "need no longer worry about the govern-

ment looking over their shoulders" and would in most cases be free to go back to indulging in the prejudices and biases that come naturally to many Americans.[25]

It is frequently added that discrimination is too difficult to prove to be attacked on an individual, case-wise basis.

This argument, too, founders on the question of justice. Preventive coercion is justified only in emergencies. It is generally agreed that the government may prevent grave wrongs clearly about to done (it can disrupt conspiracies) and more remote but potentially catastrophic possibilities, but must otherwise act after the fact. It would be regarded as impermissibly unfair to reduce the felony rate by incarcerating all eighteen-year-old males, since males who were never going to attack anyone would inevitably be swept along. To be sure, sex discrimination is sometimes described as an evil of sufficient magnitude to warrant preventive measures too extreme to be deployed elsewhere, but this supplementary argument must also await consideration of the issue of justice.

The argument from preemption is also empirically vulnerable. To stop discrimination before it occurs by enforcing the outcome that would obtain without discrimination presupposes knowledge of what the nondiscriminatory outcome would be, and if that outcome is taken to be statistical proportionality, it is being assumed that the only possible causes of aggregate differences in outcomes are malign forces. This is the complete environmentalism which we have seen to be wholly untenable.

There is a close connection between quotas conceived as preventive detention and the concept of institutional discrimination. Quotas are necessary, it is argued, because the very structure of institutions and the unconscious assumptions that accompany them result in minorities and women being excluded from certain activities. Still, in order for quotas to be an appropriate response, it must be demonstrated that the *particular blacks and women* who gain admission to otherwise structurally discriminatory institutions would have been excluded but for quotas. After all, it cannot be assumed that structural discrimination discriminates against absolutely every member of every unprotected class. Similarly, it must be somehow demonstrated that the particular white males penalized by preventive quotas are just those who would have benefitted from institutional discrimination—we cannot just assume that *every* white male so benefits. Even if there is such a phenomenon as institutional discrimination, it does not follow that quotas are consistent with justice.

Quotas as Indemnification

We come to the *nervus probandi:* quotas are not only not unjust, they are demanded by justice, for they give today's Blacks and women the jobs they would have gotten had there been no sexual or racial discrimination in the past. Judging today's Blacks and women by sex-blind and race-blind merit standards unfairly disadvantages them by allowing past discrimination to perpetuate itself. Quotas make whole today's Blacks and women by "neutralizing the *present* competitive disadvantages caused by those past privations";[26] quotas compensate Blacks and women for the competitive abilities they would have had had their ancestors been treated properly. Reserving jobs for less qualified women and Blacks is fair to the bypassed, better-qualified White males, who would not have been better qualified in a non-discriminatory world. To let better-qualified White males claim those jobs is to let them profit from wrong-doing, even if not their own. As for which White males have profited from the mistreatment of which Blacks and females, it must be assumed that every male enjoys an unfair advantage over every Black and female:

> Surely every white person, however free of direct implication in victimizing non-whites, is still a daily beneficiary of white dominance—past and present. . . . Though, of course, there are obvious and important differences, women too have been victimized as a group.[27]

This final phase of the argument may seem gratuitous paranoia, but it is actually crucial. To use any other indicator of victimhood which merely correlates with race or sex as a basis for preference—poverty, let us say— will entitle a poor White male, although a relatively rarer specimen, to the same preference as an equally poor Black woman. (And to call for affirmative action for Blacks or women to attack poverty, without claiming the support of justice, is still to call for the equally special treatment of equally poor Whites, Blacks, men, and women.) Unless race and sex are in themselves the stigmata of victimhood, racial and gender quotas are inappropriate instruments of compensation.

The Government Accepts the Compensation Argument

The compensation argument would be significant had it been taken seriously only by a handful of private employers willing to act on its implications out of sight of the Civil Rights Division of the Justice Department. As it happens, the three branches of the federal government and all state and municipal governments have embraced it. In his 1976 presidential campaign, Jimmy Carter referred approvingly to quotas as "compensatory discrimination." A decade earlier, Lyndon Johnson had compared the Black man to a runner whose ankles have been shackled and deserves a head start in a race even if the other runners were not the ones who had shackled him.

The compensation argument has been equally influential in case law, leading the judiciary to impose what it terms "remedial" quotas and backpay settlements in class-action sex discrimination cases. The courts have deemed themselves competent to determine the number of Blacks, Hispanics, and women who would have qualified for jobs had discrimination never occurred: "Affirmative Action [is successful when] eligible minority members [are placed] in the position which the minority would have enjoyed if it had not been the victim of discrimination."[28] The court's embrace of this doctrine is curious in several ways. First, even if the courts could make the aggregate determination presupposed in *Ríos,* it would not yet follow that the courts could identify the *particular* minority members who would have occupied better positions. Second, even if these particular determinations could be made, court placement of individually deserving Blacks and women over White males deprives the latter ex post facto of the benefits of discriminatory acts which were legal at the time they were done, in apparent violation of Article 1 of the Constitution. Finally, it would seem that all forms of racial or sexual preference are forbidden by Section 703(a)(2) of Title VII of the Civil Rights Act:

> It shall be an unlawful employment practice for an employer to limit, segregate, or classify his employees in any way which would deprive or tend to deprive any individual of employment opportunities or otherwise adversely affects his status as an employee, because of such an individual's race, color, religion, sex or national origin.

This ban on all racial and gender preference became permission for racial preference in *Weber.*[29] Under pressure from the Labor Department's Office of Contract Compliance Programs (see below), Kaiser Aluminum and the United Steelworkers' Union agreed in 1974 to match every White with a Black in a special training program, the Whites but not the Blacks to be chosen by seniority. The consenting parties hailed the agreement as voluntary, and *Newsweek* praised it as proof of the strength of the free enterprise system.[30] Brian Weber, a passed-over White, sued under Title VII. The Supreme Court ruled the agreement voluntary and consistent with Title VII, the nerve of their argument being an appeal to section 703(j) of Title VII, which reads: "Nothing in this title shall be interpreted to require any employer . . . to grant preferential treatment to any individual because of [his] race." The court held that if Congress had wanted to forbid preferential treatment it would have worded 703(j) as "nothing shall permit" instead of "nothing shall require"; from the principle that legislatures must intend what they do not but easily could forbid, the court inferred that Congress intended to permit racial preference.

This reading of 703(j) would have been inventive had its only background been 703(a)(2); its legislative history makes it clear beyond cavil that 703(j) was intended to forbid all race-consciousness in employment.

One of the principal supporters of Title VII, Senator Harrison Williams, anticipated and consistently dismissed the possibility that it would permit quotas:

> For some time, the fact that there is nothing whatever in the bill which provides for racial balance or quotas in employment has not been understood by those opposed to civil rights legislation. They persist in opposing a provision which is not only not contained in the bill, but is specially excluded from it. Those opposed to H.R. 7152 should realize that to hire a Negro solely because he is a Negro is racial discrimination, just as much as a "white only" employment policy. Both forms of discrimination are prohibited by Title VII of this bill.[31]

One charge that Senator Williams was particularly concerned to rebut was that "quotas will be imposed, forcing businessmen to hire incompetent and unqualified personnel." It was to address this concern, that *federal officials* might use Title VII to impose quotas by inferring discrimination from statistical disproportionality, that 703(j) was added as an amendment. Senator Gordon Allott proposed

> an amendment which I believe makes it clear that no quota system will be imposed if title VII becomes law. Very briefly, it provides that no finding of unlawful employment practice may be made solely on the basis of racial imbalance.[32]

Allott's amendment became 703(j),[33] a proviso intended to block *governmental misconstrual* of "discrimination" and irrelevant to the prerogatives of private employers, which had already been unambiguously restricted by 703(a)(2). In this context, the phrase "nothing shall require" *does* have the force of "nothing shall permit." When a law stipulates the findings of fact which are to entail a finding of wrong-doing, it exhausts the legal meaning of the wrong in question. What 703(j) means, quite simply, is that racial imbalance is not in itself discriminatory. Private arrangements like Kaiser's are already forbidden by 703(a)(2); 703(j) prevents the courts and the executive from ordering such arrangements.[34]

Gender quotas have not at this writing been tested as rigorously as racial quotas, but the judiciary has been equally ready to impose them. Its opportunities would be limited if all discrimination suits were brought by private complainants, but the EEOC has standing to sue on behalf of aggrieved parties whose complaints it finds meritorious. The EEOC can also consult informally and conciliate, and with its broad investigative powers can intimidate firms into accepting quotas by threatening expensive court action. While its policies have varied with particular administrations, the EEOC has been guided since its creation under the Civil Rights Act by the principle that workforces will, absent discrimination, be statistically representative of the underlying population. Its working attitude was forthrightly summarized by Eleanor Holmes Norton when, as EEOC commissioner during the Carter administration, she was asked on the television program *60 Minutes* whether quotas are fair to White males. She replied: "White males will just have to bite the bullet."

Congress has felt less need than the courts or the executive to justify explicitly its discrimination against White males. Without explanation, the Public Works Employment Act of 1977 reserves a proportion of federal contracts for firms whose boards of directors are more than 51 percent female. Program 8(a) of the Small Business Administration, created by the Small Business Administration Act, loans money only to such firms; in 1979 the First Woman's Bank—which is of course also eligible for the rest of the SBA's services—was kept afloat by 8(a) loans, which would not have been available to any First Man's Bank able to secure a legal charter. Most state and municipal governments set aside funds for similar purposes. In most cases, the firms covered are not required to submit closed competitive bids, and when, as very often happens, only a single firm qualifies for a reserved contract, it can charge what it wishes. Legislative history leaves it unclear whether Congress intended the PWEA as indemnification or merely as a pork-barrel. The Supreme Court, in approving the PWEA, deferred to the right of Congress to appropriate money as it sees fit.[35] Not surprisingly, White male businessmen have responded by filling bogus managerial positions with members of "protected populations" to gain eligibility otherwise denied them because of their race and sex.

The preferred government incentive for the adoption of quotas is the threat of termination of funds. Any educational institution receiving federal money must submit an institution-wide affirmative action plan,[36] as must any cultural institution receiving assistance from the National Endowment for the Humanities. Recipient states and municipalities must also have such plans. The Justice Department induces state police forces to adopt "goals and time-tables," under which the hiring of specified numbers of women is the criterion of "good faith," by threatening the loss of Law Enforcement Assistance Administration grants. It is arguable that hedging the disbursement of federal grants to localities with such measures was necessary before 1972, when the Civil Rights Act was extended to cover public employment. The persistence of these measures can only be intended to entrench quotas.

The principal support of the quota system is the Office of Federal Contract Compliance Programs of the Labor Department. The OFCCP was created in 1949 by the Federal Property and Administrative Services Act, which directed the executive branch to ensure economically efficient procurement. In 1965, under the authority of this act, Lyndon Johnson issued Executive Order 11246, requiring federal contractors to take "affirmative action" to eliminate racial discrimination. The text of EO 11246 notes, correctly, that discriminators incur excess labor costs by narrowing their labor supply. However, it was in the speech that announced EO 11264 that Johnson introduced the "shackled runner" analogy, which sanctions *in*efficiency in the interest of justice. Since then, extensions of EO 11246 have emphasized compensatory justice while ignoring questions of economic efficiency. In 1971 the Nixon Labor Department issued Order No. 4, requiring federal contractors with more than fifty employees and $50,000 in contracts to set "goals and timetables" for the appropriate "utilization" of Blacks. Revised Order No. 4 extended Order No. 4 to women in 1972. The OFCCP oversees compliance with these orders.

Estimates of the number of employees covered by the OFCCP vary from 16 to 25 million. There are 325,000 firms that hold primary federal contracts or supply primary contractors;[37] all subdivisions of all such firms fall under OFCCP jurisdiction. The OFCCP interprets its mandate broadly enough to allow it to set quotas for craft training programs, requiring for instance that 6.9 percent of all apprentice plumbers at any construction site be female. (Current OFCCP rules permit a contractor who cannot fill his quote of females for one nontraditional craft to achieve overall gender balance at a worksite by exceeding his quota for some other nontraditional craft.) OFCCP policy has recently been aligned with the EEOC policy of assuming discrimination if the proportion of protected workers falls below 80 percent of their proportional availability in the general workforce, but, like the EEOC, the OFCCP has never departed from the principle of using statistical proportionality as the test of equity. The OFCCP cannot continuously monitor every firm, and it can waive quotas for employers it deems to have made good faith efforts to meet its quotas, but—as many businessmen have told me—it is easier to avoid trouble by hiring a woman over a man if the opportunity arises.

The argument that firms who dislike OFCCP quotas need not do business with the government, it should be emphasized, overlooks the source of the money with which the government buys services. The exchange of government aid or a government contract for a promise to discriminate against males is not a free trade between private parties. The public funds used as incentives for discrimination, like all public funds, are collected coercively. The special character of government revenue is commonly understood to limit government disbursement to the support of consensus goals, or at least goals consistent with the good of all, since people should not be forced to finance what they abhor. Discrimination as such is surely not a consensus goal of contemporary American society; it is easy to imagine the outrage that would be provoked by government set-asides for Whites males. Current government eschewal of discrimination is partial, as the government also subsidizes discrimination against White males.

If to the workforce covered by the OFCCP one adds the employees of universities and cultural institutions and the 18 million nonfederal public employees, between 30 and 40 million people are controlled by government-sponsored quotas in the United States. The impact of this system is enormous, and ramifies as new dimensions of discrimination continue to be discovered. The character of jobs is changing—a federal court has ordered that 25 percent of all new West Coast longshoremen must be female until 20 percent of all longshoremen are. Equipment must be redesigned to accommodate the physical limitations of women. Economic decisions are being removed from the control of those whose investments are at stake. A federal court barred Western Electric from closing an unprofitable plant on the grounds that closure would necessitate the dismissal of women hired under an affirmative action plan.[38] Long-term investment of energy is made irrational as rights originally promised on the basis of seniority are subordinated to the need to "preserve the gains" of affirmative action. Civil as well as economic liberties are curtailed, as when the Labor Department forbids "psychologically discriminatory" words like *foreman* in want ads. This vast, intrusive apparatus is sustained entirely by the compensation argument, to which it is time to return.

Compensatory Quotas for Women

A compensation claim is a thought experiment in which we return the world to the moment when a wrong was done and imagine how the world would have evolved had the wrong not been done. What the injured party would have possessed in this ideal world is what he *should* possess in the real world; the difference between his two positions in the two worlds is what the wrong cost the injured party and what the tort-feasor owes him. Despite the obvious uncertainties that beset such reasoning, the courts are able to carry it out in limited contexts—but not merely by observing the truism that people deserve what they wrongfully lost. Five specific conditions must be met to establish a compensation claim: (1) Injury must be shown; (2) the injured party must be identified; (3) the cost to the injured party must be established; (4) those who inflicted or profited from the injury must be identified. The complainant's loss cannot be restored at the expense of the innocent. Moreover, while those who do not inflict a wrong may be compensatorily liable if they profit from it, they must profit from it *directly*. If a terrorist bomb detonated a half-mile away loosens a treasure hidden in someone's ceiling, he does not owe the treasure to the terrorist's victim. (5) Restitution must be feasible, and feasibility constraints may dictate the replacement of what has been lost by an equivalent. Since the dancer cannot get back his mangled toe, the jury awards him compensatory damages in the amount he would have earned in performance fees had the moving man not clumsily dropped the piano on his foot. Indemnificatory quotas fail all five conditions; gender quotas far more completely than racial quotas.

Was injury done? The beginnings of a case for compensating contemporary Blacks can be based on the injuries done to their ancestors by slavery, segregation, and the lynch mob. No remotely comparable injuries have been done to women. Rape is occasionally cited as such an injury, but there is no evidence that rape adversely affects female acquisition of job skills. Because no palpable, physical injuries have been done to women, advocates of gender quotas are forced back on psychological injury supposedly done by sex role stereotyping. The most able defender of the compensation argument known to me is able to marshal only the following evidence of injury to women: "The feminist movement has convincingly documented the ways in which sexual bias is built into the information received by the young."[39]

It scarcely needs repeating that, if the arguments of chapters 3 and 4 are correct, sex stereotypes are no more than reports of the inevitable manifestations of innate sex differences. Stereotypes are true, and possess little independent power. But even supposing sex stereotypes baseless, it is moral lunacy to equate them with racial animosity. Within living memory, a Black man risked a beating or far worse for drinking from a Whites-only fountain. The feelings of an employer uncomfortable about putting a woman on the assembly line bears no resemblance to the hatred that led to what newspapers of the last century shamelessly called "negro barbecues." No matter how frequently it is repeated, the comparison of the sufferings of women to those of Blacks remains offensive to reason.

Who was injured? Who inflicted the injury? Who benefited? That Blacks were actually injured in the past does not justify racial quotas today. The perpetrators of those wrongs have died, and it is impossible to trace in detail the effects of those wrongs. It is therefore impossible to determine which particular Blacks are worse off than they should have been, or by how much, or which Whites are better off. Slavery cannot be said, by the standards of law, science, or common sense, to have benefitted today's second-generation Greek-American. It is if anything more speculative to claim that a particular White man has benefitted from the wrongs which have disadvantaged a particular Black man. It simply cannot be determined whether every Black promoted over Brian Weber would have been his senior had there been no discrimination.

That the basic showing of injury cannot be sustained for women makes it superfluous to ask how the women injured by sexist discrimination, and the men who have benefitted from this injury, are to be identified. Janet Richards writes: "The only men excluded [from jobs] on this principle would be the ones who, as a far as we could tell, would not have succeeded anyway if the situation had been fair."[40] This merely restates the problem without some account of how one *is* to tell which men these are and what net advantage they enjoy over particular women.

Current Black disadvantages at least *appear* traceable to past wrongs because Blacks from a coherent subgroup within the general population. It is clear that parents may transmit handicaps to their children within coherent subpopulations (although this effect is attenuated by the social mobility characteristic of industrial democracies). Whatever slight support this transmission of handicaps may lend to the case for racial quotas, it is entirely inappropriate for women. Women do not form an autonomous subpopulation within which norms and traditions are transmitted. Women's ancestors are *everybody*. To the extent that a person's competitive position reflects that of his parents, the average woman must be assumed to have gained as much from her father's ill-gotten advantages as she has lost from her mother's undeserved handicaps. What is particularly ludicrous about the comparison of Blacks and females in the workforce is that *women marry men* whereas Blacks do not typically marry Whites. For most practical purposes a wife has full use of her husband's assets. If the average man is better off than he should have been because the average woman is worse off, they pool their resources and split the difference when they marry. Since virtually all men and women marry, gender quotas harm virtually all women. If compensatory quotas harmed a Black for every Black they helped, they would defeat their own purpose. But whenever a man loses a job, promotion or training to a woman, just because he is a man, another woman, namely the man's wife, is deprived of precisely what the quota beneficiary gained. Gender quotas self-defeatingly compensate some members of the allegedly victimized group by depriving others.

So far as I know, this self-evident point has been overlooked in the literature on quotas. This oversight is due in part to the central role played in the case for gender quotas by the young woman seeking a nontraditional career, a woman less likely than average to be married. A more fundamental cause of this oversight is the repeated portrayal of men and women as competing groups. The motif of woman-as-outsider is a staple of feminist rhetoric;[41] as I mentioned, even feminist evolutionary biology treats men and women as competitors.[42] In addition to the ambitious career woman, much attention has been given to the single mother who must support her family alone and would benefit from an affirmative-action boost to a high salary job. Quite apart from the irrelevance of her plight to the justification of affirmative action—men also have families to support, and a single mother is not usually single because of the actions of the men against whom she is competing for jobs—the single mother does not make men and women disparate groups.

What was lost? "Lost competitive ability" is too obscure to justify compensation, although again its application to race must be distinguished from its application to sex. Compensation theory emphasizes the need for tangible criteria of loss, some *goods* lost, since the career of a physical object can be relatively easily traced. If you steal my car, it is possible many years later to identify it as what I lost. There are limits even on the use of physical objects and sums of money as guides to compensation, since the identity of a (stolen) physical object can be blurred by the contributions of subsequent recipients and bystanders. The common law will not disposses the current holders of land that has been transferred in good faith for a number of generations, despite proof from a claimant that the land was stolen from his ancestors; too much honest labor is now part of the land.

Even in the racial case, "inability to compete" fails the test of identifiability. No Black can point to a successful White and claim that he would have had just *that* much competitive ability had the world been fair. Allan Bakke, a White denied admission to the University of California medical school under a racial quota system, had an undergraduate grade point average of 3.8 out of a possible 4, while the Blacks chosen over him had averages no higher than 2.38.[43] If competitive ability is operationalized as college average, defenders of the University of California quota must be prepared to claim that the Blacks selected over Bakke would have had grade averages at least 1.42 points higher had the world been fair. It is not clear how anyone could know this. And if competitive ability is not operationalized in some such way, it is not clear what advocates of compensatory quotas have in mind when they speak of it.

In marked contrast, no detours into the metaphysics of compensation are needed to see how much less substantial is the corresponding claim about women's "lost competitive abilities." Dominance-aggression, the ability most crucial for success in competitive situations, is physiologically determined and could not have been shared more equally by women in any physiologically possible world, however just it might be. Blacks and Whites want to get to the top equally badly, but Blacks lack some of the skills possessed by Whites. There is this much sense to talk of Black/White competitive abilities being discrepant. The difference between men and women is that women do not want to get to the top as badly as men do, and men do not want to do the things women prefer intensely to do.

The basic trouble with speculating about the abilities people would have had in a better world is that it ignores the constitutive contribution of competitive abilities to the human personality and indeed to personal identity.

Intelligence, persistence, a sense of detachment toward setbacks—all make a person who he is. Failure to recognize this is the profound error of the shackled runner analogy. We understand what real shackles cost a shackled runner because it is easy to imaginatively remove the shackles and speculate about how *he* would perform without them. Competitive traits are not so easily prised off their possessors. One cannot "unshackle" an ordinary person from his ordinariness by imagining him brilliant, decisive, and unquenchably ambitious; it would not be the same person. You are imagining somebody else who looks to your mind's eye like the man you thought you were imagining. Compensation arguments which posit far more gifted counterparts for various actually existing people are describing *replacements,* whose hypothetical performances imply nothing about the entitlements of anybody who actually exists.[44]

Is rectification feasible? Quotas require the award of jobs to individuals who by hypothesis are not the best able to perform them and are in some cases absolutely unable to perform them. Quotas thus violate feasibility constraints that normally limit compensation. The dancer crippled by the careless piano mover does not ask the moving company to hire him to perform *Swan Lake,* for the dancer's complaint, after all, is that—thanks to the moving company's negligence—he can no longer dance very well. He asks for the monetary equivalent of his lost skill, not the right to perform actions for which the lost skill is necessary. (There are reidentification problems even in this case, and perhaps an element of convention enters into the jury's determination of what the dancer would have earned over a lifetime had his skill level remained unimpaired by negligence; these difficulties show that estimates of lost higher-order abilities, like the ability to compete, are even less well founded than I suggested above.) It is therefore odd that compensation for Blacks and women, assuming it to be deserved, should take the form of jobs, when the grounds for compensating them is their lack of the skills necessary for those jobs. The normal mode of reparation in such cases is monetary. If, instead of money, Blacks and women deserve the very jobs they should have been but are not able to fill, if no substitutes are acceptable, Black and female students deserve the grades they should be but are not able to earn. If no substitutes are acceptable, why not allow a free felony, one major crime without punishment, to compensate each Black for all the undeserved punishments inflicted on his ancestors by a legal system once unjust to Blacks? In fact, there *are* government-mandated grading quotas. The U.S. State Department awards five extra points to Blacks taking its Foreign Service, and girls in the Australian Capital Territory receive five extra points on their college entrance examinations.

Feasibility constraints are disregarded when the subject is quotas, I suspect, because discrimination is taken to be morally special, not just one wrong among many others all competing for rectification, but the worst wrong imaginable, a sin. The world must be remade just as it would have been had this blot on humanity never happened at all. It is this assumption that elicits defense of preventive discrimination from people who would not think of preventively detaining potential murderers. Sin is a theological doctrine which cannot profitably be judged by an unbeliever, but it might be instructive to ask the actual victims of a variety of wrongs which one they think worse and in more urgent need of remedy. Would the average Black man prefer to lose a job because of his skin color, or be murdered? Would the average woman prefer to be robbed at knifepoint or be told that driving a truck is unladylike? Which does she want back first, her freedom to realize herself, or her pocketbook?

Racial discrimination seems special because people tend to reify races into entities in their own right, and think of the race itself, not merely the particular victims of discriminatory practices, as having suffered. This is a mistake in its own right—only individuals can suffer—and leads to the further mistake of forgetting that particularly grave discriminatory acts, like lynching, are grave precisely because they fall under nonracial headings like intimidation and murder. No doubt the female sex has also been reified into a victim by the ontologically careless, but, again, it remains crazy to compare the "romantic paternalism"[45] with which many nineteenth-century American males may have viewed women to the racial hatred endured by Blacks.

The Costs of Quotas

On the whole, advocates of quotas have been indifferent to the question of costs. As one puts it, "The winds of utility blow in too many different ways"[46] for quotas to be assessed on the basis of their consequences. The question is not so easily avoided, for if no case *for* quotas can be sustained, then, even prior to a precise statement of what is positively *wrong* with them, any burdens they impose on society count heavily against them.

One of the two principal obstacles to assessing the consequences of quotas is the reluctance of social scientists to discuss the topic.[47] Critics fear the epithet "racist" and businessmen fear creating legal difficulties for themselves. Only a handful of empirical studies exist, including those by Orrin Hatch,[48] Finis Welch,[49] Jonathan Leonard,[50] and Kevin McGuiness.[51] The second obstacle is confusion about the criteria appropriate for assessment. Since quotas are conceived as demands of *justice*, they carry no built-in economic goal in terms of which their "success" might be empirically specified. When in 1981 the Labor Department announced plans to cut back slightly on hiring quotas, the president of NOW objected that "a cutback on quotas is a cutback on justice."[52] If price controls are imposed to hold down inflation and inflation continues at the same rate, price controls have failed; there is no such clear test for quotas. Matters are further confused by the widespread conviction that quotas "work" if they increase the number of Blacks and women in high-level positions. This criterion is shared by critics and advocates of quotas. Leonard, a supporter of quotas, defends them on the grounds that 6 percent more White females have been hired for managerial positions in firms covered by OFCCP rules than in noncovered firms. McGuiness argues against them because their net labor market effect has been to increase the proportion of female managers by only 3 percent over projected pre-quota trendlines. *Time,* concurring with the Leonard estimate, calls affirmative action "quietly effective."[53] Thomas Sowell, another critic, argues that affirmative action does not work because it rewards well-credentialed Blacks and women whom firms are eager to hire without helping poorly-credentialed Blacks.

There is nothing but confusion here. The measure of success used by Leonard, McGuiness and Sowell measures only the amount of discrimination against Whites that the federal government has managed to achieve. All the disputants implicitly agree that *if* significantly many White males have been denied managerial positions because of their race and sex, affirmative action is vindicated. In fact, if affirmative action is wrong, success in this sense only makes it worse, and if it is wasteful, success only makes it more so. To avoid this slough of irrelevancy, I will *stipulate* that affirmative action has led to many Blacks and women being taken on in various capacities who would not have been taken on but for their race or sex. The question of costs can now be raised.

There is prima facie reason to think that affirmative action imposes inefficiencies. One need look no further than the federal government's internal quota policy as articulated in the 1978 Civil Service Reform Act to see the conflict between quotas and merit. The CSRA was intended to put the civil service on a merit basis, which is recognized to exclude biological criteria:

> Recruitment shall be determined solely on the basis of relative ability, knowledge, skills, after fair and open competition, which assures that all receive equal opportunity. Any authority who has authority to take . . . any personnel action, shall not . . . discriminate for or against any employee or applicant for employment on the basis of race, color, religion, sex or national origin.

At the same time, however, the CSRA declares an interest in producing "a work force reflective of the Nation's diversity" and mandates that "each executive agency conduct a continuing program for the recruitment of minorities . . . to eliminate underrepresentation," defined as "a lower percentage of the total number of employees within the employment category than the percentage that minority constitutes within the labor force of the United States." The CSRA also mandates that the newly created Senior Executive Service "increase opportunities for women and minorities."

In this context, a "job opportunity" cannot mean a legal right to apply for and hold the job in question, since that right is possessed absolutely by all Blacks, Whites, men, and women and is not a matter of degree. An "increased opportunity" can only mean an increased *probability* of getting the job, and increasing the probability that an applicant of one sort will get the job lowers the probability that any applicant of any sort will. An agency chief would be forbidden to focus his search on men to fill a position because so doing would clearly "decrease the opportunity" of all female applicants. And here recurs the central dilemma. If recruiting by merit raises the proportion of an "underrepresented" class, merit selection has taken care of the statistical imbalance and preference is *unnecessary;* if merit selection lowers the "opportunities" of minority applicants so far as to yield an unrepresentative workforce, eliminating the imbalance *precludes* the best workforce. Racial and sexual criteria are either redundant to merit or incompatible with it.

Two, admittedly fragmentary, empirical studies confirm this initial suspicion. In 1979, 14.8 percent of Blacks who scored between 1 and 4 out of a possible 7 on their Medical College Admissions Test were admitted to medical school, while no Whites who scored in that range were admitted; similar disparities are found in acceptance rates for all MCAT subtests.[54] Dropout rates for Blacks are correspondingly higher. It is difficult to believe that medical school resources are not being wasted on less educable students, or that inferior doctors are not being produced. Women do not share the cognitive deficits displayed by Blacks—overall, Black MCAT scores run 1.5 standard deviations below White MCAT scores—but comparable inefficiencies may be presumed to be incurred in other ways. Schmidt, Mack, and Hunter have studied the comparative productivity costs of hiring practices dictated by quotas.[55] In "top-down" merit selection for *n* open positions candidates are ranked by performance on a merit-related test, and the top *n* scorers are hired. This method confers the greatest possible gain in productivity over random hiring from the general population. Its two usual replacements under affirmative action are hiring at random from testees who achieve the mean test score, and hiring at random from testees who score at least 1 standard deviation below the mean. In a sample of eighty National Park rangers hired for a tenure of ten years, Schmidt, Mach, and Hunter found that hiring from the mean incurred a productivity loss of 55 percent relative to top-down, and that hiring from 1 SD below the mean incurred a relative productivity loss of 84 percent. In other words, affirmative action hiring foregoes from 55 to 84 percent of the productivity gains achieved by merit hiring. The authors estimate that the federal government's own affirmative action program costs $16 billion per year in foregone productivity.

Leonard disputes the negative effect of affirmative action on the grounds that the relative productivity of Black and female workers when compared to White male workers did not decline between 1966 and 1977, which, he says, it would have done had affirmative action encouraged the employment of underqualified Blacks and women.[56] Leonard's econometric argument for the constancy of these productivity ratios is extremely roundabout and circumstantial, and I would not presume to assess it. However, the constancy of these ratios, even if granted, does not support Leonard's conclusion and in fact suggest that affirmative action *has* indeed adversely affected efficiency. Whether or not every productivity gain by White male workers was matched by Black and female workers, White male workers remain *more productive* than Black or female workers, and to the extent that affirmative action replaces Whites by Blacks and females, it substitutes less productive workers for more productive ones. If affirmative action had duplicated the effect of pure merit hiring, there would have been a *jump* in productivity ratios as inefficient discrimination was eliminated. This jump has not been observed. Leonard mentions in passing that the profitability of firms covered by the OFCCP has not decreased, but that can be explained by the uniform coverage of *all* large firms by the same rules, which prevents any firm from taking advantage of a more productive labor pool and driving its competition into unprofitability. General Motors need not worry about transmitting costs to the consumer in the form of higher prices so long as Ford and Chrysler must do the same.

The most obvious tangible consequence of affirmative action, although one on which it is difficult to put a total dollar figure, is equipment redesign. When the American Telegraph and Telephone Company consented to quotas for female repairmen, it was forced to design special handcarts for carrying heavy tools. These handcarts have no marginal utility; no organization would voluntarily incur the cost that these handcarts represent to the firm and ultimately the consumer. The Labor Department worries only that job redesign will justify lower pay for women and "reinforce negative stereotypes." For this reason, and because the "immediate" replacement of all existing equipment might be prohibitively expensive, it suggests that much equipment might be redesigned for use by men and women with equal ease.[57] The prospects for unisex redesign are in fact dim, since male/female differences in strength, motor control, and skeletal structure mean that all jobs involving lifting, pulling, or pushing can be done with maximum efficiency by men, and jobs requiring fine coordination can be done with maximum efficiency by women.

A narrower but more easily measured dimension of quotas' cost is the administrative—the paperwork, litigation, special advertising, in-house communication, and new managerial positions that have to be created to oversee "equal opportunity." According to the EEAC study cited earlier, the overall affirmative action compliance cost to the Fortune 500 corporations in 1980 was $1.5 billion, of which $942 million was spent on OFCCP compliance.[58] As the cost of OFCCP compliance to all federal contractors is given by the EEAC as $1.5 billion, assuming the same ratio of total "equal opportunity" to OFCCP compliance costs put total compliance for all federal contractors at $1.83 billion. If federal contractors compose half the workforce covered by civil rights legislation, the other half incurs non-OFCCP equal opportunity costs of $680 million, for a total of $2.5 billion in private sector compliance costs. A 1975 study by the American Council on Education put the compliance costs to 250 colleges and universities at $75 million.[59] Extrapolating this figure to the approximately 3,000 institutions of higher education covered by affirmative action, and adjusting for inflation, annual compliance cost to American education is $1 billion in 1980 dollars. (Vagaries of record keeping may understate the cost. The Affirmative Action office at the author's university is budgeted at $20,000 for a secretary and related facilities. The salary of the Affirmative Action *officer,* a full-time member of the faculty relieved of all teaching responsibilities, is included in the instructional budget. Maintenance and furnishings for the Affirmative Action office itself, a large suite adjacent to the office of the president, is included in the capital budget.) To this must be added the OFCCP's 1980 budget of $51 million, the EEOC's budget of $160 million, and the $250 million budgeted to the Office of Personnel Management to oversee the federal government's internal quota system. I have seen no aggregate figures for state and local governments, but they spent $185 million in 1976 to oversee federally mandated quota programs,[60] and assuming a comparable amount spent on their own quota programs and adjusting for inflation, states and municipalities annually spend $500 million in 1980 dollars on their own quota programs. The total annual compliance costs for quotas is thus approximately $4.5 billion in 1980 dollars, a figure which excludes the costs incurred in trying the thousands of Title VII cases each year that are not litigated by the EEOC.[61] This is somewhat below Orrin Hatch's estimate of $5-7 billion,[62] but somewhat above the result of applying the Weidenbaum rule—that the total social cost of a regulation is twenty times its administrative budget[63]—to the combined EEOC and OFCCP budgets of $211 million.

Jonathan Leonard describes the $1.5 billion in compliance costs as "insignificant . . . about as much as most firms spend on annual bonuses."[64] There is, however, a considerable difference between the opportunity cost of bonuses, which spur productive effort, and money spent to ward off litigation. What *else* could have been done with the $3 billion that went for paperwork? What could have been done with the resources and engineering talent that went into AT&T's handcarts? These questions lead to more elusive but nonetheless very real problems: What productivity has been lost due to demoralization by the suspension of merit standards? What are the long-term consequences of underwriting training for women in fields in which women cannot be expected to work as steadily as men?

Women in Traditional Male Jobs is a study of 91 women in non-traditional white collar jobs and 73 women in non-traditional blue collar jobs, all "selected for their positions with great care," and in some cases recruited from outside of the firm that employed them (a procedure not likely to improve the morale of males in the workplace).[65] The study reports that over fifty percent of the white-collar women and sixty-three percent of the blue-collar women incurred extra costs for their employers in extra training, higher absenteeism, higher turnover, more frequent injuries, lost productivity and inability to perform certain tasks.[66] Although most of these women had been on the job less than four years at the time of the study, the drop-out rate, especially for the blue-collar women, was "likely to be high." Less than half the sample was married, but more than half reported of-the-job emotional problems associated with the job. Forty percent of the blue-collar women and thirty-five percent of the white collar women did not expect or seek promotion. That they are a financial liability was more likely to be reported by their first-line managers than by high-level managers more directly exposed to EEOC pressure.[67]

The report concludes from these data that there should be stepped-up efforts to "integrate" the workplace: monitoring the EEO efforts from a central vantage point in the organization, special efforts to recruit women for blue-collar jobs, follow-up counseling, additional special training, and "comprehensive, well-thought-out efforts" which may include counseling for marital problems.[68] The need for these measures underlines the inefficiency of the proposed sex "integration," which would almost certainly not survive in competition against workforces permitted to use merit standards.

The need for these measures also indicates some of the macroeconomic effects to be expected from quotas. Because more resources are used in training unsuitable workers, fewer resources are available for capital investment. This prediction is confirmed by the marked slow-down in the rate at which capital replaced labor in the United States between 1973, the year Revised Order No. 4 went into effect, and 1982, the year the Reagan administration began to ease enforcement of OFCCP guidelines. The capital/labor ratio increased by an almost constant 2.9 percent annually between 1947 and 1973; in 1973 it fell to an average annual rate of 0.7 percent.[69] The downturn in labor and capital productivity in the same period may also be partially explainable by quotas. Excluding farm labor, output per unit of labor input grew at an average annual rate of 2.7 percent between 1947 and 1965, 2.2 percent between 1965 and 1973, and 0.5 percent between 1973 and 1980; between 1977 and 1980, labor productivity fell by 0.5 percent annually.[70] Output per unit of capital input (including farming) grew at an annual rate of 0.8 percent from 1948 to 1965, but fell at an annual rate of 0.5 percent from 1973–79 and by 3.6 percent in 1980.[71] Conventional economic analyses have not been able to explain this decline in productivity by other variables.[72] Various studies have attributed as much as 36 percent of this decline to "government regulation," but none attempt to connect this decline specifically to affirmative action, an omission due perhaps to the taboo nature of the subject. It should be observed that the EEAC, Leonard, and *Time,* although disagreeing about the magnitude of the effect, all agree that affirmative action has increased the number of Blacks and females in managerial positions.[73] As any reduction in the efficiency of management multiples itself by the number of subordinates who receive the wrong orders (in the words of Sherwin Rosen, "marginal productivity [is] an increasing multiplicative function of hierarchical position"[74]), affirmative action has "succeeded" in the most sensitive area of the economy. It is hardest of all to estimate the effect of quotas on worker morale, but some survey data suggests that workers' perceptions of justice have not responded to quotas in quite the way they were supposed to. It is part of the compensatory argument that quotas are temporary and will end at some specifiable future moment when Blacks and women have been made whole. As this moment approaches, grievances felt by Blacks and women are expected to lessen, as are those of White males who realize they are entering a more just society. A study by the Office of Personnel Management suggests that things are working out otherwise.[75] In 1979 and 1980, just before and after the Civil Service Reform Act went into effect, OPM surveyed federal employees about, among other matters, their attitude toward affirmative action. The language of the survey is euphemistic—preferring a Black or a woman is "choosing a candidate for equal opportunity reasons"—but the respondents got the point anyway: sixty-one percent of supervisors reported that EEO considerations were important to them and their supervisors, and 77 percent reported that "top management took an active interest in the racial, ethnic, and gender composition of their staffs."[76] There was, not surprisingly, a widespread perception of bias on the part of White males: twenty-eight percent of the males surveyed in 1979 and 29 percent of those surveyed in 1980 felt that females are treated "better or much better" than males;[77] 28 percent of senior-level employees surveyed in both years agreed.[78] (39 percent of 1979 Whites and 35 percent of 1980 Whites felt that Blacks were treated better, the same figures as for senior-level employees.) A far more striking result was that 40 percent of the women surveyed in 1979 and 29 percent of those surveyed in 1980 felt that men were being favored over women (with 62 percent of 1979 Blacks and 49 percent of 1980 Blacks feeling that Whites are favored). OPM interpreted these figures to show a waning sense of unfairness, which the data to some extent supports, but in absolute terms a great many members of the "protected populations" continued to feel discriminated against *after* the introduction of measures favorable to them.

These results should be compared to two Gallup polls taken in 1975 and 1982 to determine female perception of bias in private employment. In 1975, 46 percent of the working women surveyed "felt that they did not have equal opportunities in employment"; by 1982 that figure was 54 percent. Perception of discrimination increased with education, with 68 percent of the college-education women agreeing in 1982 that women lack equal opportunity and 71 percent of them saying that women do not have the same chance to be executives as men.[79] It is unlikely that discrimination against women increased by 9 percent between 1975 and 1982. The greater readiness of women to report discrimination is more plausibly attributed to the volume of public discussion of discrimination in that period, most of it emphasizing its supposed subtlety and pervasiveness. If you tell people often enough that they are being cheated (a flattering message which excuses individual failure), they will believe it. The result is an aggravated sense of grievance, and an increasingly truculent workforce wedded to the mechanisms of affirmative action that were supposed to wither away.

The Trouble with Reverse Discrimination

Quotas deny benefits and impose burdens on individuals not responsible for any wrongs. They cannot be justified as compensation, inspiration, or prevention, and they decrease economic efficiency. So much alone suffices to close the case against them, but it does not clarify why quotas strike most people as *unfair*. Quotes burden innocent, well-qualified White males—But what is wrong with that?

The usual explanations are unsatisfactory. Quotas cannot sin against the right of the best qualified to a job, since, as far as I can see, there is no such right. The rights and correlative obligations that control employment are created by the mutual agreements of employers and employees. If every individual has a right to refuse to enter agreements with anyone he pleases, an employer may refuse to enter an agreement with anyone, including the person best able to perform a job the employer wants done. If the employer has no right to refuse an offer the best-qualified individual makes him, the employer is to that extent his slave, and has no right to associate *or not* with other people as he pleases. The employer may be irrational in refusing to deal with the best-qualified individual, but the employer does not *harm* him. The employer is simply *refusing to help* that individual (and himself).

For similar reasons, I do not see how White males or anyone else can have a right to be "free from discrimination."[80] Private discrimination is not a force that attacks White males (or anyone else) minding their own business. A White male is discriminated against in employment when, after he offers his services to an employer, the employer turns him down for no other reason than his sex and skin color. It was the White male who initiated proceedings. The potential employer who was minding his own business, has simply refused to enter a mutually beneficial arrangement with the White male; the White male has been made no worse off than he was before proceedings began. If the employer has no right not to bargain with White males as such, White males to that extent *own* him.

There is no injustice in discriminating against White males, *just as, in logical consistency, there is no injustice in discriminating against Black males, females, or members of any other group.* Favoritism, injustice, and moral arbitrariness enter when the government permits and demands preference for one group while forbidding preference toward another. If, as the Supreme Court held in *Weber,* preference for Blacks is a legitimate exercise of an employer's freedom of association, preference for Whites must also, in consistency, be considered a legitimate exercise of the same freedom. The unfairness of the present quota system lies in the government's disadvantaging White males by permitting—and encouraging and requiring—employer discrimination against them while forbidding employer discrimination against non-White males. The government thereby denies to White males a protection it extends to Blacks, Hispanics, females and other populations.

There are two ways to restore symmetry. It might be argued that, since there are utilitarian reasons to forbid private discrimination,[81] the government should impartially forbid preference of any sort. (If the government rejects the "right" not to be discriminated against but forbids discrimination for the general good, it might wish to rethink the equation of Blacks and women when redrawing the limits of permissible favoritism.) On the other hand, it might be argued that the government should leave freedom of association unlimited and impartially permit preference of any sort. In the latter case, employers persuaded by the arguments for quotas would be free to treat Blacks and females preferentially; employers persuaded of the virtues of merit criteria would be free to use pure merit criteria; and employers persuaded that by now White males deserve some reverse reverse discrimination would be free to prefer White males. The government would revert to a neutral, nondiscriminatory stance under either alternative.

As for the government's own hiring policies, it is clearly impermissible for the state to confer benefits like employment on the basis of race alone, and state action could easily be race blind, so long as proportionality was not the test of race blindness. It is not so clear that the state could ever be blind to sex. As I argue in chapter 12, the state will always have to impose the burden of defense on men, which is a form of discrimination against them (unless it is argued that combat positions open to male volunteers are a public benefit discriminatorily denied woman—an argument which must be withdrawn whenever the shooting starts.) It is unthinkable that the state could pursue its functions without taking some account of biological sex differences.

Notes

1. Donna Shalala estimates that 80 percent of full-time working women work out of perceived economic necessity (presentation to the National Convention of the Council on Foundations, Detroit, April 29, 1982). According to a survey conducted by *Newsweek,* 56 percent of working women say they work "for money" ("A Mother's Choice," *Newsweek* [March 31, 1986]: 51). Presumably, the figure is much higher for working mothers. For the economist, no one (except perhaps those facing imminent starvation) "has" to work; work is preferred to not working. Let us say that a woman has to work if she would not work were her husband's salary increased by an amount equal to her own (or, if she is unmarried, she suddenly acquired a suitably salaried husband).
2. On male and female commitment to employment, see June O'Neill and Rachel Braun, *Women and the Labor Market: A Survey of Issues and Policies in the United States* (Washington, D.C.: Urban Institute, 1981).
3. Barbara F. Reskin and Heidi I. Hartmann, eds., *Women's Work, Men's Work: Sex Segregation on the Job* (Washington, D.C.: National Academy Press, 1985). Cited in *The Women's Rights Issues of the 1980s,* undated pamphlet distributed by National Academy Press.
4. *Profile of American Youth: 1980 National Administration of Armed Services Vocational Aptitude Battery* (Department of Defense, Office of the Assistant Secretary of Defense for Manpower, March 1982). The ten ASVAB subtests are: Arithmetic Reasoning, Numerical Operations, Paragraph Comprehension, Work Knowledge, Coding Speed, General Science, Mathematics Knowledge, Electronics Information, Mechanical Comprehension, and Automotive-Shop Information.
5. Mechanical includes: Mechanical Comprehension, Automotive-Shop Information, and General Science. Administrative includes: Coding Speed, Numerical Operations, Paragraph Comprehension, and Word Knowledge. General includes: Arithmetical Reasoning, Paragraph Comprehension, and Word Knowledge. Electronics includes: Arithmetic Reasoning, Electronics Information, General Science, and Mathematics Knowledge (Ibid., p. 27, table 13).
6. Expressed in mean percentiles (so that a score of *n* for a group means that the average member of the group scored as well as *n* percent of the population): Mechanical-Male, 51; Mechanical-Female, 26; Administrative-M, 44; Administrative-F, 51; General-M, 52, General-F, 48; Electronics-M, 53, Electronics-F, 41 (ibid., p. 32).

7. Ibid., p. 90, table C-14.
8. Ibid., tables C-10–C-13, pp. 86–89.
9. See I. Smith, *Spatial Ability* (San Diego: R.R. Knopp, 1964), pp. 135–55.
10. See L.M. Terman and Leona Tyler, "Psychological Sex Differences," in *Manual of Child Psychology,* 2nd ed., ed. L. Charmichael (New York: Wiley, 1954), pp. 1064–1114.
11. *Estimates of Worker Trait Requirements for 4000 Jobs* (Washington, D.C.: U.S. Government Printing Office, 1957).
12. For a survey of occupationally relevant sex differences, see F.L. Schmidt, "Sex Differences in Some Occupationally Relevant Traits: The Viewpoint of an Applied Differential Psychologist," manuscript (Washington, D.C.: Office of Personnel Management, 1972).
13. *Women in Traditionally Male Jobs: The Experience of Ten Public Utility Companies,* Department of Labor Research and Development Monograph 65 (Washington, D.C.: U.S. Government Printing Office, 1978), p. 117.
14. "Panel Report Sex Disparity in Engineering," *New York Times* (December 16, 1985): A15.
15. For a discussion of EEOC rules see Phil Lyons, "An Agency with a Mind of Its Own: The EEOC's Guidelines on Employment Testing," *New Perspectives* 17 (Fall 1985): 20–25.
16. See Michael Levin, testimony, *Voting Rights Act: Hearings before the Subcommittee on the Constitution of the Senate Judiciary Committee, 1982,* (Washington, D.C.: U.S. Government Printing Office, 1983), pp. 717–47.
17. Robert K. Merton, "Discrimination and the American Creed," in id. *Sociological Ambivalence and Other Essays* (New York: Free Press, 1976), pp. 189–216.
18. Announced in a series of advertisements in *Time, Newsweek,* and other national magazines the week of January 7, 1985.
19. See Gabriel Moens, *Affirmative Action: Concepts, Justifications, and Practice,* a report critical of affirmative action prepared for the Australian Human Rights Commission, September 1984. The Human Rights Commission has refused to publish this report, but it is scheduled to be published by the Institute for Independent Studies in Sydney. Professor Moens has kindly shown me a draft copy.
20. "Title VII's": Mack A. Player, *Federal Law of Employment Discrimination* (St. Paul: West, 1981), p. 125; "The dearth": Claire Sherman Thomas, *Sex Discrimination* (St. Paul: West, 1982), p. 210.
21. See *Legislative History of Titles VII and XI of the Civil Rights Act of 1964* (Washington, D.C.: EEOC, 1965); esp. 3001–3355, 3213–34. "Mrs. GREEN of Oregon. Mr. Chairman, the additional amendments just presented from the Representative from Ohio clearly indicate that full and careful consideration were not given to the amendment last Saturday adding sex to this bill. As I said then, there were no hearings by any committee of the House; not a single word of testimony was taken; and the full implications could not have been understood" (Ibid., p. 3231).
22. *Women on Patrol: A Pilot Study of Police Performance in New York City* (New York: VERA Institute, 1978).
23. *The Sceptical Feminist,* p. 111.
24. *Rostker v. Goldberg* 101 SCE 2646, 453 US 57 (1981).
25. "Around City Hall," *New York* (September 18, 1981): 161.
26. George Sher, "Justifying Reverse Discrimination in Employment," *Philosophy and Public Affairs* 4 (Winter 1975): 163.

27. Haywood Burns, "The Bakke Case and Affirmative Action: Some Implications for the Future," *Freedomways* (First Quarter 1978): 6.
28. *Rios v. Enterprise Ass'n Steamfitters Local 698*, 501 F.2d 2nd Cir. (1974).
29. *United Steelworkers of America v. Weber*, 433 U.S. 1983 (1979).
30. "Victory for Quotas," *Newsweek* (July 9, 1979): 78.
31. *Legislative History of Titles VII and XI*, p. 3189.
32. Ibid., p. 3187.
33. "The sense of Allott's amendment was incorporated in the Dirksen-Mansfield compromise and appears in sec. 703(j)," ibid.: "This subsection [703(j)] does not represent any change in the substance of the title. It does state clearly and accurately what we have maintained all along about the bill's intent and meaning" (remarks of Senator Hubert Humphrey, ibid., p. 3005).
34. Justice Rehnquist also emphasizes the twisting of 703(j) by the majority in his *Weber* dissent.
35. *Fullilove v. Klutznick*, No. 78-1007 (1980).
36. Before the 1984 *Grove City* decision, any institution receiving federal money for any purpose had to have an affirmative-action program, so that if, for instance, a college receiving no other federal revenues of any sort received a grant to construct a physics lab, every phase of the college's operation fell under the quota system. As this is written, Congress has before it legislation to override *Grove City*, but it has shown no comparable interest in overriding *Weber*.
37. Kevin McGuiness, "An Analysis of the Cost of OFCCP's Compliance Activities and Its Impact as Measured by National EEO-1 Forms," (Washington, D.C.: Equal Employment Advisory Council, 1982), p. 1.
38. *Kyriazi v. Western Electric*, 527 FSupp 18 (1982).
39. Sher, n. 6.
40. Janet Richards, *The Sceptical Feminist* (Boston: Routledge & Kegan Paul, 1980), p. 118.
41. "I am not real to my civilization. I am not real to the culture that has spawned me and made use of me" (Vivian Gornick, "Woman as Outsider," in *Woman in Sexist Society*, ed. Vivian Gornick and Betty Moran (New York: Mentor, 1971), p. 144.)
42. See Chapter 4, fn. 15.
43. *Bakke v. University of California Regents*, 438 U.S. 265 (1978), in which the Supreme Court approved race-conscious admissions policies.
44. For further discussion of these points, see Michael Levin, "Reverse Discrimination, Shackled Runners, and Personal Identity," *Philosophical Studies* 37 (1980): 139–49. It is sometimes argued that the biologically determined differential success rates of men and women are unjust since, had women been treated fairly over the milennia, the market would have evolved to reward female talents as much as it now rewards male talents. Trying to substantiate a conditional this counterfactual is like trying to determine whether Julius Caesar would have used atomic weapons had they been available 2,000 years ago.
45. U.S. Commission on Civil Rights, 1980, p. 9.
46. Sher, pp. 159–60.
47. See Frederick Lynch, "Totem and Taboo in Sociology," *Sociological Inquiry* 54 (Spring 1984): 121–41; also Frederick Lynch, "Affirmative Action, the Media, and the Public: A Look at a 'Look-Away' Issue," *American Behavioral Scientist* 28, 6 (July–August 1985): 807–27.

48. Orrin Hatch, "Loading the Economy," *Policy Review* (Spring 1980): 23–27.
49. Finis Welch, "Employment Quotas for Minorities," *Journal of Political Economy* 84, 4 (1976): S105–39.
50. Jonathan Leonard, "Anti-Discrimination or Reverse Discrimination: The Impact of Changing Demographics, Title VII and Affirmative Action on Productivity," Working Paper No. 1240, National Bureau of Economic Research, November 1983; id. "Splitting Blacks? Affirmative Action and Earnings Inequality within and across Races," NBER Working Paper No. 1327, April 1984.
51. "An Analysis of the Cost."
52. Quoted in Beverly Stephen, "Affirmative Action: Women Feel the Pinch Again," *New York Daily News* (September 10, 1981): 42.
53. "Every Man for Himself," *Time* (September 7, 1981): 7–8.
54. Steven Shea and Mindy Thompson Fullilove, "Entry of Black and Other Minority Students into U.S. Medical Schools," *New England Journal of Medicine* 313, 15 (October 10, 1985), table 4, p. 938. The authors themselves accept these disparities as "unfortunate but acceptable costs of the transition to educational equality," p. 939.
55. John Hunter, Frank Schmidt, and Murray Mack, "Selection of Utility in the Occupation of U.S. Park Ranger for Three Modes Test of Use," manuscript (Washington, D.C.: Psychological Services, April 1983); see also John Hunter, Frank Schmidt and John Rauschenberger, "Fairness of Psychological Tests: Implications of Four Definitions for Selection Utility and Minority Hiring," *Journal of Applied Psychology* 62, 3 (1977): 245–60. In New York City, the Police Department was forbidden by a federal court to use its sergeant's test, designed in response to a previous Title VII lawsuit, as too many Blacks were failing it. The NYPD currently selects Black sergeants at random from the applicant pool.
56. Working Paper No. 1240.
57. *Women in Traditional Male Jobs,* p. 123.
58. "An Analysis of the Cost," section 1.
59. Cited in Hatch, p. 34.
60. Ibid.
61. See Finis Welch, "Affirmative Action and its Enforcement," *American Economic Review* 71, 2 (May 1981): 129.
62. Hatch, p. 35.
63. See Murray Weidenbaum, *The Future of Business Regulation* (New York: American Management Association, 1979).
64. Working Paper No. 1240, p. 16.
65. *Women in Traditionally Male Jobs,* pp. 1–8.
66. Ibid., p. 84.
67. Ibid., p. 75–76.
68. Ibid., pp. 115–26.
69. See Richard A. Goodman, "U.S. Productivity" (New York: W.R. Grace, October 1982).
70. Goodman.
71. See "Multiple Input Productivity Indexes," *American Productivity Center* 2, 3 (Houston, Texas, February 1982).
72. See Karen Arenson, "Study of Productivity Implies a Dim Future," *New York Times* (May 31, 1981): D1–D4.
73. The EEAC estimates that the total net effect of affirmative action has been to

put 3.1 percent more females in managerial positions than would have been there had the trendline for increased female presence in management in the 1960s continued.

74. Sherwin Rosen, "Output, Income, and Rank in Hierarchical Firms," (Stanford University, Working Papers in Economics no. E-81-10, August 1981), p. 4.

75. *Federal Employee Attitudes: Phase 2: Follow-Up Survey 1980* (Washington, D.C.: Office of Personnel Management, doc. no. 139-38-6, 1981).

76. Ibid., p. 34.

77. Ibid., p. 35, graph 6.

78. Ibid.

79. "Poll Says Most Women Perceive Job Sex Bias," *New York Times* (August 15, 1982): 28.

80. John Bunzel speaks of "the right to be free of discrimination" in "Rescuing Equality," in *Sidney Hook,* ed. Paul Kurtz (Buffalo, N.Y.: Prometheus, 1983), p. 179. "Mr. Celler: The bill seeks simply to protect the right of American citizens to be free from racial and religious discrimination." *Legislative History of Title* VII, p. 3283.

81. This position is defended in Kent Greenawalt, *Discrimination and Reverse Discrimination* (New York: Borzoi, 1983).

6

Comparable Worth

The feminist critique of the market extends beyond hiring practices to the wages paid to women for the jobs they actually hold. Just as discrimination in hiring is taken to require extraordinary government remedies, so too is wage discrimination. With more than 30 million America women working full time, the scope of this issue is enormous.

The theory that women are underpaid rests on a statistical disparity between the average wages of full-time working women and full-time working men; the former are, on average, 60 percent of the latter. This wage gap had narrowed to 37.5 percent by the early 1980s from 41 percent in the 1970s, but the slogan "59¢ to the dollar" has continued to encapsulate the issue. It must be emphasized that the question being raised is not whether women are receiving the same pay as men for the *same* work, which was settled in 1963 when the Equal Pay Act made it illegal to pay a woman less than a man for the same job. The problem, rather, is that men and women tend to do different jobs, and jobs dominated by men tend to pay more than jobs dominated by women. Feminists are quite explicit about having shifted the issue: "Equal pay for the same work is ineffective when equal work, in practice, means the same work, and most women are not doing the same work as most men."[1] People who profess sympathy for the feminist demand for "equal pay for equal work" are choosing a side that has disbanded.

The comparable worth theory is the contention that male-dominated jobs pay more than female-dominated jobs because the pay for female jobs is not proportional to the "intrinsic value" or worth of what women do. Women's wages would rise if compensation were determined by "real," not market value—if, in short, comparably valuable jobs received identical salaries: "The goal of pay equity is accomplished by raising the wages of predominantly female jobs in a workplace to match the wages of similarly valued male jobs."[2] The undervaluation of female jobs is thought to be immediately evident from a group of cases regularly cited in the comparable worth literature, such as the considerably higher wages paid to mostly male tree surgeons than to mostly female librarians and nurses. The National Organization of Office Workers cites a bank offering $745–1,090 per month for general clerks, who must analyze invoices and have "good telephone etiquette," and who are usually female, while offering $1,030–1,100 per month for shipping clerks, who need only write legibly and be able to "lift equipment in excess of 100 lbs," but who are usually male. It is thought obvious that the ability to talk on the telephone entitles one to at least as much money as a strong back.

Diffidence about any unclarities in this theory does not deter its advocates from insisting that the theory be applied:

> Although most policy-makers believe research should inform the development of effective policy, it is more often the case that policy development stimulates new research. The area of pay equity is no exception.[3]

Indeed, the idea of comparable worth is virtually never raised without an accompanying demand that it be made law. The idea first came to broad public notice in strikes by municipal workers, and has been sustained mainly by court action. In *Washington v. Gunther,* a case involving female prison guards of female prisoners who claimed that their work was as valuable as that done by better-paid male guards of male prisoners in higher security prisons, the Supreme Court ruled that litigants could test comparable worth in federal courts under Title VII.[4] *AFSCME v. Washington State* tested the theory, and a federal court awarded four years back pay and raises to 15,500 female employees of Washington State.[5] Strictly speaking, *AFSCME* did not find discrimination in the wages Washington paid its workforce, but in the state's failure to implement a previously commissioned comparable-worth study after having resolved to abide by its results.[6] Washington had hesitated because it had estimated the cost of implementation to be nearly $65 million;[7] ironically, the cost imposed by *AFSCME* ran close to $1 billion. *AFSCME* was overturned on appeal but, in exchange for a promise from *AFSCME* not to appeal further, Washington agreed to a settlement costing an initial $482 million and $75 million per year thereafter. Despite the clear warning of *AFSCME* that undertaking a comparable worth study invites adversary litigation and burdensome settlements, dozens of states and hundreds of municipalities have commissioned such studies of their workforces.

Other state actions commonly demanded in the comparable worth literature include EEOC guidelines on wage bias, a Labor Department "crackdown" on private employers through its OFCCP and Women's Bureau, and repeal of prevailing wage laws. In 1983 the National Committee on Pay Equity issued nine recommendations for elected officials, which included, in addition to those just mentioned, "the enforcement of wage discrimination laws" (there is currently no statutory recognition of comparable worth), "education of the public through speeches, publications, conferences, and all other avenues," and "provision of the necessary funds to achieve pay equity" by state and local governments. Sheila Blumrosen has argued that women who hold "traditionally segregated" jobs have a prima facie case for wage discrimination under Title VII, with the burden of disproof falling on the employer.[8] It would clearly be impossible for most employers to sustain this burden; since wage discrimination was unheard of until very recently, no employer could have taken affirmative steps to prevent it. In 1982 the leadership of the Democratic Party endorsed "equal pay for work of comparable social value,"[9] a doctrine that goes further than equal pay for comparable economic value, and the 1984 Democratic presidential candidate publicly called for "equal pay for comparable effort,"[10] more radical still.

Apart from the need to remedy injustice, a consideration cited with increasing frequency in the comparable worth literature is the single mother who cannot support her family on the wages paid by the jobs such women typically hold:

> The "pay equity" I am going to talk about is whether or not what somebody makes is adequate to support a family. . . . Twenty-seven percent of all divorced and separated women are on welfare. Half of all black babies, in some urban areas more than half of all black babies, are born out of wedlock. . . . The problem, of course, in the welfare system is that most of these poor women can't get jobs that pay enough to support their families, and welfare is really a better deal financially for them.[11]

This consideration may safely be ignored. The *need* of single mothers for higher wages has nothing to do with the value of the work these women do, which is the gravamen of the comparable worth argument. It may be prudent or compassionate to raise wages for the jobs that single mothers tend to take, but it would be equally prudent and compassionate to raise the wages for the jobs men do, since at least as many men need higher wages to support *their* families. Socialism may be indicated, but language should not be tortured into calling it equity.[12]

Why Do Women Earn Less Than Men?

Why do women earn so little if the human capital they embody is so valuable and their work so important? The answers given by comparable worth advocates may be ordered by the degree of conscious malevolence they attribute to employers. At one extreme is the accusation that (male) employers actually conspire against women to reduce labor costs ("to maximize profits" is the preferred equivalent). This charge runs that "big corporations" profit from "herding" women into a "reserve army" of "cheap labor," to use the language employed by Ellen Cassedy of Working Women in testimony before the EEOC. Cassedy explained:

Employers interested in profits and not averse to capitalizing on discriminatory patterns can be expected to carefully control the entrance of women into
certain positions. Obviously, there is no point having highly-paid men with
high expectations as bank managers if women can do it just as well for a
lower wage—*so long as overcrowded female job ghettos can be preserved.* If
women had the opportunity to compete equally for *all* jobs, of course wages
would have to rise in the currently crowded jobs—as the demand for clericals
rose overwhelmingly in relation to supply. But if a small number of women
can be siphoned off into the upper jobs without disturbing the basic immobil-
ity of most women workers, then a formerly male job can be turned into a
female job, and its wages depressed. With the enormous influx of women into
the job market, this can be done with an increasing number of jobs. We
predict that it will be done.

Cassedy went on to assert that employers "colluded to hold down wages,"
her evidence being that bank presidents meet regularly for lunch and that
men arguing with female union organizers use "cultural stereotypes."

Conspiracy theories are not taken very seriously even within comparable
worth circles. For one thing, the practices they ascribe to employers violate
Title VII and the Equal Employment Opportunity Act, and comparable
worth advocates have been unable to adduce conspiracies actually plotted in
the last two decades. The evidence for wage discrimination remains entirely
statistical. Second, the wage gap was 36 percent in 1955, and it is unlikely
that intentional discrimination against women has increased since 1955. (It
is more likely that a higher proportion of women who worked in 1955 had
motives for entering the labor force other than perceived necessity, and bar-
gained up wages because they could afford to be choosier about the jobs
they took.) Third, the sort of conspiracy that would have to be attributed to
employers makes no economic sense. If employers are willing and able to
rig substandard wages for women—why would they not also rig substandard wages for men? For discrimination against women alone to work,
employees would have to establish (illegal) wage-fixing cartels perpetually
vulnerable to raids by independent firms. Suppose a group of firms were to
conspire to keep female potential engineers employed as secretaries to
depress secretarial wages to $5/hour while continuing to pay its male
engineers $10/hour. An independent would be able to get female engineers
for, say, $7.50/hour, reducing his labor costs below those of the cartel.
Luring female engineers will drive up the independent's secretarial wages,
to be sure, *by precisely the mechanism that is already driving up the cost of
male engineers for the cartel.* The conspiracy has no point in the first place.
If the conspirators can somehow depress secretarial costs without raising
engineering costs, why would they have let wages for engineers rise above
$5/hour in the first place? The final reason that the wage gap cannot be due
to conscious discrimination is, simply, that, until recently, nobody ever

dreamed that the value of disparate jobs could be compared. It would have been impossible for any employer to have intended to compensate women's jobs less than men's jobs of comparable value when it could never have occurred to him that the jobs were comparable. The idea of comparability, if valid at all, became available only in the last decade with the invention of the statistical techniques (discussed below) used in specifying the comparable worth argument.

Any account of wage discrimination must thus posit unintended mechanisms. Serious comparable worth advocates cite two. The first, already mentioned, is the herding of women into job ghettos, which floods the market for those jobs and depresses their wages.

> An alternative hypothesis places the reason for sex-related pay differentials on the traditional sex-segregation of most jobs. Under this hypothesis, the results of "crowding" of females into the clerical and service occupations is an oversupply of labor in these occupations, with resulting lower wages. Traditional programs of salary administration, and particularly the job evaluations by which wage rates are determined, are seen as maintaining and contributing to this pattern of discrimination.[13]

But this hypothesis rests most uneasily with the charge of discrimination, for it concedes that at bottom female wages are determined by the market forces of supply and demand, which in turn express the decisions of the individuals who constitute the market. If women enter the labor force primarily to supplement family income, they will tend to seek employment like clerical work, which permits periodic withdrawal from the labor force without serious impairment of earning capacity. The more would-be secretaries there are, the less an employer must offer to attract secretarial help, but the same is true of *all* jobs. Secretarial wages are discriminatory, and the supply of secretaries an *over*supply, only if "crowding" is not a metaphor but a literal description of employers forcing women into some jobs and barring them from others—a reversion to conspiracy theory.

"Crowding" theorists are able to point to supply and demand and yet charge conspiracy because they treat the vocational choices of women as central components of the conspiracy. According to AFSCME spokesman Winn Newmann, "the marketplace is discriminatory. . . . The system of wages was set up by a grand conspiracy, so to speak, that has held down the wages of women to minimize labor costs."[14] This is a theme encountered previously: women are not really free (and men have profited from women's bondage) because their choices are improperly limited by socialization. Because of their upbringing, the expectations currently made about them, and the overall nature of society, women who choose clerical work might as well be barred outright from the executive suite. To cite Barrett again:

> Economic gender roles in the traditional family work against economic parity in several ways. First, of course, they perpetuate gender-based stereotypes and stereotypical self-images. . . . Second, women's household responsibilities compete for time and energy with labor force activities; while for men, household (financial support) responsibilities are complementary to labor force activities. . . . The relative positions of men and women in the labor force are not the outcomes of supply and demand in the conventional sense. Rather, they are the outcomes of a complicated set of traditional expectations that have to be analyzed in a model in which gender confers a set of distinct property rights on certain activities.[15]

While belief in "conspiracies" may be expected to lead to hostility to the family in the comparable worth case, the correctness of this belief would still not show that market wages for female jobs are incommensurate with their value. The pools for these jobs may be inflated by the socialization given females, but *given* those market conditions, the wages for female-dominated jobs are being determined by standard market mechanisms, and, according to classical economic theory, the wages of *all* workers in a market reflect their marginal productivity no matter what prejudices their employers may harbor. Indeed, the adverse socialization hypothesis itself predicts that, since women have been denied proper preparation for public activities, their work *should* be of lower value than that of men. Why then does the market not accurately measure the productivity of women?

The extra factor is said to be society's disdain for women. According to Sharon Shepala and Ann Viviano, "the value of an activity or characteristic can be lowered simply through its association with women (or minorities)."[16] In consequence, "Women may be put into equally demanding and valuable jobs, but these are evaluated by the employer, the society or the worker as being less worthy, valuable and demanding, so they are paid less well."[17] One commonly cited example of this process is the Labor Department's rating of the job of zookeeper as requiring more skill than nursery school teacher.[18]

This is probably the most persuasive argument in the comparable worth case, but the correlation in question must be properly understood, and its bearing on market operations carefully assessed. The association of female participation with lower status is best seen as the *result* of the male's greater tendency to pursue activities that are antecedently accorded higher status. To the extent that association with women *causes* an activity to lose prestige, this is a second-order effect of male dominance-aggression mediated by inductive extrapolation; since typical high-status activities are dominated by males (because of male dominance-aggression), any further female-dominated activity is accorded lower status. To the extent that these mechanisms are at work, lower social valuation of nonmaternal female tasks is not "sexist prejudice." In any case, these mechanisms and the valuations they generate do not seriously affect market wages. Take the zookeeper example. Care of children is certainly a more important activity than care of animals, but nobody needs special training in how to feed a child without having a finger bitten off. A "skill" is an ability that is scarce relative to demand. Knowing how to feed human children and being able to count to fifty are both remarkable abilities, compared to what most living creatures can do, but since just about every member of human society exhibits them, they are not skills. Zoos are paying for the rarity of the ability to feed gorillas, not its value to society.

Most significantly, the "cultural bias" theory is not supported by the relevant empirical data. Female sex-typed jobs are not only not perceived as less prestigious than male sex-typed jobs, they are perceived on average as slightly *more* prestigious; Linda Gottfredson reports the coefficient of correlation between perceived status and male sex-typing to be -.06.[19] While the most prestigious jobs are perceived to be and indeed are male,[20] so are the least prestigious jobs, such as groundskeeper. Female sex-typed jobs hover in the middle. High status attracts men, but most men fail to achieve high status. In light of this data and psychological studies of children, Gottfredson rejects the idea "that sex differences in preferences reflect perceptions by girls that some of their options are 'foreclosed,' and they are already accepting their less favored status in society."

Job Surveys

Comparable worth advocates maintain that direct empirical evidence of an artificial depression of female wages is supplied by job evaluation surveys used by students of management. A particularly influential review of these surveys by the National Academy of Science concludes that

> in many instances . . . jobs held mainly by women and minorities pay less at least in part *because* they are held mainly by women and minorities. . . . [T]he differentials in average pay for jobs held mainly by women and those held mainly by men persist when the characteristics of jobs thought to affect their value and the characteristics of workers thought to affect their productivity are held constant.[21]

WWW expresses this conclusion by means of a linear regression, a mathematical formalism which in this instance tends to obscure the nonformal assumptions required for its construction. Suppose a given variable W (wages, say) has been found to depend on a set of factors $F_1 \cdots F_n$ in a finite number of empirically observed cases. The relation between W and the Fs as given in these cases can be expressed by a term, called a "regression," of the form $a + b_1F_1 + b_2F_2 + \cdots + b_nF_n$, where each b is the weight of its associated factor. If the Fs are the only factors affecting W, further observed values of W may be expected to satisfy the regression formula, which for this reason is also called "W_e." Any deviation of W from W_e for subsequently observed data points indicates the influence on W of further factors not among the Fs. If in particular wages are predicted on the basis of all characteristics that affect wages other than gender, and W_e overpredicts the wages paid women, the further factor of "proportion female" on a given job must be added to the regression, and its coefficient $-c$ will express the negative correlation between the wages paid for a job and the proportion of females who hold it. Relative to the factors chosen by WWW, c turns out not to equal 0.

The tricky part, of course, is being sure before beginning to calculate the regression that one has identified all the characteristics other than proportion female that actually affect wages. In practice, this means hiring a team of management experts, like the Arthur Young Co. or Hay Associates (the designers of the Washington study). It also means, in practice, linking the question of what factors do determine wages to the quite different question of what factors, in the opinion of management experts, ought to determine wages, an ambiguity cloaked by reference to characteristics "thought to affect" value and productivity. What management consultants typically do is to resolve all jobs into a few standard factors—skill, effort, responsibility, and working conditions, or variants thereof—and assign jobs a numerical rating on each factor. Jobs with equal combined point totals are regarded as equally valuable and hence equally compensable. It was in terms of such evaluations that WWW found women to be victims of wage discrimination. In the Washington study, for example, Hay Associates gave 197 points to the job of electrician and 209 points to the job of "attendant counselor III," which involves helping disabled children, although the predominantly female attendant counselors earn about $600 per month less than the predominantly male electricians. This and similar data prompt WWW to call $-c$ the "coefficient of discrimination." Most comparable worth studies using this sort of methodology assign c a value near .2.

There are obvious and unobvious difficulties with this procedure. The subjectivity of point assignments is admitted by the firms involved in job evaluation, and by WWW: "Job evaluation rests ultimately on judgements." The degree of reliability—intersubjective agreement—of these assignments is fairly high (although far from perfect), but unlike the reliability of measurements taken by physical instruments, which is most plausibly attributed to the presence of objective quantities the instruments are measuring, the reliability of job scores is as easily explained by similarities in the training and preconditions of the management experts. These experts are, after all, expected by their contractors to find discrimination, and, being aware of the sex-typing of jobs, they are aware of which assignments will produce findings of discrimination. In this case, reliability is not a sign of responsiveness to any quantity objectively present in the phenomena being studied.

What is less frequently appreciated is the mathematical meaninglessness of comparing the ratio of salaries for pairs of jobs to the ratios of their point-totals. Ratio comparisons are well-defined only between cardinal scales; value in dollars does not form a cardinal scale unless certain very strong assumptions are met, while evaluation point assignments never yield anything better than an ordinal scale.[22] In particular, the assignment of cardinal numbers to a domain of objects requires the existence of an additive operation on the domain. An object weighing fourteen pounds can meaningfully be said to be two-fifths as heavy as an object weighing thirty-five pounds, because five fourteen-pound objects combined will balance two 35-pound objects. Ordinal scales, in contrast, are purely comparative. To say that being a repairman rates 15 in responsibility and being a salesman rates 30, means only that there are fourteen jobs of intermediate responsibility. It makes no sense to say that being a repairman is half as responsible as being a salesman, because there is no way to combine two repairmanships into a single job independently determined to be as responsible as a single sales position. Thus, even if the ordinal assignment of value to electricians and counselors were perfectly objective, it would make no sense to say that an electrician's job is 6 percent less valuable than a counselor's and should be compensated at a rate 6 percent lower. The most that can be demanded is isomorphism between wages and point totals.

Advocates of comparable worth insist that, whatever their flaws, job surveys are so widely used in modern management that there can be no objection to using them as *WWW* does. However, the systems used in the business world involve few or no a priori decisions about what characteristics should affect wages or the weights to assign to these characteristics. Some firms scale wages for jobs by monitoring the wages for those jobs prevailing elsewhere in the market. These scales usually involve high-low ranges to allow personnel managers flexibility and employers incentives, but there is no pretense that these ranges are determined objectively, and at their core such systems remain dependent on the market. Other firms use "policy-capturing" scales: Factors are selected a priori as relevant to compensation, (ordinal) numbers with respect to these factors are assigned to the jobs currently done within the firm, a W_e coinciding with the actual pay for these jobs is calculated, ordinal numbers for the predetermined factors are assigned to any *new* jobs created within the firm, and the new jobs are given the salaries predicted for them by W_e. In other words, factor weights derived from extant jobs are taken as normative for future payrates. The firm determines how much it has been paying for risk or responsibility, and resolves to go on doing the same. This method involves an element of the a priori, and some acceptance of "comparable worth" in seeking to assure consistency within the firm. Other firms use policy-capturing regressions based on the market wages for benchmark jobs. Still, under either format, policy-capturing regressions remain functions of the market: The salaries for jobs used as data-points, whether in-house or benchmark, are determined by the market, and so therefore are the factor weights. For these reasons, WWW explicitly rejects the use of policy-capturing regressions for the estimation of job worth: "Job evaluation involves judgements, making it possible for well-known processes of stereotyping to result in an undervaluation of jobs held mainly by women."[23] In context this argument is quite surprising, for if their limited reliance on judgement vitiates policy-capturing evaluations, the far more extensive reliance on judgement of a priori evaluations must surely be far more suspect.

But even assuming the objectivity and cardinality of the numbers assigned in a priori factor analyses, it still would not follow that discrimination explains the wage gap. WWW concludes that "differences in education, labor-force participation, labor-force commitment, or other human-capital factors believed to contribute to productivity" explain at most half the wage gap, yet this failure to explain the wage gap by a given set of variables is consistent with the operation of undiscovered variables having nothing to do with discrimination. Given the softness of the original data, such a hypothesis has to be taken seriously. This point is, unfortunately, beclouded by word play: Discrimination is construed as a "residual." Certain variables are selected as relevant ("believed to contribute") to wages, and discrimination is then *defined* as what these variables cannot explain. The epistemological policy recommended by WWW is effectively equivalent to taking discrimination as a residue:

> The burden should rest on the designer of the job-evaluation system to identify and explicitly incorporate all factors regarded as legitimate components of pay differences between men and women, not merely to assert the possibility that including unspecified and unmeasured factors or improving the measurement of existing factors could reduce the "discrimination" coefficient.[24]

By fiat, a heavy presumption is created against the possible relevance of such factors as differences in competitive drive and family sex roles. In practice, wage discrimination becomes identical with the wage gap itself, an outcome difference then regarded, like the sex-segregation of the workforce, as impermissible whatever its cause.

I observed earlier that the traditional "intent" test for discrimination in effect has yielded on many fronts to the more dubious "effect" test. The "residue" test goes far beyond "effect." Stigmatizing a practice as discriminatory in effect requires at least that one identify some specific human activity and show that it has some definite impact on the sexes. The residue test uncontrollably conflates all situations in which gender differences are observed, possibly including those caused by innate biological sex differences with subtle societal consequences.

Causes of the Wage Gap

Open-mindedness about the causes of the wage gap is not just good methodology. *WWW*'s challenge to identify further factors is easily met. Only one of the studies it reviewed attempts to control for the "double burden" borne by working women with children,[25] and it finds this factor to explain 44 percent of the wage gap. However, even that study counts divorced or widowed as "single," whereas the proper counterpart to the average man is the woman who has never married and has worked full time all her adult life.[26] Such a woman is as free from family burdens as, and has demonstrated the career commitment of, the typical working man. It is perhaps unfair that it takes spinsterhood to free a woman for work as much as marriage frees a man, but that is irrelevant to whether marriage does in fact depress female wages, and this nondiscriminatory factor indeed explains much, perhaps all, of the wage gap. In the 30–44 age cohort in 1971, "single women who had worked every year since leaving school earned slightly more than single men."[27] A 1973 study found that American single women between 25 and 34 with continuous work histories earned 93 percent of what comparable men earned, and in the 55–64 cohort women earned 6 percent more than men.[28] Single academic women earn more than single academic men when area of specialization is held constant.[29] In 1979 the ratio of wages for strictly single Canadian women to Canadian men in the 30 and over cohort was 99.2 percent.[30] (Surely if a male chauvinist ideology were at work in society, women who defy conventional stereotypes by refusing to marry and pursuing careers would be the ones most penalized, whereas these women are not economically penalized at all).

Marriage interacts with other factors relevant to wages. One is continuity of workforce participation. In 1978 the average male had spent 4.5 years with his current employer and the average female 2.6 years.[31] A second such variable is the number of hours per week that men and women work. The average full-time working man works 44 hours per week, while his female counterpart 35.7 hours per week.[32] Summarizing a variety of studies in O'Neill and Braun and O'Neill, June O'Neill[33] concludes that at least two-thirds of the wage gap is explainable by variables already identified, and some economists place the figure closer to 90 percent. According to Jacob Mincer, what remains is "a measure of our ignorance."[34]

The effects of marriage are subtle. To take one example, the lower salaries of academic women are explainable by the demographics of marriage.[35] When two academics marry, both tend to place the husband's career first, and when they move both partners prefer large metropolitan areas that offer jobs for both. This limits job choice. Since female academics like other females are hypergamic, more female academics enter two-profession marriages than do male academics; the constraints on the mobility of two-profession couples therefore affect a greater proportion of female academics than male. Mobility is important to academic advancement, and because female academics are less likely to move than their male counterparts and more likely to live in large cities with crowded job markets, their average wages tend to be lower. (Conversely, a rural campus need not be "underutilizing" women if it has fewer female Ph.D.'s than the average.)

The foregoing data only suggest and do not by themselves demonstrate wage effects for sex differences in motivation and the impact of marriage; more substantial evidence is supplied by a natural experiment known as "The XYZ Affair."[36] XYZ was a pseudonymous Fortune 500 company experiencing legal difficulties for not hiring "enough" female managers despite a vigorous affirmative action program. XYZ commissioned Hoffman Research Associates to determine why it could not find enough women. XYZ was committed to equalizing the number of its male and female managers; Hoffman Associates specialized in utilization studies for affirmative action programs; and Carl Hoffman himself is skeptical about sex differences in behavior. It was, in Hoffman's words, an "ideal experiment" to determine what impedes women.

After interviewing hundreds of managers, and male and female clerks in a position to rise to management rank, Hoffman Associates concluded that the gender difference in promotion rate was due entirely to differences in motivation. Female clerks were significantly less willing than males to relocate for promotion, less willing to work longer hours, and less inclined to see their job as the first rung up the corporate ladder. Eighteen percent of male clerks, but 44 percent of female clerks, reported they "would prefer to have a part-time job, if possible." These differences could not be attributed to differences in perception, as male and female clerks agreed about the consequences of promotion for increased job hours and decreased flexibility. On a composite index of motivation, Hoffman Associates found 61 percent of the male clerks as opposed to 31 percent of feminists to be "highly motivated." Marriage affected XYZ men and women differently:

The largest difference between men and women . . . is that between highly motivated married men and highly motivated married women. Marriage appears to increase promotion-seeking among highly motivated men and to decrease it among highly motivated women. . . . In general, the effects of parenthood were like those of marriage, only more so.

"Did the relatively low proportion of women among those promoted reflect discrimination?" ask Hoffman and Reed in conclusion:

Clearly the answer, from our survey, is no. It reflected differences in the behaviors and attitudes of male and female clerks—differences the company and its policies had no part in producing. These differences decrease as one moves up the organizational ladder, reflecting self-selection at each step: those women who are prepared to seek and accept responsibility are promoted like men who behave in the same way.[37]

Advocates of comparable worth have shown no inclination to drop the charge of discrimination as it has become more apparent that the wage gap is due to basic difference in family sex roles. Rather, these differences are interpreted as further injustices and further proof of oppression. One sociologist has described the finding that married men spend more time on the job than married women as proof that "marriage is good for men, not so good for women,"[38] an interpretation which assumes that women want to spend as much time on the job as men do. When *Fortune* asked why lower wages were an injustice to a cohort more likely to leave the workforce, Susan Sharp replied:

Criticizing women for "lower labor force participation than men, moving in and out of the labor force more frequently than men, and being more likely than men to be seeking part time work only" fails to take certain fundamental facts into account. For instance, among Fortune 500 executives, who is taking care of the children? Whose responsibility is it to juggle career demands with child-bearing and child-caring? Did it ever occur to you that the reason women seem less committed to careers is that they don't have the luxury of a wife to take care of home and children while they blaze their career paths?[39]

This rage at basic differences in male and female roles suggests that the real grievance actuating claims for comparable worth is not any isolable inequity in the wage system, but the family and the "social conditioning" taken to cause sex differences in labor market behavior. Unfortunately, economists critical of comparable worth often accept wholly environmental explanations of sex differences in economic behavior, and seek other mitigations of the market. Hoffman objects to comparable worth because it penalizes employers who "had nothing to do with producing . . . female inhibition."

Lee Smith writes that "in large part, the [wage] disparity stems from traditions and prejudices that have channeled women into low-paying jobs."[40] John Bunzel conjectures that "greater interests and responsibilities in the home" may explain the number of women in lower-paying jobs, but adds that these interests may in turn "reflect socialization toward traditional roles that, for many women, begins in childhood." Walter Block explains sex differences in economic characteristics in terms of a "fear of success" which besets girls in high school. Cotton Lindsay cites only two factors which limit women's "access to high paying occupations": "Discrimination against women in admission to technical and professional schools. . . . More important may be the subtle socialization process beginning in childhood, which orients women toward domestic careers."[41] Such concessions leave unchallenged the core of the comparable worth case. If an adolescent girl's socialization really inhibits her into choosing a low-paying job, her employer may not have wronged her, but she has in some way been deprived. It is a small step from here to recognizing a governmental right to intercede for the general good by preventing such situations from arising.

It is therefore important to reemphasize the virtually certain contribution of innate factors to the wage gap. Money is a sign of status in societies which use conventional means of exchange. The amount of money a worker commands is a measure of the esteem in which others hold his labor and by extension the laborer himself. Money has enormous symbolic value as an indicator of status. In *The Right Stuff,* Tom Wolfe recounts the fuss over small pay increments made by pilots risking their lives for what, by civilian standards, is a pittance. Males, with their greater innate drive for extrafamilial status, will gravitate to where the money is. A substantial wage gap, if not any precise figure, would thus seem to be inevitable.

WWW operationalizes wage discrimination by asking whether low-paying female jobs would still be low-paying if men held them.[42] On its face this is the right question—and on its face the answer is "yes," for the same reason that football fans would presumably like football just as much if women played it, *so long as women played it just like men.* That latter supposition, however, is wildly inconsistent with biological laws, and it is this same inconsistency which renders the *WWW* test ill-formed. The key question assumes, radically contrary to the facts, that all variables but sex can be held constant. Baby-sitting would pay as little as it now does if it were done by men who did it for the same reason women do it, if the pool of male baby-sitters were as large as the pool of female baby-sitters is now, if people felt as comfortable entrusting their children to the care of men as they do to the care of women, if teen-age boys liked babies and saw baby-sitting as an agreeable way to earn pocket-money . . . if, in short, men were women. Environmentalists will think they understand this because they assume it could be realized with suitable socialization, but, as character and preference are inseparable from biology, the *WWW* test is ill-formed

To say that men want more intensely than women to be in a position to perform highly remunerated tasks is not to say that men deserve to do these tasks or that men do them better. There is no cosmic cashier dispensing wages for having a virilized brain. Nobody gets paid without performing. But because men try harder more often, they will, if not forcibly prevented, succeed more often than women in attaining highly-paid positions.

What Is Really Wrong with Comparable Worth

Critics of comparable worth tend to concentrate on the biases inherent in any list of factors "deserving" compensation. For instance, all job evaluation systems I have seen assume that a college degree enhances a worker's instrinsic value, an echo of feminist indignation that female college graduates typically earn less than men who have only completed eighth grade.[43] (One wonders whether this indignation is shared by successful high-school dropouts.) Yet this arbitrariness is not what is fundamentally wrong with comparable worth. For while the range of objective judgements about "training" or "responsibility" is too narrow to support sweeping doctrines like comparable worth, such judgements can nonetheless be made. Planning space shuttle missions plainly carries greater responsibility in terms of lives and hardware than teaching philosophy. And planning space missions is plainly harder than adding up columns of figures, because the latter skill is subsumed within the former.

For the sake of argument, then, let us assume a skill which is objectively difficult, reflects much objectively measurable training on the part of its practitioner, and is dangerous as well; but let us also suppose it is a skill no one is interested in. Consider a person who is adept at throwing arrows high into the air and catching them with his teeth. This is extremely difficult to do, and takes endless practice. Basketball players earning six-figure salaries do nothing so demanding. And our man could hurt himself. Unhappily, nobody wants to hire him to throw and catch arrows. He must eke out a living as a street entertainer. Is he somehow being denied his intrinsic worth by passers-by who flip him quarters? Does a circus scout who offers him a pittance undershoot what the knack entitles him to? The answers would seem to be no. Moral and aesthetic merit aside, the skill is economically worthless—unable to command other goods and services—if no one will pay for it. Only someone willing to trade something for this service can confer economic worth on it.

This crucial point is easy enough to see in connection with material substances. It would be absurd to maintain that copper deserves to cost more than gold because it conducts electricity better; gold and copper, absent people's actual desires for them, would just be stuff in the ground. The point is also reasonably clear in relation to the "just price" of money—that is, permissible interest rates, to which medieval theologians devoted much thought. I suspect that the market determination of wages meets greater resistance only because it puts the value of each of us so squarely in the eyes of our beholders.

Money itself is merely the conventional measure of the capacity of a thing to prompt people to exchange their own goods for it. A thing's price summarizes the ebb and flow of its performance in exchange, and has no independent meaning.[44] And here is the black hole at the center of the comparable worth doctrine: There is no such thing as intrinsic economic value. It is a chimera. And this point rings another variation on a by-now familiar theme. Supplanting the market price of labor means overriding the liberty of exchange, association, and contract this market price reflects. For each comparable worth proposal, the question is only one of determining just where it suppresses freedom.[45]

Intrinsic Value

The example of the arrow catcher may be dismissed as a contrivance. Contrived it is, which proves its point. The skill seems freakish, worthless, precisely because no one has ever valued it or is ever likely to. Our very perception of skillfulness is determined by the market. The ability to draw, set bones, or fix automobiles seems naturally compensable because we are used to the existence of a market for such skills. But the once naturally compensable ability to make buggy whips does not seem so today, when people no longer want them.

A long line of thinkers, extending back through Marx to Ricardo, have attempted to devise nonmarket criteria of economic value for labor; almost every proposal in this tradition can be found in the comparable worth literature. The straight Marxist appeal to the "social value" of work founders on the need to specify "social value." If something is "socially valuable" because a great many people are willing to pay top dollar for it, we are back to the market—and there is no other way to tell that society wants something than its willingness to try hard to get it.

A more common proposal equates the value of a job with its contribution to the employer's profit. We may overlook the obvious difficulty that this proposal would make wages fluctuate wildly with exogenous factors—think of proofreaders becoming superfluous when a publisher's profits are due to a single bestseller. Let us, instead, consider wage rates. Classical economics holds that each employee tends to get the marginal return on his product as he bargains continuously and omnisciently with his employer: If Jones's labor is worth $10/hour to Smith, Jones can return Smith's wage offer of $5 with a counterdemand for $6, which is still attractive to Smith. But then Jones can hold out for $7, $9, $9.50—until Smith must agree to pay the full $10. But in this case the market itself already bestows a wage equal to contribution to profit. In reality, of course, communication and mobility are imperfect, and an employer must retain some portion of his employee's product if he is to have any reason for hiring him. But then the contribution criterion means deciding what portion of a businessman's profit he deserves to keep, and any decision is bound to be arbitrary.

One such decision seems somewhat less arbitrary than the others. It might seem simplest and most equitable to give each worker in a firm the *same* return on his product, thereby ensuring at least that females get the same return men do, whatever the "right" return might be. A secretary would be entitled to 90 percent of her product if holders of male-dominated benchmark jobs, like engineers, got 90 percent of theirs. Unfortunately, the benchmark figure must be determined independently, which once again means by the market. A firm finds that to secure the labor of scarce engineers it must pay engineers 90 percent of what they earn for the firm. But if so, what fairness requires is not that the return for secretaries be proportionate to that for engineers, but that it be determined *in the same way*—by the market. Making the availability of engineers a factor in compensating secretaries is neither equitable nor rational.

What lends an air of unreality to every version of the contribution-to-profit test is the fact that several jobs may each be necessary for a firm's profitability. Since it is logically impossible to give all the profits to each of several job categories, what does and must happen in the real world, in which a firm needs secretaries and engineers, is recruitment of secretaries and engineers at market-clearing wages they all agree to accept. As the English economist Thomas Hodgskin wrote, there is no "principle or rule for dividing the produce of joint labor among different individuals who concur in producing, but the judgment of the individuals themselves."

A cognate difficulty undermines the related test of basing a job's wages on its contribution to the "organization's objectives," to use the formulation of the Michigan comparable worth study. This measure is often suggested for nonmarket organizations like universities, governments, and philanthropic entities. Yet the attainment of nonmonetary goals also requires the cooperation of many people whose contributions cannot be isolated a priori. In any case, to compete with profit-seeking organizations in attracting a sufficiently talented work force, nonprofit organizations must also heed market decrees about wages. So much is recognized by management consultants like Hay Associates, which cautions its clients that "your compensation program should be competitive in the various marketplaces in which you compete for executive talent."[46] Finally, determining the contribution of some government position to the "overall objectives" of the government presupposes clarity about those "overall objectives," a goal that has eluded political philosophers for many centuries. If governments have accommodated comparable worth more readily than private organizations, this is not because governments have found comparable worth easier to construe, but because governments can finance their mistakes by taxation without having to worry about consumer loyalty.

Comparable worth tests that use job characteristics like working conditions face difficulties like those besetting the use of worker traits. Collecting refuse may be unpleasant, but it is pleasant enough to attract applicants at current rates of compensation. We need no elaborate analysis to see that the market adequately rewards refuse collectors for what they put up with; and again, our very perception of working conditions is shaped by the market. Most American farm workers would find intolerable the backbreaking chores that constituted farming a millenium ago.

It is admittedly hard to shake the conviction that worker traits like training and effort should count. Yet using these traits to determine compensation would yield curious results. Should a widget manufacturer pay an employee more, the longer it takes him longer to learn to run the widget machine? (If the manufacturer should reward mastery, training drops out as irrelevant.) What of natural aptitude? It hardly seems just to reward the more gifted *less* than the less gifted, on the grounds that the more gifted need less training—a policy which would in any case discourage the use of natural gifts. Similar problems arise about effort: Should an energetic tailor who makes the pants too long be paid as much as an equally energetic tailor who also knows what he is doing? Should Mozart's patrons have paid him less than Salieri because Mozart could write a symphony in a few weeks? Had Mozart's patrons been silly enough to propose this arrangement, they would simply have lost his services to others, assuming the Viennese judiciary had not previously imposed comparable worth.

Effort and training do play a role in determining wages. Someone who has invested much time preparing for a hard job will drive a hard bargain. More importantly, the harder the job and the training for it, the fewer competitors he will have, strengthening his hand to bargain wages further up. This naturally high correlation between difficulty, training, and salary helps explain the intuitive feeling that demanding jobs "deserve" higher pay. In the end, however, these factors raise wages only by influencing the free decisions of bargainers.

One irony in the current reanimation of theories about the value of labor is the limited enthusiasm shown by comparable worth advocates for rewards for skill or effort in contexts in which these measures might be well-defined. The suspicion is voiced that sexism leads many more men than women to be judged exceptional performers:

> More and more public and private workpalces are instituting performance evaluations to reward "productive" workers by paying them higher wages within a wage bracket. It is essential to analyze whether supervisors rate men and women differently and how their ratings are influenced by the sex-type of a job. Past research would indicate this to be the case.[47]

Costs and Consequences of Comparable Worth

Appeal to the free market may appear slightly musty in a time of the minimum wage, banking regulation, the National Labor Relations Act, and cancer warnings on cigarettes. Yet these familiar measures are modifications of laissez faire, while the rationale and scope of comparable worth make it a frontal assault on any form of economic liberty whatever.

To begin with, none of the extant labor laws rests on a nonmarket theory of value. The minimum wage was intended to ensure everyone a "decent" wage, without pretense that every worker's output is "really" worth $3.35 per hour. The National Labor Relations Act banned "antiunion animus" on the part of management not because collectively negotiated wages were thought to reflect value more accurately, but to secure "labor peace." And, while the minimum wage does truncate the range of possible bargains, and the National Labor Relations Act does affect a wide range of negotiations, both measures still permit very extensive play to market forces. Unionized steelworkers may not get strict market wages, but their wages are linked to the market, as may be seen in the willingness of domestic unions to moderate wage demands in the face of overseas competition to heavily unionized industries.

Overall, the many regulations that control banking, trucking, the airlines, mergers, workplace safety, and the like are industry-specific or activity-specific, and are intended, rightly or wrongly, to preserve the free market against its own excesses. Wage and price controls, when imposed, are usually justified as temporary measures to curb inflation. Even socialism itself was originally conceived as a more efficient way of harnessing the productive capacity generated by capitalism. And because New Deal-type regulations purport to secure specific results, they contain built-in standards against which they may be assessed.

But comparable worth, like affirmative action, contains none of these self-limitations. Its scope includes every job in the work force; since most jobs are sex-segregated, most pay scales would be open to challenge. Nor does comparable worth pretend to facilitate the best tendencies of the free market; it explicitly seeks to bypass the market. It does this, moreover, without clearly specifying what positive goal is to be achieved beyond "justice"; under this loose mantle, the pursuit of comparable worth can ignore any economic havoc it wreaks as irrelevant to its "success" as long as the wage gap is closed. If comparable worth is "a feminist road to socialism," as Penn Kemble has called it,[48] it is socialist planning without a plan.

Like other feminist goals, comparable worth can never be realized through voluntary agreements. If a firm can get secretaries at a market-clearing wage, so can its competitors. Were it to raise its secretarial wages for ethical reasons, its labor costs would rise without any gain in productivity, its products would cost more than those of its competitors, and it would slide into failure. Comparable worth presents a coordination problem of the sort which tends to get solved by governemnt. In short, whether or not the marketplace offers an appropriate ideal of justice, wages will converge to their market value so long as people retain anything like their accustomed economic liberty. Comparable worth can be implemented only by endless government intervention, in the words of a pre-*Gunther* court, "pregnant with the possibility of disrupting the entire economic system of America."[49]

These words are not overly dramatic. In 1983 figures, there were 49 million full-time working men, whose median income was $20,683, and 31 million full-time working women, whose median income was $12,172. The raw gap to be closed is thus about $8,500 per woman, or about $260 billion—about 15 percent of all wages paid in 1983. In theory, pay equity demands the closure of only the residual of the raw wage gap: As *WWW* observes, the "net effect of sex composition" can be nullified if "$-c$ dollars are added to the pay rate of each job for each additional percent female among the incumbents."[50] The price tag for this modified proposal is still large. Comparable worth studies that control for factors deemed legitimately compensable generally place the net cost to women of discrimination at about 20 percent of the wage gap; redeeming this much discrimination would involve an annual transfer of $50 billion. In practice, it seems unlikely that comparable worth advocates, having articulated their issue in terms of the raw statistical gap—"59¢ to the dollar" is the slogan, not "the unexplained residue of 59¢ to the dollar"—will be able to press for less than the absolute equalization of wages. Comparable worth advocates like Ronnie Steinberg have been somewhat defensive about the bill handed Washington State in *AFSCME*.

> It is the backpay award, and not simply the correction of the underevaluation of women's jobs, that has created the high price of the Washington State ruling. [Presiding judge Jack] Tanner's order will cost about . . . $75 million per year in the future . . . without back pay, it amounts to roughly 5 percent of the annual payroll.[51]

Miss Steinberg was writing before *AFSCME* was overturned and settled out of court, and it is indicative of the magnitude of comparable worth claims that she nonetheless understated *AFSCME's* eventual cost. The ultimate settlement did involve $75 million per year in raises. Miss Steinberg gave $375 million as the back pay award under the Tanner decision, whereas Washington State settled for paying $482 million. About 15,500 women were involved in the original *AFSCME* case. Altogether, Washington State employs about 25,000 women. Projected over the 14 million women in the public sector workforce, $75 million for 25,000 puts the annual pricetag for just compensation at $42 billion; projected over the entire workforce, the figure comes to nearly $90 billion. If every governmental entity is liable for back pay on an *AFSCME* scale, the total initial bill for past inequities in the public sector will be astronomical. The scale of comparable worth back pay awards against private firms has been equally lavish. Three thousand five hundred stewardesses won $52.5 million in six years' back pay from Northwest Airlines.[52] These settlements average about $3,800 in back pay per female work-year, a standard which, extrapolated over the entire workforce at five years of back pay per woman, yields a back pay bill of $570 billion, about 15 percent of the current gross national product.

Comparable worth advocates promise that the wage gap will not be closed by cutting male salaries, and it might appear that the gap could be closed slowly and painlessly by freezing or retarding the growth of men's salaries until women's salaries caught up. This is now the policy of the San Jose municipal government under an agreement reached with AFSCME. Surely, however, a man who gets a smaller raise that he otherwise would have gotten has, so far as he is concerned, suffered a pay cut because of comparable worth. The argument that comparable worth assists working women struggling to help their families with a second income once again erroneously portrays men and women as competing groups. It helps no one to hold down a husband's wages so that his wife's can be artificially boosted. Failure to appreciate this leads to the absurdity of urging that "men must face the propsect of lower pay, so their wives can move ahead."[53]

It seems unlikely that men or their unions would tolerate a wide-scale arrangement so costly to them. The likeliest short-term effect of comparable worth would be to boost everyone's wages, flooding the market with new money in the absence of new goods—the standard recipe for inflation. (This might be the occasion for the government to begin coordinating wage policy to assure the proper closure of the wage gap.) The longer-run consequence of inflating female salaries and holding down male salaries in defiance of the market would be a massive disincentive to work. Women would already be getting more without having to work harder, and men would not be permitted to get more even if they did work harder. Why, then, should anyone work harder? Work forces would not become more "integrated," since women would have no incentive to leave traditional female work once it paid as much as less pleasant male work. If anything, men would try to invade the newly well-payed female sphere. And at the same time men were queuing up for the typing pool, there would be no reason for a man to undertake unpleasant jobs like collecting refuse if high wages for it were no longer available as an inducement—so there would almost certainly be critical job shortages. Add to this a quota system which would prevent management from replacing women with possibly more desirable men, and a crisis of considerable proportions would be upon us.

The attitude of the business community toward comparable worth is epitomized by the American Compensation Association: "Planning for the inevitable appears to be the appropriate response."[54] Like John Bunzel's classification of comparable worth as part of "the revolution of rising entitlements," the ACA's bemused comment does not come to grips with what is distinctive about the comparable worth campaign. It looks like the agitation of one more pressure group, but it is unique in being a movement without potential beneficiaries. Interest groups normally push for policies that help their members. In theory, each group's balancing the interests of the others places all the groups in Pareto optimum equilibrium. Comparable worth, while it may benefit a few women in the short run, serves the middle- and long-run interests of no one—not the married woman nor the career woman already ensconced in a remunerative "nontraditional" position. At best, it gratifies the sense of justice of a small number of ideologues. In practical terms, this means that these ideologues cannot be restrained by the usual interest-balancing mechanisms. Unlike farmers seeking price supports, say, who will moderate their demands in the face of countervailing threats to their interests, comparable worth advocates have no interests to protect. Having nothing to lose, they have no reason to compromise.

Notes

1. Francis Hutner, "Facts and Figures: Wage Discrimination and Job Segregation" (Washington, D.C.: Women's Legal Defense Fund, n.d.). The judiciary has slowly extended the Equal Pay Act to cover "similar" but not identical jobs. See Mayer Freed and Daniel Polsby, "Comparable Worth in the Equal Pay Act," *University of Chicago Law Review* 51 (Fall 1984): 1078–1111.
2. Joy Ann Grune, "Pay Equity Is a Necessary Remedy for Wage Discrimination," *Comparable Worth: Issue for the 80's* (Washington, D.C.: U.S. Civil Rights Commission, 1984), p. 165.
3. Nancy Perlman and Bruce Ennis, "Preliminary Memorandum on Pay Equity: Achieving Equal Pay for Equal Work" (Albany, N.Y.: Comparative Develop-

ment Studies Center, Graduate School of Public Affairs, State University of New York, 1980), p. 16.

4. *Gunther v. County of Washington,* LW 2175 (1979).

5. *AFSCME v. Washington,* 578 FSupp 846 (1983).

6. The court's animadversions in AFSCME—presiding judge Jack Tanner referred to "direct, overt, and institutionalized" discrimination against women—make it difficult to divide the narrow procedural basis given for the decision from endorsement of comparable worth itself.

7. Undated Memoradum, Washington State Personnel Office.

8. Ruth G. Blumrosen, "Wage Discrimination, Job Segregation, and Title VII of the Civil Rights Act of 1964," *University of Michigan Journal of Law Reform* 12 (Spring 1979): 399–502.

9. *Rebuilding the Road to Opportunity,* Report of the Democratic Caucus, U.S. House of Representatives, September 1982, p. 69.

10. Statement of Walter Mondale, Hunter College, New York, April 1, 1984. Cf. also Walter Mondale's televised debate with Ronald Reagan, October 7, 1984.

11. Nancy Barrett, "Poverty, Welfare, and Comparable Worth," in *Equal Pay for UNequal Work,* ed. Phyllis Schlafly (Washington, D.C.: Eagle Forum Education and Legal Defense Fund, 1984), pp. 26–27.

12. Raising the wages for jobs currently held by welfare mothers would make these jobs more attractive to better-qualified applicants, leaving welfare mothers again with only low-paying jobs to choose from.

13. *A Comparable Worth Study of the State of Michigan Job Classifications: Executive Summary,* prepared by Arthur Young and Co. for the Office of Women and Work, Michigan Department of Labor, n.d., pp. 2–3.

14. Quoted in John Bunzel, "To Each According to Her Worth?" *Public Interest* 63 (Spring 1982): 81.

15. Nancy Barrett, "Obstacles to Economc Parity for Women," *American Economic Review* (May 1982): 163–64.

16. Sharon Shepela and Ann Viviano, "Some Psychological Factors Affecting Job Segregation and Wages," in *Comparable Worth and Wage Discrimination,* ed. Helen Remick (Philadelphia: Temple University Press, 1984), pp. 47–58.

17. Perlman and Ennis, p. 8.

18. See Mary Witt and Patricia Nahmey, *Women's Work: Up from 878: Report of the DOT* [Dictionary of Occupational Titles] *Research Project* (Madison, Wis.: Women's Educational Resources, University of Wisconsin-Extension, 1975).

19. Linda Gottfredson, "Circumscription and Compromise: A Developmental Theory of Occupational Aspiration," *Journal of Counseling Psychology* Monograph 8, 6 (November 1981): 545–97.

20. Gottfredson reports that as of 1975 there was a .85 correlation between the perceived sex-type of a job and the percentage female employed at it.

21. *Women, Work, and Wages* (Washington, D.C.: National Academy Press, 1981). Henceforth *WWW. WWW* was prepared by the National Academy of Sciences for the EEOC. Also see the interim report leading up to *WWW:* Donald J. Treiman, *Job Evaluation: An Analytic Review* (Washington, D.C.: National Academy of Sciences, 1979).

22. For a classic discussion of the conditions for measurability see Carl Hempel, *Fundamentals of Concept Formation in Empirical Science* (Chicago: University of Chicago Press, 1950), pp. 58–69. More recent work suggests that the homomorphism condition can be induced by appropriate constraints on the ordering of the domain.

23. *WWW*, p. 74.
24. *WWW*, p. 85.
25. That study is Mary Corcoran and Gregory J. Duncan, "Work History, Labor Force Attachment, and Earnings Differences between the Races and Sexes," *Journal of Human Resources* 14 (Winter 1979): 3–20.
26. See Thomas Sowell, "'Affirmative Action' Reconsidered," *Public Interest* 42 (Winter 1975): 47–65.
27. "The Economic Role of Women," in the *Economic Report of the President* (Washington, D.C.: U.S. Government Printing Office, 1973).
28. James Gwartney and Richard Stroup, "Measurement of Employment Discrimination according to Sex," *Southern Economic Journal* 39, 4 (April 1973): 583.
29. Thomas Sowell, "Weber, Bakke, and the Presuppositions of Affirmative Action," in *Discrimination, Affirmative Action, and Equal Opportunity*, ed. Walter Block and Michael Walker (Vancouver: Fraser Institute, 1982), p. 51.
30. Walter Block, "Economic Intervention, Discrimination, and Unforeseen Consequences," in Block and Walker, pp. 111–12.
31. June O'Neill and Rachel Braun, *Women and the Labor Market* (Washington, D.C.: Urban Institute, 1981), p. 46, table 19.
32. Ibid., p. 24, table 8.
33. *The Determinants of Wage Effects of Occupational Segregation* (Washington, D.C.: Urban Institute, 1983).
34. Cited in O'Neill and Braun, p. 71.
35. See Gerald Maxwell, Rachel Rosenfeld, and Seymour Spilerman, "Geographical Constraints on Women's Careers in Academia," *Science* 205 (September 21, 1979): 1225–31.
36. Carl Hoffman and John Reed, "When Is Imbalance Not Discrimination," in Block and Walker, pp. 187–216.
37. Ibid., p. 206.
38. Viviana Zelizer, quoted in "A Rousing *Oui* for Married Men," *Time* (May 31, 1982): 75.
39. Letter to *Fortune* (September 6, 1982): 19.
40. Lee Smith, "The E.E.O.C.'s Bold Foray into Job Evaluation," *Fortune* (September 11, 1978): 58.
41. Cotton Lindsay, *Equal Pay for Equal Worth* (Miami: Law and Economics Center, University of Miami, 1980), p. 22.
42. *WWW*, p. 93.
43. Hutner. In 1979, the mean annual earnings of a full-time working White female college graduate was $13,186, that of a full-time working White male with eight years of elementary education was $14,580. See *Current Population Reports P−60, no. 129 (Washington, D.C.: Bureau of the Census, Department of Commerce, 1980), table 53*.
44. Let T_1 and T_2 be traders, and B, C, and D (bananas, coconuts, and dates) be goods. Let $[x/y, z, w]$ be the exchange ratio for goods x and y with respect to traders z and w. Two separately necessary conditions jointly suffice to impose a cardinal scale on a barter system, whose unit is the unit of currency. The proof can be indicated by an example. First, there must be no trader T_3 such that $[B/C, T_1, T_2] \neq [B/C, T_1, T_3]$. If such a T_3 exists and one banana is the unit of currency, one trader will eventually own everything. Suppose that 1 coconut is worth 2 bananas between T_1 and T_2, but 4 bananas between T_1 and T_3, and that T_2 starts out with 2 bananas. He trades with T_1 for a coconut, gets 4 bananas

for this coconut from T_3, runs back to get 2 coconuts from T_2 . . . Second condition: if B/C and C/D are exchange ratios constant across traders, it will again be possible for someone to own everything unless $B/D = B/C \cdot C/D$. Suppose that, for everybody, 2 bananas are worth 1 coconut, 4 coconuts are worth 1 date, and one date is worth 12 bananas, so that $B/C > B/C \cdot C/D$. T_1 exchanges his live savings of 12 bananas for 6 coconuts from T_2. T_1 saves 2 of these coconuts, and uses the other 4 to get a date from T_3. With that date he gets 12 more bananas from T_2 and 6 more coconuts from T_3. He now has 8 coconuts, and can use them to get 16 bananas from T_2 . . . The additivity requirement preserves a fixed number of units of currency across transactions, since letting the unit go proxy for goods in a chain of exchanges leaves everything as it would have been under pure additive barter. This sustains the illusion of something constant—*value*—preserved across currency transactions.

45. Several federal courts recognized this before *Gunther*. The court in *Christiansen v.Iowa* (417 FSupp 423 [1976]) maintained that comparable worth would "abrogate the laws of supply and demand."
46. "The Analysis, Design, and Installation of an Executive Compensation Program," Hay Associates, n.d.
47. Perlman and Ennis, p. 19.
48. Penn Kemble, "A New Direction for the Democrats?" *Commentary* (October, 1982): 37.
49. *Lemons v. City and County of Denver*, 620 F.2d 228 (10th Cir.), 1980.
50. *WWW*, p. 89.
51. Ronnie Steinberg, "Identifying Wage Discrimination and Implementing Pay Equity Adjustments," in *Comparable Worth: Issue for the 80's* (Washington, D.C.: U.S. Civil Rights Commission, 1984), p. 113.
52. "Airline Must Pay Women $52 Million," *New York Times* (December 1, 1982): A16.
53. Andrew Hacker, "Why Women Still Earn Less Than Men," *Working Mother* (October 1983): 36.
54. "Comparable Worth: A Few Thoughts on the Issue," *ACA News* (February 1984): 11.

7

Education: The Lower Grades

Like other ideologies, feminism has an ambitious educational agenda. This agenda has become institutionally entrenched with remarkable speed. Unlike other educational reforms, feminist pedagogy does not aim primarily at changing the way in which knowledge is transmitted to children. Rather, it aims at changing children's personalities and attitudes toward each other, in the hope of producing children not crippled by sexism, children open to nontraditional goals and the adoption of characteristics once arbitrarily linked to sex. Typical of this pedagogy is a pilot project course recently introduced into some New York City public schools. The course material follows neutrally named teen-agers ("Jan," for instance) on a visit to the airport and other familiar activities. The point stressed throughout is that some of the girls are "assertive" and some of the boys "sensitive," an effect achieved by obscuring for the reader the sex of the individual characters. Concern that this deliberate sex neutrality will be a distraction is beside the point, since the material is clearly intended not so much to communicate information or critical skills as to persuade the student that the distinction between male and female is unimportant. This material has lately been supplemented by classroom posters showing females repairing cars and males operating sewing machines.

Government at all levels presses for these programs, a matter I discuss in chapter 9, and educational theorists have enthusiastically embraced them. The textbooks currently used in education courses and at teachers' colleges endorse the full range of feminist proposals, from trying to get boys interested in dolls[1] to getting teachers to work systematically to change what are invariably called "sex role stereotypes."[2] These tests labor rather transparently to incorporate the feminist message in ways that make it seem natural and taken for granted. One recurrent technique is the tendentious example. In *Kindergarten and Elementary Schooling,* for instance, Dorothy Cohen and Marguerita Rudolph are concerned to remind the reader that ideas about proper behavior are learned and may not be "objective":

> Let us take as an example learned attitudes about what boys and girls may or may not do. Boys are not supposed to cry, even when little. They should be

brave, defend girls, and never hit them. Girls may be tomboys and get away with it, but boys pay a heavy price for gentleness and non-aggressive attitudes. Are teachers guided by these old-fashioned standards, learned in childhood, when they judge the actions of boys and girls? Are teachers likely to be furious when a sturdy little boy hits just as sturdy a little girl in absolutely justifiable anger, because gentlemen do not hit ladies? Or can she be impartial regardless of a child's sex?[3]

By now the original point has been lost to the completely unrelated topic of sexual impartiality. (We will have further occasion to observe the subterfuge and indirection integral to feminist pedagogy.)

Publishers' Guidelines

As these initial citations may begin to suggest, feminist pedagogy covers every aspect of schooling. The effort to change the classroom begins with the guidelines issued to authors of textbooks by McGraw-Hill, Macmillan, Harper and Row, Lippincott, Rand McNally, Silver Burdett, Scott-Foresman, Laidlaw Brothers, and South-Western, among many other major publishing houses. Virtually identical in substance, wording, and format, these guidelines are in fact not suggestive but mandatory, as authors who do not follow them quickly discover. The stated aim of the guidelines is "fair representation of women" (Silver-Burdett) and "the equal treatment of the sexes" (Harper and Row); but the aim is also given as "improving the image of women" (Scott-Foresman) and "creating positive sexual images" (Macmillan). This vacillation points up an underlying tension that surfaces repeatedly in these guidelines: Is the idea to show the world as it actually is, the world as it should be, or to pretend that the world is as it should be in order to make the way it should be into the way it will be?

On balance, the third alternative—high-minded deviousness— predominates. The pull of this compromise is felt in Macmillan's guidelines, which urge acceptance of the unusual—"It is unrealistic and unfair to imply that all single-parent homes are 'broken' homes"—but falsification of the norm: "We are more interested in emphasizing what can be, rather than the negatives that still exist." South-Western is as explicit as textbook publishers are likely to be when endorsing what amounts to Plato's "Noble Lie" approach to education: "Emphasis is on what can be and should be rather than mirroring what the society is." In this, publishers are merely following the lead of theorists like Marcia Federbush (writing before NASA's affirmative action program): "What is desirable is realism (female taxi drivers) plus a little exaggeration (female astronauts)."[4] This double standard for accuracy permits the plea of realism to defend the portrayal of trends agreeable to feminists, and the plea of idealism to defend the suppression of trends disagreeable to feminists.

Unsurprisingly, the very distinction between truth and falsity is quickly lost. "Textbooks which avoid male and female stereotyping will more accurately represent reality," says Silver-Burdett in justification of its demand that "no occupation should be shown as reflecting the masculinity or femininity of people pursuing it." The Harper and Row guidelines say that "economic texts should not always assume that the consumer is a woman . . . it should not be assumed that all women have marriage and motherhood as goals." (In fact, women in these guidelines never have such goals.) Scott-Foresman asserts that "because such characteristics [as rudeness and timidity] are shared by males and females in reality, textbooks that classify them as 'masculine' or 'feminine' are misrepresenting reality." The question of whether these generalizations might be true about a significant majority of cases goes unaddressed. Quite apart from questions of innateness, it must be as obvious to publishers as it is to everyone else that most consumers *are* in fact women and that the typical rambunctious child is a boy. To deny this intentionally is to lie. Macmillan attempts to meet this point by calling generalizations about the sexes "tyrannical, irrelevant, inaccurate, and outdated." What the guidelines offer in place of a reasoned defense of their presuppositions is prescription—"Women and girls should be shown as having the same abilities, interests, and ambitions as men" (McGraw-Hill)—and invention. One of Scott-Foresman's examples of a "stylistic" change is that a sentence like "An ex-stenographer got a job as a stewardess with an airline" be replaced by "the ex-stenographer got a degree in accounting." (Second-stage feminists have not been conspicuous for contesting the publishing industry's uncritical embrace of environmentalism.)

The pronoun *he* receives much attention. "It may sometimes be best to use the generic *he* frequently," McGraw-Hill notes, "but to add, in the preface and as often as necessary in the text, emphatic statements to the effect that the masculine pronouns are being used for succinctness and are intended to refer to both females and males." McGraw-Hill does not indicate who might be unaware that "he" denotes both males and females, nor does it show concern about inducing in young people an aversion to something as pointedly associated with masculinity as the pronoun *he*. This quest for equality in language has the ironic effect of making these guidelines for writers promote bad prose. The wish to avoid "he" moves South-Western to recommend the passive voice over the active, so that the phrase "why he should feature the merchandise," for example, is to be replaced by "why the merchandise should be featured." Another favored circumvention of English pronominalization is the repetition of antecedents. A sample "bad" paragraph runs:

> A farmer may have harvested 10,000 bushels of wheat. If the price of wheat is $3 a bushel, *he* may sell all his wheat; but if it is only $2 a bushel, *he* may sell only enough to supply *himself* with sufficient cash until he can dispose of the rest at a better price.

The approved paragraph runs:

> A farmer may have harvested 10,000 bushels of wheat. If the price of wheat is $3 a bushel, the farmer may sell all the wheat; but if it is only $2 a bushel, the farmer may sell only enough to provide sufficient cash until the rest can be sold at a better price.

This is not only wretched writing, it is inaccurate. The phrase "to provide sufficient cash" does not say who gets the cash, as the phrase "to supply himself with sufficient cash" does. The usual aim of instruction in writing is to foster the exact use of words; the approved prose here promotes clumsiness and turgidity as standards to emulate.

When these guidelines acknowledge gender differences at all, they attribute these differences exclusively to socialization and discrimination: "Where representation in proportion to share of population would be contrived or a distortion of history, notice may be made that the imbalance results from suppression or exclusion of a group's contributions" (Rand-McNally). MacMillan goes further. It asks with some urgency: *"What about real-life events where women really were in a passive role?* History is replete with instances where women were treated as second-class citizens; current events, too, reflect this lingering bias. We want to depict these facts clearly in our illustrations." The treatment of science is especially tortured, since Macmillan cannot quite bring itself to admit that most scientific discoveries have been made by men. Instead, it presents the dilemma this way: "Because of the societal roles that have been traditionally assigned in our culture to women and minority people, white males are *credited with* [emphasis added] most of the significant achievements in science." Even so, artwork for science books "should depict women and minority people at least 50 percent of the time, avoiding sexual and racial stereotypes."

These guidelines do not merely indicate a general direction for authors to follow; they demand strict score-keeping. On one page Macmillan says "equal treatment in classroom materials is not a 'numbers game,'" but on another it tells illustrators to *"Maintain a 50–50 balance between the sexes*—numerically and in terms of the significance and prominence of the activity illustrated." This again follows once "radical" orthodoxy.[5] The guidelines leave no part of the text, no representable activity, unsupervised. The colors blue and pink are taboo; girls must not be shown "mostly indoors and hovering near doorways, sheltered from the elements, carrying umbrellas when boys are not." The requirements imposed by this strict and specific unisexuality extend all the way to Macmillan's advice that "cosmetics, hair coloring, and other artifices can be discussed for both sexes."

For all the pretense of balance, the one activity never depicted favorably in these guidelines is motherhood. Some allow that motherhood itself is "one option" for women, but ban the words *mother* and *housewife.* "Homemaker" is permitted, presumably because it does not imply womanhood. Scott-Foresman allows that "showing some women in traditional roles is not sexist if women are shown in other roles as well," but it is never suggested that "nontraditional" depictions need be balanced in the same way. It is not too much to say that a decided animus against motherhood and the family informs these guidelines. Lippincott, for instance, offers some samples of "acceptable" and "unacceptable" drawings. One "acceptable" illustration shows a father beaming at his son as his son looks up in adoration at a Black woman sitting behind a large desk. The draftmanship in this picture is razor sharp and accurate. On the other hand, the perspective in the "unacceptable" picture, a family outing at the zoo, is so distorted as to cause queasiness.[6] This contrast cannot be inadvertent. The very gesture which consigns it to oblivion treats the family as unpleasant and disturbing.

Schoolbooks

Given these guidelines, the books that result are unsurprising. In *People Need People,* a Holt-Rinehart second-grade reader, the story "Wet Albert" typifies the treatment of males (even six-year-old ones). Hapless, passive, dopey-looking Albert is followed everywhere by a rain cloud until one day there is a drought and by chance he becomes useful. One may compare this with the portrayal of girls in the Holt third-grade reader *Never Give Up.* A story called "Do You Have Time, Lydia?" described in the teacher's guide as a "realistic story about a busy, creative girl," concerns a heroine—she lives with her father and seems to have no mother—who takes on too many obligations. The story ends when, after many triumphs, Lydia also manages to build a go-cart for her helpless younger brother. Another story, "The Hole in the Tree," praises birth, but stresses that brother Scott is just as enamored of baby animals as is sister Paula. Similarly dutiful are the practice sentences that follow the lesson: "Jill seems very grown up"; "Judy doesn't like to set the table"; "Mother and Daddy like to kiss the baby"; and—lest the other half of the lesson be forgotten—"Bobby has chocolate on his face." Laidlaw Brothers' *Good English* program uses sample sentences that are if anything more heavy-handed: "Mrs. Ito was the referee"; "She and José shared an adventure with a bear"; and "Meg was practicing karate." To "show that males can be passive," it offers "The boys have lain in hammocks all afternoon."

"Christina Katerina and the Box" is another example of the feminist paradigm from *Never Give Up.* Christina does have a mother, but one so shadowy as to be absent from the summary of the story in the "Teacher's Overview":

> Christina Katerina is a little girl who uses her imagination to convert a big box into several creative playthings in her front yard. With her father's help, she changes a TV box into a castle. When the castle collapses, Christina makes a clubhouse of what is left of the box. [More examples of Christina's ingenuity follow.] Watson, the boy next door, is at first jealous of Christina's imaginative resourcefulness and destroys her creations. Later, he tries to help but ends up inadvertently destroying more of her creations. In the course of the story, Christina's imagination overcomes each obstacle, and in the end, Watson shows that he has entered the fun.

The curious emphasis on father-daughter relations in these books is not, as might be thought, designed to encourage fathers to spend more time with their families. Rather, it is dictated by the theory that mothers cripple their daughters through "passive" values. In the interest, apparently, of encouraging cross-sex identification and a general belittlement of the family as normally understood, children are repeatedly told—but not told they are being told—that single-parent families are numerous and happy. Childrearing is never described as a task in any way especially suited for women.

The changes in books do not end with elementary school. Typical of high-school pedagogy is *Viewpoints,* a ninth-grade literature reader from Houghton-Mifflin. A poem by Marge Piercy about her love of hard work and hard workers is followed by "The Perfect Shot," a autobiographical essay by Billie Jean King. "I expect to win every time," says this aggressive, achieving heroine, "I still want to be number one."

Another story in *Viewpoints* sounds a related message, but this time with a male "role model" as protagonist. Teruo, the hero of "Say It with Flowers," works in Mr. Sasaki's flower shop; his problem is Mr. Sasaki's insistence that he lie to customers about the quality of the flowers being sold. Teruo is too upright and appreciative of beauty for what the story implies is fairly ordinary business practice. In the end, Teruo gives away some choice roses to a girl who admires them, and leaves happily when Mr. Sasaki fires him. This particular story is a marvel of compression, offering a minority group, an exquisitely sensitive male, and a businessman who casually resorts to fraud.

As to what may be in store, a recent curriculum report of the National Association of Secondary School Principles suggest that forthcoming high-school texts may be even more extreme. Under the heading "Back to

Basic," the report describes a "new emphasis on traditional themes" in high-school curricula. (The vocabulary of "basics" has reentered educational debate as dissatisfaction with American education has intensified; new wine must sometimes be poured into old bottles.) One example of the new emphasis are "U.S. history texts that emphasize the World War II home front more than its battlefields." This translates into a shift of attention to Rosie the Riveter at the expense of other actors of the period at least as significant. The most cursory glimpse at high-school social studies texts shows them emphasizing virtually any woman that can be found to have had any connection with any topic discussed. If the topic is seventeenth-century religious freedom, Ann Hutcheson is more likely to be discussed than Roger Williams. Amelia Earhart is given more prominence than Charles Lindbergh.

These changes have by no means been confined to schoolbooks. Children's books of every sort have been transformed, and may now be relied on to feature women in conspicuous if improbable positions of command, physical strength, and expertise. Princesses slay dragons and rescue princes. Female firefighters shovel coal, "man" work crews, and serve as subway engineers and railroad inspectors.[7] In books about flying the paradigm flight engineer is female, and dialogue is so arranged that every bit of information supplied by a male character is matched by an equally knowing comment from a female character.[8] Richard Scarry's classic books for children have been revised to suggest that the police force of the average town is largely female. A children's classic like *Make Way for Ducklings,* with its firm assignment of "traditional" roles to the mother duck and the drake, would have difficulty finding a publisher today.

Space limitations preclude an exhaustive survey of all the books for children published in the last decade. Some books are not quite as doctrinaire as those described here, others are far more so. The books I have mentioned, however, are entirely typical of the sea change that has come over children's literature. Paul Vitz has recently analyzed the contents of 670 stories in twenty-two basal readers for grades third through sixth, and Vitz too finds in these stories a complete reversal of the roles of male and female.[9] This reversal is so extreme that in a certain sense it has left everything precisely as it was. Boys in the new books are shown acting as boys always have, and girls are shown acting as girls, except that the boys are given girls' names and long hair while the girls are given boys' names and short hair.

For the longest time books have depicted boys as active and successful; to do the same for girls, it is argued, is merely the fair play of turnabout. The difference, of course, is that in the past the representation of the sexes has not been determined by a conscious desire to manipulate evidence for the purpose of inculcating false beliefs—a process ordinarily called propagandization.

The Nonsexist Classroom

The search for bias in classroom conduct is as thorough as the search for bias in books, with, again, any difference in the treatment of boys and girls the effective criterion of discrimination. There are studies of the proportion of boys to girls who raise their hands, of boys who take German to girls who take French—the preference of boys for German and girls for French being discriminatory because German is better preparation for a technical education—and of the parts of automobiles that shop teachers are more likely to ask boys to fix.[10] The discovery that boys ask more questions and are scolded more often, a manifestation of innate male aggressiveness familiar to teachers, is taken to reveal that girls are "invisible members of classrooms."[11] In one informal experiment,[12] a teacher intentionally called on girls instead of boys in an attempt to achieve numerical parity, but at the point at which the girls-called-on to boys-called-on ratio reached 72 percent, the boys became too disorderly for class to continue. (The teacher concluded with some indignation that "the boys perceived her efforts as favoritism.") Even the superior performance of girls in the lower grades is construed as discrimination, on the grounds that "teacher criticism, a seemingly negative response, may actually lead boys toward greater independence, autonomy, and activity."[13] According to Judith Wirtemberg:

> The most easily identifiable indicators of equity (or inequity) are enrollment and graduation rates in traditional and nontraditional fields of study, course, and extra-curricular activities, participation in athletics, and a few indicators of outcomes such as grades and aptitude tests.[14]

The indicators cited virtually exhaust all aspects of school life; one hesitates to ask what inequities more recondite indicators would reveal. It should not be thought, however, that Wirtemberg and her associates take absolutely every gender difference to reveal bias. They do allow that the greater prevalence of learning disabilities among boys may be a real sex difference (for correcting which Wirtemberg displays little enthusiasm).

The classroom protocols necessary for correcting this entrenchment bias are described in David and Myra Sadker's *Sex Equity Handbook* and *Microteaching Skills for INTERSECT (Interactions for Sex Equity in Classroom Teaching)*, a handbook-videotape package intended primarily for instructors but also advertised for "supervisors and administrators."[15] The Sadkers emphasize that all aspects of the classroom must be subject to scrutiny:

Nonsexist teaching is a total process. It should involve all aspects of the classroom environment. Nonsexist teaching involves the total classroom including: The physical arrangement and organization of your room; verbal and nonverbal classroom language and interaction; selection and use of print and audiovisual curricular materials; development of classroom lessons, units, and learning centers.[16]

They do not dispute that this regimen would displace all instructional aims in the classroom, leaving little time or energy for anything but the elimination of sexism, and the specific exercises they propose are appropriate to their sweeping purpose. Most are designed for all grades from kindergarten to twelfth—already an anomaly, since no activity having properly to do with learning can be suitable for beings as disparate in cognitive capacities as six- and eighteen-year-olds. The Sadkers would have the student look for sex role stereotyping in magazines, write essays on women's changing roles, and write letters of complaint to broadcasters and publishers. They advise the instructor to "sponsor a contest for the best student slogan on roles and rights for women and men." A preferred assignment in composition class is "to write a nonsexist story" beginning with the sentence "Nadine put on the boxing gloves and stepped into the ring." High-school social science students are to be asked to discuss an incident in which a young man is criticized by a young woman for whom he opens the door, with the associated study questions "Why do some women object to this social custom?" and "Should a woman ever open a door for a man?"

Microteaching explicitly advocates the manipulation of teachers and children. Teachers are urged to recognize that "you will need *consciously* and *intentionally* to keep in mind" the two dozen rules of nonsexism. Some of these are harmless tautologies—"Boys should not receive more reprimands than girls unless their behavior clearly warrants this response"—but others, such as an injunction against overpraising girls for "excelling in neatness," disregard sex differences that do invariably prompt different responses from teachers. The Sadkers are particularly concerned that teachers wait longer for boys to answer questions. They advise teachers to be careful that waiting time be equitably distributed, and supply a chart on which to record how "during a short period (5 to 10 minutes) teachers allocate wait time in seconds to males and females." They do not explain how such data are to be collected without the distracting presence of assistants in the classrooms, or how in day-to-day teaching the instructor is to tick off fractions of seconds while still heeding what is being said by the children she has recognized. The Sadkers are not altogether prepared to dismiss the possibility that boys get more attention because they are innately more aggressive, but they believe that it is "wrong" to let it influence the classroom, and is best counteracted by the "planned ignoring" of boys' more intense attention-seeking.

Sex equity skills become their most intrusive when applied to the most serious obstacle to sex equity: the preferences of children themselves for "voluntarily sex-segregating themselves." The recommendation most frequently reiterated in *Microteaching* is that the teacher disrupt voluntary groupings:

> If students self segregate or stereotype their own activities, you may find it necessary to intervene and make a special effort to achieve classroom integration. . . . In some cases, students will volunteer for and select sex stereotyped activities, tasks, and roles. Then it may be necessary to intervene and make assignments on a non-stereotyped basis.[17]

Coercion is not to cease should it produce dissatisfaction: "If students are uncomfortable with non-stereotyped assignments, you may choose to discuss the issue of sex stereotyping with individual students or with the whole class." If turning the distribution of assignments into an occasion for consciousness raising does not work, discipline must take over: "In order to eliminate single sex groups formed by students, teachers may wish to establish some ground rules to insure that both sexes are included in these groups." The Sadkers explain that these measures are necessary because separating students by sex is as intolerable as separating them by race.[18] What is more, "Teachers don't let children do whatever they want in class. Teachers can't let children just hit each other if they feel like it."[19] The Sadkers do not regard all sex segregation as the moral equivalent of fighting or playing with fire, however. They allow that it might be permissible to form single-sex remedial groups, which, they strongly imply, will be composed of boys.[20]

The connection between classroom dynamics and innate gender dimorphism was widely recognized by educators before the subject became taboo. Since girls get information from words while boys get information by manipulating objects, have a shorter attention span, and begin to act up when forced to listen to teachers, the classroom situation overwhelmingly favors girls. Four decades ago this was "the problem of the feminized classroom." While it remains possible to acknowledge gender differences unflattering to boys, and feminists have been willing to defend all-girl schools (without regard to the consistency of this position with their other commitments), the question is otherwise no longer discussed.[21]

Autonomy Again

Advocates of censorship and falsification have been unapologetic because they conceive these measures as necessary for the "creation of options." A Department of Education anti-sexism program called Born Free offers to "help educators to create settings that encourage students to explore and pursue a wide range of career and life-style options." Marjorie U'ren explains:

> It would be better if young girls could look to the role of mother and house-wife as something they might *choose* to be and could see this role as only one of a number of possibilities in life. In the word "choose" lies the key. . . . Girls are not so much told that they cannot do something as *not* told that they can.[22]

A certain amount of fabrication may be necessary to help children overcome the "internal barrier" of thinking that certain activities are not for them.[23] By being told that certain possibilities are more open to them than they in fact now are, children will feel free to act on those possibilities.

Encouragement of personal autonomy is a goal shared by many people who would never endorse the obsessive extremes of the Sadkers, and these people might consequently describe themselves as opposed to feminist means but nonetheless sympathetic to feminist ends. In this instance, however, means and ends are not easily separated. Once one's depiction of the world ceases to be an unconscious transmission of what one sees, *any* depiction becomes a matter to be decided on the basis of policy. Let the number of females in a picture of a little league game become an issue, and a choice must be made: One token girl? As many girls as boys? A number proportional to the number of female little leaguers in the United States? The number of girls there should be? Any answer entails specific numerical do's and don'ts.

The numbers game is not simply the use of fabrication as a means to an end, autonomy or any other. It arises from a wholesale rejection of pedagogy as ordinarily understood. Educators are usually thought to foster autonomy best by giving students the unvarnished information they will need to make up their own minds about the problems they will encounter as adults. The educators in any viable culture will transmit their culture's values, but there is transmission and transmission. The values carried by ordinary pedagogy are inseparable from the subjects studied, not lessons anybody makes a point of giving. Objectivity, for instance, is integral to the study of science itself. Second, the virtues ideally instilled by ordinary pedagogy are general traits of intellect and character, like curiosity and diligence, whose chief function is to allow children to grow into adults capable of thinking for themselves. These ideals have never included the installation of specific preferences based on erroneous factual assumptions.

The life path a girl chooses when she encounters the actual world is no doubt somewhat different from the one she would have chosen had she encountered a somewhat different world (if not as different as environmentalists suppose possible). That marks no barriers on her autonomy, which is impaired only when the world she is responding to has been surreptitiously manipulated for the purpose of getting her to make one decision rather than another. Feminist pedagogy refuses to allow children to form their own ideas because it sees the ideas of children as manipulated in just this way by sexist ideology. The only hope for restoring autonomy to children then becomes countermanipulation, and if all education is at bottom brainwashing, the only serious question concerns ownership of the laundry. Sometimes the theory that *all* education is indoctrination is stated with uncompromising explicitness:

> While some of us no doubt have been intentionally indoctrinated, most of the indoctrination we receive—into racism, sexism, capitalism, for example—is simply not a deliberate activity of someone wanting us to develop unshakable beliefs and act accordingly.[24]

Because they assume that all children's books are meant chiefly to communicate "lifestyle options" and that purportedly objective depictions of the world are endorsements of the status quo, feminists can insist that their educational materials alone confer freedom while admitting that their educational materials alone are the products of conscious calculation. If all education manipulates, with or without premeditation, it makes no difference that some programs do so consciously and others do not. Once any material presented in perfect faith is considered propagandistic if from it children can infer that boys and girls differ, the purposeful manipulation of evidence to induce contrary beliefs is no worse than fidelity to facts. It follows from the feminist theory that if traditional materials restrict girls by making it too likely that they will see themselves mainly as future mothers, increased autonomy requires that girls become *less* likely to see themselves as such. One of the aims of pedagogy then becomes to make motherhood less appealing. Traditional materials endorsed motherhood through their many depictions of it; the planned exclusion of depictions of motherhood from counterprimers must be intended as an attack on motherhood to neutralize that endorsement.

Still, would the world not be a *better* (if not freer) place if girls believed they could happily do more things than they currently believe they can happily do? And if convincing girls of this takes a little fibbing, so be it. This argument begs the fundamental empirical question of *why* it should be necessary to lie in order to convince girls that they could be happier if they made less traditional choices. Lies might be necessary because sexist propaganda is drowning out the truth, or lies might be necessary because the message they carry is false. The second hypothesis is the simpler; girls form their conceptions of what will make them happy from their perception of a social order in which people are in fact following their most basic impulses. Ironically, if the feminist message is false, purveying it is the surest way to *obstruct* autonomy. Should you take a wrong turn on a highway because you mistakenly thought it was the way to Cleveland, you have not driven to Toledo by choice.[25] Should the ideal of career plus effortless motherhood be unrealistic for most women, encouraging little girls to follow it will not make them free.

I have frequently encountered the response that traditional educational materials also lie in the service of important ends. After all, children are not harmed by stories about talking frogs. The disanalogy between fairy tales and feminist tales remains, however. Fairy tales are meant to be taken as literally false but metaphorically true,[26] while feminist tales make no claim to metaphorical insight and are meant to be taken as literally true. Children know that frogs do not talk; the characters in children's stories are given animal form to add to their charm and distance them psychologically from the world of the young listener. Feminist tales *are* supposed to be taken at face value; children are supposed to come away from them believing that women are airline pilots and batting champs. Conversely, the patently human actions of the creatures in children's stories communicate important truths: that love redeems *(Beauty and the Beast)*, that courage is good *(Pinocchio)*, that one's reach may exceed one's grasp *(The Sorcerer's Apprentice)*. There can be no similar resonance from stories basically false to the human condition.

Effects

Social scientists have yet to investigate the long-term effects of feminist pedagogy. This incuriousness is striking in a discipline normally eager to study any cultural innovation, the more so as the onus lies with its advocates to demonstrate, and on educators to demand that they demonstrate, that unisex course material is at worst harmless. Innovations introduced solely for their pedagogical promise often fail. It would be an extraordinary coincidence if material introduced solely for the extrapedagogical purpose of justice should have instructional merit without adverse side effects. Most educational innovations now widely adopted first had to prove themselves in extensive tests—itself not an infallible sign of merit, since innovations are frequently tested on small groups of children by teachers dedicated to the new methods. Feminist practice lacks this backing as well. Relative to the usual waiting time for curricular reform, it arrived overnight.

Systematic study may be lacking, but a few observations seem warranted. The gap between the way people actually behave and the ways they behave in the new books is bound to disconcert children. It is never made clear whether children are supposed to notice the unisex message of these books or ingest it subliminally, but if children do notice they are being preached to they will think their books lie, and if they do not notice they are being preached to they will be puzzled by the world's persistent violation of what they are being taught to expect. Feminist pedagogy would seem in theory to demand pictures and accounts explicitly labeled "ideal" in juxtaposition to pictures of the "real" world, but its advocates are reluctant to admit a gap between the real and the ideal. It is not even possible to communicate an ideal of neutrality by having neuter figures go about human activities in books, since the boys must be distinguished from the girls if the message that they are similar is to be properly formulated. (Governmental and corporate iconography is moving toward asexual neutrality, but stick figures still look male unless accoutred with stylized skirts or breasts—in which case they look female.) The most committed text must thus rely on the usual signs of gender. To get the message across, long hair must poke dutifully out from one-third of the baseball caps, with these compromise creatures doing things that children almost never see females do. Girls do not swing a bat with a form Hank Aaron would envy, as one does in another Lippincott "good" drawing, and children know this. One way or another, confusion is sewn. Of course, the faith of feminist educators in the power of image over reality, their preoccupation with the atypical, might simply underestimate the child's capacity to come to his own conclusions despite his elders' mendacity. On the other hand, there is always the chance that a few children will take their unisex counterprimers seriously. It is a commonplace of developmental psychology that a strong sense of gender identity is necessary for strong ego formation. It makes no psychological sense for a child to regard himself as "a human being" and only secondarily a male or female. Educational reformers impressed by the feminist case are obligated to demonstrate that their innovations are not harming children's sense of gender identity. This outcome may not be particularly likely, but ignoring it is irresponsible.

Then there are the cognitive effects of distorting reality. Feminist pedagogy creates discord. Alongside the nominal subjects of the text runs a second lesson. As the child is being taught about how houses are built, he is also being taught that women are—can be? should be? have been stopped from being?—electricians. Nor is he told that he is being taught a covert lesson. Because the hidden lesson is unrelated to the official one, the child must process an irrelevancy every time his book calls the electrician "he or she." Learning proceeds most efficiently when the material to be learned is easily integrated into the cognitive set the learner has constructed from prior experience. One supposes that the net effect of a message as counterexperiential as antisexism is distraction and impairment of concentration. The distractive effect of ideologically shaped iconography has been observed in another context by cartoonist John Saxon. He reports that "most art directors now request the inclusion of blacks and women in office scenes," but notes (with regret) that cartoons drawn in accordance with this request do not work. One of his own cartoons involving a businessman checking out a library book misfired because the Black librarian he was required to insert raised "irrelevant questions" in the mind of the viewer. "It remains difficult to include women and blacks in normal office cartoons," Saxon writes, "because their presence draws too much attention and the point of the idea gets sidetracked."[27]

Perhaps some evidence of the disruptive effect of unisex inconography can be found in the decline in SAT scores that began at about the time androgynous texts were being introduced. Obviously preferable to such inferences would be experimental determination of the effects of feminist materials on memory, attention, and reasoning. Appropriate experiments are not difficult to design.

1. *Effects on attention and short-term memory.* Show children a picture of a woman driving a truck and a man mending a dress. Ask them about details of the picture immediately after it has been removed. Compare their performances with that of a control group shown the same scenes but with the man driving the truck and the woman mending the dress. Vary the exposure time. Analyze by sex.
2. *Effects on long-term memory.* Ask the subjects in the foregoing experiments about details of the pictures fifteen minutes later, a day later, a week later. *Hypothesis:* especially under short exposure time, children will notice comparatively less about the unisex scenes apart from their unisexuality than the controls.
3. *Reading.* Administer age-appropriate reading comprehension tests, giving the experimental group a passage using the "he or she" construction and controls the same passage in standard English. Vary by using "he or she" in the testing instructions. Administer the tests to children of different ages, including children reading above and below their grade level.
4. Administer reading tests normed at a level of difficulty just above that achieved by the subjects, to test the effects of "he or she" and allied constructions on students pushed to the limits of their reading competence.
5. *Mathematical Aptitude.* Mathematical aptitude may be insensitive to the content of word problems, but nonchance results might be found for the effect of unisex language on speed of solution of word problems.

The aggressive use of unisex material may be uncorrelated with performance. Children may just ignore it. It might correlate negatively with performance. It seems unlikely that it will correlate positively with performance; not even the most ardent feminist claims that children learn to read better on stories about strong females rescuing passive males told in the "he or she" idiom. No doubt better tests than these can be designed, and should have been designed and administered long ago, and their results widely discussed.

Notes

1. See Sharon Papalia and Sally Olds, *A Child's World* (New York: McGraw-Hill, 1979).
2. See e.g. Robert Biehler, *Psychology Applied to Children,* 3rd ed. (New York: Houghton-Mifflin, 1978).
3. Dorothy Cohen and Marguerita Rudolph, *Kindergarten and Elementary Schooling* 2nd ed. (Englewood Cliffs, N.J.: Prentice-Hall, 1977), p. 338. New editions of books on child psychology brought out since 1970 often differ from previous ones only in incorporating concessions to feminist ideology.
4. Marcia Federbush, "The Sex Problems of School Math Books," in *And Jill Came Tumbling After: Sexism in American Education,* ed. Judith Stacey, Susan Bereaud, and Joan Daniels (New York: Dell, 1974), pp. 178–83.
5. "A good rule of thumb is to divide all roles and activities 50:50 whenever possible." Ibid.
6. Lippincott threatens legal action against reproduction of these pictures.
7. See for instance Peter Lippman, *Busy Trains* (New York: Random House, 1978).
8. See Dinah L. Moché, *We're Taking an Airplane Trip* (New York: Golden Book, 1982); Kennon Graham, *My Little Book about Flying* (Racine, Wis.: Whitman, 1978).
9. Vitz's study will appear as technical report NIE-G840012 for the NIE under the title "Religion and Traditional Values in Public School Textbooks: An Empirical Study." He has kindly shown me an advance copy. Also see his "Textbook Bias Isn't of a Fundamentalist Nature," *Wall Street Journal* (December 26, 1985): 6.
10. For mention of other studies see Karen DeCrow, "Hardlining Title XI," *Perspectives* (Summer 1980): 16–23.
11. See Myra and David Sadker, *Sex Equity Handbook for Schools* (New York: Longman, 1982).
12. See Ann Snitow, ". . . and the Rest Are Girls," *The Nation* (May 28, 1983): 697.
13. Betty Levy, "Do Schools Sell Girls Short?" in Stacey Bereaud, and Daniels, p. 144. See also C. Etaugh and V. Hughes, "Teachers' Evaluations of Sex-Typed Behaviors in Children: The Role of Teacher, Sex, and School Setting," *Developmental Psychology* 11 (1975): 394–95; J. Wirtemberg, *Expanding Girls' Occupational Potential: A Case Study of the Implementation of Title IX's Anti-Sex-Discrimination Provision in Seventh Grade Practical Arts* (Ann Arbor, Mich.: University Microfilm, 1979).
14. Judith Wirtemberg, Susan Klein, B. Richardson, and V. Thomas, "Sex Equity in American Education," *Educational Leadership* (January 1981): 311–19.
15. Prepared under a grant from the Department of Education. The Sadkers' evidence for discrimination against girls includes the wage gap discussed in chapter 6, the greater discouragement experienced by girls at initial failure, which they call "learned helplessness," and the perceived association of males with traits perceived by both sexes as more socially valuable. They dismiss as

far-fetched the hypothesis that these phenomena might manifest the male's greater innate competitiveness and drive for extrafamilial status.

16. *Sex Equity Handbook,* p. 136.
17. *Microteaching,* pp. 50–51.
18. Ibid., p. 49.
19. Letty Pogrebin, an advisor to the New York City Board of Education as well as an author, concurs: "You'd intervene if [children] were doing something physically dangerous or if it became necessary to break up a fight. You should also intervene when one three-year-old tells another that she can't sit in the pretend truck because 'ladies can't drive trucks,' intervene when someone chants 'no boys allowed,' intervene when you hear a jump rope chant that offends," *Growing Up Free* (New York: McGraw-Hill, 1980), p. 355.
20. *Microteaching,* p. 53.
21. See D. McGuiness, "How Schools Discriminate."
22. Marjorie U'ren, "The Image of Women in Textbooks," in *Women in Sexist Society,* ed. Vivian Gornick and Betty Moran (New York: Mentor, 1971), p. 327.
23. David and Myra Sadker, "The One-Percent Solution? Sexism in Teacher Education Texts," *Phi Delta Kappan* (April 1980): 550–53.
24. Jane Martin, review of *New Essays in the Philosophy of Education* (London and Boston: Routledge & Kegan Paul, 1973), *Philosophical Review* 85 (October 1976): 569.
25. If freedom is acting from desires one does not mind having, actions done in ignorance cannot be free, since nobody wants his desires to be formed in ignorance of relevant facts.
26. For a discussion on the symbolic meaning of fairy tales, see Bruno Bettlehiem, *The Uses of Enchantment* (New York: Vintage, 1977).
27. John Saxon, *Honesty Is One of the* Better *Policies* (New York: Viking, 1984), p. x.

8

Education: The Universities

The entrenchment of feminist ideas in higher education in the United States and other Western countries, like its entrenchment in primary education, has involved government intervention facilitated by the acquiescense or active support of academics themselves. It is now a commonplace on campuses to find curricula assessed by reference to numbers, with women equated with racial minorities. A dean at Columbia College regretfully summarizes problems of his institution this way: "If you look at our curriculum, it is probably fair to say that it is massively Euro-centered white male."[1]

Feminist protocols for the postsecondary setting mirror those applied to high school and elementary school. College texts are expected to follow the publishers' guidelines. It is no longer "all men" but "all humans" who are mortal in logic books. Females in a typical text like Hocutt's *The Elements of Logical Analysis and Inference*[2] are almost always "quick" and "strong" and occupy positions like judgeships, while males are usually "handsome" and verging on failing courses. Textbook iconography conforms similarly. The cover of A.C.C. MacKenzie's *The Major Achievements of Science* features a picture of Marie Curie larger than those of Newton and Einstein, implying that she was the most important of the three.[3] Professional associations, among them the American Anthropological Association, the American Philosophical Association, and the American Psychological Association, have resolved to purge sexism and "sexist language" from their disciplines. The American Political Science Association has formulated an Evaluation Questionnaire for detecting "sex bias in the treatment of women in politics in textbooks."[4] The principles of this questionnaire are essentially those of the guidelines for kindergarten readers: The chief faults marring political science textbooks are said to be use of "he" and failure to "showcase women in important political roles and processes." All texts are expected to pass one test: "Does the author explain institutional sexism?" It is not thought permissible for a text to ask whether there is such a phenomenon, nor is the APSA concerned that "showcasing" women might distort the actual character of the political process—an especially pressing

173

danger if, as these guidelines also assume, women have been excluded from important political roles.

Score-keeping about women is now central to course design. After resisting pressure to include at least one woman in the syllabus of its Humanities course, which is intended to survey the fifty most important thinkers of history, Columbia University has recently added a unit of ideas about women. It was not made clear during debate on this change whether some woman as important as Aristotle had previously been overlooked, or whether the need to include a woman transcended considerations of historical significance. (Whether or not this circumstance is construable as further evidence of "cultural sexism," the major figures of the Western tradition like Hume, Kant, Aristotle, Hobbes, and Montesquieu pass only scattered and wholly convention remarks about women which have nothing to do with their most influential ideas.)

Demands for changes in personal conduct analogous to those made for kindergarten children are made for the college environment. A 1982 report by the Project on the Status and Education of Women of the Association of American Colleges[5] found that females were less likely to be called on in class than males, that teachers "use terminology that excludes women" (i.e. "he"), and that teachers asking questions make eye contact primarily with males. PSEW recommends that teachers increase eye contact with females and "use language that does not reinforce limited views of men's and women's roles in career choices." Difficult as the classroom situation is for women, a follow-up PSEW study found, "it may be *more* egalitarian than other college settings" because of additional informal "microinequities."[6] There is the same "lack of eye contact" outside class, but there are also "disparaging comments about lesbians" and "highly assertive speech" on the part of men, who make "sex-based assumptions" about women and emit "physical gestures that express comfortableness, dominance, and control." Finally, "activities sponsored by women students' organizations . . . are avoided or belittled by faculty, staff, and students." Not taking the view that these behaviors and feelings lie beyond conscious control, PSEW recommends a 78-point program for dealing with them, including a requirement that "all students take at least one course on sex roles," the adoption of "a non-sexist language policy to cover all written and verbal institutional communications," the use of videotapes to alert members of the college community lest they "inadvertently treat students differently on the basis of sex," and an attempt by all members of the college community to "balance more 'masculine' skills of analyzing [and] clarifying . . . with traditionally 'female' skills of listening, reinforcing and facilitating other speakers' participation."[7]

It would be easy to observe that these protocols, like those of the Sadkers, would leave no time for any instructional activity, perhaps an embarrassment to an organization like the AAC which describes its mission as the "strengthening of education." The AAC might also be uncomfortable about the tension between its demand that everyone on the college campus disregard sex with its energetic support for gender quotas. But these protocols also highlight more general problems with the "liberal" goal of suppressing sex-based preconceptions. In the college setting, this liberal ideal is said to mean, for instance, that a medical school admissions officer ought not to ask a female applicant how she plans to handle her family if she becomes a doctor unless he also asks this of male applicants.[8] Yet to ask simultaneously for adjustments for the differences in the cognitive and communicative styles of the sexes is to concede that men and women may reasonably be expected to respond differently to the same treatment, in which case perceptual coding by sex is not prejudice and "preconceptions" about women's vocational prospects need not be "outmoded."[9] Whether the difference is acquired or innate, a difference in the response of men and women to parenthood makes it reasonable for an admissions officer to take this factor into account when evaluating male and female applicants. You cannot have it both ways. If a guidance counselor finds that a discipline like philosophy demands a high degree of aggressiveness, a will to control the topic of conversation, and the skills of "analyzing, clarifying, and evaluating," it is inconsistent to protest both that philosophy as it is currently constituted is too "masculine" *and* that academic advisors who recognize these facts are "communicat[ing] sex-typed expectations about a field of study" if they warn females away from philosophy as temperamentally unsuitable. We may thus expect academic feminists to interpret "equal opportunity" as feminists understand it elsewhere: lower standards for women to compensate for sex differences.

Women's Studies: Origins

Establishment of the subject of women's studies has left the deepest feminist mark on the academy. Between 15,000 and 20,000 women's studies courses are currently being offered on almost 500 American campuses. A few institutions like Denison University require it for graduation. A great many others include women's studies among their small "core" of courses from among which all matriculants must choose.

The essentially and distinctively ideological content of women's studies courses was implicit in their creation. After Black studies introduced political equity as a basis for curriculum design in the 1960s, other groups were able with equal justice to demand their own "studies," and those declaring themselves to represent women demanded women's studies and a wide range of interdisciplinary courses like "Philosophy of Women." Judith Waltzer writes in retrospect of the "unusual genesis" of women's studies, "the spark of anger that charged the early projects in women's studies."[10]

In some cases the wholly political character of these projects was frankly acknowledged by the administrators who granted them academic credit. In hearings before the Educational Policy Committee of Kalamazoo College, one member of the faculty defended the recognition of women's studies over Black studies on the grounds that women are 51 percent of the population while Blacks are a minority.[11] Nor could academic officials have doubted the ideological freight this new subject was to carry. Many of the programs now called "Women's Studies" began as Feminist Studies. Florence Howe, a founder of the discipline writes "Feminism and women's studies . . . for me the two terms are interchangeable."[12] A report for the Department of Education prepared under Howe's supervision recognizes "the necessity that all who teach women's studies be not only singularly prepared in the relevant academic area but also *in feminism*," and it stresses that Brooklyn College requires its women's studies courses to incorporate "feminist analysis."[13]

Women's studies, then, was not called into existence by significant new discoveries or a new type of thinking that needed to be communicated to students, of the sort, say, that have generated courses in molecular biology and computer science. Academic feminists have announced major discoveries, to be sure, some of which will be examined presently, and periodicals like *Feminist Studies* and *Signs* publish the work of academic feminists. However, this putative body of knowledge was not cited, nor does anyone claim that it existed, when women's studies was founded and accredited. Nor did women's studies undergo the scrutiny to which far more modest academic innovations are normally subjected. So far as I have been able to determine, the only institution at which a women's studies course met initial resistance was Brown. The course in question was entitled "Biology of Women," described by its avowedly radical instructor Anne Fausto-Sterling as less concerned with scientific research on gender per se (as its title suggests it might be) than with the "political motives behind" this research.[14] Biology of Women is now firmly in place, and elsewhere women's studies have proliferated with great vigor.

A curious index of the leniency accorded women's studies emerged as the present chapter was being prepared. I asked reputable instructors of women's studies at several universities for references to the best statement they knew of the rationale of their subject, by then almost two decades old. Some told me they knew of none; others referred me to the April 1982 number of *Change* which I have been citing. None mentioned anything earlier. (Nor did any academic feminist I consulted feel prepared to offer a concise descriptive definition of "feminism.") Just as with feminist innovations in secondary education, it would be a remarkable coincidence if women's studies, created for wholly nonacademic reasons, should have turned out to be academically sound.

Books and Classes

The desire to win the game while playing by special rules is vividly evident in the content of women's studies courses. Contending that they have been barred from the rigorous, prestigious disciplines by various pressures overt and covert, and given a free hand and much administrative support, academic feminists have produced little more that consciousness raising in the classroom punctuated by advocacy of a policy agenda—undisguised restatements of feminism itself.

Among the textbooks that appear repeatedly in women's studies syllabi are: *Our Bodies, Ourselves,* a manual published by the Boston Women's Health Collective (largely concerned with lesbianism, masturbation, and rape); *The Second Sex;* novels such as Margaret Atwood's *Surfacing* (about the author's dissatisfaction with male lovemaking), Kate Chopin's *The Awakening* (an older novel on a similar theme) and Alix Kate Shulman's *Memoirs of an Ex-Prom Queen.* In one women's studies class I attended, Shulman's book, which concerns a girl's seduction by her professor, was the occasion for an exhortation by the instructor that females are as entitled to be as promiscuous as men. Shulamith Firestone's *The Dialectic of Sex* remains widely used. Its inclusion is usually defended as providing an example of "one phase" of feminist thinking, and it must be agreed that the seriousness once accorded to Firestone's advocacy of incest raises disturbing questions about the culture which received it. The fact is, however, that the ideas Firestone advocated, not the significance of their reception, remain the topics of study.

Some women's studies books do observe the forms of academic respectability. Sheila Ruth's anthology *Issues in Feminism* includes numerous charts and graphs to document the allegedly disadvantaged position of women. The readings it contains, however, emphasize Engels, Betty Friedan, and advocacy literature for the ERA, material that would normally be considered insufficiently rigorous for college classroom. The picture presented by Ruth herself of the women's studies class is certainly harsher than any critic would propose:

> [Teachers] come frequently from counterculture organizations, from consciousness-raising groups and feminist organizations, from political parties and equal rights agencies. . . . One is apt to find group projects, credit for social change activities or for life experiences, contracts for self-grading, diaries and journals, even meditation and ritual.

This description is reinforced in *Seven Years Later,* which praises the women's studies classroom for being "a place in which anyone may say anything, however private or political, . . . both of intellect and feeling, qualitatively different from most college classrooms . . . mainly because of the reliance on a unique combination of scholarship and the experience of classroom participants." *Seven Years Later* mentions "menstruation, machismo, and rape" as examples of the "unusual subject matter treated."

Women's studies course materials ignore other customary features of instruction at the university level, principally the presentation of both sides of disputed issues. The most objective texts, like Jane English's *Philosophy and Sex,* balance twenty or thirty selections by feminists with one or two short selections by critics. Many other texts freely admit to being partisan: On the first page of *The Women's Movement,*[15] Ruth Deckard announces "Chapter 1 documents prevalent sexual stereotypes and explains how they function as ideology. It is the explanation of the political functions of this ideology that sets the analytical framework of this book."

Probably the most salient feature of women's studies courses is failure to include the objective study of women. Williams College's "Foundations of Feminism" treats pornography and the compatibility of feminism with "personal adornment," but not fetal hormonalization. When scientific studies are mentioned at all, one of the "major components [of] the new scholarship on women" is stress on "the importance of null findings."[16] Womanhood is considered principally in terms of the student's subjective response to it. The "major project" for a passing grade in "Women in Contemporary Society," the basic women's studies course at the University of Indiana, is "a critical and analytical essay on the subject 'Myself as a Woman' or 'Myself as a Man.'" Students enrolled in this course may choose the grade they will aim for. Students seeking an "A" can write a short paper on "How do you feel about the way you were told and how would you tell your daughter about menstruation?" or they can "Compare and contrast early lesbian literature with recently written literature by reading Hall's *The Well of Loneliness* and then [Rita Mae] Brown's *Ruby-Fruit Jungle."* One may also "critique Firestone on Racism." Should the academic forms of comparing, contrasting, and critiquing prove burdensome, the less ambitious student satisfied with a lower grade may "keep a journal for two weeks wherein you record your daily experience as a woman or as a man." Those who might suppose that such ruminations lack rigor are rebuked: "A journal is not a place to jot down or muse randomly but it is a place to think seriously on paper."

The one feature of women's studies courses that students appreciate readily enough is how easy they are in comparison to standard college courses on Shakespeare or organic chemistry. Male enrollees in women's studies courses have told me that they are there for an easy "A." It would seem difficult not to succeed in a course whose main requirement is a diary or a report on oneself, and in which grades are based on sincerity. The women's studies final at one New York university asks "What do you think of Women's Liberation?" Women's studies instructors are notorious for penalizing students critical of feminism.[17] It is a backward scholar who cannot answer a women's studies examination.

The reader who finds it difficult to believe that women's studies courses are typically conducted in the ways described may wish to consult the women's studies texts in the bookstore of the nearest university. Should field work still leave him with the feeling that "every movement, every academic area has its excesses," he should ask himself whether any other academic subject admits the possibility of, let alone displays, comparable excesses. Are there calculus courses which use meditation, literature courses in which ritual is deemed appropriate? Why does women's studies generate a uniquely pathological fringe, if fringe it is?

The Case for Women's Studies

The most common justification for women's studies are mutually incompatible and internally incoherent. The basic tension springs from the recurrent question: Must the curriculum incorporate the work of women because *men and women experience the world differently?* If so, it is admitted that some disciplines, perhaps the hard sciences, may really be "masculine" and others "feminine," so that the relative absence of women from some and predominance in others does not reflect bias. If not—if, that is, liberated women will produce art, science, and literature indistinguishable from that produced by men—the creation of courses in "Women's History" or "Women in the Visual Arts" is arbitrary gerrymandering. It might be replied that there is a distinctive female view of the world, one caused by women's oppression. But in that case, once again, there being no *natural* cleavage between the worlds of men and women, the appropriate courses to give would bear titles like "The Visual Arts from the Perspective of Oppressed People." If there are no innate sex differences, women's studies must simply comprise whatever happens to have been done by women in any given field, consistency then requiring left-handed studies, men's studies—a study for any group whatever.

The standard reply to this observation is that the current curriculum already is, in effect, men's studies; virtually every extant subject has been developed by men. It is time women had a fair go. Florence Howe calls it a "political act" not to mention women in a class, and she proclaims "the right of women to a place in the curriculum that will allow them images of achievement and aspiration." Elizabeth Minnich writes:

> If our notion of history leaves out well over half the human race, it is not human history, and we need to get busy figuring out what we need to do and know to create a human history—for the first time in human history.[18]

This argument cannot be taken seriously, for the university curriculum is already sex-neutral. Material is taught when it is judged by competent students of the relevant discipline to be interesting and significant. Courses in calculus are offered because calculus is important in describing nature, not because a man invented it. If a woman had written *The Critique of Pure Reason,* there would have been just as many seminars devoted to it as there are now. There is no evidence that the work of female figures deemed important, like that of Margaret Mead, has suffered neglect. If the work deemed academically significant is usually done by men, it is more profitable to ask why this is so than to apply political categories to the phenomenon.

While a great many academic feminists do belong to the It-was-really-Mrs.-Newton-who-discovered-gravity school, the more sophisticated do not claim that male curricular authorities have consciously conspired to exclude important achievements by women. Rather, these officials are said to be unconsciously influenced by the maleness of various figures. A "gender-balanced perspective" (in the words of Wheaton College) is needed to balance the masculine bias of the tests of academic significance themselves. While this improves upon the conspiracy theory, no evidence has ever been marshaled that conventional academic standards are biased, beyond their failure to select women in proportional numbers. Bias is once again given an operational meaning that requires abandonment of all canons of value and pertinence in favor of sex. It is not surprising that Elizabeth Minnich calls "dishonest" the thoughts of Pythagoras, Augustine, Aquinas, Aristotle, Spinoza, Kant, Rousseau, Shakespeare, Tolstoy, and Freud because they did not embrace the ideas of modern feminism. Gloria Bowles and Renate Klein unflinchingly draw the logical consequence of thus rejecting traditional standards wholesale: "*Every* issue is a Women's Studies Issue."[19]

The equity justification of women's studies, which admits the subject's ideological character, reaches the heart of the argument, namely that, since *all* instruction is political in nature, there can be no objection to the particular politics represented by women's studies. In the words of a participant in a workshop on Integrating the Study of Women into the Liberal Arts, "ideology does play a role in any teaching program . . . one's politics are apparent in both the choice of topic and its treatment."[20] "Is this feminist perspective, is this teaching about woman, a political act?" asks Florence Howe:

> In the broadest context of that word, teaching is a political act. . . . In a university whose goal is that abstraction called truth, no political act ought ideally to be excluded, if it might shed light on the ultimate goal. And the study of half the human race—the political act we call women's studies—cannot be excluded without obvious consequences to the search for truth.[21]

The idea that all teaching is political or ideological is flatly untrue, unless those words are used so broadly that all meaningful distinctions are obscured. The decision to communicate new knowledge or drop old is a judgement of value, to be sure, but *epistemic,* not political or moral value. Science faculties that offer computer science clearly think recursion theory is worth knowing and teachers of the subject communicate their enthusiasm for it in the classroom. This is hardly politics, which means the allocation of resources and power. Treating all values as part of some ideology, the argument from politics goes on to confuse what may be *inferred* about a person's values from what he does with the explicit *advocacy* of those values. Clearly, an art history teacher lecturing animatedly about Picasso thinks it is good to know about modern art, but he is not explicitly encouraging his students to become artists or art historians, or to subsidize Matisse exhibitions. Exhortations to students to do such things would be recognized as violating professional ethics. In fact, conscientious instructors try as far as possible to disguise their preferences (a conscientious teacher of American history will leave his students in doubt as to whether he thinks Franklin Roosevelt an angel or a devil) and when this is impossible, to lay out their own assumptions explicitly, to be treated as postulates for the sake of discussion.

The advocacy of values and programs in women's studies course therefore cannot be justified by the inherently confused idea that *all* instructors make value choices. In fact, the idea that all inquiry is perspectival cannot survive the sheer admission that there is such a thing as objective truth, discoverable and communicable regardless of the norms of the investigator. It should be no surprise, when we look below at the frontiers of feminist research, that its central discovery is that truth is a male invention.

A final justification for women's studies is the therapeutic: "Male students must know the injustice done women," and the "emotional repression" done by "the American emphasis on a certain masculine ideal."[22] In practice, this conception of women's studies leads to academic encounter groups, role playing, the formation of grievance committees for academic credit, and other forms of self-dramatization. One university course asks the female taking it to pretend she is the wife of a plantation owner who has sired ten mulatto children, or to pretend "you are a middle-class woman talking to a working woman, and both of you are unhappy with the status of women." For Florence Howe, the chief goal of women's studies is "to raise the consciousness of students."

Personal growth is no doubt desirable, but giving it a central role in the defense of women's studies is in considerable tension with the claims of women's studies to cognitive value. No other college subject is intended to help students pursuing it grow as persons.

Women and feminism can certainly be subjects of respectable course work, but such work is more appropriately undertaken in traditional departments. If the writing of women truly reveals a distinctive sensibility, it can best be taught in the English department. The nature and ramifications of gender differences are empirical questions of biology, psychology, anthropology, sociology, political science, and history. Their dispassionate study will differ greatly from the drawing of foregone conclusions of the sort expounded in women's studies courses. Feminist themselves offer an interesting subject for the social sciences. Who are they? What is their typical income, religion, age, marital status, sexual orientation, number of children, education, health, and political outlook? Works such as Claire Fulenwider's *Feminism in American Politics,* cited in chapter 2, show how profitably such inquiry can be undertaken within the confines of traditional disciplines.

Reclaiming "Herstory"

With the possible exception of psychology, no discipline abrades egalitarian sensibilities as harshly as history. What historians study is at once so amorphously defined and so close a reflection of what a culture deems important as to be a natural magnet for feelings of neglect. Because historians usually chronicle war, revolution, statesmanship, and exploration, all predominantly male activities, it is easy to accuse history of bias. Even social history—about, say, changes in the workplace—although a reaction to classical historiography, has also ended up being largely about men. Feminists argue that it is time "to re-envision the lost culture and history of women."[23]

There are two fundamental reasons why an equal-time principle is useless for assessing historical significance. First, the world's women do not form a coherent group. To speak of a group's history presupposes that it bears the marks of group identity: geographic isolation, cultural distinctiveness, special institutions such as myths, art, or language, and a relatively discrete gene pool. Obviously, women have none of those things; marriage means that what happens to women happens to men, and vice versa. Those events that have most affected women have been the wars and technological developments that affect everyone. Women do not share any myths, art, or language that is not also shared by the men of their culture. All that a modern American woman shares with the wife of a fifth-century Chinese peasant are those biological and biologically based traits that feminism minimizes or denies.

Most fundamentally, equity is irrelevant to historical inquiry because some periods and groups have exercised a disproportionate influence on mankind, and these groups must assume disproportionate prominence in historical accounts. Geoffrey Partington has proposed a five-fold criterion for the significance of a historical phenomenon: its effect on the development of rationality, human control over nature, personal autonomy, personal security, and equality of considerations between persons.[24] One cannot decide on moral grounds that predominantly male activities like technology, war, and law fail to meet this criterion more fully than the activities of women. Indeed, those phenomena most significant for women have largely been the work of men. The invention of the sewing machine changed the lives of more women in more fundamental ways than the franchise.

No doubt Partington's criterion can be accused in turn of masculine bias toward rationality and control, but it must be recognized sooner or later that the nature of historical inquiry imposes its own objective criteria of importance for historical events. The aim of history is explanation, in particular explanation of how the human world got to be the way it is, just as the aim of natural history is explanation of how the living world got to be the way it is. History is the reconstruction of the causal lines leading to the Peloponnesian War, the predominance of Islam in North Africa, the names of American cities. Microhistory seeks explanatory understanding within its own limited domain: The history of garlic, for instance, is concerned with why garlic is used in different ways in different cultures, how the present world distribution of garlic came about, and what influence garlic may have exerted on the development of trade routes. Historical importance is a completely objective matter, however difficult it may be to determine in particular cases. Historically important phenomena are those that have had the most to do with creating the present. History can no more decide who *should* be important than geology can decide what *should* cause earthquakes. Even if there were no women at Appomatox, solely because of sexism, the events there became a major determinant of the nature of American society, and that is how these events must be taught.

Philosophers are apt to object, with some justice, that there is no such entity as "the world" to be understood historically, only various phenomena within it. Some prior principle is needed for selecting the phenomena whose causes are to be sought (and perhaps there is male bias in this prior principle that needs to be redressed). But the admission that explananda must themselves be choosen injects no serious relativism into historical inquiry. *Given* a circumstance to be explained, its major causes are a question that remains completely objective. One can if one wants study fruit preserving rather than the manufacture of automobiles, but what led to the use of mason jars is not itself a matter of anybody's values (nor are the antecedents of mass production). I am in any event far less sure than are philosophical relativists that there is no such thing as "the world," at least as history understands it. The world is the system of societies that exist, on which are superimposed the grid of nation-states that constitute the political world. In an absolute sense, it is the origin of this world that historians are trying to understand, and it is not clear a priori that the preservation of fruit, and the other activities of women studied by those who feel that women's activities deserve emphasis, changed this world as profoundly as the invention of the steam engine. Many of the studies that appear in journals of scholarship about women are methodologically sound, but taken as a whole they confirm one of the oldest and most deeply entrenched of sexual stereotypes: Women provide the stability in society while men provide the change.[25]

Women have no culture, lost or otherwise. Within each society a sorority of mothers transmits a special lore to its daughters, just as fathers transmit a different lore to their sons. It is quite possible to study this universal sisterhood, how ordinary women lived in different epochs and the effect of ordinary women on their culture and nation. But tracing these strands of tradition does not create a new subject. Such work has been and continues to be done by many historians and economists without ideological preconceptions. Barbara Tuchman's discussion of the effects of medieval childrearing practices on the medieval personality is a case in point.[26] There might be some reason to call research into the lives of unknown women a "new kind of history" if it produced evidence or theories at variance with ordinary facts or the standard ideas of history, anthropology, and psychology. So far it has not.

The Research Frontier

Like other academic fields, women's studies has a frontier of research. In addition to the periodicals mentioned earlier, a reputable academic publisher has brought out a collection of essays on feminist epistemology and metaphysics.[27] The University of California, among other institutions, offers an advanced degree in women's studies. Feminist scholars themselves are not modest about their collective achievements:

> It looked occasionally as if the discoveries were so different in kind from other, conventional work as to point toward a new way of studying people and things altogether.[28]

> Over the past decade and a half, feminist activists and scholars have begun a revolutionary movement in thought and behavior so profound and so rooted in a transformed consciousness that it will not stop until all Western consciousness and civilizations are transformed.[29]

Academic feminists are not talking about recent work in brain physiology or behavioral genetics, which has been conducted in accordance with standard methodological rules and which, as we have seen, undermines femin-

ism itself. Academic feminists have shown some interest in Carol
Gilligan's work on sex differences in moral thinking—more as part of the
case that society ignores women than for its possible implications about
gender dimorphism—but Gilligan's work is hardly a Copernican revolu-
tion.[30] More typical of feminist academic research are the activities of the
Stony Brook College Society for Women in Philosophy, whose 1985
Conference on Women and Moral Theory featured papers on "The Curious
Coincidence of African and Feminist Moralities" and "The Acceptability of
Hume's Ethics to Women." During its 1979–80 Series on Feminism: The
Present and the Future, this same colloquium presented a lecture entitled
"Images of Lesbian Sexuality in the Fine Arts," described in the accom-
panying literature as "images of women loving women." The lecturer, Tee
Corinne, was credited as the illustrator of *I am My Lover* and *The Cunt
Coloring Book.*

Readers accustomed to academic circumspection may again wonder if the
Stony Brook group is representative. My own sense is that their emphases
are fairly typical—about one-third of feminist research concerns
lesbianism—but let us turn to other "important breakthroughs" that are said
to be "challenging conventional scholarship."[31] One repeatedly finds this
challenge to amount less to the discovery of anything new and important by
standard criteria of importance, than to rejection of the criteria themselves.
One recently announced discovery is that the Renaissance was not a time of
progress, since women were oppressed by the rejection of medieval
chivalry.[32] A related discovery is that Periclean Athens has been

> overrated: It may be suggested, on the basis of comparison between Archaic
> and Classical Athens and between Athens and Sparta or Roman society, that
> some women—at least those of the upper class—flourished in aristocratic
> society, while none fared as well under the democracy. . . . It may also be
> suggested that after the class stratification that separated individual men
> according to such criteria as noble descent and wealth were eliminated, the
> ensuing ideal of equality among male citizens was intolerable. The will to
> dominate was such that they then had to separate themselves as a group and
> claim to be superior to all nonmembers; foreigners, slaves and women.[33]

A third discovery, announced at a conference of eighteenth-century historians, is that Montesquieu was a "phallocentrist" (not surprising, perhaps,
since, if one accepts that category, everyone in human history has been a
phallocentrist.) Perhaps the most familiar such discovery is that quilts and
diaries are just as valuable as "fine arts," a judgement often paired, inconsistently, with the proviso that "questions of value must be suspended" until
all the hitherto neglected work of women is sorted out.

Reevaluations of historical periods cannot properly be called discoveries
unless they rest on some new information, which these purported

discoveries do not. Any moderately well educated person knows that wives counted for relatively little in ancient Athens (just as most males were slaves in that society), and that the chivalric ethos passed with the Middle Ages. The adverse judgements passed on these epochs by feminists are not based on newly authenticated manuscripts, reattributions, revised chronologies, or the highlighting of previously unsuspected features of Greek or Renaissance political institutions. They are simply expressions of dislike toward an entirely familiar past.[34] Similarly, everyone already knows what quilts look like. It would be a matter of scholarly interest if claims about quilts were accompanied by the sort of sea change in perception that accompanied Picasso's neoprimitivism. The claim that "accused witches groped in their confession of guilt to understand human life just as Descartes did with his Cogito"[35] would be important if based on a newly discovered diary in which an accused Salem witch pondered the mind/body problem. These necessary supplementations have not been forthcoming. The isolated corrections made by feminists in the historical record—Merino sheep breeding in Australia may well have been founded by the wife of the man usually credited with it—does not amount to a new way of studying anything. Indignation is not a methodological advance.

As in history, the standards of evaluation in the other scholarly disciplines are determined by the problems the disciplines are trying to solve and not by the subjective commitments of their practitioners. This is obviously true of the sciences. It is true of philosophy as well; there is far more agreement than outsiders might suppose on the goodness of arguments. It is equally true of the modes of aesthetic criticism. Art historians and literary critics are not especially interested in what is "good." Merit is, in Nelson Goodman's phrase, a means to further understanding—of the problem the writer or painter himself was trying to solve, of his influence on his followers, of his place in the tradition.

We thus arrive at the core of the feminist challenge to conventional scholarship: rejection of the idea of objectivity. Renate Klein writes:

> The postulate of *value free research*, of neutrality and indifference [sic] toward the research objects, has to be replaced by *conscious partiality*. . . . The contemplative, uninvolved "spectator knowledge" must be replaced by *active participation in actions, movements, and struggles* for women's emancipation.[36]

Barbara Du Bois characterizes the "Passionate Scholarship" of feminists similarly:

> Traditional science reacts to and builds on a consensual construction of reality; that construction of reality is seen as given, real, graspable. It is to be

known, from the outside, objectively, neutrally, impersonally. Feminism withdraws from the patriarchal construction of reality.[37]

Feminists have made their most extraordinarily relativistic claims about science in both popular publications and nominally more responsible outlets. Elizabeth Minnich finds that as women are "more conversational, more interested in collective thinking, more interested in building support than antagonism," they can change not only social relations between scientists but the content of what they discover. The maleness of most scientists "undoubtedly has affected the content of science."[38] Elizabeth Fee claims that the liberal view of science depends on a "series of sexist dichotomies":

> We find that the attributes of science are the attributes of males: . . . cold, hard, impersonal, "objective." . . . If we accept the radical feminist view, science itself must be transformed, not simply to permit the acceptance of women, but more importantly, to conceptualize new kinds of relationships between human beings and the natural world [than those] in our existing forms of knowledge.[39]

For Ruth Bleier,

> truth, reality, and objectivity are all in trouble from our point of view; we see a male-created truth and reality, a male point of view, a male-defined objectivity.[40]

Inevitably, these claims are given a conspiratorial twist:

> Aperspectivity is revealed as a strategy of male hegemony. . . . The male epistemological stance, which corresponds to the world it creates, is objectivity.[41]

Catherine MacKinnon argues that "the male mind is assumed to be like a penis. . . . Feminists are beginning to understand that to know has meant to fuck."

Without question, the illusoriness of objective truth is the discovery that feminist scholars themselves regard as their most significant. (Their position resembles that of the misogynist who also denies that women are capable of putting aside their emotions, differing only in that the misogynist values "thinking like a man" while feminist scholars abhor it.) To evaluate this epistemological doctrine, one needs some positive account of what female science would be like, and some evidence that objectivity is impossible—assuming that "evidence against objectivity" is not a contradiction. There is a long tradition of epistemological relativism, but its arguments have nothing to do with the genitals of inquirers and are consequently unavailable to feminist relativists. Unfortunately, one finds little sustained defense of distinctively gender-centric relativism. Elizabeth Fee says "there is no way of imagining in advance [what] feminist science" would be.[42] Those who have tried to imagine it emphasize "process, change, and interaction," in Ruth Bleier's words, replacing masculine concern for linear causation. Evelyn Fox Keller, somewhat less extreme, suggests that no woman would have invented any idea as connected to "domination" as the "master molecule" theory of DNA.[43] Fee also cites, by way of general argument, the money received by scientists from the military and "corporate interests," and the fact that scientists feel emotions about their work.[44] I do not wish this summary to sound shallow and dismissive, for that might leave the reader suspecting that these authors offer more substantial arguments that I have slighted, and that impression would be inaccurate. The arguments cited are the most substantial I have encountered.

The more feminist epistemologists emphasize the radical difference between male and female thinking, the harder it is to explain these differences in terms of socialization. But let us overlook considerations of consistency (and the penchant of these authors for overstating the differences between male and female cognition more grotesquely than any follower of Ruskin ever did) and consider the arguments themselves. It is, first, difficult to see the difference between "interaction" and causation, or how, if men cannot weigh complexity, male mathematicians developed factor analysis, multiple regression analysis, control theory, the calculus of variations, and other tools for describing the interaction of several variables. Second, not only is there no evidence that a woman could never have invented the "master molecule" theory—female molecular biologists like Barbara McClintock vehemently reject the idea that they do not think like male molecular biologists—the genesis of a hypothesis has nothing to do with its *evaluation*. However a hypothesis is contrived, the predictions drawn from it must be compared to observations—which are never so skewed by competing preconceptions that a consensus cannot be made to emerge in reasonable time. A scientist's choice of the problems he wishes to study is not doubt influenced by extrascientific factors (and this is as true for female scientists as male), but not the soundness of his solutions.

The breathtaking view that DNA, subatomic particles, and the rest of nature would have been different had women studied them—and there is no other interpretation to put on the words of Hubbard, Fee, MacKinnon, or Bleier—denies the existence of a world independent of our beliefs about it. If the overparticipation of males has distorted science, it is impossible to understand why airplanes, built on the basis of distorted male physics, should stay up. Would airplanes designed in accordance with incompatible holistic female aerodynamics also stay up? Would they stay up only if women flew them? The greatest discovery of feminist scholarship is so patently foolish, the arguments enlisted for it so meretricious, that, had its partisans been men unprotected by the guilt feelings of critics, it would have been laughed to silence.

The Roots and Flower of Feminist Relativism

Feminist relativism has three sources. One is the embarrassment caused feminists by the biological and behavioral sciences. The only remaining barrier against the tide of evidence for important innate gender dimorphism is rejection of the idea of evidence. When reason goes against a man, said Hobbes, the man goes against reason. The second source is Marxism, which also rejects the idea of a world independent of human praxis. The third is unfamiliarity with science, including the work of female scientists. It is doubtful that many feminists who laud the "soft" female style of thinking are acquainted with Emmy Nöther's treatment of algebraic ideals, which differs from the work of most male mathematicians solely in its superior rigor.

Once reason and objectivity are banished, and the question becomes not what hypothesis is true but which side to take, the way is opened for the ungoverned exercise of the will, and with it violation of the norms of academic conduct. A group called Coalition of Women's Art Organizations, having concluded that men exclude women from art history, has organized a boycott in university art history departments of Jenson's *History of Art,* Gombrich's *The Story of Art,* and other standard texts on the subject, an effort endorsed by The Association of American Colleges. One wonders what Ernest Gombrich, who survived the Nazis, makes of this latest attack on books for reasons of biology. For the first time in universities not fettered by officially imposed state ideologies, one group of self-described scholars is attempting to boycott and suppress the academic work of other scholars—behavior not surprising from people who profess to believe that truth is to be decided politically.

Notes

1. Michael Rosenthal, quoted in "Panel Debates Women's Studies," *Columbia Spectator* (January 31, 1986): 1.
2. Max Hocutt, *The Elements of Logical Analysis and Inference* (Cambridge, Mass.: Winthrop, 1979).
3. A.C.C. MacKenzie, *The Major Achievements of Science* (New York: Simon & Schuster, 1973).
4. Beverly Cook, "Evaluating Textbooks for Sex Bias," *News for Teachers of Political Science* 30 (September 1981): 1–25.
5. Roberta M. Hall with Bernice Sandler, *The Classroom Climate: A Chilly One for Women?* (Washington, D.C.: Project on the Status and Education of Women,

Association of American Colleges, 1982). PSEW is funded by the Carnegie Corporation and the Ford Foundation.

6. Roberta M. Hall and Bernice Sandler, *Out of the Classroom: A Chilly Climate for Women?* (Washington, D.C.: PSEW, AAC, 1984).

7. For similar proposals, see "Statement on Educational Diversity, Equality, and Quality" (Washington, D.C.: Office of Women in Higher Education, American Council on Education, June 1984); Cynthia Berryman-Fink, "Male-Female Interaction Patterns," a summary of "Communication Training as a Prevention of Sexual Harassment," Fifth Annual Communication, Language and Gender Conference, Athens, Ohio, October 16, 1982.

8. *Chilly Campus Climate*, p. 6.

9. Ibid.

10. Judith Walzer, "New Knowledge or a New Discipline?" *Change: The Magazine of Higher Education* (April 1982): 21.

11. Harold J. Harris, "How Women's Studies Came to Kalamazoo," manuscript, Department of English, Kalamazoo College, Kalamazoo, Michigan. See also Elizabeth Lilla, "Who's Afraid of Women's Studies?" *Commentary* (February 1986): 53–57.

12. Florence Howe, "Feminist Scholarship: The Extent of the Revolution," *Change* (April 1982): 19.

13. Florence Howe, *Seven Years Later: Women's Studies Programs in 1976* (Washington, D.C.: Department of Education, 1977).

14. Fausto-Sterling describes her course thus in "The Myth of Neutrality: Race, Sex, and Class in Science," *The Radical Teacher* 19 (1981): 21–25.

15. Ruth Deckard, *The Women's Movement* (New York: Harper & Row, 1979).

16. Howe, p. 15.

17. "One teacher tells of learning that a student in the women's studies course was asked to defend her decision to dress in a noticeably feminine manner. Other students have complained of having their grades lowered if they fail to use the 'he/she' form in their papers. (The provost makes a point of requiring that all papers for his courses be free of 'exclusive language.')." Lilla, p. 55.

18. Elizabeth Minnich, "A Devastating Conceptual Error: How Can We *Not* Be Feminist Scholars?" *Change* (April 1982): 8. The error in question is a failure to realize that women are human beings: "We have not studied women except from the perspective of men, who took themselves to be the whole, all there is, *humans*, leaving no room for other humans unlike them." Ibid., p. 7.

19. Gloria Bowles and Renate Klein, "Introduction," in *Theories of Women's Studies*, ed. Gloria Bowles and Renate Klein (New York: Routledge & Kegan Paul, 1983), p. 3.

20. Marylyn Rands, summary of the Wheaton College Psychology Department's 1981 workshop, "Toward a Balanced Curriculum." This workshop was funded by the U.S. Department of Education.

21. Howe, pp. 12–20.

22. John Schilb, "Men's Studies and Women's Studies," *Change* (April 1982): 401.

23. Howe, p. 15.

24. Geoffrey Partington, "What History Should We Teach?" *Oxford Review of History* 6 (Summer 1980): 157–76.

25. See for instance Joanna Stratton, *Pioneer Women* (New York: Simon & Schuster, 1981).

26. Barbara Tuchman, *A Distant Mirror* (New York: Ballentine, 1980).

27. Sandra Harding and Merrill Hintikka, eds., *Discovering Reality: Feminist Perspectives on Epistemology* (Boston: D. Reidel, 1983).

28. Walzer, p. 22.

29. Ruth Bleier, *Science and Gender* (New York: Pergamon, 1984).

30. See ch. 2.

31. These phrases are used in "Scholars Face a Challenge by Feminists," *New York Times* (November 23, 1981): A1–B6.

32. At other times, of course, feminists bitterly criticize chivalry for idealizing female bondage.

33. Sharon Pomeroy, *Goddesses, Whores, Wives, and Slaves* (New York: Shocken, 1975), p. 78.

34. There is, coincidentally, a reasonable case against the claims of the Renaissance; many of the inventions characterizing the "modern world" were made well before the fifteenth century. Considerations like that are no part of the feminist argument.

35. *Times* (November 23, 1981). Another recent discovery about Descartes is that the first-person sceptical perspective of the *First Meditation* is "feminine," while the objective scientific standpoint of Bacon is "masculine."

36. Renate Klein, "Towards a Methodology for Feminist Research," in Rowles and Klein, pp. 122–24.

37. Barbara du Bois, "Passionate Scholarship," in Klein and Bowles, p. 112.

38. Minnich and Hubbard, cited in *Times* (November 23, 1981).

39. Elizabeth Fee, "Women's Nature and Scientific Objectivity," in Hubbard and Lowe, pp. 13–22.

40. *Science and Gender,* p. 196.

41. MacKinnon, p. 537.

42. "Women's Nature and Scientific Objectivity," p. 22.

43. Evelyn Fox Keller, "Feminism and Science," *Signs* 7, 3 (1982): 589–602.

44. "Women's Nature and Scientific Objectivity," pp. 18–22.

9

Feminism, Education, and the State

If feminist pedagogy were being offered in the marketplace of ideas, it would be fair to let it rise or fall according to its popular acceptability. It is not being so offered, however; government at all levels has thrown its weight behind feminist pedagogy. This may well be more true in other Western countries than in the United States. England's Equal Opportunity Commission has proposed that every school playground have a monitor to watch for "sex stereotypical play activity." The Swedish government, whether socialist or conservative, is completely committed to sex-neutral education. But this trend is sufficiently advanced in the United States to confine our attention here.

State Laws and Public Education

The most effective tactic for giving feminism access to the primary classroom has been the outlawing of books that violate feminist guidelines from the public schools of California, Massachusetts, and other states. Beyond securing local legal monopolies for feminist materials in public education, mandating these materials in a state as populous as California makes it uneconomical for publishers to defy feminist requirements elsewhere. It is pointless to produce a book banned in so large a market. A national monopoly is thus ensured.

The endorsement of feminism in the public school systems of the most populous states goes beyond textbooks. The regulations of chapter 622 of the State of Massachusetts, which prohibits discrimination in public schools, cover course requirements, guidance, curricula, extracurricular activities and "evaluation practices that result in affirmative action." The states of Alaska and Washington have passed laws with similar language. These laws and their implementing regulations are predictably attentive to minutiae. California's Department of Education circulates questionnaires to determine why girls do not take business education. It urges "revising the English curriculum to use non-sexist language," and issues career guidance pamphlets almost half of which—including one entitled "I Can Be Anything"—are designedly nontraditional in content. California authorities

192

have expressed concern about high-school students breaking up into "sex-segregated teams and games." In 1981 the Sacramento Unified School District warned that ridicule of male dancers by "male weightlifters" violated the principle of "equal access to classes."

The injection of feminism into the curriculum is equally hefty in what is sometimes called "Middle America." Section 257.25, paragraph 1 of the Iowa Code, enacted in 1978, reads: "The State Board shall promulgate rules to require that a multicultural, nonsexist approach is used by school districts. The education program shall be taught from a multicultural, nonsexist approach." Section 257 gave local school boards one year to develop a plan for "multicultural, nonsexist approaches to education" (a phrase that recurs as a single unit throughout relevant portions of the code) and five additional years to effect the plan. Paragraph 3.5(5)c(3) requires evidence of "systematic input by men and women, minority groups, and the handicapped in development and implementation of the plan," where "women" is clearly intended to refer to feminist groups. Integration of the races, the sexes, and the handicapped are treated by section 257 as entirely similar goals.

The areas of instruction to be covered are specific, the manner all-encompassing. Paragraph 3.5(6) of Iowa School Standards 670-3.5 (257) says: "The curriculum structure, content, instructional materials, and teaching strategies shall reflect the contributions and perspectives of women and men and diverse racial/ethnic groups." The same paragraph also provides for evaluation of "each pupil's progress" in learning that the English language has "sexism and cultural, racial bias." "Objective (b) of goal 1" is that "Students will be exposed to language patterns in the classroom through which they see broad potentials for themselves . . . regardless of their sex, race, culture, or disability." A mandated "self-evaluation checklist" to be used concurrently asks, "Do classroom teachers avoid oral language patterns which may be sexist or ethnocentric?" So far as I know, civil libertarians have not expressed concerned about Iowa's restrictions on the freedom of expression of its teachers.

The Iowa statutes share the obscurities of the publishers' guidelines. Males and females are supposed to be each unique without actually differing. In the interests of "help[ing] students develop positive and realistic self-conceptions regardless of race, sex, cultural background, or disability," schools are required to "foster the knowledge of, and respect and appreciation for the historical and contemporary contributions of men and women to society." If this is not to be the pleonastic demand that students appreciate society per se, the contributions of men and women to society must be assumed to be distinct. Yet Iowa schools are also instructed to minimize this distinctness:

> Do Life Science and Biology Curriculum include . . . the role science can play in promoting sex equality and how it may also be misused as a basis for promoting sexism? . . . Students will demonstrate an awareness of the common characteristics of men and women as well as of the physical sex differences which make each sex unique. These real sex differences should be taught in a manner which does not exaggerate them or reinforce traditional sex role stereotypes.

It is ultimately required that even these nonsocial, physical differences be downplayed:

> Goal 3: To help students understand that all persons have common needs, feelings and problems, while at the same time stimulating their respect for the uniqueness of each individual and cultural group. Inherent in this goal is the awareness that racism, sexism, and cultural bias and bias toward the disabled are social phenomena. Students will recognize when real sex differences, racial/cultural differences, or effects of disability are exaggerated in order to promote racist and sexist philosophies or discrimination against disabled citizens.

At no point is it suggested that acknowledgement of any nonanatomical sex differences might be legitimate, or that the misuses of racial differences have been incomparably more vicious than any use of sex differences. By the maxim that a law excludes what it easily could but does not include, it is illegal for a teacher to assert in an Iowa public school that any feature of society is the product of innate, nonanatomical sex differences.

When it injects highly controversial doctrines into the classroom, the state abandons the neutrality long regarded as essential to its role as educator. Public education forces parents to send their children to either a state-administered and financed school or to a privately supported school required to meet state standards. Teacher certification is occasionally proposed.[1] The original justification for this coercion was not the rights of children, but the duty of children to learn enough to become responsible democratic citizens. This argument limited state authority in education to those means deemed necessary to achieve the aim stipulated. The state can legitimately press literacy, numeracy, and basic factual information on children, because children will grow up to vote on matters affecting everybody; beyond that, the state has no right to abridge parental control. In particular, the basic rationale for public education confers on the state no right to impose empirically dubious ideologies.

Worries about public education have long focused on the danger of the state abusing its educational monopoly by indoctrinating children. Aware of this danger, the nineteenth-century founders of the common school system insisted that public schools confine themselves not only to basic subjects, but to values that were unanimously embraced by the surrounding society.

The public schools could teach industriousness and honesty, but they could not take sides in controversies. This neutrality has proven relatively easy to observe about the many emotionally charged issues which have no direct bearing on classroom procedures. Teachers need say nothing about tariffs or the gold standard. Feminism has been able to breach this neutrality because its totalistic character constantly puts teachers and administrators on the spot. As there is a distinctively feminist way to do everything in the classroom (and everywhere else), to fail to do things the feminist way is to do things the antifeminist way; feminism, unlike other issues of the day in the larger world, cannot be avoided in the classroom in the interests of amity.

The Federal Role

Numerous regulatory and judicial initiatives have placed the federal government firmly in support of feminist educational innovations.

Most federal initiatives derive from three laws: Title IV of the Elementary and Secondary Education Act (ESEA) of 1965, Title IX of the 1972 Education Amendments to the Civil Rights Act, and the 1974 Women's Educational Equity Act Program (WEEAP), designed in part to prepare the country for Title IX. Title IV of ESEA is a natural handmaiden of the publishers' guidelines. Under it, the federal government supports certain "exemplary" experimental programs that have the stated intention of "changing the values" of schools and students, and disseminating these programs through federal channels. It seems unlikely that a publisher would bring out a book that would risk being stigmatized as insufficiently "exemplary" or "experimental."

Among its many activities, WEEAP disburses millions of dollars to feminist organizations for the purpose of bringing sexism in schoolbooks to the attention of local authorities. WEEAP also funds the development and evaluation of curricula, textbooks, and other educational materials, its 1978 reauthorization including grants for "model projects" to "eliminate persistent barriers to educational equity" for women. WEEAP has given $300,000 to NOW for its "National Title IX Grass-Roots Action Campaign," $110,000 to the Rural Alternatives Institute of Huron, South Dakota, for developing a Title IX Puppet Kit for disabled first-grade girls, and $46,000 to the University of Delaware for "Reducing Discrimination in Educational Institutions," which may occur in "neural processing of information, such as credentials and performance records." A woman received $35,000 from WEEAP to write three "one-act plays about American women's historical achievements, the format for each a historical television 'talk show.' "[2]

A small sample of the titles available from the WEEAP publishing center conveys something of the character of the books, manuals, guides, and videotapes produced under these grants.[3] There is *Physical Educators for Equity*, about "the effects of sex role stereotyping"; *Thinking and Doing: Overcoming Sex-Role Stereotyping in Education; Together We Can*, on sex stereotypes and "sex-role assignments"; *Venture beyond Stereotypes; Teacher Skill Guide for Combatting Sexism; Sex Stereotyping in Education*, "with suggestions for minimizing sex-role differences"; *Beyond Pictures and Pronouns; Sexism in Teacher Education Textbooks; Checklists for Counteracting Race and Sex Bias in Educational Materials; Stereotyping in Curriculum; Becoming Sex Fair; Revising the Curriculum.* In the event that anything about "the effect of sex stereotyping in physical education" has somehow been omitted, *Physical Education for Equity, Eliminating Sex Bias in Physical Education,* and *Equity in Physical Education* are also available.

It might seem that WEEAP funding does nothing more than sustain the repetition of a single message, but WEEAP occasionally goes beyond that, as when it gave $244,000 to the Council on Interracial Books for Children (CIBC) for its Equity Models for Basal Readers project. CIBC had already prepared its own *Guidelines for Selecting Bias-Free Textbooks and Storybooks,* which, in addition to providing help in detecting sexism—defined in the *Guidelines* as failure to advocate role-changing—also observed that "Racism, sexism and economic exploitation are not occasional aberrations of the U.S. system, but deeply ingrained mechanisms of the national, social, and economic order." In view of these evils, the guidelines recommended that teachers emphasize illegal action as an effector of social change throughout American history. WEEAP funded CIBC to embody these principles in a "feminist model of a basic elementary textbook" which would seek to "mold human beings without counter-values that may help to restructure society." The resulting third-grade reader tells the story of the Gonzalez girl, whose father is jailed for punching a man about to repossess his truck. "I thought daddy was right to fight," she concludes, and the reader is invited to contrast her unhappy situation with life in Fidel Castro's Cuba. It is amusing to reflect that, in order to condemn American society with sufficient vehemence, the CIBC reader must endorse an extreme example of male aggressiveness.

Federal agencies also fund much of the research that inspires feminist classroom materials. I have already quoted from a 1980 NIE request for proposals for research on the "subtle classroom processes" that affect "sex equity in classroom interaction" and the "attempt to alter those classroom processes as a possible model for later widespread intervention efforts in the direction of greater equity."[4] The NIE is frank about the scope of the intervention that may be needed:

To the extent possible, intervention strategies should not depend upon exceptional environmental circumstances such as extraordinarily supportive
administrators, an unusual community, or the availability of particularly sex
fair curriculum materials. The intervention experience we do have suggests
that it may be necessary to adopt a strategy which helps teachers or students
learn about their own behavior.

Given the scope of these programs, it seems almost impertinent to mention that most of them are illegal. The authoritative statute covering this
area, the General Education Provision Act, expressly forbids the "direction,
supervision, or control" of curricula by a grantee, contractor, or employee
of the U.S. government. Yet, as the 1980 report of the President's
Advisory Committee for Women notes, WEEAP was created "to improve
instructional materials and approaches." Of the programs developed by
WEEAP between 1976 and 1980, 75 were devoted to "Curriculum
Development." (The leading category, subsuming 180 programs, was
"Awareness."[5]) WEEAP funding of a series of textbooks entitled *Sex and
Gender in the Social Sciences: Reassessing the Introductory Course* is certainly at odds with the spirit of the GEPA. And the National Endowment for
the Humanities must have been working in ignorance of the GEPA when it
funded the American Historical Association to train 200 teachers to
"integrate women's history into high-school curricula" and to "revise curricula in women's history." *Seven Years Later* recommends federal support
for "the development of new curricular materials" and "increased financial
assistance to women's studies programs." The Department of Labor spon-
sors a secondary school curriculum designed to weave lessons about avoiding sex stereotyping, and the need for early planning for nontraditional
careers for girls, into everyday subjects. GEPA is blatantly violated by the
federal funding of forty state-run "Sex Desegregation Centers" throughout
the United States, in which public school officials are helped to "identify
sex bias and sex-role stereotypes in books and other curricular materials
and develop methods of countering their effects on students," and in which
"non-discriminatory counselling materials and techniques" are provided.

The federal commitment to feminist pedagogy is relatively small in dollar
terms. WEEAP is budgeted at about $10 million annually. Yet the influence
of government support is not linear with funding. A dollar of Social Security, once spent, is gone forever. A dollar spent on a nonsexist reader is
preserved forever in the school library. The question of money becomes
more pertinent, however, in connection with Title IX. The federal government transfers over $13 billion yearly to colleges and universities alone;
conditions attaching to this disbursement are clearly consequential. Title IX
says that the money cannot go to sex discriminators: "No person shall, on

the basis of sex, be excluded from participation in, be denied the benefits of, or be subjected to discrimination under any education program or activity receiving federal financial assistance."

The case made for Title IX rested primarily on statistical studies—of the proportion of female to male elementary school principals, for instance—and it was perhaps inevitable that discrimination be given the meaning that generally accompanies use of statistical data. (The Department of Health, Education, and Welfare had already begun to extend the scope of Title IX by ruling that any institution that receives federal funds in any way is forbidden to discriminate throughout all its operations.[6]) The wording of Title IX suggests sex-blindness, and so it was sometimes interpreted. It was for instance understood to require the same dress code for boys and girls at any recipient institution, effectively ending all dress codes in the United States. (This implementing regulation has since been deleted.) In most cases, however, Title IX was understood to mandate whatever procedures are necessary to ensure statistical equality of outcome for the sexes. Guidance counselors were required to apprise students of the advantages of nontraditional careers and forbidden to apprise them of the psychological discomfort that might accompany pursuit of nontraditional careers. Course requirements with "differential results" were barred, so that in principle an institution cannot require calculus for engineering if no girls have taken calculus. (I know of no actual threats to defund on the basis of this provision.) Just as the clear antiquota language of the Civil Rights Act was interpreted to permit quotas, the clear antidiscrimination language of Title IX was interpreted to permit single-sex programs to remedy the effects of past discrimination, programs which invariably amount to preference for females. Title IX became the statutory justification cited by university administrators for imposing limits on the employment of men. It has had extensive consequences for athletics, as schools have been required to treat female athletes better than males of equal ability, and forbidden to extend sex-blind equity wherever equity threatened to yield unequal results. When Colgate College was reported to be spending more on boys' athletic footware than on girls', it was required to convene a committee to verify that this difference was due to the greater stress imposed on footwear by Colgate's physically heavier males. It should once again be emphasized that more parties are involved in Title IX exchanges than government, and the educational institutions who are free to avoid the constraints of Title IX by refusing to accept government funding. The funds used to induce schools to discriminate against men are coercively collected from the public.

There have been increasingly bold calls to use Title IX to override the First Amendment. The constraints on the words of guidance counselors would already appear to violate the Supreme Court doctrine that the denial of public benefits on the basis of speech is as violative of the free expression clause of the First Amendment as the imposition of state burdens on the basis of speech. The Sadkers tersely note that the federal government refuses on First Amendment grounds to use Title IX to forbid traditional textbooks, and the reader will not find an endorsement of this refusal by the Sadkers.[7] According to Riane Eisler, a central goal of Title IX and ERA, to "Equalize and strengthen the position of women in education," means that "Counselling, texts, and curricula must be re-examined and, where necessary, adjusted to the contemporary needs and aspirations of women."[8] Civil libertarians have shown no interest in these developments.[9]

The University

Assessing the impact on the university of the alliance of feminism and the state requires an understanding of academic freedom. Its basic components are freedom in admissions, curriculum, hiring, and promotion. Knowledge is best pursued when colleges may admit whomever they believe would best contribute to a spirit of intellectual community, a principle recognized in the continued existence of all-female and all-Black colleges. The same principle applies to the hiring of colleagues thought most likely to contribute to intellectual community, a freedom that includes the granting of permanent employment or tenure. Secure against dismissal for all but the most outrageous infractions, the tenured instructor can investigate and publish what would otherwise be taboo. (Even unorthodoxy that proves erroneous encourages the valuable thought that no holds are barred, and inspires further inquiry.) Freedom to hire and confer tenure requires confidentiality; public deliberation about tenure would jeopardize candor.

Truth is attainable only when scholars are free to follow their own standards, which have as little to do with equity as the standards of a monastery or an army. In recent years the judiciary and regulatory agencies have invaded academic freedom to further sexual egalitarianism and other values. Princeton University was obliged to convince a federal court of its right to discipline a student for plagiarism. Freedom of admission has been lost to claims of a right to admission backed up by Title IX, which bans any admission standard which, however unintentionally, adversely affects a protected group (but also permits and encourages special programs and admissions for these same groups). Curricular freedom was damaged by the decision of a federal court in *Lynn*[10] that the University of California at Irvine discriminated against women in downgrading its Women's Studies Program, a decision which curtails freedom of hiring as well, for UC Irvine is now legally required to hire someone to teach women's studies. Integral to all the forms of academic freedom is the university's right to allocate funds, also challenged by the court's decision that the failure of the University of California to provide day care is sex discrimination.

Perhaps because of its great size, the University of California has attracted considerable federal attention. In 1980, in response to an anonymous complaint by a female student that her course at the Law School at Berkeley was "too conservative" and contained "too much talk about violence," the Labor Department sent an investigator to audit courses at the Law School secretly, on the grounds that the complaint involved affirmative action "in the broadest sense."[11] The auditor predictably found sex discrimination and advised Berkeley to hold a consciousness-raising seminar. Berkeley protested, albeit more against the surreptitiousness and prejudgement of the Labor Department than the basic issue of its right to intervene in any manner.

Curtailment of the freedom to hire by the quota system does not differ in essentials from the general curtailment of the freedom to hire described in chapter 5. The present author, and I suspect any reader who has ever served on an academic hiring committee, has more than once been told by senior administrators that some appointment "has to go to a woman." Every hiring decision at every university must be approved by its Affirmative Action Office. One former graduate student of the present author was offered a position, then told a few days before he was to move his family to his new university that his appointment had been overruled by that university's Affirmative Action Office, which demanded a woman in his place. This man is now employed outside the academic world. Joseph Adelson's memoir of "living with quotas" captures the double-think by which academics deny to themselves that the quota system is omnipresent and discriminatory.[12] There is little reason to doubt that the incidents reported by Adelson and the incident just related by the present author are typical of the way all hiring decisions are now made, but even if they represent unique abuses of affirmative action, one need only imagine the outrage that would be expressed had some federal regulation even once lent itself to comparable discrimination against a woman. In the university, discrimination against men has become a matter of course.

Comparable worth has also been instrumental in bringing hiring decisions under the control of the state.[13] The Labor Department has sued Northwestern University for paying members of its mostly male departments, such as physics, more than members of its mostly female departments. In 1982 the clerical staff of Southern Alabama University was awarded $1.3 million in a federal comparable worth suit. In 1983, a federal court awarded women at the City University of New York $4.7 million solely on the basis of statistical evidence of wage discrimination, an award which unavoidably included payments to women who could not demonstrate any individual wrong. Many universities have preempted government action by equalizing salaries for ranks across departments.

Certain features of academic life make comparable worth litigation especially destructive. The Equal Pay Act, under which comparable worth litigation takes place, permits an investigation to be opened on the basis of a telephone call or anonymous tip. The EEOC, which is now responsible for enforcement of the Equal Pay Act, allows anonymity for complainants until there is a court case. (In few others areas of Western law is the accused not permitted to know his accuser during the preliminary stages of state action.) The university is more dependent on informal trust than most other institutions, and therefore more vulnerable to people who harbor grievances. The frictions caused by resentful students with low grades or colleagues who feel their work has been slighted are no different in kind from the frictious that erode morale in other organizations, but they are more destructive when the purpose of the organization is the pursuit of inquiry. In addition, private universities, unlike many other private organizations also vulnerable to comparable worth decisions, must compete against public purveyors of the same services in the form of state universities. A private university must pass along increased labor costs and court settlements as higher tuition, but state universities can secure more generous appropriations from state legislatures.

Government intervention in hiring decisions has received what should have been the unlikely support of the American Association of University Professors, an organization founded by Arthur O. Lovejoy and John Dewey to further academic freedom. The AAUP has testified at federal hearings in favor of "goals and timetables."[14] Most of the studies and advocacy literature it produces appeal only tacitly to the government for enforcement of quotas, but the appeal is occasionally more explicit. A position paper entitled "Guidelines for Equality: A Proposal," urges colleges to prepare statistical data for litigation—presumably against themselves—and it urges the EEOC to be more ready to sue. It also suggests that the EEOC rule that charges of discrimination may be brought "without naming an individual complainant" in order to "prevent intimidation and retaliation."[15] Since all legal action creates the possibility of reprisal against complainants and witnesses, the AAUP was remiss in failing to explain why all criminal and civil proceedings should not be conducted anonymously. One must conclude that the AAUP now values equality, pursued if necessary by Star Chamber methods, over academic freedom.

Tenure would normally have provided an insurmountable barrier to assaults on appointive freedom, since it allows colleges to dismiss, after a suitable trial period, any incompetent it is forced to hire. In recent years, however, the judiciary has also curtailed this prerogative in the name of fighting discrimination. It is not surprising that feminists should have appealed to the judiciary to overthrow the tenure system, since no sooner was affirmative action established than the claim was made that women were second-class academic citizens because they were not getting tenure in proportion to their numbers.

The courts have listened sympathetically to this claim. Although they have yet to find the Ph.D. requirement itself inherently discriminatory because of its disparate impact on women, the courts have on several occasions awarded tenure to women who have not met department or institutional requirements of an advanced degree or additional course work. The courts have been extremely sympathetic to the argument from statistical underrepresentation. In 1981 the New Jersey Superior Court ruled that since only 11 percent of the faculty of Stockton State College was female, Stockton State was obliged to grant tenure to Jeanne-Andrée Nelson, a French instructor. Stockton State had previously sought to limit the size of its tenured faculty, but the court held that Stockton State's affirmative action program superseded this normal faculty prerogative. The presiding judge concurred with a union arbiter that Nelson was a "prime tenure candidate" on the basis of "the facts shining through conflicting academic judgements." Those familiar with academia will recognize "conflicting academic judgement" as a euphemism like the theater world's "mixed reviews," frequently enough by itself to disqualify a candidate for tenure. The court, in this case, overrode the faculty on a point of academic judgement.

The most widely publicized tenure case involved James Dinnan, a member of the committee of the Department of Education of the University of Georgia which denied tenure to Maija Blaubergs. Miss Blaubergs claimed that she had been discriminated against because she was a feminist, and demanded, contrary to confidentiality, to know the vote of each member of her committee. When Dinnan expressed willingness to disclose to a federal court the criteria by which he had voted, but refused to disclose the vote itself, he received ninety days for contempt. The Supreme Court refused to hear Dinnan's case, and the AAUP declined to assist him on the grounds that the case involved "two good principles in collision." The AAUP identified one as "fighting discrimination," but declined to identify the other.

When Brown University denied tenure to four female instructors, these women countered with a Title VII lawsuit. As the implementing regulations of Title VII subject universities to the same rules as other workplaces, Brown was estopped from dismissing the complainants until their suit was heard. Pretrial setbacks convinced Brown that, despite its considerable endowment, it could not afford to defend itself further. The ensuing out-of-court settlement conferred tenure on the four complainants and $252,000 in legal fees. All told, Brown had spent over $1,000,000, mostly in legal fees, in a case that did not get to court. No doubt administrators at other universities drew appropriate conclusions about the prospects of success in denying tenure to their female applicants.

The ground rules for discerning discrimination in the university may change in the near future. It has become increasingly common to encounter the claim that standard promotional criteria are discriminatory because they emphasize published papers, conferences, attendance at conferences, peer recommendation, and similar evidence of scholarly achievement. These criteria favor men over women who temporarily leave teaching to have a child. It is admitted that bearing a child hinders scholarly production as normally understood, but, so it is now being claimed, childrearing may make a woman a better teacher when she returns to her position, and should be treated as equivalent to several scholarly articles. This argument is likely to be developed in tandem with an (incompatible) appeal to compensation. I have asked academic feminists who profess to equate children with learned articles whether having a child is not, after all, a voluntary decision to forgo the advantages of scholarly activity for the alternative advantages of motherhood; one replied that because of the pressures applied by the expectations of her father and husband, having a child had *not* been a free decision on her part. It is not unthinkable that the courts will eventually be asked to decide whether motherhood contributes to one's scholarly abilities, and, if not, whether it is fair to deny tenure to female scholars, forced by social pressure to bear children, for not publishing as much as men.

Sexual Harassment in the University

In addition to the more traditional academic freedoms, freedom of speech in the classroom has fallen under challenge in the course of the battle against "sexual harassment." There are undoubtedly objectionable practices that "sexual harassment" might denote, such as threatening to withhold a high grade from a sexually uncompliant student, but this term is customarily stretched to cover a good deal more.

In 1979 the National Advisory Council on Women's Educational Programs (NACWEP) followed its "Call for information on the Sexual Harassment of Students" with *Sexual Harassment: A Report on the Sexual Harassment of Students*.[16] *Sexual Harassment* contains numerous undocumented accounts of intimidation and exploitation; some of them may strain the credulity of the reader, but it would be surprising if a score of obnoxious incidents could not be culled from the experiences of the 6 million females enrolled in American universities. The crucial question is the typicality of these incidents. The section of this 86-page document entitled "Frequency" is 150 words in length, and concludes that "estimates of frequency are beyond the scope of this report." Nor does *Sexual Harassment* explain why, even assuming such incidents to occur frequently, they should be a matter for the law. The capacity of the university to discipline itself in matters other than public order has long been recognized, and universities themselves have always understood the impropriety of exchanging sex for grades—just as it has had the wisdom to disregard anonymous complaints. (In fact, the university's traditionally hard line against sexual fraternization was softened by the conviction, urged by feminists among others in the 1960s, that the *loco parentis* doctrine was an antiquated, repressive pillar of patriarchy.) *Sexual Harassment* nevertheless outlines elaborate steps by which universities can, in concert with their Affirmative Action offices, use Title VII and Title IX to "publicize prohibitions . . . increase awareness and conduct consciousness raising among faculty and students."

And indeed actions have been brought, and warnings posted on all campuses. An entire wall of a classroom building at the University of Adelaide is covered by a poster reading "Sexual Harassment Is Everywhere." This campaign does not seem to be taken very seriously, but it does raise serious questions of principle (some of which I discuss in chapter 12). NACWEP finds "great promise" in treating "words and acts causing mental or emotional disturbance" as tortious, and is satisfied that a remark is harassing if, regardless of intent, its effect is to "interfere with the learning environment," an implication drawn from *Continental Can Co. v. Minnesota*.[17] It is also taken as clear from *Miller*[18] that institutions are strictly liable for sexual harassment and must act affirmatively to prevent it, which is why universities must establish grievance procedures. Failure to provide an "equitable solution" of complaints is itself construable as sex discrimination. Complaints may remain anonymous.

The definitions of "sexual harassment" supplied by those who find it a problem seem tailored to conflict with the emotions distinctive to the academic setting. The feminist conception, which lies a considerable distance from the sex-for-grades paradigm, involves "psychological coercion" and "power relations":

> Sexual harassment in the classroom is harassment in which the faculty member covertly or overtly uses the power inherent in the status of a professor to threaten, coerce, or intimidate a student to accept sexual advances.[19]

This concentration on "power relations" leads Adrienne Minnich to urge the government to recognize that "in any classroom situation where a man grades a woman, a sexual advance of any sort constitutes harassment."[20] On this definition, a teacher who innocently asks a student for a date has committed an actionable offence. While not fully endorsing this proposal, NACWEP defines sexual harassment quite broadly as *exploitation of a difference in authority to compel a choice between unwelcome alternatives.* . . . It is not sex so much as the exploitation of power which can lead to problems. . . . "A department head and a teaching assistant aren't evenly matched."[21]

NACWEP is prepared to accept the implication that if a department head asks a graduate teaching assistant for a date and gracefully accepts rejection, *that alone* constitutes harassment: "The student wonders if her response to his question will affect her grade."

Indeed, academic criticism of feminism might well be construable as harassment under current regulations. An instructor's intent to make a merely theoretical point (say, that boy babies act differently from girl babies) would not absolve him, since intent is irrelevant. His words might cause distress and be construed as "directed at students of only one sex"—a further NACWEP criterion—if, as is generally the case, all the feminists in his class are female. The interpretation of "sexual harassment" that will eventually become binding on the academic community lies entirely in the hands of the federal judiciary, charged with interpreting Title IX and Title VII, under which the EEOC's sexual harassment regulations (see chapter 12) have been issued.

Beyond an obvious desire to make sexual relations problematic, one detects in these expansive understandings of sexual harassment an echo of the "radical" doctrine that the extant "power relations" between the sexes that force her compliance make any sexual overture to a woman by a man essentially rapacious. In plain fact, the great numbers of women in higher education guarantee romances between men and more junior women. No coercion of any sort is involved in the vast majority of these matches, and the happy marriages that many of these matches have produced are less likely to occur in an atmosphere charged with hostility to sexual awareness.

The campaign against sexual harassment, like the other feminist intrusions onto the campus, has been marked by the silence of academics, who are not usually known for their uncritical approval of government policies that affect the university. Many campuses permit the use of facilities by feminist organizations that keep confidential files on "sexist" professors. Male academics above all seem disposed to interpret the initiatives of their feminist colleagues as temporary distortions of a fundamentally sound idea. These male academics assume that their feminist colleagues share an allegiance to the values of free inquiry that would, in a showdown, lead them to subordinate their ideological agenda to the preservation of institutional autonomy. This is a mistake. Adherents of an ideology which repudiates objective truth can be expected to shape their research for political ends, and academic feminists have not hesitated to advocate just this course. According to a joint resolution of the Coordinating Committee on Women in the History Profession and the Conference Group on Women's History of the American Historical Association: "We believe as feminist scholars we have a responsibility not to allow our scholarship to be used against the interests of women struggling for equity in our society." A number of feminist historians have urged that it not be said publicly that women tend to make different life choices than men, *even if this is true,* lest the "political consequences" of such candor be adverse to their goals.[22] The loyalty of such individuals to the ideals of the university is very much open to question.

Notes

1. "The Department of Education should develop incentives to encourage States to promote the development of sex-fair practices by requiring educational personnel to demonstrate their knowledge of nonsexist practices as a basis for certification and periodic recertification." *Voices for Women* (Washington, D.C.: U.S. Government Printing Office, 1980), p. 32.
2. See *Annual Report of the Women's Educational Equity Act Program 1980* (Washington, D.C.: U.S. Department of Education, 1981).
3. See *Resources for Educational Equity,* 1981–82 (Newton, Mass.: Educational Development Center, 1982).
4. National Institute of Education Requests for Proposal RFP-NIE-R-80-0018 (Washington, D.C.: Department of Health, Education, and Welfare, April 30, 1981).
5. *Annual Report of the National Advisory Council on Women's Educational Programs* (Washington, D.C.: Department of Education, 1981), Appendix A.
6. According to the National Advisory Council on Women's Educational Programs, "The impact of Title IX has been felt throughout the nation at every educational level [because] virtually all school districts and most colleges and universities received Federal financial assistance through grants, contracts, or loans under programs ranging from school lunch subsidies to college housing constructions."
7. David and Myra Sadker, *Sex Equity Handbook for Schools* (New York: Longman's, 1982), p. 45.
8. *Equal Rights Handbook,* p. 193.
9. In 1984 the Supreme Court ruled (*Grove City v. Bell,* 459 US 1199) that Title IX is "program-specific," so that a university need apply its implementing regulations only to those of its operations which receive federal funds. Congressional critics of *Grove City* have proposed a bill to restore and extend the pre-*Grove City* meaning of Title IX by requiring that Title IX regulations cover all recipients by "transfer" of federal funds. This proposal, designated "House Resolution 1" to indicate the importance accorded to it by the House leadership, does not exempt recipients with fewer than fifteen employees, as does Title VII of the Civil Rights Act.
10. *Lynn v. University of California,* 656 F 2nd 1337 (1983).
11. See *Welcome to Federal U., Campus #1037: Regulation and Academic Freedom* (Washington, D.C.: House Republican Research Committee, April 22, 1980).
12. Joseph Adelson, "Living with Quotas," *Commentary* (May 1978): 23–29.

13. See Bernice Sandler, "A New Weapon in the Fight for Equal Pay," *Chronicle of Higher Education* (February 26, 1973): 6.
14. See "Affirmative Action Plans," *Academe: The AAUP Bulletin* (January–February 1982): 15a, fn. 2.
15. Mary W. Gray and Alice T. Schafer, "Guidelines for Equality: A Proposal," *Academe* (December 1981): 351–54.
16. Washington, D.C.: Department of Education, August 1980.
17. Minn. S.C. 1980.
18. *Miller v. Bank of America,* 20 FEP Cases 462 (9th Cir. 1979).
19. This definition is attributed by NACWEP to the assistant vice-president of the University of Minnesota.
20. Adrienne Minnich, "Seduction in Academe," *Psychology Today* (February 1978): 82–108.
21. NACWEP attributes the quoted remark to a memo distributed by Stanford University in 1978.
22. See "Scholars' Conflict in Sears Sex-Bias Case Sets Off War in Women's History," *Chronicle of Higher Education* (February 5, 1986): 1–8. Cited in this article is feminist historian Ellen DuBois: "We, as women's historians, owe our jobs and our ability to pursue our scholarship to feminism. We have an obligation to remain honest to our feminist origin by, at the very least, ensuring that our scholarship is not used for an anti-feminist purpose." Also cited is Alice Kessler-Harris, another "historian of women," on whether it was morally permissible to testify on behalf of Sears, Roebuck, & Company in a sex discrimination case in which Sears contended that the underrepresentation of women in its managerial levels is due to the different life choices made by women: "If Sears wins this case, the political consequences will be to help the Reagan Administration war on affirmative action. Those political consequences should not be taken lightly." The suggestion that truth is primary—that the "war" in question might be justified if statistical underrepresentation is due to differences in life choices—is never addressed.

10

Sports

You put together a bunch of 10-year-old boys and girls and they'll choose up teams, and with rare exceptions they'll play among themselves. They will not cross sexually unless somebody comes along and forces them too—they know better.[1]

It is sometimes said that sports are too important to be tampered with by social engineers, and that forcing young boys to compete against young girls may impair the development of male confidence. Both claims are plausible, particularly the second, but they are not my reasons for discussing the topic of sports. Rather, sex equality in sports offers an unusually pure study in feminist dialectic.

Literally understood, sex equality as applied to sports is the claim that females are as innately gifted at athletics as males, that all female performance deficits are caused by girls' having been socialized away from strenuous activities like hitting baseballs and throwing footballs, and that in a world free of sexist stereotyping half the quarterbacks in professional football would be women. This claim may seem too preposterous to be plausibly attributed to anybody, and it is not the pivot on which arguments for equal opportunity or government policy turn, but it is nonetheless regularly propounded and must be considered at the outset. I mentioned in chapter 2 that NOW views sex differences in basketball skill as a "legacy of the past." It has been confidently asserted that "if we gave little girls footballs to play with and gave little boys dolls, girls would grow up to be big and muscular like the stereotypical man, and boys would grow up to be soft and nurturing, like the stereotypical woman."[2] At the time contemporary feminism was coming to the fore, popular magazines ran numerous articles to the effect that the "muscle gap" was closing. (Much of the evidence for the coming closure was the performance of fillies in horse races.) Air Force undersecretary Antonia Chayes testified before Congress in 1979 that the military academies were closing the gap in strength between men and women.

Feminists who do not accept this hypothesis nevertheless respect it. Brenda Feigen-Festeau admits that her husband beats her at squash, but "that may have been as much a matter of opportunity as biology: he's been able to play squash whenever he's wanted to and on courts where I wasn't allowed because of my sex."[3] She allows that the average man will "probably" beat the better-than-average woman, noting that "scientists chalk this up" to physiological factors, as if it were an arcane matter divorced from everyday experience. Letty Pogrebin has this explanation for her husband's superiority at softball: "Bert spent every day of his childhood playing outdoors while I was guarding my reproductive organs."[4]

The same idea is accorded serious consideration by feminist scientists. Marian Lowe, a member of the Chemistry Department of Boston University, declares "there is growing evidence that differences in physical strength come as much from life experience as from innate factors."[5] (Lowe does not cite the evidence.) Lowe might be charitably understood as suggesting that the heritability of anatomical factors relevant to size and strength is .5. This would still be incorrect—the heritability of height, for instance, is .9—but in fact Lowe believes it to be an open question whether *any* physical difference between the sexes is genetic in origin:

> I do not mean to suggest that if females and males were raised in the same way there would be no average difference in strength or height. At this point we have no way of knowing what would happen under those circumstances.[6]

I have been unable to locate a single feminist source which unconditionally acknowledges an innate sex difference in the physical factors relevant to athletic performance, and I frankly doubt that the reader knows of any, even though the most radical feminists are *supposed* to admit anatomical differences. The reason for this reluctance is plain. If the general features of society are not supposed to be due to biology to any significant extent, *all* biological sex differences must be minimized to the point of denial. Once differences in outcome for men and women in any facet of society are conceded to be based on biology, common sense armed with Occam's Razor will want to explain other facets of society similarly. As the psychomotor skills involved in athletic performance are continuous with the skills involved in other activities, it is extremely unlikely that innate sex differences manifest themselves in sports and nowhere else. To suppose that a sports difference alone is innate is on a par with positing an innate ability to draw landscapes but no other subject. Either there are innate sex differences with broad manifestations, or there are no innate differences. Faced with this dilemma, feminists seize the second horn.

Sex Differences Relevant to Athletic Performance

Men are taller, heavier, and more muscular than women, and these advantages are nearly wholly genetic. If men and women were raised under identical conditions, the male means for these variables would exceed the female means by about as much as they do now. The mean male-female height difference is constant across tall and short families: Phenotype varies as genotype varies, with little regard for environment. Between-race mean differences in IQ are sometimes explained by the hypothesis that the within-population heritability of IQ is high while between-population differences are environmentally caused, but whatever the merits of this hypothesis as it concerns IQ, the within-sex heritability of height cannot be high while the between-sex difference is environmentally caused unless (as is the case with Blacks and Whites) the sexes constitute separate breeding populations, which they manifestly do not. Girls could probably be made as strong as boys if the environments in which both were raised were *un*equal—if for instance boys were bound hand and foot for the first ten years of their lives while girls received two hours of athletic training every day—but that is irrelevant to whether the sexes are innately similar with respect to strength. (It is also irrelevant to equality as a normative goal: If it is permissible to manipulate environments differentially to reduce the manifestations of innate sex differences, it is equally permissible to manipulate the environment to expand observed sex differences; why not hogtie girls at birth and give every boy weight training?)

Because many of the sex differences relevant to athletics are also relevant to military task performance, they have been studied extensively by the U.S. Army. It has ben found that women have only 55–58 percent of the upper body strength of men; due to the higher fat/muscle ratio in female bodies, the average woman is only 80 percent as strong as a man of identical weight. Average female leg extensor strength is 65 percent of male, and average female trunk flexor strength is 68 percent of male.[7] Again controlling for body size, women exhibit only 60 percent of the shoulder strength of men. Average female aerobic capacity is 78 percent that of the male. Extended training does not narrow the male/female difference in muscle strength and aerobic power.[8]

Preadolescent girls are as large as preadolescent boys in terms of overall weight and height, but preadolescent boys already have a lower fat/muscle ratio. A study by the Youth Sports Institute of Michigan State University found that boys were stronger than girls and ran faster by the age of seven and a half, while girls were more flexible by that age.[9] As every parent observes, boys are more interested than girls in throwing. That girls "throw like girls" from an early age is apparently due to sex differences in neural control of the throwing motion. Sex differences in accuracy and distance of throwing appear by age three and a half; by five, right-handed boys but not girls begin to throw balls in a vertical plane from the side of their shoulders by shifting their weight from the right foot to the left.[10] (Presumably the mirror-image change occurs for left-handers as well.) This is the familiar motion of the baseball pitcher, and it is also involved in throwing footballs, javelins, and right crosses; coordination of the same shift in weight from back to front foot is necessary for hitting baseballs, golfballs, tennis balls, handballs, and hockey pucks.

These raw mean statistical differences are compound in their significance for sports, since most sports require a combination of size, strength, speed, and coordination. Let us say that the ideal high-school running back should weigh 200 pounds, bench-press 200 pounds, and run 100 yards in 12 seconds. If among adolescents there are 50 males for each female who can perform each task, and 20 200-pound males for every 200-pound female, there will be *50,000* males capable of being outstanding running backs for every female. Even this understates the resultant difference, since the relevant variables interact; because of sex differences in the muscle/fat ratio, there will be many more fleet 200-pound males than fleet 200-pound females.

The closing of the muscle gap has been very partial, occurring mainly in long-distance running events. There has been no appreciable closing in any sport requiring strength, jumping, or throwing, except when females have masculinized their bodies with steroids. It would also be a mistake to extrapolate the improvement in female track time linerarly into the future. The fall in best female times is proportionally greater than the fall in the best male time in the same events in the same periods when women began to participate in previously all-male activities. Top female performance may be expected to stabilize as women approach their physiological limits. The relative performance levels of men and women at tennis stabilized about forty years ago; the best female time for the marathon appears to be stabilizing at about 11 percent below the best male time. There are few quantum leaps in male performance because men are already near their physiological limits in a number of events. Human bones would shatter under the stress of a 7.5 second 100-yard dash. Quantum improvements like Bob Beamon's 28-foot, 6-inch long jump are bound to become ever rarer.

There might be a handful of females who could hold their own with the college basketball varsity in some divisions of play, but it is doubtful that any female could play in the National Basketball Association. No female has even finished in the top fifty of a marathon. Probably the best evidence for male athletic superiority is the newsworthiness of a female trying out for a male team. A number of females have won places on male teams by clever legal footwork, but just about the only girls cited in the egalitarian literature as having made teams on merit are Mary Ellen Garrity of Pompton Lakes, N.J., who competed on her high-school fencing team,[11] and two girls from Post Falls, Idaho, who were on their high-school wrestling team (although they are not reported to have wrestled any boys). No female has ever made the college varsity in any major sport.

Equality

To end the reader's embarrassment at being asked to take nonsense seriously enough to see it criticized, let us turn to two more modest notions of "sex equality in sports." The first is one the average person would be happy to endorse. The second probably exceeds what the ordinary person would endorse, but it is entailed by the percept that each person is to be treated as an individual, without regard to sex. Feminists categorically reject both.

First, most people would agree that girls should be allowed to play anything they want to. The average parent probably approves of sex-discriminatory rules against females on public high school football teams, but he would certainly not object to girls having a private game of tackle football. Parents are just as interested in their daughters' health as their sons', and many women enjoy athletic activities of all sorts. School girls were playing field hockey by the beginning of the twentieth century, and a 1922 magazine advertisement for gingham shows five little girls playing vigorously with a ball, as if the sight were entirely unremarkable.[12] (A number of advertisements from this period have similar themes.) The average parent does not expect boys and girls to be interested in the same activities, and he would never dream of forcing them to play together, but he is otherwise egalitarian.

This broad egalitarianism cannot be what feminists are advocating. They describe equality in sports as a distant dream rather than an everyday reality, as a goal opposed by many rather than accepted by all. Unless they are completely uninformed about what most people think, feminists must have something else in mind.

Second, since people are to be evaluated only as the basis of their individual abilities, boys and girls of all ages should be allowed, perhaps made, to play together. Boys and girls should be judged by uniform sex-neutral standards and compete for berths on the same teams.

This is what feminists have demanded for small children, and what governments at various levels have mandated. No single-sex team composed of children under 12 may use public facilities in Minnesota. A state court determined that females have a right under the Fourteenth Amendment to try out for previously all-male teams fielded by public schools.[13] Since it is natural to suppose that feminists would stigmatize any other arrangement as "sexist," it is surprising to find that feminists firmly reject this version of sex equality. To be sure, denial to a girl of the right to try out for a boy's team still causes indignation, but feminists do *not* wish to see boys permitted to try out for girls' teams, and the government has followed this lead by forbidding sex neutrality in adolescent and postadolescent school sports. And the reason feminists reject sex-neutral standards in sports is, quite simply, that men outperform women. What Brenda Feigen-Festeau calls "pure" equality is undesirable because

> the very best girls are not as good as the very best boys. In any high school or college, integrating teams on an "ability only" basis could [sic] result in a new form of exclusion of women players.[14]

The new basis of exclusion would, of course, be merit. But if sports are not to be "integrated" on a merit basis, what is left? "[W]e're left with the separate-but-equal solution"[15]: Separate teams for boys and girls, with boys' teams competing amongst themselves and vice versa. Although Feigen-Festeau's chief worry is that under this arrangement girls good enough for boys' teams would be penalized, it is more realistic to worry about the many boys good enough for the girls' teams but forbidden to try. Feigen-Festeau's slogan obscures her suggestion, which ought to read "separate but unequal."

It is difficult enough to reconcile this proposal with sexual equality, but Feigen-Festeau goes further: "Equal financial attention must be paid to both sexes. . . . Coaches of women's teams must be paid as much as coaches of men's teams. . . . Scholarships must be equalized." These further demands immediately raise questions of practicality and equity. Colleges profit from their major sports, and girls' sports do not, with rare exceptions, attract the gate of boys' sports. Attendance for girls' basketball is often boosted by scheduling games between regular boys' events, but it remains weak. It has proven extremely difficult to put all-female athletics on a paying basis at any level: A woman's professional basketball league folded the year it was formed despite support from a major bank, Manufacturer's Hanover Trust. Asking male and female athletics to be funded at equal levels is asking male athletics to subsidize female athletics, or, since resources are limited, for the termination of some male athletic programs.

Feminists are impatient with this problem. Letty Pogrebin asks: "Even if schools did show a profit on male-only policies, since when is making money an excuse to discriminate?" But raising the banner of justice leads one to ask how just it is for female athletes to be supported at the level of superior male athletes by the male athletes themselves. Such subsidization is far removed indeed from rewarding persons according to individual ability. A British court implemented this new idea of equity by interpreting the will of Cecil Rhodes, which clearly reserves Rhodes scholarships to *men* displaying outstanding athletic and academic qualities, to mean "men and women." This would have been no more than judicial usurpation had the Rhodes Foundation subsequently held men and women to the same standards, but it has not. Female applicants are only required to excel in female athletics, while males must excel in male athletics. Assuming a continuous distribution of academic achievement throughout the population of male and female candidates, Rhodes scholarships are awarded to females who are academically no better than, and athletically inferior to, male Rhodes scholars, and athletically inferior to as well as academically no better than some males who do not quality.

Or consider the distribution of prizes for the New York Marathon. As its primary condition for providing the municipal services necessary for holding this event New York City demanded in 1984 that the female winner's prize money equal the male's, a demand made and accepted by the organizers of the Marathon in full knowledge that dozens of men would beat the best female and yet win nothing. As no more than 18 percent of the field in the New York Marathon has ever been female, the winning female thus receives, for beating 18 percent of her competitors, precisely what the winning male receives for beating all his competitors.

Equality for women in sports has thus evolved into equal support and reward for inferior performance. It would be a mistake to credit feminists with partial fidelity to their official standard of sex neutrality for urging that preadolescent sports be completely unisex. It is more likely that feminists simply do not know how early sex differences in athletic performance appear.

The Government Concurs

Like so many feminist arguments, the demand for equity in sports could be dismissed as a curiosity had it not become public policy, in this case through the regulations implementing Title IX. Rather than requiring recipient institutions to let boys and girls compete for positions on the same teams, these regulations forbid the practice as discriminatory. Recipient institutions are required instead to maintain separate teams for males and females to be funded at equal levels, with the girls' teams permitted to use standards below those of the boys'. (In practice this invariably happens.) Colleges are thus legally required to reserve scholarships for females who are inferior in ability to hundreds of males who, presumably, would eagerly compete for these scholarships if the law allowed sex-neutral standards.

The Title IX Regulations presume differences in expenditures for equipment, training facilities, and per diem allowances to be prima facie discriminatory. Total funds actually spent by schools for female athletics remain less than those for male athletics because contact sports are exempt from those regulations. The exemption was granted over strenuous objections by feminists, who seem prepared to admit only those sex differences in athletic performance that can be cancelled by legislation disadvantageous to men.

The contact sport issue continues to vex sexual egalitarians. In October 1985 a federal judge overturned a New York State Regents rule barring girls from play on boys' contact sports teams in high school, and the State Regents subsequently revised their rules to allow girls to try out for boys' football teams. At the same time, it deferred deciding whether to permit boys to try out for girls' teams, which in consistency it would seem committed to doing. At about the same time, a New Jersey high-school girl won in court the right to play on her no-cut high-school football team under a state law against sex discrimination, which prompted a New Jersey boy to sue his high school for sex discrimination for removing him from the girls' field hockey team. An administrative judge ruled for the boy, but the New Jersey Commission of Education ruled against him on the grounds that *even though excluding boys from the girls' field hockey team apparently violates state law,* it is "substantially related to accomplishing an important government goal," namely increasing the participation of girls in sports.[16] This decision may be ascribed the single virtue of making clear that the animosity toward men characteristic of "radical" feminism has become institutionalized in the law.

Sports, Merit, Quotas

The feminist idea of equality in sports highlights the conflict between sexual egalitarianism and merit. Sports have always been the preeminent activity in which talent shines through. Willie Mays was unarguably a better hitter than Willie Stargell because Mays hit more home runs, drove in more runs, and batted for a higher average. And sports, more than any other activity, connects merit to reward. The race may not always be to the swift, commented Damon Runyon, but that is the way to bet. Clumsy duffers sometimes beat opponents with impeccable form; the strongest weight lifter may lose a tournament when weakened by a head cold. Harvey Haddix once lost a perfect game. But these anomalies are memorable precisely because of their rarity.

This is why sports continue to embarrass advocates of racial and sexual preference. When quotas in sports were offered in *DeFunis* as a reductio ad absurdum of all quotas, the NAACP, an amicus party to the case, accused the plaintiff of stirring passions but did not address the argument.[17] The idea of minimal competency commonly proposed in the quota literature as a basis for hiring, is absurd when applied to sports. Standards are clear there, the outcome vital, and all are striving to excel. Were a professional basketball team to hire the best available Jew with a minimally competent jump shot, team performance would fall below a competitive level. The resulting coordination problem could be solved by legally requiring every other team to hire a Jew with a minimally competent jump shot, thereby depressing the level of play still further, perhaps below that needed to attract paying customers. Athletic excellence is readily detectable and detected by fans eager to pay to see it.

A second lesson of sports disagreeable to egalitarians is that small differences at the margin make large differences. Nobody remembers the man who ran second to Roger Bannister, or the team that has lost the most superbowls. The "small" difference between the best male and female marathon times ("small" compared to that between the best female marathon time and that of your next-door neighbor) guarantees that dozens of men will always beat the fastest woman—and that, as Steven Goldberg points out, any woman who sets her heart on running the world's fastest marathon is going to be disappointed. The lesson that small differences in skill or effort make all the difference when everything is on the line is not lost on people at other important junctures in their lives. The difference in skill between an excellent and a merely competent brain surgeon is small compared to the difference in skill between a merely competent brain surgeon and your next-door neighbor. But what do you want when you have a brain tumor—competence or excellence?

The law of the margin is another way of saying that the failure of socially observed group differences to match the statistical contours of the underlying innate group differences may easily be a further effect of those differences rather than an arbitrary social artifact. If the average Blue runs 15 percent faster than the average Green, it is in no way "natural" that the Blues win 15 percent more frequently than the Greens in a long series of races. That will happen if the competitors assort themselves randomly, but after it becomes clear that Blues are "good at" running, running will attract the fastest Blues, who are faster than virtually all the Greens, while the fastest Greens, who can beat most Blues but not the fastest Blues, will direct their energies to other pursuits. Over time Blues will come to dominate running to an extent disproportional to their initial advantage. (This mechanism may currently be turning basketball into a "Black" sport.) The Blues' eventual near-monopoly on running is *no less natural* a product of the gene which controls the relevant differences in Blue/Green musculature than are the proteins produced by this gene. The social effects of the genetic difference might seem artificial rather than natural because they can be blocked by tampering with races between Blues and Greens, but the distinction is unreal. The chemical effect of a gene can also be blocked by tampering with cell chemistry. The biochemical effects of a gene are no less exaggerated than its social effects; biochemical consequences differ from the social only in the number and kind of mediating mechanism they require. The chemical environment which mediates the gene's protein production is itself partially determined by the gene, to be sure, and for this reason one might wish to deny that this environment is an external factor mediating the action of the gene. But the feedback which transmutes the raw physiological Blue/Green differences into socially observed differences—like the feedback which transmutes raw sex differences into socially observed differences—is itself partially determined by those physiological differences and, for the same reason, is not an external factor mediating those differences. As Goldberg says, there is no outside experimenter for society.

Merit, Reward, Justice

Reserving for girls scholarships that are denied to superior boys not quite up to the level required for male scholarships seems almost designed to confirm the cynical belief that reward depends on birth and connection. A familiar line of criticism of liberal democracy ridicules success as a matter only of knowing how to play the game, and dismisses any form of objective testing as indicative only of test-taking skills, acquired by a middle-class birth. The system, assert the critics, is rigged all the way through.

Sports have long served to rebut this criticism. There could be no gainsaying the Irish, Italian, Jewish, Black, and Puerto Rican slum kids who reached the apex of boxing and other sports solely through skill. Southern White baseball players who in 1940 would not have stayed in a hotel admitting Blacks were by 1960 eager to have Black teammates, after it had become clear that Blacks could help win pennants. This practical vindication of democratic culture does not tolerate equal reward for unequal talent. Egalitarians have claimed the fix is in, and then proven their point by inserting the fix themselves.

The doublethink needed for believing that legally protected lower standards amount to equality is also useful when extolling the fivefold increase in female participation in high-school sports and twofold increase in college sports that has occurred since 1971.[18] In that same period, 1,100 boys' teams have been dropped by schools unable to afford matching girls' teams. When mentioned at all, these and similar costs to males are usually dismissed as "the price of equity," much as are the costs to male victims of quotas. The large number of medals won for the United States by its female athletes in the 1984 Olympics was widely cited at the time as vindicating Title IX. Some recognition was given to the decency of Eastern Bloc athletes for staying home; less recognition was given to those American males who might have won medals had funds for their training not been diverted by Title IX. Unless in a world without Title IX those males would have gotten those funds as a direct result of discrimination against the very females who actually did get them under Title IX, the denial of training to those males is a burden imposed on them by the state just because they happen to be males.

Realizing Your Full Potential

Something deeper than "equal opportunity" must undergird equity conceived as "separate and unequal but by law equally funded and rewarded,"
since no degree of inattention can suppress the fact that all that is equal here
is money. As it happens, the conflict of this concept with meritocracy is
said to be one of its virtues, giving girls an "equal opportunity" to gain
emotional intangibles while helping to undermine the destructive masculine
emphasis on winning.

To understand this final twist, it must be remembered that sports as they
currently exist, like everything else, are conceived as oppressing women.
Sports teach competitiveness and self-improvement, valuable traits monopolized by men. Sex role stereotyping has encouraged boys to participate in
improving rough and tumble while telling girls it is unladylike. As a result,
young men are prepared for success while young girls fear it, and boys feel
comfortable with their bodies while girls fret about their looks. Little girls
need sports to derive this same psychological payoff:

> An adolescent girl should be encouraged to take part in sports, *whether she is
> good at them or not,* because they build her general health and accustom her
> to competition. The emotional lessons learned on the baseball field or the vol-
> leyball court spill over to relationships later in life, so that as an adult the girl
> is less inclined to accept passive, non-competitive roles. Likewise, boys who
> see girls participating actively in athletics are more likely to grow into men
> who are unafraid of strong, equal female partners.[19]

Let us overlook the dubious empirical assumptions of this theory—that
competitiveness can be learned (in a rather mechanical fashion) and that
men respond positively to women who compete against them. The fact is
that feminists are unable to maintain it consistently, since the right of
women to the exuberant confidence men are thought to derive from sports
collides immediately with disapproval of male exuberance in sports. Brenda
Feigen-Festeau is concerned lest sports

> become for women what they have been for many men: a display of aggres-
> sion, a proof of toughness, and a kind of primitive communication that
> replaces emotional intimacy. Sweating, swearing, and grunting together as
> they play, men manage to create a fellowship which they find hard to sustain
> elsewhere. And sports provides men with yet another vehicle to test domina-
> tion and preeminence.

The dilemma is unavoidable, given environmentalist assumptions: Sports
must have the same effect on women as they have on men, if men and
women will respond identically to identical stimuli. The words just cited are
especially puzzling in their context, in which Feigen-Festeau has just grown

"angry and sad" at the exclusion of girls from the sort of macho ritual she is about to deplore:

> For the first few weeks of the season, two eight-year-old girls longingly watched the practice sessions of a Montgomery, Alabama boys' football team. . . . When you're that young it's hard to see the value of being female because males are permitted to do almost everything girls do, but not vice-versa.

What are the girls being denied, if the activity they wish to take part in, as it is presently constituted, leads to undesirable traits?

This problem is frequently resolved in traditionally male terms. The values of sports are male, and by participating in sports, girls will become more like what men actually are:

> I've never seen women as strong, as well developed. They have a long, lean, confident look. They arrive here outgoing, confident, with a good self-image. It's beginning in their home-towns, where athletic scholarships have become status symbols. They're not hiding in their rooms with people saying "Oh, those phys-ed majors." They're like male athletes.[20]

This is not the solution given by most feminists, however. They more often say that girls participating in sports will become more like men while retaining their femininity. Girls will humanize sports while becoming toughened by controlled competition, at the same time that boys will learn not to regard sports as an occasion for dominance. This idea assumes an implausible degree of plasticity in male aggression as manifested in physical tasks, along with an innate gender dimorphism in insisting that females bring something unique to sports. The idea makes little sense in terms of sports themselves, which are inseparable from competitiveness. As soon as the aimless games of infancy are abandoned, there is winning and losing, and the point of playing becomes winning. Competition tends to become increasingly fierce because, at any given level of skill, otherwise adequately talented participants who do not care about victory are eliminated from the field, leaving only the more competitive to move on to the next level. Once again, the upshot is a coordination problem: Sports can become noncompetitive only if everyone simultaneously ceases to care about victory. Men would have to cease behaving competitively, so much so that they would have to cease noticing who wins in any competition. Marcia Federbush has proposed, as a step toward eliminating preoccupation with male performance, that all records of performance differences between males and females be suppressed by combining the girls' team's score against the opposing girls and the boys' team's score against the opposing boys into a single team total. It should be clear that no such formal arrangement could prevent informal score-keeping by spectators and male participants. Boys who consistently beat their opponents but were denied the more tangible fruits of victory by the losses of their female counterparts would feel victimized. Informal single-sex contests would probably be arranged, and male competitiveness would reemerge uninhibited.

Noncompetitive sports would likely be no more enjoyable than they are practical. Few people enjoy aimless exertion. Sports become fun only when the warm-ups end and the game begins. Close friends with no desire to dominate each other off the tennis court work harder at set point than during a practice volley. Joggers compete against their own best times. A changeless regimen of calisthenics, about the closest analogue now imaginable to noncompetitive sports, is usually undertaken for some external purpose, like weight control or muscle development, rather than as an end in itself.

The goal of psychologically strengthening girls through acquainting them with victory does not, in the end, escape the need for doublethink. How are girls to derive a sense of competence, assuming that this is something girls are badly in need of, when they know, and know everyone else knows, that they are inferior to a multitude of boys who are legally barred from competing with them? Making the little-league team by lawsuit can hardly instill pride, and is the farthest thing from a lesson in self-reliance. "Sex-equality in sports" as currently conceived amounts to the receipt of legally protected privileges to compete for a payoff precluded by the terms of the competition.

Advocacy of artificial victories for girls rests on the confusion of effect with cause that supports comparable worth and textbook censorship. Sex differences in sports cause the perception of sex differences. By suppressing the circumstances under which sex differences become perceptible, it is thought that the sex differences themselves can be made to vanish. Letting children alone, or allowing local institutions to fund athletics as they please, or maximizing intersex competition, would all underline sex differences. The only solution is to require girls to compete against girls in uniforms modeled on those of boys, give them equal money for scholarships and facilities, and avoid questions of ability. That way the girls will *look* like boys.

Notes

1. Cited in David Monagan, "The Failure of Coed Sports," *Psychology Today* (March 1983): 58–63.
2. Cited in Thomas H. Middleton, "Boys and Girls Together," *Saturday Review* (May 1980): 26. This assertion was made on a television talk show; Middleton reports that it met with general consent from the other participants.

3. Brenda Feigen-Festeau, "Giving Women a Sporting Chance," *Ms* (July 1973): 56–108.
4. Letty Pogrebin, *Growing Up Free* (New York: McGraw-Hill, 1980), p. 362.
5. Marian Lowe, "The Dialectics of Biology and Culture," in *Women's Nature,* ed. Marion Lowe and Ruth Hubbard (New York: Pergamon, 1983), p. 42.
6. Ibid., p. 48.
7. D. Kowal, J. Voegl, D. Sharp, and J. Knapik, *Analysis of Attrition, Retention, and Criterion Task Performance of Recruits during Training,* U.S. Army Medical Research and Development Command Technical Report TS/82, 1982.
8. W.L. Daniels et al., *The Effects of Two Years' Training in Aerobic Power and Muscle Strength,* U.S. Army Institute of Environmental Medicine, Report no. M-12/80, 1980.
9. Summarized and tabulated in Monagan.
10. See Lulu Jenkins, *A Comparative Study of Motor Achievements of Children of Five, Six, and Seven Years of Age* (New York: Teacher's College, 1930). See also A. Gesell et al., *The First Five Years of Life* (New York: Harper & Row, 1940).
11. Her case is discussed in *Title IX: The Half Full, Half Empty Glass* (Washington, D.C.: Department of Education, 1981).
12. See Bryan Holme, *Advertising: Reflections of a Century* (New York: Viking, 1982), p. 84.
13. See Feigen-Festeau, p. 58, for details.
14. "Giving Women a Sporting Chance," p. 58.
15. Ibid., p. 103.
16. See "Lawyer: Gender Cost Boy a Spot on HS Girls' Team," *New York Daily News* (January 14, 1986): 9; "Regents to Let Girls Compete with Boys in the Contact Sports," *New York Times* (January 14, 1986): A1–B4; "State Panel Confirms Ruling: Girls Can Play on Boys' Teams," *Newsday* (January 23, 1986): 17; "Jersey Bars Schoolboys from Girls' Athletics," *New York Times* (May 22, 1986): B3.
17. *DeFunis v. Odegaard* 416 US 812 (1974).
18. *Sports Participation Survey,* 1971 and 1979, of the National Federation of State High School Associations: "Comments of the NCAA on Proposed Policy Interpretation of the HEW Regarding Application of its Title IX Regulation to Intercollegiate Athletics," 1975, p. 11.
19. Cynthia Cooke and Susan Dworkin, *The Ms Guide to a Woman's Health* (New York: Doubleday, 1979), p. 27.
20. Linda Lopiano, Director of Women's Athletics at Texas A&M, quoted in "Old Images are Fading Rapidly," *New York Times* (October 29, 1982): B12.

11

The Forces of Order

Playing Soldier Like the Boys

Social life is a compromise between freedom and order. Private persons can enjoy liberty only when confident that criminals will be punished and invaders repelled. Free societies like all others must thus maintain institutions for forcibly preserving peace. This framework of security is provided by the police and the military, and supported by emergency services like firefighting. Because the maintenance of order requires physical strength and aggressiveness, it has been a male task in every society that has ever existed. It has generally been pursued by small bands of males whose camaraderie bonds them into effective fighting units; the basic unit of modern mechanized armies remains the small group of males. Policies based on feminist ideas may be expected, therefore, to depart radically from previously established practices, and to reorient the very aim of the protective services.

Precisely because innate gender differences are nowhere more apparent than in armed combat, it has been a particular focus of the debate surrounding sex integration. A fully integrated military, in which women have the "right" to engage in combat, is a paramount goal of NOW and the Women's Equity Action League. This emphasis is vital to the conceptual purity of feminism for the same reason that equality in sports is: If the protective role has fallen to males for biological reasons, there ends the theory that *all* role differentiation is a social artifact, and it would be woefully unparsimonious to suppose that all other role differentiation is social in origin. Correlatively, if women can be accepted in an environment as hostile to traditional femininity as combat, there can be no objection to changing any other sex role.

The argument for the complete sexual integration of the military hinges on a strong version of environmentalism. There is some talk of women being "different but better," but none of the vacillation characteristic of "second-stage" feminism about the origins of sex differences. There are occasional verbal concessions that women may be on average somewhat weaker and less aggressive, but it is insisted that in essentials "women have

222

the same skills and talents as men."[1] "Much of the difference between the physical strength and endurance of males and females is due to social conditioning rather than inherent physical strength."[2] Might there be a greater female aversion to killing which would inhibit females in battle? Richard White, chairman of the House Subcommittee on Military Personnel, quizzed Air Force undersecretary Antonia Chayes on this matter during Congressional hearings on women in the military in 1979:

> Mr. White: . . . Now, is there going to be a difference in performance, do you feel, between the male or the female [in] dropping bombs that will kill children?
>
> Secretary Chayes: . . . I do not see that there is any sex or gender difference in the degree of pacifism or unwilingness to go to war in anything I have noticed. Nor did I notice when I was a college dean during the Vietnam war, when there was great resistance, any difference in attitude that was remarkable as between men and women.
>
> Mr White: We are talking about a person that has a finger on the trigger, bomb release . . . unfortunately, war calls for destruction and for killing.
>
> Secretary Chayes: I think that is a cultural concept that really does not necessarily accord with the truth now. I think there are creative people. [Women] are capable of having babies and men are not. I really do not see what that has to do with their choosing a military profession.
>
> Mr. White: I am not talking about choosing a military profession. I am talking about the finger on the trigger . . . I am talking about something visual.
>
> Secretary Chayes: I think that women throughout history, even in mythology, have taken up arms, and very effectively. Look at the Amazons. They were women.[3]

Feminists willing to grant mean statistical differences between the sexes with respect to factors relevant to combat generally seek to dismiss these differences by comparing them to racial differences or contrasting them to within-sex variances:

> Oriental men are also significantly lighter and shorter than Caucasians on the average, but this in no way precludes their use in the military, nor has it precluded various Asian nations from fielding very effective fighting forces.[4]
>
> We do not know how much men and women of the ages relevant to combat differ in aggressive behaviors. More important, the implications of any differences for using women in combat are not clear. . . . [V]ariations *among males* are not felt to affect combat effectiveness.[5]
>
> It must be remembered that racial integration of the military was accompanied by these very arguments: troop morale will fall, unrest will be rampant, and our forces will be ineffective. Such fears were not credited or acted upon when racial integration was an issue. They should not be credited in this instance.[6]

At the same time, feminists insist on special measures to compensate for the female deficit at tasks associated with violence: easier physical requirements for women or physical standards lowered to allow women to pass them; emphasis on paper-and-pencil skills, at which females excel; inattention to comparative data on male and female task performance. Ultimately, the functions of the forces of order are reconceived to conform to female abilities. It is contended simultaneously that women can fight as well as men and that women bring a valuable gentling influence to the military. Betty Friedan writes of girls at West Point "playing soldier like the boys . . . without turning themselves into men," and she suggests that a combat officer who weeps during battle makes a more effective leader than one who puts on a façade of courage.[7] At times the contradictions latent in trying to have it several different ways become explicit. In November 1979, Antonia Chayes told the House Armed Services Committee:

> It is not sensible to shut out 50 percent of a dwindling manpower pool. . . . The Air Force would be pleased to exceed its goal. Many of the most critical shortages—engineers, scientists, pilots—can be filled by qualified women.

In December 1979 she told a private conference on the All-Volunteer Force:

> The fact is, we don't find large numbers of women to fill the technical areas, neither enlisted nor officers. It's very hard to find women engineers. This, I think, is a product of our educational system and cultural bias.[8]

It should be clear that the issue is not whether women have a place in the police or military. They obviously do. Police departments need women to guard female prisoners, for surveillance and undercover work where men would be conspicuous, and for performing administrative chores to free men for patrol. Similarly, military women in all-female units can free men to fight, and have served admirably in medical and intelligence services. There can be nonideological debate about the appropriate extent of female participation in the police and military, although there would seem to be no room for women in firefighting unless they can meet the same exacting standards men are expected to meet. But these matters have nothing to do with the demand for an integrated 50 percent female armed services with women in the combat arms and included in any future draft:

> Our nation's defense system would gain the talents and skills of the 50 percent of its young people who have been arbitrarily excluded. We would have a more effective, efficient military force—with a higher educational level—if women were accepted on an equal basis with men.[9]

> Combat duty, horrendous as it is, must be shared on a gender-neutral basis. Until it is, women not only will be deprived of the important opportunity for full participation in the military but they will also continue to be considered less than full-fledged citizens.[10]

These professions cannot always be taken at full face value. The president of NOW wishes to see women conscripted so that they can undergo the "politically maturing experience" of *resisting* the draft. The ACLU simultaneously litigates for the inclusion of women in any future draft, and for the outright abolition of the draft on the grounds that conscription impermissibly invades individual liberty. The ACLU either believes that the scope of impermissible state action should expand so long as the action continues, or it considers sexual equality more important than logical consistency.

Just as raising questions about female strength and aggressiveness is considered inimical to equality of opportunity, so it is considered prejudiced to note that all past armies have been male. Appeals to experience are replaced by hypotheses and unevidenced extrapolations about the possible performance of women. A strongly proegalitarian article by Sgt. Maj. Bruce N. Bant in the official magazine of the U.S. Army summarized the entirety of the cases for and against "the complete integration of women in military service" as follows:

> Those against the complete integration of women in military service say that no country in modern history has ever put women in combat unless the homeland was threatened. Those in favor say just because it has never been done doesn't mean that it couldn't or shouldn't be done.[11]

Considering that the human race has been waging war for thousands of years, any practice that has never emerged very probably *is* unfeasible. Bant's argument too clearly seeks to evade induction by hypothesis to warrant extended consideration were it not for the accuracy of his observation that this integration is "not that far from Army policy," which at the time he wrote included the use of women " 'to defend their unit or participate in a counterattack or something like that,' " in the words of "a D[epartment of the] A[rmy] expert on women personnel management programs" cited by Bant. I have been informed that the editor of *Soldier* was instructed to insert Bant's article by Clark Clifford, the Secretary of the Army at the time the article appeared.

Women in the All-Volunteer Force

Egalitarian assumptions have determined American military manpower policy since the early 1970s. Over the last fifteen years, one of the major aims of manpower policy has been to place great numbers of women in the services and to direct them toward nontraditional military occupational specialties (MOSs). The immediate occasions of this revolution were the end of conscription in 1973 and, simultaneously, the anticipated passage of the ERA. The end of the draft ended a guaranteed supply of men and, as noted earlier, most legal experts agreed that the ERA would end differential treatment of women in the military, particularly exclusion from combat or any MOSs. Faced with these extramilitary constraints, the Pentagon prepared to accommodate unprecedented numbers of women. The General Accounting Office was clear about the situation:

> With the advent of the All-Volunteer Force and the anticipated passage of the Equal Rights Amendment, the Department of Defense intensified efforts to recruit women and to increase their use in a wider range of occupational specialties, including some previously restricted to men.[12]

Air Force and Navy women were, and still are, forbidden combat assignment by Title X of the U.S. Code, and Army women remain barred from combat by Department of the Army regulation. This combat exclusion policy was the only restraint on the expansion of the female presence in the military between 1973 and 1981.

Otherwise, the Armed Forces proclaimed themselves "Equal Opportunity Employers" and made every effort to live up to this promise. Recruitment advertising was targeted to young women. The iconography of official Pentagon publications became scrupulously unisex: A fixed proportion of all figures shown are now female and nontraditional but, per a request by the Defense Advisory Committee on Women in the Services (DACOWITS), also feminine. The Women's Army Corps, the WAVES, and the Women Marines were abolished. The Army dropped as discriminatory its requirement that female enlistees be high-school graduates (thus compromising the argument that females would raise the educational level of the AVF). At the same time, a steady narrowing of the definition of combat opened more MOSs to women, and women were assigned to such elite units as the 82nd Airborne Division. The service academies were opened to women in 1976 by the Stratton Bill, which was ostensibly passed to create "equal opportunity" for women, but it also permitted "minimal" adjustments in existing standards to accommodate "physiological differences" between the sexes. To make it as clear as possible that the real meaning of "equal opportunity" was the admission of women to the academy whether qualified or not by some neutral standard, Congress further mandated an approximately 10 percent admissions quota for women—a doubly curious step in view of combat exclusion, since the main purpose of the academies is to train combat officers. These quotas are proving difficult to fill: The admissions director of West Point conceded in 1980 that "this doesn't allow us to be as selective as we otherwise would, and that adds to our drop-out problem."

With equity a dimension of manpower policy, the courts have taken a stand. In 1978, a federal court ordered the Navy to place women on non-combat ships, arguing that such service was necessary to guarantee women job-training opportunities to which they are entitled under the Fourteenth Amendment.[13] Considerable litigation currently surrounds limitations on homosexuality in the Armed Forces. In 1984, a group of unwed mothers brought suit against the Army's policy of excluding single parents. (The Armed Forces had accepted unwed mothers in the early 1970s, but discontinued the practice after finding them too unreliable.) The suit concedes the sex-neutrality of Army policy, but the policy is said to affect women and Blacks disproportionately, and to stem ultimately from "the attitudinal and institutional sexism that remains deeply entrenched in military policy and tradition."[14] The suit is unresolved at this writing.

The pace of sex integration accelerated during the Carter administration. President Carter himself urged registration of women for the draft when he reinstituted draft registration in 1979, and his appointees argued vigorously for repeal of combat exclusion.[15] The Defense Department integrated the Army's basic combat training in 1978. By the end of Clifford Alexander's tenure as Secretary of the Army during the Carter administration, only 38 of the Army's 349 MOSs remained classified as combat-related, thus excluding women. When it left office, the Carter administration was projecting a 12 percent female Armed Forces by 1985, including an Air Force as high as 15 percent female and an Army employing 87,500 female enlisted personnel and 12,500 female officers.

In 1981 the Reagan administration paused in these integration efforts on the grounds that the Carter projection "was not based on any empirical analysis." It set a ceiling of 65,000 enlisted women for the Army and stabilized female recruitment for the other services. In 1982 it reintroduced separate ("gender-pure") basic training because the lower standards adopted upon integration were not challenging male recruits. According to the director of the Army Initial Entry Training at Ft. Monroe:

> You get a group of young males together who want to prove their manhood and we found they would be beyond the criteria. We call this the "stretch factor." We found that women couldn't keep up . . . because of [their] physical structure.[16]

This pause, however, may more accurately be termed a deceleration; shortly after the pause was announced, the Army raised its female recruitment ceiling to 70,000, and by October 1983 the ceiling was 72,500. By mid-1983 the Defense Department was projecting a 10 percent female active-duty officer corps in the Armed Forces as a whole for 1987, and 12 percent for the Army.[17] It also drew up (without submitting) legislation authorizing conscription of female medical personnel.

The expansion of the female role in the military has been a smashing success by numerical standards, the Reagan pause notwithstanding. Whereas in 1971 only 1.3 percent of the active-duty enlisted personnel in the Armed Forces were female, by the end of Fiscal Year 1984 the figure was 9.4 percent. The Air Force's enlistees are now 11 percent female, while the Army's 70,000 female enlistees represent a more than sevenfold increase since 1965. In the Navy, 10,000 of 42,000 enlisted women serve in non-traditional areas: about 3,500 of them serve aboard ship, along with nearly 200 female officers. Women can be assigned to mobile logistics support force ships, and female helicopter pilots can be deployed with explosive ordinance disposal detachments. The Air Force has made similar changes.[18]

Inevitably, the criteria by which the military judges itself have changed. Army combat training at Ft. Benning now includes a course on sexual harassment. Cadets at West Point are instructed to refrain from bad language to plebes and are rated on "attitudes toward equal opportunity." Marine combat training includes discussions of equal opportunity. I have been told by field officers that filing a field report raising questions about the performance of women can harm an officer's career. Given the tradition of deference to civilian command in the American military, it is not surprising that career officers have raised few objections to these changes, and there is some evidence of efforts to paper over difficulties that have arisen. "WAC 77," the report on the performance of women during the 1977 REFORGER war games exercises, managed to conclude both that "10% women has negligible impact on unit performance in a 10-day field exercise for the types of companies tested," and that "a number of leadership and management problems involving women were observed." These changes in criteria have made it difficult for the military to form an objective internal assessment of its unprecedented experiment.

Precedence and Population

Unprecedented it is, and radical, when viewed in historical perspective. Contrary to a widespread misconception, no nation, including Israel and the USSR, has ever employed women to the extent to which they are now employed in the American military. The USSR has 10,000 females in a total active force of 4.4 million, performing traditional medical and clerical chores, and the paramilitary branches of the KGB are also virtually all male. There is not a single female general officer in the Soviet forces.[19] Israel has fewer than 3 percent women in its military, all of whom are used in traditional ways. Deeply committed to sex equality, Israel sent women into battle in the relatively low-intensity 1948 war, and withdrew them in three weeks. (Feminists interpret this withdrawal as evidence that Israelis "are not as committed to equal opportunity for women," [20] which suggests that feminists treat their military assumptions as unfalsifiable.)

To be sure, the Soviets used women in combat—sparingly—during World War II. It must be remembered, however, that the Soviets had lost several million men at the outset of hostilities and were facing conquest by a brutal invader. The units in which Soviet women served were all-female, and were disbanded after the war. Some of these units, particularly the "Night Witch" fighter wing, achieved considerable fame, but so far as I can determine the Soviet government has never released reliable data about their performance. In any case, these precedents are irrelevant to the American experiment. No doubt every woman must pick up a gun when the enemy is charging through the gates. East Germany, at a time when it had no women in its military, had plans for drafting women in cases of "national emergency." But the American military is not now facing any external crisis; its sexual integration marks the first massive peacetime increase in the number of women in any army, and the first indiscriminate mixing of the sexes in military units.

It is frequently maintained that the American military does face an emergency of sorts in the shortfall in the number of men available for service, soon to become very serious with the end of the baby boom. This worry is not supported by demographics. During World War II, an American population of 150 million sustained a force of 12 million men; the present U.S. population of 240 million could surely sustain a comparable force. Defense Department projections of hypothetical threats estimate future American manpower needs not to exceed 5 million men, and at any time the U.S. population includes at least 9.5 million males between the ages of seventeen and twenty-one. There is no demographic need to enlist women. Nor does the increasing dependence of some aspects of war on technology require the enlistment of women, since men continue to dominate science and technology.

The manpower situation is complicated by the current dependence of the American military on volunteers. It is sometimes argued that the AVF is failing to attract enough qualified male volunteers, a shortfall that will become critical should the unemployment rate fall below 5 percent. I cannot enter that debate here,[21] but if the AVF is unable to attract enough men, an obvious solution is return to all-male conscription, which has been *proven* to work in the only sense in which lessons of military history can be regarded as proven: Conscripted males won two world wars.

Many critics of the AVF who are reluctant, on grounds of equity, to endorse a male-only draft, also recognize that conscription of females would be too unpopular to be proposed seriously. The compromise emerging among such critics is universal national service, the conscription of all eighteen-year-olds for work deemed vital to the nation, with military service included as one option. The UNS plans of Yvonne Burke, Senator Peter McCloskey, Margaret Mead, and Gary Hart all either stipulate the inclusion of women or conspicuously fail to exclude them, and the weakness of the arguments for preferring UNS over a male-only draft suggests that the inclusion of women is their real if unstated purpose. It is argued, for example, that a male-only draft would be unfair to the 25 percent of eighteen-year-olds actually taken. However, as every eighteen-year old runs the same risk of being selected, an all-male draft fairness—just as lotteries are fair to losers so long as the losers had an equal chance to win before the drawing. Any felt ex post facto unfairness could be alleviated by taking all eighteen-year-old *males* for national service with a military option. There is no reason to involve women in any way in such a scheme.

Some UNS advocates seem genuinely unaware of the ramifications of their proposal. When asked what he would do about young mothers in a UNS system, Peter McCloskey replied: "I'll have to think about that. I haven't thought that one out."[22] Others, like Margaret Mead, are more candid about using UNS to further feminist aims:

> The inclusion of women on the same basis as men is absolutely essential . . . a failure to include them will promote a split in the experience of men and women at a time when it is essential that they should move in step with each other, economically and politically. . . . [I]t should be possible for a choice to be made by each girl; for a sheltered and protected environment within which she could carry out her national service . . . or for contraception. In either case, pregnancy could be treated as a severe breach of contract, comparable to going AWOL in males. Part of the institution of UNS would be the postponement of marriage until the service was completed, if universal service takes the form of a nationwide call-up at 18, or the possibility of the entry into national service as a working couple if proposals for extending the service period into the late 20's were to be adopted. UNS would replace for girls, even more than for boys, marriage as the route away from parental home, and provide a period of responsible and directed reappraisal before marriage and parenthood were assumed.[23]

National service does not seem likely in the United States in the foreseeable future, but discussions of it typify the contortions required by conformity to feminist precepts.

Sex Differences Relevant to Military Service: WITA

The Reagan pause occurred because, despite the optimistic face put on sex integration by the Defense Department, problems had emerged by the late 1970s. Since women, such as those in the Signal Corps, had been stationed near battle zones during the Carter administration, heavy female casualties appeared inevitable in the event of war in Europe. A more concrete problem was the female strength deficit. Most of what soldiers do is physical. They carry, erect, chop, dig, drive, march, run, and above all, fight. The U.S. Army's light machine gun, the M-60, weighs twenty-nine pounds, and anyone who doubts that soldiering requires strength should carry an M-60 for an hour. (Its West German counterpart weights forty pounds.) French Foreign Legionnaires are expected to be able to run five miles in forty minutes with a full pack.

In the previous chapter I discussed some significant sex differences in muscle strength and aerobic power. These differences suggest pronounced limitations on possible female participation in the military, and it is not surprising that the female strength deficit should have become a pressing problem for the Pentagon. Commanders of combat support and combat service support units were encouraged to use women in unit training programs but to exclude them from grenade training, for example, because most women have difficulty throwing a grenade far and accurately enough. ("If you want to commit suicide," one officer told me, "be near the range when the girls are taking grenade practice.") Not only were women restraining men in basic training, they were proving too weak to perform many of the nontraditional MOSs to which they had been assigned. It became clear that strength tests would have to be developed and administered to allocate military jobs more efficiently.[24] In May 1981 the Army undertook just such a review of its assignment of women to physically demanding MOSs and positions near combat. The results of this study appeared as *Women in the Army Policy Review,* or WITA.[25]

WITA found that over 90 percent of the Army's MOSs call for upper body strength, that 74 percent of Army personnel must lift at least 65–85 pounds, and that a number of very heavy MOSs require lifting over 100 pounds, with frequent lifting of 50 pounds. (A box of ammunition for the Army's M-16 weighs about 90 pounds.) Even though only 3 percent of women can perform very heavy tasks, as opposed to 80 percent of men, the Army had assigned 42 percent of its women to very heavy tasks.[26] Not surprisingly, perhaps, 50 percent of females assigned to heavy or very heavy MOSs attrite, compared to 31 percent of males. In light of these findings, WITA recommended development of a gender-neutral Military Entrance Physical Strength Capacity Test (MEPSCAT) to help in assigning MOSs to recruits. WITA also recommended closure of twenty-three additional MOSs to women, due to the probability that soldiers assigned to them "will routinely engage in direct combat."

The angry opposition of WEAL and DACOWITS to these quite modest proposals illustrates the obstacles that impede the evaluation of even purely physical female characteristics. Military egalitarians may concede in theory that gender-neutral testing might legitimately exclude women from some MOSs, but in practice they remain prepared to find any evaluation which reveals any sex difference to be inherently discriminatory. DACOWITS and WEAL charged WITA with neglecting the possibility of equipment redesign and of alternative ways of performing tasks to offset the need for strength. A woman unable to lift a 100-pound truck tire, it was maintained, might be able to roll it. When I asked a WEAL staff counsel if any new methods had emerged for dragging an unconscious 180-pound man from a burning helicopter, I was told that a woman might possibly drag a man from a wreck more slowly than another man, but her female level-headedness might help her administer first aid more expeditiously.[27] It is WEAL's position that the difficulties experienced by women in nontraditional MOSs are due entirely to sexual harassment. For its part, DACOWITS demanded the formation of a new study group to study the WITA study, which, it said, had eroded female morale.

It should be noted, incidentally, that the WITA statistics and similar statistics found in the secondary literature tend to overstate female strength as it relates to military service. These statistics are frequently based on single-trial tests rather than repetitions performed under time limitations. For instance, 11 percent of the females tested in the WITA study could lift 100 pounds, as opposed to 92 percent of the men tested; a more realistic question is the proportion of women able to lift 100 pounds on a sustained basis, as soldiers must do in combat. It is one thing to lift a 155mm howitzer shell and then break for a rest period, another to lift 155mm shells as fast as one can for as long as one can. Given the known differences in muscle mass, aerobic power, and endurance, repetitions of the tasks defined in the WITA study would probably disclose greater sex differences.

Despite the overwhelming confirmation of what common sense would have predicted, officials of the Reagan administration tended to side with the more radical critics of the WITA study. Sharon Lord, then the Defense Department's top equal opportunity officer, said that the end of coed basic training was "highly unfortunate [and] smacks of the old argument of 'separate but equal.'"[28] Other administration officials were, at best, defensive. Lawrence Korb, the Defense Department's assistance secretary for manpower, promised "career-enhancing assignments" for women—including "close monitoring" of the promotion of women lest combat exclusion slow their rise through the ranks—and he expressed oblique opposition to combat exclusion itself. Even before WITA appeared, Ronald Reagan, when quoting from George C. Marshall in a speech at West Point, carefully replaced all of Marshall's references to "men" with "men and women."

In the end, the second thoughts expressed in the WITA report came to very little. In October 1983 the Army reopened thirteen of the MOSs closed by WITA, while closing one additional MOS. It also announced that MEPSCAT, the physical strength test, would go into effect "only as a guideline":

> For example, prospective enlistees may be unable to lift the 80-pound weight found to be the best predictor of success in jobs classified as "heavy" or "very heavy" in terms of their physical demands. If they chose [sic], the prospective enlistees may still enlist for jobs in that category if other classification criteria permit.[29]

Changing the Standards: Costs and Consequences

Objective evaluation of male and female capabilities cannot realistically be expected in the near future. Results of tests are viewed by the civilian command primarily in terms of their impact on women rather than on their implications for the total force structure. Sharon Lord objected to the end of coed basic on the grounds that "the male soldier might feel apprehensive about being supported by a woman who did a different training"[30]—as if it were unreasonable to worry about support troops who could not have kept up in ordinary training.

The dismantling of military job standards is of a piece with the view that civilian job standards are presumptively discriminatory if they differentially affect women, a test that sexual egalitarians would like to see applied to the military. A counsel for WEAL informed me that a possible route to equal opportunity would be a Title VII challenge to the WITA task analyses. In a similar vein, Antonia Chayes told the Senate Judiciary Committee that, under the ERA, physical standards in the military that selected fewer qualifying females would have to be "justified" and "demonstrably related" to job performance: "I would ask whether 40 push-ups or 60 push-ups are required to do most jobs."[31]

As I have noted, the services themselves do not conceive sex equity as the impersonal application of stringent standards to all. When a federal court found height and weight requirements for police candidates violative of Title VII, West Point promptly eliminated height and weight requirements. Since very few women can do chin-ups, West Point requires its female applicants to perform one "flexed arm hang" while continuing to require its male applicants to perform six chin-ups. West Point women do not take hand-to-hand combat training with men, and when only 14 percent of the females at West Point proved able to achieve a passing time in the two-mile run, as against 96 percent of the males, the females were permitted to "pace themselves." The Air Force Academy has eliminated push-ups from its training and lowered its obstacle course, as has West Point, so that women—or, in the language of the official authorization of the change, "shorter people"—can clear it. Female Army recruits are required to do sixteen push-ups, fewer than half of those required of men, and to run two miles in the leisurely time of 22:14. A 26-year-old male in the Army is expected to do forty push-ups, a 26-year-old female sixteen. The Navy asks its 20-year-old men to do twenty-nine push-ups in 2 minutes, its 20-year-old women eleven.

The most common defense of these relaxed standards, that women can do whatever men can do if given extra time and training, ignores two critical features of warfare. First, the law of the margin operates more drastically in war than elsewhere. Every second counts in battle. Lives depend on whether a box of M-16 ammunition is being carried or dragged over exposed ground. If NATO responds even slightly less quickly and flexibly than the Warsaw Pact, there will be no second chances after a rest break. Second, the planning of military maneuvers assumes a high degree of certainty about the capabilities of each soldier. Only if a commanding officer is sure that all his men can run three 7:30 miles can he confidently order his men to be at a point three miles away in twenty-three minutes, and only uniform and stringently applied training requirements can allow him to be certain.

The controversy surrounding WITA also illuminates, if less directly, the cost of combing the female population for a few standouts when enough capable men are available. There is little information to be gained from a test that only 3 percent of an antecedently identifiable population can pass (assuming that Title VII considerations do not thwart the test at the outset). It is not clear why millions of dollars must be spent to find the one woman in a thousand able and willing to lift heavy truck tires when there will always be someone in an all-male motor pool who can lift them.

Speaking more generally, the U.S. military has already spent a great deal of money on a wide variety of special provisions for women essential to sustaining the proposition that the sexes are militarily interchangeable. Most of these provisions are necessitated by physical differences, which do not end at strength. The smaller skeleton and wider pelvis of the female makes her less well suited to the thirty-inch stride basic to all military drill and marching. Combined with the greater narrowness of the female heel, this has meant that, even in narrow sizes, the standard Army booting, which has proved satisfactory for men, has created proneness to injury in women, and so has been changed.[32] Prolonged sitting in standard helicopter seats was found to cause back pain in women, necessitating the redesign of the seats. Lost time due to urinary tract infection, to which females are prone in the filth incidental to field conditions, has necessitated the redesign of underwear and trousers. Among other items that have required redesign are flask vests, gas masks, helmets, gloves, cold-weather jackets, and uniforms (maternity uniforms have also been added). The formerly male-oriented supply system has had to be amplified to include a wider range of uniform sizes. Problems were created by the Colt .45-caliber pistol, which is too large and heavy to be fired effectively by many women. This weapon, in use since 1912, was replaced in 1985 by a smaller Beretta. (The Army Office of Public Affairs has told me that this change had nothing to do with difficulties experienced by women in handling the .45.)

The requirements of female privacy have led to the duplication of field clothes-changing units, baths, and latrine facilities. Shipboard living quarters have had to be altered so that male personnel do not routinely pass through female latrine and sleeping quarters. Female soldiers serving in isolated areas must be protected, adding to the troop strength that must be deployed, paid, equipped, and maintained. The reduced stamina of some women during their menstrual cycles increases the workload on male soldiers, a problem exacerbated by the tendency of women in groups to menstruate synchronously. The medical support base of the military has had to be expanded to include physicians with expertise in gynecological problems. To all this might be added that $20,000 were budgeted at Ft. Jackson for teaching female recruits how to apply makeup.

Pregnancy is a further "friction factor"—to use Clausewitz's phrase— unique to a sexually integrated military. At any time, 10 to 15 percent of the females in the Army are pregnant. Pregnancy is no longer grounds for discharge, and NATO must contend with female soldiers who do not report for duty because they are unable to find babysitters. I have been told that the orderly rooms in Europe at midnight resemble nurseries. In the event of emergency, pregnant female soldiers in critical positions will have to be evacuated, and others will be absent from duty seeking shelter for their babies. Such a prospect corrodes unit morale and degrades readiness,[33] but the issue of pregnancy has yet to be faced squarely by the Defense Department. WITA avoided the issue on the grounds that it concerns all the services, not merely the Army, and advised the Defense Department to initiate a "Joint Study effort."

The other protective services have also been forced to abandon the use of stringent, sex-neutral standards. The initial promise of "unbiased" testing that accompanies the introduction of affirmative action programs for police and fire departments invariably yield to double standards, lower standards, or the elimination of standards. No longer permitted to set minimum size requirements, most police departments ask only that recruits be "proportional in height and weight," which, because of the lower muscle/fat ratio in women, favors relatively corpulent women. Instead of hiring the highest scorers on its combined written and physical tests, the New York Police Department hires at random from among candidates whose combined scores exceed a minimum cutoff. In 1985 the NYPD announced that it intended to make its physical test easier, since 30 percent of female applicants, as opposed to 1 percent of males, fail it. It argued in particular that the ability to climb a fence, which used to be part of the test, was no longer deemed relevant to police work (good news to felons fleeing on foot), and that the NYPD would be sued if it kept the test. The New Jersey Highway Patrol, under court order, instituted a special training and recruiting program to attract women, which included letting women train only with other women in hand-to-hand combat and giving female troopers more attractive pensions that male troopers.

Unable to find suitable women even after lowering its physical standards in 1975, the Seattle Fire Department began in 1979 to recruit

> at job fairs, schools and colleges, utilizing sound-and-slide presentations and . . . advertisements over local television stations as well as in local newspaper [for] women who had been active in intramural sports [with] 120 lbs. of lean body mass.[34]

In two years the SFD found twenty-seven such women who could also pass the written civil service examination. The SFD then gave these women fourteen weeks of weight training, at the end of which they were asked to press 95 pounds and curl 100 pounds once each—strength sufficient for all firefighting duties, according to a kinesiologist retained by the Seattle municipal government to advise on their affirmative action program. All twenty-seven women passed this preliminary test and were given a further six weeks of pretraining in mechanical skills. The women received full fireman's salaries during these twenty weeks. At the end of this period all twenty-seven passed the (lowered) SFD physical ability test and were hired. The permanence of the strength gain was not determined by retesting.

Familiar questions of prudence and justice arise. If public funds are to be used for SFD talent hunts, should the hunt not also target male athletes, some of whom are bound to be stronger, more mechanically adept and easier to find than the SFD's twenty-seven women? In terms of equity, the Seattle program is biased against the thousands of Seattle males more qualified than the twenty-seven women eventually hired, whom the SFD made no effort to find, and against the additional thousands of Seattle males *precisely as trainable* as the twenty-seven females, whom the SFD made no effort to locate and who would have been ineligible for the special training had they presented themselves.

The tests designed to ensure the hiring of women do not always claim to predict the best performance; their designers frequently claim predictive validity for no more than the ability to meet the physical challenges presented by routine engine-company and truck-company work,[35] or routine policework. These tests thus ignore the extraordinary tasks for which police and fire services ultimately exist. A woman can write a parking ticket or inspect a fire exit as easily as a man, but not so easily subdue a psychotic with a knife or carry a heavy adult from a burning building. One group of firemen declared pubicly that "the women now on the job are proving every day that they are not qualified."[36] Many policemen refuse to accept female partners because they do not trust females in difficult situations. Voicing criticism may have results opposite to those intended, as a federal court has held that criticism of female firefighters is sexual harassment impairing their ability to perform at capacity, and that therefore performance deficits are not grounds for removal. Quelling violence is indeed nonroutine police work, but that is (now) because of the deterrent effect of the visibility of police conspicuously able to outmuscle troublemakers. As female police officers are overpowered on duty,[37] this deterrent becomes less credible.

Proponents of placing large numbers of women in the protective services might have been expected to insist on detailed records of female performance, if only to refute stereotypes about female shortcomings. In fact, no such records are kept, and advocates of sex equality are adverse to record keeping. Kathleen Carpenter and Antonio Chayes warned the House Armed Services Subcommittee that Defense Department testing would "create a goldfish bowl atmosphere." The VERA Institute reported in 1978 that the felony arrest rate for New York Police Department females was several times below that for males, and that female absenteeism was more than twice as great.[38] VERA has since ceased tracking female performance. The NYPD Public Affairs Office informed me that the department is "unisex" and keeps no comparative statistics, and this appears to be the position of other police departments. Very probably, organizations covered by the Civil Rights Act fear that keeping comparative statistics might create Title VII liability. The Defense Department, not covered by Title VII, does follow sexual differences in attrition rates, but it no longer attempts to measure the effect of women on combat effectiveness: "The question of whether women can perform as well as men in combat service support type skills is no longer at issue. It is recognized that women do perform as well as men in these jobs."[39] This attitude should be contrasted with the military's normally close monitoring of weapons systems and other aspects of its operations.

This disregard of empirical data has necessitated a gradual shift in the announced functions of the protective services. When asked how a small female police officer is to disarm a 200-pound psychotic, the NYPD Information Office replied that "the purpose of the Police Department is to serve the public." The New York Board of Education justifies the use of female guards in its violence-plagued schools on the grounds that children feel comfortable with women around. The Seattle firefighters union maintains that "today, there's a lot of first-aid work, a lot of code enforcement. The criteria for the job is changing. We have to have smart, articulate people."[40] Some observers of women in the Armed Forces, like Helen Rogan, imagine the Army transformed into a kind of large-scale Civilian Conservation Corps. And inevitably, the military has begun to lose a clear sense of its mission. The service academies have replaced an emphasis on withstanding stress with an emphasis on academics. As previously noted, it is now impermissible to physically punish or use "abusive language" to a plebe,[41] and "equal opportunity" is now a part of combat training. The New York City Department of Sanitation recently so altered its physical test in the direction of "sex fairness" that, of 44,000 applicants who took the test in 1986, 43,300 achieved a perfect score. From this pool, 127 applicants, of which 2 were female, were hired at random.

There might be no decisive objection to an unlimited expansion of the female presence in the military if the military were never expected to fight anybody. However, as Clausewitz reminds us, "the whole of military activity must be related directly or indirectly to the engagement. The end for which a soldier is recruited, clothed, armed, and trained, the whole object of his sleeping, eating, drinking, and marching is simply that he should fight at the right place and the right time." The issue of combat is unavoidable.

Combat

The full integration of women into combat units and the conscription of females for combat duty is defended on a variety of empirical and normative grounds, but a major part of the case for women in combat is to caricature the opposing case as sentimental nonsense. According to Judith Stiehm, a member of DACOWITS, men have kept women from combat because they have felt that "it exposes the vessels of life—women—to untimely death" and because men have felt that "women should not be subject to the suffering of war."[42] This version of the issue has entered the popular debate; according to the *New Yorker,* those opposed to women in combat believe "the bearers of life should not be its takers."[43] Acknowledged experts also have difficulty focussing. Charles Moskos identifies the "major dilemma" that "precludes the utilization of women in the combat arms for the foreseeable future" in this way:

> To allow women the choice of whether or not to volunteer for the combat arms would lead men to ask for the same prerogative, including the option of not serving in the combat arms. If regulations are changed so that women could be compelled to serve in the combat arms, as is presently the case for men . . . the end result would almost certainly be a sharp drop in the number of women who would volunteer to join the Army in the first place.[44]

These invented issues sidestep the real one: the danger of lowering our war-fighting capabilities in the face of as tough a potential opponent as the Warsaw Pact.

At this point emerges probably the most familiar egalitarian argument, one that may seem plausible to those familiar with changes in weapons technology since World War II: The next war will be fought by technicians pushing buttons at consoles, and women are just as capable as men in this regard:

> [T]echnology has changed the nature of warfare dramatically. It is no longer exclusively the hand-to-hand combat in which exceptional physical strength and size are absolute prerequisites. The development of new bombs, missiles, and high-powered guns has moved a good part of war out of the trenches and fox-holes and into the hands of trained technicians.[45]

This argument has been found persuasive by the Defense Department, which has assigned women to the crews of ground-launched cruise missiles in Europe, and DACOWITS is at this writing pushing for the assignment of females to MX crews. Yet this argument overlooks sex differences in motivation that go far beyond mere differences in physical strength. Females are more likely to see their target as people, a response which might inhibit females from pushing the button at the critical moment. Given the known sex differences in sociality, this possibility cannot be ignored. The assignment of women to button-pushing positions is a gamble, and an unnecessary one given that men, and not women, have historically demonstrated the perhaps morally deplorable but nonetheless militarily invaluable readiness to treat war as a game and kill impersonally on command.

In any event, combat has not changed as much as advertised. The push-button wars of the future stubbornly remain where they are set—the future. Modern technology has changed only the levels of firepower that can be brought against individual soldiers. Mutual nuclear deterrence has made long-distance strategic exchanges far less likely than conventional warfare, and, at the operational level, tactical atomic weapons have ended the long-term massing of troops. According to FM-100-5, the Army's official operational manual, the next war will be fought by small, quasi-independent units, with the outcome resting on the offensive spirit of individual soldiers and unit leaders. FM-100-5 emphasizes *"initiative, depth, agility and synchronization . . . maneuver and surprise . . .* leadership, unit cohesion, and effective independent operations."[46] The combat situation in the next war is expected to be fluid, with a "nonlinear" front, aircraft ranging far to the rear, and supply convoys subject to interdiction. Casualties will be heavy in support areas, and "distinctions between rear and forward areas will be blurred."

It is a military axiom that the capabilities of every soldier will be critical in future wars. Recent military history has confirmed the importance of the preparedness of every soldier to fight. The German counterattack in the Ardennes in 1945 was stopped because clerks, cooks, and telephone operators fought effectively. Much the same happened at the Chosin Reservoir during the Korean war. As FM-100-5 puts it,

> Forward deployment forces may have to fight on a few hours notice. Other components of the force may have only days or weeks to make final preparations for war. . . . The Army may be forced to fight a come-as-you-are war, with the soldiers, weapons systems, and supplies already on hand.

Curiously, egalitarians cite the fluidity of modern warfare as a reason for repealing combat exclusion. Some claim that women need "protection" from being plucked from their assignments. Others, like Antonia Chayes, maintain that since there are bound to be numerous female casualties anyway, women may as well be allowed to better their chances for promotion by fighting. As she told the House Armed Services Subcommittee in 1979:

> In any future war, I have no doubt that women will face more severe risks of injury just as U.S. civilians will. What we achieve by barring women from combat roles is an obstacle to career advance, and little enhancement of protection.

Miss Chayes was still blunter in her testimony four years later on the military implications of the ERA:

> It is time to recognize the fact that women have performed well, and are here to stay. . . . If we want to protect women from high risk of casualty, we will have to bury them underground.

If it were an unalterable fact of nature that there are going to be women in combat zones no matter what, such reasoning might be appropriate. If, however, combat is no place for women, the more appropriate conclusion is simply to exclude women from combat zones, defined as broadly as necessary to allow for the indefiniteness of modern combat.

The view of combat as a route to career advancement accords with the claim that women have a *right* to engage in combat, often made in conjunction with the claim that conscription and combat are "societal obligations and duties" which women must assume if, in the words of the ACLU, "true equality" is to be possible. These claims sometimes fuse, as when M.C. Devilbiss explains that women's "right to fight" has been "taken away from them by the first-class citizens (men) [who] wanted these jobs for themselves." As a result, "women constitute a 'special category' of citizens,

those who do not have either the rights or the duties of full citizenship."[47]
This position is not coherent, since no status can be both obligatory—that
is, owed *to* other—and entitled, which means owed *by* others. Combat cannot be an evil kept from women by men seeking to monopolize good things.
It must either be a good to which women are entitled, or an evil which
women are obligated to assume. Since no one is prepared to assert publicly
that combat is a good, can combat for women plausibly be regarded as an
obligatory evil? The best that can be said for so framing the issue is that it
ignores the decisive weight of utilitarian considerations in military matters.
When the existence of society is at stake, the fighting must be done by those
who fight best. If women *cannot* fight as well as men, there is no clear
sense in arguing that they *ought* to fight, and only men have ever proved
themselves capable of the steadfast murderousness required to engage in
combat over extended periods. It is worthwhile here to have a realistic
description of the phenomenon:

> I have personally participated in hand-to-hand combat and have seen men
> fight and die on the battlefield. The combat environment is an ugly one. For
> the ground soldier it is characterized by loneliness and desolation, weary
> marches, at times relentless heat, bitter cold, torrential rains, filth, pestilence,
> disease, the slime of dripping dugouts, and the stench of human carnage, all
> coupled with feelings of depression which stem from fear, uncertainty, and
> long separation from loved ones. It calls for an antic toughness that women
> do not normally possess. The soldier's feelings fluctuate from despair to
> extreme hate and bitterness, and these emotions tend to bring forth his most
> animalistic instincts.
>
> One early July during the Korean war, we had to move quickly to secure a
> position on Pork Chop Hill. The composition soles of my shoes burned my
> feet as I watched my weary men moving up in staggering columns, bending
> under soggy packs, almost sapped of all their strength . . . at about 3:20
> a.m. mortar and artillery fires began to fall again and build up to an
> extremely rapid rate. At the height of this fire holocaust, the startling voice
> of my forward platoon leader frantically rang out over the sound-powered
> telephone—"Captain, they're coming up the hillside, hundreds of them. My
> God, black figures, they are everywhere." As I called for my final protective
> line fires, I looked up from the trenches—the enemy seemed to blanket the
> whole hillside. Men were screaming and shouting—I still remember some of
> the cries such as "I'm blinded, help me, don't let them take me," as some
> soldiers were dragged away. The fight was mass confusion and exhausting.
> We were like vicious animals in the hand-to-hand fighting that followed. As
> daylight broke that morning, we could see the hill was covered with bodies,
> some of which had been there several days from previous battles. Our first
> task was to clean out the trenches by throwing the dismembered hands and
> limbs, caused from grenade and artillery explosions, over the top of the para-
> pet. . . . This description covers only two days of my experience on Pork
> Chop Hill. Without physical strength, none of us could have made it.[48]

The recent Falklands campaign confirmed this basic picture. While Argentina had the preponderance of futuristic weapons (some of British manufacture), the British had morale, leadership, and—what proved decisive—old-fashioned infantry stamina. The decisive action of the campaign was a fifty-mile march by Royal Marines packing 100 pounds through freezing rain and over the rocky terrain of East Falkland Island, a feat the Argentines had not considered possible.[49]

Many egalitarians say they respect this empirical argument, but appeal to what they regard as the rights of unusually tough females who wish to be considered for combat, and the correlative need for gender-neutral testing to determine combat capability:

> Gender-neutral tests can and should be devised and administered to determine whether persons of either sex are physically capable of the duties required of a given military occupational speciality. . . . [T]o the degree they have been tested, women have proved themselves capable of a wide range of combat duty.[50]

One may reasonably doubt, in light of the WITA experience, that any such test could be devised or applied. Any test would almost certainly be judged by a disparate impact standard, and complaints of inequity raised if officers at the front ordered mostly men to fight as a command decision. The chief uncertainty at present is whether a statistical preponderance of male fatalities would be taken as discrimination against men or women.

Allowing the best faith in the world to sexual egalitarians, their claims about tests for combat effectiveness are empty. No physical or psychological tests for combat fitness exist, and there is no reason to believe that any could be devised. Combat is so different from any other environment that psychological simulation of it is impossible. Equipment can be fairly reliably combated-rated under simulated conditions, because a tank can not tell whether it is being test-driven or driven to meet Warsaw Pact troops. Any test for readiness can be validated only in actual combat, when it is too late to correct errors. If the ability to perform very heavy tasks is a proxy for the physical strength necessary for combat, there are 3 sufficiently strong women for every 80 men. If the same ratio holds for aggressiveness, there will be one sufficiently strong and aggressive woman for every 711 men. It seems absurd to develop costly and uncertain predictors to detect this minuscule population when it is *known* that men can form effective fighting units.

Morale, Bonding, and Other Intangibles

There is wide agreement among military men that the effects on morale of "integrating" the military are more serious than the effects on economy and efficiency of force that arise from ignoring physical sex differences. Mixing males and females in the army adds an additional abrasive element into an environment already containing numerous intangible factors that may prevent a military organization from functioning adequately even though supplies are plentiful and planning brilliant.

One such new friction factor is "sexual harassment." Over the centuries, male soldiers have undergone various forms of hazing that has been part of the honing process that fits them physically and psychologically into the war machine. These rites of initiation have no counterparts in groups formed by women and may be perceived by them as harassment when it has no such function.[51] Army regulations that refer complaints of harassment through the chain of command, such as those now in place, shift command concentration from operations and training to an artificial problem. Then, too, building the concept of "sexual harassment" into standard procedures tends to strengthen the hand of critics who use "sexual harassment" as an all-purpose explanation of any shortfall from complete equality, again miring the military command in a nonmilitary bog.

Another morale problem arises from the reluctance of many men to subordinate themselves to women, a difficulty that may arise when female officers and NCOs are placed in command over male personnel. Orders given by women may lack the psychological weight that attends orders given by men seen as being capable of backing up words with more tangible measures; this is an important consideration in situations of great stress. Moreover, the vernacular used by male NCOs to galvanize male solders may be perceived as anomalous when used by women.[52] This problem is not critical so long as female commanders can count on higher male authorities to back them up in their dealings with male subordinates, but this causes female officers to rely more heavily on the code of military justice than "leadership by example," the traditional basis of military discipline. In fact, military publications do explicitly urge female officers to secure obedience by using their rank.[53] It is overwhelmingly likely that the difficulties experienced by women trying to command men, unlike any difficulties that might once have been encountered by Black men trying to command White men, are rooted in biology. One manifestation of male dominance-aggression is the male desire to dominate male-female encounters, an urge complemented by the stereotyped willingness of females to let the man be the dominant partner.[54] To the extent that these innate factors are at work, problems of insubordination in armed forces with a large female officer corps will not yield to management techniques.

The morale problem dealt with least realistically by egalitarians is male competition for women. Conventional military wisdom takes male-female bonding to be a disruptive matter of chemistry against which regulations are powerless. Anyone who has ever fallen in love understands the power of this emotion to distract attention from goals not of immediate concern to the lovers. As such, there is nothing to be done about sexual fraternization beyond limiting the conditions under which it is likely to occur. This course has not recommended itself to egalitarians. Sue Berryman finds it "self-evident" that sexual rivalry can be reduced by "constituting units with roughly equal numbers of men and women,"[55] as if numerical balance will preclude jealousy and other forms of amatory dissatisfaction. As for males protecting females in disregard of unit goals, which can occur just as easily after pairings have defused male-female rivalries, Berryman suggests that "we may have already observed the limits of [protectiveness] in past wars with all-male combat units." She speculates that integrating the service academies has created "role models of a brother-sister relationship with romantic entanglements excluded." Similar hypotheses are deployed to explain away male bonding in military units, which makes men willingly fight to the death for their friends. Unlike male-female bonding, which excludes competing loyalties, male bonding is inclusive and builds small groups of men into effective fighting units. The brawling, drinking, athletic rough-house, vulgarity, and sexual braggadocio of young men in groups, incomprehensible to most women, are the rituals that cement the male bond. Young men in groups often risk death rather than be thought "screw ups" by their companions and male authority figures, another aspect of male bonding important in combat and incomprehensible to most women. To be sure, not everyone acknowledges the phenomenon of male bonding: "Claims that women interfere with crucial 'male bonding' processes are specious, based on subjective and biased reporting, not on fact. Such ideas should be laid to rest."[56] Others who recognize the phenomenon, like Sue Berryman, explain it as an adaptation to sex-neutral roles which women will display once they are "trained in the formal role of the soldier":

> What is described as "masculine" represents a collection of attitudes and behaviors that make considerable adaptive sense for anyone in combat—whether male or female. . . . [W]hat have been identified as behaviors specific to males seem specific to a situation in which only males have routinely participated. . . . [I]n high stress . . . both sexes will manifest these responses.[57]

Berryman cites two pieces of evidence for this adventurous contention: Females talk more about their emotions than males do and show a greater capacity for emotional closeness, and "the data show that the ideals of manhood and loyalty to the primary combat group affect combat performance."[58] The first point is irrelevant, since the issue is not whether women feel emotions as intensely as men do, but whether they feel the same emotions. The second patently begs the questions, which is precisely whether women can be expected to react as men do to the stresses of combat. There is no reason to think that male bonding is adaptive for individuals, since it often leads men to sacrifice their lives. It is, however, an inclusively fit adaptation for the male of a K-selected species seeking to outdo his rivals.

There are egalitarians who tentatively admit that men act differently with each other than they do with females nearby, and that this factor contributes to combat effectiveness.

> The antics of a hero might look objectively foolish, even childish, but they do much to drive combat forward; and it might be that men would be less excessively masculine in the presence of women.[59]

As this unflattering language might suggest, Stiehm finds this situation a "problem," which

> would seem to lie not with the women but with the men, or with the group leader who lacks the ability to fuse a heterogenous group of individuals into an effective, purposeful fighting unit. Again, does the problem really lie with the stimulus or with the response?

Calling male rituals by derogatory names does not diminish their importance. A handful of women might be physically and psychologically suited for combat, but if their introduction into male units disrupts the intangible bonds that keep a unit effective, egalitarians will have to decide whether being defended by male boors is too high a price to pay for survival.

Deterrence and Credibility

A little-discussed friction factor abrading a sexually integrated military is the universal aversion to seeing women slaughtered. Environmentalist explanations of the taboo against exposing women to battle *must* be conspiratorial, since it has no apparent social as opposed to biological effect beyond denying weapons to women.

> But society forbids them to use its legal force. Why? Is it possible that this represents the collective oppression of one sex by the other, just as rape is said to be a "conscious process of intimidation by which all men keep all women in a state of fear?" Isn't the placing of virtually all weaponry in the hands of men basically an intimidating policy? When one is not permitted to have weapons but is "protected" by someone who does have weapons, it begins to sound like a protection racket is in full swing.[60]

This explanation inherits all the general objections to environmentalism: Why does "society" (which is half female) associate weapons with males? What started the association if women really want access to weapons as badly as men do? It also leaves this taboo a phenomenon disparate from the chivalric imperative "Women and children first," which normally benefits women, rather than, as it clearly is, a special case of the imperative. A better explanation of the taboo begins with the relative unimportance of males for reproduction. A group can survive the loss of most of its males but not any significant number of females. A group which did not evolve chivalric norms would be at a competitive disadvantage against groups which did; chivalric norms are always selected for in the course of social evolution—whatever the official reasons offered for them within a society—and by this point may have a biological component, just as the distress experienced by human beings watching a child die unquestionably has a biological component.

Tracing chivalry to biology is not to endorse it, but it is to point out the difficulties, perhaps the impossibility, of waging war with a significantly female force. Faced with choosing between surrender and the commitment of a heavily female force to battle, any public and any leader may be forced to choose surrender. At least 2,500 of the 25,000 women stationed with NATO forces in Europe will be killed or wounded at the outset of full-scale hostilities with the Warsaw Pact, according to the Pentagon's scenario for this eventuality. Could an American president commit troops to battle with the prospect of such a loss? It is possible that the United States has already passed the point at which it has begun to deter itself from fighting by the exposure of more women to danger than it would tolerate losing.

The message being sent to our allies and potential enemies by persistence in the unisex experiment is a question little discussed within the American military and intelligence community, whose overall estimate is that no one knows how others see this experiment. The egalitarian consensus is that "a nation signals the defensive nature and moral rectitude of its actions" by using women in combat (Judith Stiehm), which hostile governments will take "as a sign of determination" (Sue Berryman). This reading depends on there being a mortal threat to the United States and an insufficiency of men to meet it, which other nations can plainly see is not the case. A more natural construction to put on the signal sent by visibly subordinating military exigency to ideology is absence of the will that must accompany capability if the armed forces are to deter credibly. There can hardly be a senior American officer who does not realize this, or realize that his Soviet counterpart realizes that he realizes this. A sure signal of unwillingness to fight is persistence in a course of action that one's potential enemy is known to consider a signal of unwillingness. When I asked a senior member of the American intelligence community for his best guess about foreign perceptions of the unisex experiment, he replied, "They think we may have lost our marbles."

There is a logical peculiarity in the push for unisex protective services. No one seriously maintains that a unisex military will be *more* effective under conditions of engagement than an all-male military; at best it will be as good, and at worst it will be worse. What is more, no one, not even those who claim that women are fully as capable as men of discharging the functions required of the protective services, is willing to claim that there could be an all-female military or an all-female enforcement hierarchy ranging from patrol person through judge up to prison guard. To admit that an all-female military is inconceivable already closes the theoretical case against egalitarianism, since *all* the order-preserving organizations in human history have been all-male. It also begins to close the practical question of the limits to the use of women in the military and police. The use of women in these services will always depend essentially on the presence of men to back them up. All that remains uncertain is the point at which the female presence begins to render these services ineffective, a question about which the current experiments may supply some empirical data.

The sexual integration of the forces of order may seem more than an experiment because the visual appearance of successful enforcers is easily mimicked. It is easy to dress women in uniforms, issue them rifles, camouflage their faces and hang nightsticks and handcuffs from their belts. The visual plausibility of the result has nothing to do with what will happen when the shooting starts. Claims about women's latent *furor teutonicus* will have to await the first victorious female army.

Notes

1. Marietta Tree, cited in *Women in the Military: Hearings before the Military Personnel Subcommittee of the House Armed Services Committee,* November 13, 15, 16, 1979 and February 11, 1980 (Washington, D.C.: U.S. Government Printing Office, 1981), p. 189.
2. Richard Knox, "Growing Pains for Women Cadets," *Boston Globe* (June 19, 1978): 20.
3. *Women in the Military,* pp. 55–56.
4. Federal Judge Max Rosen writing for a three-judge panel that overturned male-only draft registration in *Goldberg v. Rotsker,* a decision reversed by the Supreme Court in 1981.
5. Sue Berryman, *The Social Composition of American Enlisted Forces* (New York: Ford Foundation, 1983), p. 105.
6. Diana Steele, "Women in the Military: Substantial Barriers Remain," *Women's Rights Report of the American Civil Liberties Union* 3 (Winter 1981): 1.
7. "Reality Test at West Point," in Betty Friedan, *The Second Stage* (New York: Simon & Schuster, 1981).
8. Panel Discussion, in *Registration and the Draft,* ed. Martin Anderson (Stanford, Ca.: Hoover Institution, 1982), p. 42.
9. "Women in Combat," (Washington, D.C.: WEAL, 1981).
10. *Women's Rights Report.*

11. Bruce N. Bant, "Working Together: The Army's Assault on Sexism," *Soldier* (October 1980): 6.
12. GAO Report FPCD-76-26, *Job Opportunities for Women in the Military,* 1976.
13. *Owens v. Brown,* 455 FSupp 291.
14. See "Single Mothers Join Suit to Enlist in the Military," *New York Times* (December 25, 1984): B2.
15. See the testimony of Antonia Chayes, Kathleen Carpenter (then Defense Department Undersecretary for Equal Opportunity), and Robert Pirie (then Defense Department Undersecretary for Manpower) in *Women and the Military.*
16. Allen Carrier, "Defense EO Chief Decries End of Army Coed Basic," *Army Times* (July 12, 1983).
17. Randall Shoemaker, "Women Officers Expected to Increase to 12%," *Army Times* (June 12, 1983).
18. *Going Strong: Women in Defense* (Washington, D.C.: Department of Defense, 1984).
19. See "Women in the Soviet Forces," under "Military Affairs Abroad," *Air University Quarterly* (January–February 1983).
20. Diana Steele, ACLU counsel, *Women in the Military,* p. 269.
21. See Michael Levin, "Reluctant Heroes," *Policy Review* 26 (Fall 1983): 94–98. See also idem, "Women as Soldiers: The Record so Far," *The Public Interest* 76 (Summer 1984): 31–44.
22. Anderson, *Registration and the Draft,* p. 210.
23. Margaret Mead, "A National Service System as a Solution to a Variety of National Problems," in *The Military Draft,* ed. Martin Anderson (Stanford, Ca.: Hoover Institution, 1982), pp. 439–42.
24. The problem was brought into focus by two articles by retired brigadier general Theodore Metaxis: "How Realistic are Female PT Standards?" *Army Times* (March 21, 1977): 15–33, and "WAC Training Needs Scientific Evaluation," *Army Times* (March 28, 1977): 15–17.
25. *Women in the Army Policy Review* (Washington, D.C.: Department of the Army, November 12, 1982).
26. Larry Carney, "Recruit Strength," *Army Times* (April 11, 1983).
27. Interview with author, June 15, 1983.
28. Carrier.
29. News Release no. 522-83 (Washington, D.C.: Office of Assistant Secretary of Defense [Public Affairs], October 20, 1983).
30. Carrier.
31. *Hearings before the Subcommittee on the Constitution of the Senate Judiciary Committee on S.J. Res. 10,* pt. 1, p. 371.
32. D.M. Kowal, "Nature and Causes of Injuries in Women Resulting from an Endurance Training Program," *The American Journal of Sports Medicine* (1980), reprinted as Appendix C of WITA.
33. See Michele McCormick, "Soldier-Mothers Create a Feeling of Concern," *Army Times* (July 4, 1983).
34. Owen Platen, "Women in the Ranks," *Firehouse* (March 1983): 47–49.
35. Michael Daly, "Firewoman," *New York* (January 10, 1983): 25. See also *Berkman* cases.
36. "Fire Retardant," *New York* (February 7, 1983): 9.
37. See "Fem Cop Beaten on Subway," *New York Daily News* (April 28, 1983): 5.
38. *Women on Patrol* (New York: VERA Institute, 1978), pp. 50–58.

39. See Jean Yarborough, "The Feminist Mistake," *Policy Review* 33 (Summer 1985): 52.
40. Cited in "Women Firefighters Still Spark Resentment in Strongly Macho Job," *Wall Street Journal* (March 3, 1983): 25.
41. James Webb, "Women Can't Fight," *Washingtonian* (November 1979). Reprinted in *Congressional Record* (September 3, 1980): S11894–S11897.
42. Judith Stiehm, "Women and the Combat Exemption," *Parameters* 10 (June 1980): 51–59.
43. July 28, 1980, p. 23.
44. Charles Moskos, "Serving in the Ranks," in *Registration and the Draft*, p. 131.
45. "Women in the Military," p. 2.
46. FM-100-5 (revised August 20, 1982), pp. 1–2.
47. M.C. Devilbiss, "Women and the Draft," in *The Military Draft*, p. 87.
48. *Women in the Military*, pp. 276–80.
49. See William Fowler, *Battle for the Falklands (1): Land Forces* (London: Osprey, 1982).
50. "Women in the Military."
51. See Judith Mann, "Is It Really Discrimination, or Just Hazing?" *Philadelphia Inquirer* (June 3, 1982): D1.
52. See "Male Voice Carries Authority, Says Study," *New York Times News Service* (February 5, 1981).
53. See e.g. Marianne Lester, "When the Boss Is a Woman," *The Times* (January 14, 1980): 4–8.
54. See Goldberg, pp. 37–40, 72.
55. "Social Composition," p. 105.
56. *Impact*, p. 369.
57. Berryman, pp. 112–13.
58. Ibid., p. 111.
59. Stiehm, p. 55.
60. Ibid., p. 57.

12

Language

Words are wise men's counters, they do but reckon by them: but they are the money of fools.

—Thomas Hobbes

Of all feminist initiatives, the attempt to alter language is the most apt to provoke derision. It is difficult to suppress a smile when "manholes" become "personholes." The Labor Department's replacement of "fisherman" and "newsboy" by "fisher" and "news carriers," the National Weather Service's scrupulous alternation of male with female names for hurricanes (which begins with male and female "A" names in alternate years), engage the sense of the absurd by their strenuous pursuit of the trivial.

Absurd or not, this campaign has been markedly successful, well beyond the embrace of linguistic guidelines by publishers and professional organizations. Executive officers have become chairpersons and chairs. Businessmen have become business professionals. Ships are no longer manned, but crewed by crewmembers. Hockey defensemen are "defenders" and "defensive players." "He/she's" populate public utterances and private memos. There are computer programs to insert "or she" after inadvertent "he's" (and to delete such words as *virile, manly,* and *manhood*). Schools encourage teachers to call their charges "children" instead of "boys and girls." "Man" as the inclusive name for the human biological species has become taboo, with parallel efforts under way to change other languages.

That natural language infuriates feminists is clear enough:

> Sexist language is no less noxious than racist language. As Kett and Underwood say in their recent book, "Avoiding *he* is equal to taking down the 'whites only' sign in a restaurant."[1]

What precisely is wrong with the inclusive use of "he" and related features of natural languages is less clear. These usages are said to be "biased," but language, which distributes nothing and takes nothing, cannot be directly assessed by the canons of justice. Speaking more analytically, there are four standard objections to current speech patterns: (1) They reflect the inferior state of women; (2) they perpetuate this inferior status; (3) they menda-ciously represent women as inferior to or different from men; and (4) they insult women by making them "invisible." Many of these charges are made in *The Right Word*, a booklet prepared by the National Committee of the American Society for Public Administration. According to *The Right Word*, current language presents a "danger" to working women by its "perpetua-tion of myths and false generalizations . . . 'active' and 'passive' are descriptive of individual personality—not gender; sometimes men are quiet [and] women are insensitive." The pronoun "he" is objectionable because it results in "misleading and inaccurate communication" and "reinforces the perception of woman as an appendant to generic 'man,' " as well as "rein-forcing inequity based on gender." Or, as Marie Shear puts it, "Male pro-nouns . . . imply that everyone who is anyone is male."[2] Similar theses are maintained in more scholarly works.[3]

These charges cannot all be leveled consistently. If women enjoy lower status than men and have been pushed by socialization from society's main-stream, it is not a lie to represent women in this light—assuming that it is *language* that can be properly said to represent anything, rather than *speak-ers* who represent things by use of the means language supplies. If some traits are for whatever reason more prevalent in one sex, it is not mytholo-gizing to reserve the appropriate epithets for that sex. One cannot coherently complain that "he" refers basically to men, and that the mascu-line "he" refers to *both men and women*. In fact, before going further, we may dismiss the idea that masculine pronouns are misleading. Words are misleading when they mislead. If nobody is misled by a turn of phrase, it is not misleading, and there is no one over the age of three who has been fooled by "he" into thinking that women are unpersons. It is not possible to produce a woman who believed (until feminists cleared things up) that "He who hesitates is lost" did not apply to her. It is universally understood that "he" is used with the intention of referring to both men and women, and that this intention has settled into a convention. Nothing more is required for a purely designative expression like "he" to *mean* men and women both.

Possibly because the only difficulty created by ordinary language is that feminists do not like it, feminist linguistic reform has become a kind of ongoing referendum about feminism itself. In the absence of any clearer purpose, substituting "person" for "man" is a concession made to feminists just because feminists demand it. As a result, whatever thought is to be con-veyed in the act of communication is consciously subordinated to equity, with the collateral effect of obscuring whatever is actually being said. When clergymen refer to "Our Father and Mother who art in Heaven," or "The God of Abraham and Sarah," as many now do, or when contemporary reworkings of the New Testament change the "Son of God" to "The Human One," they shift attention from religion to the struggle against sexism. Feminist linguistic reform is an attempt to make all thought whatsoever concern feminism to the exclusion of everything else.

Feminist linguistic reform is for this reason far from inconsequential. Linguistic change legislated to conform to a worldview makes people self-conscious about their own language, an uncomfortable state of mind that may properly be called oppressive. Language is the vehicle of thought, and in an important sense speakers must be unconscious of choosing their words if they are to express their thoughts. When we become entangled in decisions about how to talk, we lose contact with the reality our talk is supposed to be about. Like playing the piano, language is largely a system of acquired habits, and fluent speech accompanied by constant conscious decisions about which words to utter is as difficult as fluent pianism accompanied by constant conscious decisions about which keys to hit. The most uncomfortable moments in life—emotional scenes, first dates, delicate negotiations with the boss—are distinguished by precisely this need to anticipate what to say. There is no need to think about words when things go smoothly—the right words come unprompted. The distraction occasioned by the felt need not to offend the notional feminist watchperson hovering nearby makes everyone just that much more self-conscious about talking. As *The Right Word* admits, "the newly sensitized administrator is frequently tongue-tied." Feminists insist that this self-consciousness passes in a few weeks. The reader must judge the plausibility of this guarantee for himself.

Language and Thought

At the end of this chapter we will look at attempts to enforce feminist linguistic reform by law. For now it suffices to remember that enforced ideological linguistic reform has been tried before, and failed. During the Reign of Terror that succeeded the French Revolution, all persons were addressed as "citizen" and "citizeness." Russians became "comrades" after the Bolshevik Revolution. In both cases these conventions swiftly became empty, for reality is not so obliging as to follow language. The ordinary worker may be officially entitled to address the First Secretary of the Party as "comrade," but that has not made them friends or equals in any substantial way. Russians must still privately distinguish genuine comrades from pro forma ones, thus undercutting the reform. The failure of "comrade" and "citizen" to induce political equality suggests that language does not and cannot shape thought in the manner or to the extent supposed by egalitarian reformers. Attempts to alter putatively biased thinking by altering the language which expresses this thinking reverse cause and effect. At the same time, these attempts have negative short-term effects of the sort mentioned in the previous section.

The beginning of wisdom on this complex subject is to reject the idea, advanced by a number of contemporary anthropologists and philosophers, that language shapes rather than reflects reality, and the related thesis, usually called the Whorf hypothesis, that a speaker's language is a significant factor in determining his conception of the world, particularly the social world.[4] In my view, the Whorf hypothesis completely reverses the direction of the causal arrows connecting language, thought, and reality.[5]

Speakers mark a distinction linguistically when the distinction becomes important, and name a phenomenon when the phenomenon becomes salient; things do not *become* important *because* the means to describe them have been enlarged. Imagine a community of cavemen who call all furry animals by the single word *furry* (or, to avoid anachronism, a word best translated into English as "furry".) Suppose that one kind of furry animal begins to attack members of the community. The community would almost certainly coin a special name for that special animal—"leopard," say. Cave children would thereafter be warned about leopards, and the next generation of adults would see leopards as particularly dangerous. It is surely implausible to attribute these changes in outlook to the addition of "leopard" to the communal vocabulary. The cavemen fear leopards because leopards attack them, not because "leopard" has fearsome connotations; quite the reverse—the coinage "leopard" acquired fearsome connotations because leopards themselves are menacing.

Feminist monitoring of language can be simulated in this situation by a shamanistic injunction to remove "leopard" from the cave vocabulary because using "leopard" is sinful. In that case, a viable cave community would simply *reinvent* a synonym for the old world *leopard,* or some handy descriptive device for capturing the difference between harmless and dangerous furry animals. The least likely outcome would be for speakers of the newly "leopard"-less language to cease fearing leopards. Speakers desirous of obeying the shaman would experience short-term difficulties in heeding the distinction between leopards and other things, to be sure, and aversion to the guilt attendant on verbalizing leopard-thoughts would generalize to aversion to leopard-thoughts themselves. No one would want to think about, much less talk about, leopards. Even though the use of "leopard" does not cause leopard-thoughts, thoughts are sufficiently associated with words for both to come to control a response originally keyed on just one. George Orwell was right to think that tinkering with language disrupts thought, but wrong to think that this was because language determines thought. The disruption is in fact the product of two vectors: positive reinforcement by reality for calling things as they are seen, and fear of pain conditioned by harassment for calling things as they are seen. The effect Orwell identified might be compared to the flickering of a flame caused by a blockage in the ventilation shaft.

The perception- and reality-dependence of language is illustrated by anthropological data commonly thought to illustrate the language-dependence of perception. Take the variety of Eskimo words for snow. In fact, Eskimos differ from speakers of English not in seeing as different what speakers of English see as similar, but in having short phrases for the different kinds of snow that speakers of English can distinguish only clumsily. The availability in Eskimo of distinct words for differently textured snow is a linguistic adaptation to the importance of weather in Eskimo life. English speakers can say whatever Eskimos can say and describe any kind of snow Eskimos can describe, albeit more longwindedly. There has been no pressure on speakers of English to compress the description "dry, powdery snow that cannot be packed into snowballs" because, in the environments in which the typical speaker of English finds himself, the texture of snow is unrelated to vital interests like the location of food. Or consider the Hopi, who use different words for the spilling and pouring of powders, but the same word for the spilling and pouring of liquids.[6] It is better to explain Hopi usage in terms of the Hopi sense of similarity—the Hopi find the spillage of different substances less similar than they do the spillage and pouring of the same substance—than to explain the Hopi sense of similarity in terms of Hopi usage. The latter explanation cannot address the question of where the Hopi usage itself came from, while numerous non–question-begging explanations can be suggested for the origin of particular similarity spacings. To have interesting empirical content, the Whorf hypothesis must predict that the Hopi *disregard* the difference between spilling and pouring liquids—that, for instance, Hopi mothers punish their children for naughtily pouring water from jugs *and* for accidentally spilling it, in contrast to English-speaking mothers who punish water mischief but not water accidents. So far as I know, this has not been observed to be a trait of Hopi behavior. In fact, so many observations are at variance with the Whorf hypothesis—primitive people with no word for "jet plane" notice and become quite worked up about the first jet plane that flies low over their heads—that its defenders usually reformulate it in terms of *inclinations* created by language to heed or ignore phenomena. It is not clear that hypotheses about inner mental models of the universe that lack behavioral manifestations are empirically significant.

I believe social scientists are led to suppose that speakers of differing languages see the world differently through identifying the expressibility of a thought in a language with the presence in that language of a single word for the thought. That this *is* an error in plain enough from the undoubted expressive equivalence of French with English despite the French use of pairs of syncategorematic particles to express negation. Neither "ne" nor "pas" means quite what "not" means, yet "Je ne danse pas" means exactly what "I do not dance" means (to the extent that synonymy can survive the attacks of the philosopher Quine). Social scientists sometimes stumble over this point in their very attempt to describe incompatible linguistic frameworks. Carol Eastman writes: "American English does not have a kinship term which refers to one's daughter's husband's brother."[7] It does, of course—"one's daughter's husband's brother."

Still, might not concepts for which no single word exists be more *difficult* to utilize than those for which there is a single, familiar word? (So that it would be *harder* to be sexist in a gender-neutral language.) There is evidence that this is not so when the environment is sufficiently demanding. The Nigerian language Wolof contains no single word for "blue," a single word denoting both "red" and "orange," and a vague word most nearly equivalent to "yellow." Bruner, Greenfield, and Olver[8] found that children who speak Wolof classified toy trucks with respect to color and function just as French children do.

A language expresses a culture and its patterns of thinking—"A language is a form of life," in Ludwig Wittgenstein's Whorfian apothegm—in the sense that much may be inferred about the culture and environment of a group from its language, particularly its vocabulary. An observer can infer a great deal about the Eskimo's world from the large number of Eskimo words for "snow." In this sense, but in no stronger sense, language is continuous with culture. An observer, then, who knew nothing of the human race, could infer from its "sexist" languages that human beings perceive the sexes to be dimorphic. And, just as he would conclude that Eskimos would not have coined so many words for different kinds of snow unless there *were* different kinds of snow, he will conclude that human discourse probably reflects some truth about sex dimorphism. What really bothers feminists about language is that virtually every natural language records a fundamental recognition of sex differences. The feminist quarrel is not with language, but the reality behind language and the human recognition of this reality. When the demand is made that "men working" signs be replaced by "people working" signs (as the state of New York is spending ten million dollars over a ten-year period to accomplish), the aim is not fairness but the denial of sexual dimorphism. Feminists want language to be the way it would have been had the sexes been the same. Because the feminist argument reverses the causal arrow between the perception of sex differences and the origin of this perception, it is not altogether clear whether feminists expect a neutered language to change the reality behind it, or whether they simply regard the avoidance of acknowldgement of this reality as intrinsically desirable.[9] Either expectation is an attack on the messenger.

Examples

An example of the confusion of words with their referents is Robin Lakoff's observation that people look askance at men who have mastered the vocabulary of sewing. This observation, although correct, has nothing to do with language. People take mastery of any specialized vocabulary to indicate familiarity with its subject. Since in our culture most men are unfamiliar with seams, hems, and other details of sewing, a man who speaks competently about them is anomalous, and draws the suspicion normally directed at any anomaly, because he shows an anomalous familiarity with sewing itself. This is a fact about people's attitude toward men and sewing, not their attitude toward men and words about sewing. Assuming it desirable to change this attitude, this change cannot be induced by encouraging people to say "John fingered the damask" with a straight face (as Lakoff herself seems at times to realize.)

An extensive subgenre of feminist writing on language is directed against sexual slang.[10] Feminists correctly observe that sex described from the male point of view is always active (men "conquer" and "score," "screw" and "hump") while sex described from the female point of view is passive (women "put out" and are "satisfied"). The anger provoked by these idioms is probably beyond the reach of reason, but it is worthwhile pointing out that in sex men *do* aggress while women are receptive. A man must achieve erection and a woman must relax. The ability to sustain an erection no matter what is a point of pride for many men, whereas women do not regard the ability to relax sexually as a comparable achievement. It is hardly surprising that metaphors for sexual intercourse should reflect these facts, or that these metaphors should involve the insertion of prongs into orifices. Parental investment theory predicts that sex for men will be accompanied by feelings of mastery, and sex for women by feelings of surrender—psychological realities merely reflected in language.

The neologism *Ms.* also puts the linguistic cart before the horse of reality. "Ms." was explicitly introduced by feminists as a device to mask the marital status of women just as "Mr." does for men, it being felt that the "Miss./Mrs." distinction disadvantageously "defines" women in terms of their relations with men. More recently, there have been efforts to replace "Ms." by the even more sex-neutral convention of designating women by their last names alone in contexts in which men are so designated. Whether these notational changes can contribute to making marital status no more important for women than it is for men depends on the function of "Miss." and "Mrs." As the most adaptive strategy for K-selected males is the aggressive pursuit of many females, while the most adaptive strategy for females is monogamous surrender to the male who vanquishes his competitors, it must be the K-selected male who initiates courtships. So as not to waste calories pursuing already mated females, a male must be able to gauge the availability of females he encounters. The female, who does not initiate courtship needs no such gauge; a male's initiation of mating rituals—showing off his tailfeathers, requesting a date—is itself a signal of his interest. Every human society will evolve a device to signal the male about the availability of females. (Male philanderers send false signals by approaching females as if unattached; on the whole, married women are less inclined to stray because one mate is all a woman needs for maximum reproductive success. In any event, social signals evolve to fit the average.) The wish to collapse "Miss." and "Mrs." into Ms.'s who resemble Mr.'s is the wish that women be thought of as selecting sexual partners in the way and with the purposes characteristic of men. It is a wish for the terms of address and marital status that would have evolved had there been no differences in the sexual nature of men and women. (I suspect that the conventional prefixing of some title to female names reflects an unconscious desire to soften the harsh functionality of bare name reference, which *is* thought appropriate for men.)

The more deeply language is probed, the more traces it reveals of the beings that produce it. The cases of nouns in languages with masculine and feminine words are usually appropriate; "house" is usually feminine and "key" masculine. The neuter in classical Greek coincides with the masculine more often than with the feminine, and never with the feminine alone—perhaps reflecting some dim perception that men have a greater affinity with neutral things. The *absence* of cases from a language has no correspondence with a cultural history in which women experience unusual political equality with men or are accorded unusually extensive participation in male spheres. Turkish lacks cases, but Turkish women lack many rights enjoyed by women in countries with more "sexist" native tongues.

Does Language Insult Women?

That natural languages reflect sex differences makes natural languages anti-woman only on the assumption that typically male traits are better than typically female ones and that any reflection of sex differences is a reminder of female inferiority. In fact, language cannot be misogynistic (or be biased against anything else) for the simple reason that anything at all about men and women, indeed anything at all about anything, can be said in any natural language. Take the word *shrew,* whose presence in English is sometimes cited as an instance of linguistic bias against aggressive women. Now, English cannot force anybody to believe that there are strident women, for if it did it would be impossible to say in English that there are no shrewish women, which is easily done by uttering the sentence "There are no shrewish women." Nor does the admitted negative weight of "shrew" compel dislike of certain forms of female behavior, for English and other natural languages contain devices for neutralizing evaluative connotations. Anyone who does not mind the behavior normally called shrew-ish need only say "I don't mind the behavior normally called 'shrewish.'"

There remains the charge that "he," "mankind," and their cognates slight women by referring to them by words that are also used to refer to men alone, thereby implying that women are not important enough to deserve a name of their own. This charge is silly for the same reason it is silly to say that "he" does not refer to women. Just as reference is secured by a mutu-ally recognized intention to refer—so that "he" refers to women as well as men because everyone realizes that it does—so an insult is a word or ges-ture used with the *intention* of causing affront through the recognition of that intention.[11] In the all-important point of their history, words like *he* and *man* are neutral names for the human race as a whole; whatever the reason that the collective name for males is also the collective name for males and females, nobody ever adopted this usage *with the intention* of causing feel-ings of shame and inadequacy, or with the intention of expressing contempt. The word *nigger*, by contrast, *is* intended to affront by expressing con-tempt. It has acquired this conventional force because its original usage was known to be accompanied by contempt, so that its continued use by a speaker, who would be presumed to know that feelings of contempt would be imputed to him, amounted to the intention of expressing contempt. The generic "he" has no similar history.

No matter what distress it may cause, a word or gesture is not insulting unless accompanied by or known to be conventionally associated with mal-ice. If my passing remark about your tie causes chagrin because of some event in your childhood unknown to me, I have not insulted you. Were ordinary pronouns insulting to women, every utterance ever voiced in English before 1970 was an insult. It would follow that Shakespeare unin-tentionally insulted women when he had Hamlet say "I'll make a ghost of him who lets me" without threatening Ophelia. The idea of an unintended insult makes no more sense than that of unintended discrimination.

The use of "he" has doubtless *become* provocative, but only because the feminist movement has made it so. By announcing that they will respond belligerently to "he," feminists have turned it into a fighting word. They have so raised linguistic consciousness that some decisions on pronouns have become unavoidable; if one is not profeminist in one's usage, one declares oneself defiantly antifeminist. It is of course the feminists' privilege to transform a previously inoffensive pronoun into a fighting word, as it is the privilege of the saloon brawler to announce that touching an intrinsically inoffensive chip on his shoulder will henceforth be con-strued as a challenge to fight. It is, however, quite absurd for feminists to decide to take offense at the English language and then complain that offensive remarks are constantly falling on their ears.

What Feminist Reform Accomplishes

Embedded sex differentiations do not desensitize language to social change. World War II produced "Rosie the Riveter," just as the popularity of Charles Dana Gibson's drawings produced the "Gibson girl" in a previous era. But such changes cannot be predicted, let alone dictated, for they arise from the same unconscious depths as speech itself and in response to the unpredictable contingencies in the extralinguistic world.

Because language reflects reality and not vice versa, universal adoption of feminist usages will do nothing to "upgrade" women. Indeed, there is an inconsistency between the claim that such coinages will beneficially raise consciousness and the demand that these coinages become the unconscious standard, for if "he or she" comes to be used as "he" now is (or was until very recently), namely as an indexical device, it will prompt no thoughts of sexual equality. The change will simply sprinkle a great many "she's" where none would otherwise have been found, a protocol as empty as calling everyone "comrade." If sprinkling "she's" is to have a point, the point must be kept in mind; if "he or she" becomes the *un*conscious norm, it will leave everything as it is. The same perceptions which once created "he" will continue to operate. Suppressing one or many of their linguistic manifestations will simply leave these perceptions in temporary tension with a language forbidden to express them—temporary, because they will find other expressions.

These points are unintentionally illuminated by an experiment taken by its designers to show that "he" suppresses thoughts of women.[12] It was found that people are more likely to think of a man first when "he" is used in sentences than when "he or she" is used. An alternative interpretation of this experiment comes to mind when its unsurprising result is redescribed as the greater readiness of people to think of a woman first when "he or she" is used than when "he" is used. It is surely more plausible to suppose that "he or she" prompts previously unentertained thoughts of women than that "he" quashes previously excogitated thoughts of women ready to enter consciousness. Consider the same experiment with "she" replaced by "a kangaroo." No doubt people are more likely to think of a human being first if "he" is used than if "he or a kangaroo" is, but does this mean that "he" inhibits thoughts of kangaroos, or that "he or a kangaroo" produces thoughts of kangaroos that would not otherwise have existed? The experiment as conducted relies on the current novelty value of "he or she." There is no reason to think the effect would continue should "he or she" simply *replace* "he" as the standard, unconscious conventional mode of reference used by English speakers from birth. People would continue to think first of whomever experience showed to lead the way in most activities, which would still be men.

It is extremely unlikely that "he or she," "he/she," "s/he" or similar neologisms will acquire purely indexical status, since they are syntactically complex. The mind seeing an "or," overt or disguised by a slash, wants to construct the meaning of the complex or-phrase from its components. The only practical replacement for "he" would have to be a completely new word bearing no syntactical relation to "he." The prospects for injecting such a word into a natural language by fiat are nil.

While its oppressiveness and clumsiness may sink feminist newspeak of its own weight, this tampering with language can, as noted, carry important negative consequences. Punishing words creates an aversion to the thoughts these words normally express, and while nothing can make people permanently disregard what they see, people can be made to *worry* about acknowledging what they see. This happened during the Victorian era, when an unwillingness to acknowledge sex openly drove people to clothe the "limbs" of tables and devise elaborate euphemisms for anything vaguely corporeal. Considerable damage was done in the way of hysteria and repression (although sex itself seems to have survived). Feminists seek to make taboo the acknowledgement of anything having to do with sex differences, and particularly with masculinity. For all their good words for forms of sexual behavior the Victorians would have abhorred, feminists are rather akin to Victorians.

Language and Government

Insofar as the feminist invasion of the mind is a private effort, there is nothing further to be said about it than to point out the errors on which it rests. It is up to each individual whether or not to lower his mental portcullis. The extent to which the government has taken the feminist side in this invasion is so far relatively minor. Still, neutering language is presented as a matter of rights, and the censoring of "discriminatory language" is increasingly equated with antidiscriminatory legislation.[13] Some feminists hold "sexist language" to violate Title VII and Title IX; during a television discussion in which I participated, it was asserted that control of the language of textbooks was a matter of "civil rights."[14]

The state has, somewhat tentatively, accepted the invitation to enter. In 1980, the secretary of health and human services prohibited the use of "sex biased" terms in departmental communications, and sent copies of *The Right Word* to all regional officers. A "right to be free of sexist language" is cited in Iowa's ban on language that "excludes women" in its public schools. This right is also cited in section 1604.11, the federal ban on "sexual harassment," which gives legal effect to the theory that language may serve as an oppressive force against women. As I noted in chapter 9, "sexual harassment" conjures up images of sexual blackmail, and there might be a case for treating sexual blackmail as a problem of some sort, if not perhaps a federal tort, if a precisely and narrowly defined case could be made for its prevalence. This condition is not met in section 1604.11, whose central provision run as follows (emphasis added):

> Section (a)(3): *verbal* or physical conduct of a sexual nature constitute[s] sexual harassment when such conduct has the purpose *or effect* of unreasonably interfering with an individual's work performance or creating an intimidating, hostile or *offensive* work environment.
>
> Section (c): an employer is responsible for its acts and those of its agents and supervisory employees with respect to sexual harassment regardless of whether the specific acts complained of were authorized or even forbidden by the employer and *regardless of whether the employer knew or should have known* of their occurrence.
>
> Section (e): An employer may also be responsible for the acts of non-employees.
>
> Section (f): An employer should take all steps necessary to prevent sexual harassment from occurring, such as affirmatively raising the subject, expressing strong disapproval, developing appropriate sanctions, informing employees of their right to raise and how to raise the issue of harassment under Title VII, and developing methods to sensitize all concerned.[15]

This language is aimed less at sexual blackmail than at any communication involving sex which, intentionally or unintentionally, bothers someone. It is consistent with (a)(3) that use of the epithet "bitch" is a tort; whether it actually is such will depend on the discretion of the federal judiciary. It is consistent with (a)(3) that an epithet need be directed at no particular individual to be harassing; if a woman is offended by an argument in the workplace using off-color language, she has standing and a prima facie case, as does a woman being pestered for a date. If a woman in a workplace dislikes a male coworker's sexual boasts, or the pin-ups in his locker, she may have a legally sound complaint; its "reasonableness" is a matter for judicial determination. Heated insistence on sex differences in an office argument will also be tortious if the federal courts see it as sufficient grounds for offense. (When section 1604 was issued for preliminary public comment before publication in the Federal Register, feminists argued strenuously for the deletion of the (a)(3) reasonableness test.)

The strict liability created by (c) for an employer for any sexual harassment by an employee or, per clause (e), any passerby, codifies *Miller,* in which the Bank of America was found responsible for a supervisor's firing a subordinate for denying him sexual favors. The application of a strict standard of liability is notable beyond its transformation of a tort that one would have thought inherently intentional. Strict liability, the threat to inflict punishment for events beyond the tort-feasor's control, is rare in the law. Some jurists regard it as a holdover from a time before the concept of individual responsibility had been developed. Jurists who do see a place for strict liability in Western law regard it as a means for promoting vigilance against serious mishaps. A restaurant owner is held strictly liable for his patrons' food poisoning even if he has taken reasonable precautions against it, on the theory that food poisoning constitutes such grave harm that restaurant owners must be made to take extraordinary precautions against it. In effect, section 1604 holds that remarks capable of giving sexual offense are as harmful as food poisoning.

Clause (f) outlines the measures an employer must take to maintain this heightened vigilance. In tandem with strict liability, the affirmative obligations of clause (f) strongly encourage employers to raise a commotion when there is no prior evidence of a need to. One thinks of the shock the required steps might bring to the average male and female office workers. They are probably not bothered by "sex harassment," and perhaps have never heard of it. They may enjoy the mild flirting that goes on, and, if unmarried, may hope to find a marriageable partner at work. Suddenly, on government orders transmitted by the local AA/EEO office, comes a flood of memoranda, posters, videotapes, lectures, warnings, instructions for bringing lawsuits and incitements to file anonymous grievances. An employer who takes section 1604 seriously may make periodic sweeps of the janitor's locker room, and to be on the safe side dismiss any employee who asks a co-worker for a date. Chase Manhattan Bank, fearful of 1604 litigation, now forbids all physical contact between employees and discourages "verbal pats on the back." The employer must still anticipate inadvertently offensive remarks by nonemployees who happen onto the premises. The owner of a diner might feel safest by putting signs around his parking lot warning "Don't whistle at our waitpersons."

This neo-Victorian obsession with sexual misbehavior is designed to mix everyone's awareness of sex with the thought of legal reprisal, to suppress speech with any sort of sexual content, and, ultimately, to chill normal relations between men and women. It is difficult to understand a "civil rights" policy which insists via quotas on "sexually integrating" the workplace, and then threatens reprisal when men and women placed in proximity, often in situations of stress, refuse to pretend they are neuters.

To place 1604 in perspective, the reader might recall the Supreme Court doctrine that no speech, however disrespectful, contemptuous, or advocatory of violent change, can be prohibited unless it is inciteful of and imminently likely to produce lawless action.[16] Under this doctrine the Supreme Court has protected topless dancing, American flags worn on the seat of the pants in public schools, and neo-Nazi marches through Jewish neighborhoods. Yet making a pass at work is no longer protected against state action.

Notes

1. Marie Shearer, "Solving the Great Pronoun Problem: Twelve Ways to Avoid the Sexist Singular," *Perspectives: The Civil Rights Quarterly* 13 (Spring 1981): 18.

2. Ibid.

3. See e.g. Robin Lakoff, *Language and Women's Place* (New York: Harper & Row, 1975); Mary Vetterling-Braggin, ed., *Sexist Language* (Totowa, N.J.: Littlefield, Adams, 1981).

4. See Benjamin Whorf, *Language, Thought, and Reality,* ed J.E. Carroll (Cambridge, Mass.: MIT press, 1956).

5. See Michael Levin, *Metaphysics and the Mind-Body Problem* (London: Oxford University Press, 1979), pp. 152–56.

6. See J.B. Carroll and J.B. Casagrande, "The Function of Language Classifications in Behavior," in *Communication and Culture,* ed. A.G. Smith (New York: Holt, Rinehart, & Winston, 1966), pp. 489–514.

7. Carol Eastman, *Aspects of Language and Culture* (San Francisco: Chandler & Sharp, 1975), p. 88.

8. *Studies in Cognitive Growth* (New York: Wiley, 1966), p. 385ff.

9. Robin Lakoff does acknowledge that "social change creates language change, not the reverse" (*Language and Women's Place,* p. 59), a conclusion very vexing to Virginia Valian: "While we are curing the disease, no overnight affair, we can use a little relief from the symptoms . . . not only is reduction of suffering a good in itself, it often gives the patient the strength to fight the disease more effectively. . . . The disease . . . is not social inequality but lack of power over one's life; all forms of oppression—be they economic, psychological, social, or linguistic—are merely symptoms of it" ("Linguistics and Feminism," in Vetterling-Braggin, p. 76). As the example mentioned at the beginning of the next section indicates, it is not clear that Lakoff herself is always consistent on the direction of the causal arrow.

10. See e.g. Barbara Lawrence, "Four-Letter Words *Can* Hurt You," in *Philosophy and Sex,* ed. Robert Baker and Frederick Elliston (Buffalo, N.Y.: Prometheus, 1975); Stephanie Ross, "How Words Hurt: Attitudes, Metaphors, and Oppression," in *Sexist Language,* pp. 194–216; Robert Baker, " 'Pricks' and 'Chicks': A Plea for Persons," in *Sexist Language,* pp. 161–82.

11. A large philosophical literature has developed a theory of linguistic meaning in terms of nested intentions; its primary contributors are H.P. Grice, P.F. Strawson, John Searle, Jonathan Bennett, David Lewis, J.L. Austin, and Stephen Schiffer.

12. Janice Moulton, George M. Robinson, and Cherin Elias, "Sex Bias in Language Use," *American Psychologist* (November 1978): 1032–36.

13. See Susan Salliday, Letter to the Editor, *Proceedings of the American Philosophical Association* 52 (August 1979): 869.

14. *Straight Talk,* WOR-TV, New York, June 21, 1982.

15. *Federal Register,* 45, 219, sec. 1604.11 (November 10, 1980), p. 74667. Sec. 1604.11 was issued by the EEOC as an implementing regulation of Title VII.

16. See *Brandenburg v. Ohio,* 395 US 444 (1969).

13

Sex, the Family, and the Liberal Order

> *Women's traditional role—and in particular their responsibility for child care—constitutes a significant barrier to equal opportunity.*
>
> —*Child Care and Equal Opportunity for Women,*
> U.S. Commission on Civil Rights, 1981

Contemporary feminism first gained wide public attention with its attack on marriage, motherhood, and conventional sexual relations. Its admirers are now somewhat rueful about the tone of these attacks:

> The slogans were extraordinary: marriage was hell, sex was political, coitus was killing, married women were prostitutes, babies were traps, intercourse was rape, love was slavery, families were prisons, and men were enemies.[1]

Feminists have for the most part moderated their tone, but not the substance of their views, which continue to influence public policy and conventional "wisdom about marriage, child rearing, and the female ' need ' for occupational achievement and independence from men."

Sex

Part of the oppression of women is that they are not allowed to enjoy sex.

> Sexual repression is one of the ways in which women are oppressed and one of the ways in which patriarchy is maintained. On another level, restraining sexuality is a very powerful way of controlling people—as Wilhelm Reich understood in his analysis of the Nazis.[2]

It is not made clear how denying sexual pleasure to women has made them obedient to men, but a big part of the liberation of women will be the removal of emotional, social, and biological obstacles to fulfillment.

> Women can never be sexually actualized as long as men control the means of production and reproduction. Women have had to barter their sexuality (or

264

their capacity for sexual pleasure) for economic survival and maternity. Female frigidity as we know it will cease only when such bartering ceases. Most women cannot be "sexual" as long as prostitution, rape, and patriarchal marriage exist, with such attendant concepts and practices as 'illegitimate' pregnancies, enforced maternity, "non-maternal" paternity, and the sexual deprivation of the "aging" woman. From a psychological point of view, female frigidity will cease when female children are surrounded by and can observe non-frigid female adults.[3]

The primary obstacle to fulfillment is the stereotype that men and women experience sex differently, men having a greater readiness for sexual arousal and casual sex, while female enjoyment of sex requires emotional closeness. To the extent that this difference is acknowledged, it is attributed to socialization, particularly the stricter sanctions most societies impose on female promiscuity. (At the same time, feminists laud female sexuality for its humaneness and describe male sexuality as if it were the frenzy of a barbarian invader.[4])

Women are additionally oppressed by the myth that penile penetration is the most satisfying form of sex, when in reality female sexual pleasure resides in the clitoris rather than the vagina. Just as the "primary male sex organ is the penis, so the primary female sex organ is the clitoris," said Alix Shulman, whose valedictory advice was "Think clitoris."[5] Freud is still excoriated for suggesting that enjoyment of vaginal intercourse is a sign of emotional maturity. These views lead naturally to masturbation:

> I think it's wonderful that women have discovered masturbation, because it will enable us to keep apart from men as long as necessary. . . . Some of the women I know are so pathetic. They run around looking for a man, any man, just because they don't know how to masturbate.[6]

Although more recent feminists avoid this unsavory tone, those who do discuss the mechanics of sex still find little good to say about vaginal penetration:

> It hardly seems necessary to point out the self-serving aspects of the theory of the vaginal orgasm, since the vagina is central to most men's sexual satisfaction. If the clitoris is recognized as central to many women's sexuality, it is a challenge to both phallic and male supremacy since it means fingers, or tongue *or* another woman can do better. Given the economic and political equality women were seeking, women might dispense with men altogether if left to their clitorality.[7]

The final obstacle of female sexual fulfillment is the unfair confinement of the danger of pregnancy to women. "It is not inevitable that women, not men, should bear the main consequences of unintended pregnancy and thus that their sexual expression should be inhibited by it."[8]

The removal of these barriers will lead to women becoming more like men with regard to sex, and men more like women. High-school sex education will "enable [a girl] to say 'yes' and feel good about herself," according to Letty Pogrebin, while "for a boy, good-bye to Mr. Macho, Don Juan, 'Get any lately?'"[9] Sexual liberation will mean the end of the idea of men as promiscuous aggressors tamed in marriage by women with more diffuse but emotionally richer erotic natures. As a result, men will become more aware of their obligation to give pleasure to their sexual partners.

Motherhood

Apart from a dwindling band who expect the replacement of maternity by technological surrogates, feminists concede gestation to be biologically innate to women. Their dissatisfaction concerns the institutions built thereon, which in their view needlessly keep women responsible for children after birth. "The institution of motherhood, as [poetess Adrienne] Rich shows, is indeed oppressive to mothers and those who are not mothers."[10] A large part of the problem is the disgusting nature of children, whom Elizabeth Janeway calls "tiny ogres of ferocious greed" and other feminists have described as "incontinent mental defectives." Shulamith Firestone wrote in *The Dialectic of Sex;*

> Like shitting a pumpkin, a friend of mine told me when I inquired about the Great-Experience-You're-Missing.   What's-wrong-with-shitting-shitting-can-be-fun says the male School of the Great Experience. . . . But-look-what-you-get-as-a-reward, says the School: a-baby-all-your-own-to-fuck-up-as-you-please.[11]

Dorothy Dinnerstein blames the "semimonstrousness" of human adults on "mother-dominated infancy":

> The deepest root of our acquiescence to the maiming and mutual imprisonment of men and women lies in the monolithic fact of a human childhood: under the arrangements that now prevail, a woman is the parental person who is every infant's first love.[12]

In considerably adulterated form, the idea that it is not good for a child to spend too much time with his mother has become very widely accepted.

Death and deformity remain ubiquitous themes in feminist writing on motherhood. Of the fifteen essays, stories, and poems in the June 1978 special issue of *Feminist Studies,* entitled *Toward a Feminist Theory of Motherhood,* all but three concern the death of babies or mothers. "Washing

Blood," the introductory essay by its editor, Rachel du Plessis, sets the tone:

> I dreamed that the best gift for a new mother was to come and help her wash the blood . . . There is so much death, for example, in the poems, in the "personal essay." Which makes me wonder about the topos of the dead baby in nineteenth century women's poetry. . . . Why? Because the social organization of motherhood is destructive, because motherhood under patriarchy means the death of the self.

In the essays that follow, Mary Oppen describes her daughter's crib death following the still-birth of a boy; Arlene Stove writes of her attempt "to defecate a child"; and Sandra Gilbert offers an allegorical reading of *Frankenstein,* according to which "Victor Frankenstein has a baby." (Mary Shelley was secretly expressing "woman's helpless alienation in a male society.") Faye Moskowitz's "A Leak in the Heart" describes the death of a baby with a bad heart. Alicia Ostriker's "The Mother/Child Papers," a diary of the birth of her baby kept at the time of the Kent State incident, concludes with the reflection: "I have read that in all wars, when a city is taken, women are raped, and babies stabbed in their little bellies and hoisted up to the sky on bayonettes." Judith Garner's concluding essay is entitled "A Wake for Mother: The Maternal Deathbed in Women's Fiction."

I do not mean to minimize the pain of childbirth nor to ridicule the suffering that some of these authors have experienced. Mary Oppen's memoir will break the heart of any parent. But it is necessary to emphasize feminist preoccupation with the most negative aspects of motherhood. One can read the entire corpus of feminist writing without learning that most women find motherhood their greatest satisfaction.

The Family

The family under patriarchy is a one-sided sexual bargain in which the wife settles for exploitation, brutality, rape, incest, and madness:

> The traditional marriage is basically a private employment contract, the terms of which specify that a woman shall exchange her sexual and homemaking services for her husband's support. This is the contract that women have been traditionally socialized to.[13]

The extreme tones of these first denunciations of the family have not moderated, as witness this assessment of the family by an academic feminist historian writing as recently as 1982:

Feminist rethinking has not only demystified the home as a work place but as a locale of intense intimacy, of close encounters not always of the loving kind. . . . It has x-rayed the greeting-card image of the smiling family to reveal the bared teeth of rage and pain; cases of incest, rape, battering, murder of the soul—not isolated, but remarkably widespread. The family has been unmasked in its oppressive relations. . . . It has been revealed, among other things, as a political arena.[14]

Housework is the object of particular scorn. For Janet Richards it is "so inherently mediocre [that] most women should not confine themselves to work in the home." Betty Friedan in *The Feminine Mystique* considered it "tasks for feeble-minded girls and eight-year-olds," reducing women to "animals" in a state like that of soldiers suffering head wounds.

The idea that marriage is a spontaneous bond between naturally complementary partners is dismissed out of hand. There is nothing good whatever to be said about male impulses, and the asymmetries of marriage are understood exclusively in terms of the husband's superior physical strength.

There are several more or less standard pieces of armament used in this assault upon wives, but the biggest one is generally the threat of force or . . . force itself. At a minimum it begins by a man's paling or flushing, clenching his fists at his sides or gritting his teeth, perhaps by making lurching but controlled motions. And, of course, the reconciliation of this scene, even if he has beaten her, may require his apology, but also hers for provoking him. . . . To take as an example . . . she may be tired of and feel insulted by her husband's belching or farting at the table. Can you imagine her husband's fury if it got back to him that she told someone he farted at the table?[15]

Janet Richards presents a similar theory in more urbane prose. Marriage cannot be instinctive, she argues, because it benefits men only and requires "a colossal super-structure of law and convention to keep [women] in place." Yet the purpose of marriage cannot be to force women to have sex with men, she says, "since a group so supremely confident of its strength as men appear to be could have relied on getting women's sexual co-operation by rape." Miss Richards concludes that the purpose of marriage was to secure "a breeding territory from which other men would be excluded."[16] It is little wonder that feminists have not only contested the cultural universality of so destructive an entity as the family, but occasionally have denied even its very existence.

Sex, Motherhood, and the Family in Biological Perspective

As usual, we must consider whether these theories are true before turning to the policies built upon them. There is doubtless some truth to the breeding territory theory, in that men become murderously jealous if their wives have sex with other men, and the only biological function such jealousy could serve is assurance that the offspring to which a man devotes his energies are his own. That K-selected males would behave in this way is predicted by parental investment theory, since a man who could in principle be elsewhere siring many copies of his genes is committing genetic suicide if the children he helps to raise are not his. However, it makes no ethological sense to suppose that he must *forcibly* monopolize the attentions of his mate to be sure this does not happen. In principle, it will be recalled, the fittest male ought to be the one who mates with as many females as possible while remaining with none. Human males care about the paternity of the children they help raise, although it is not in their prima facie genetic interest to raise children at all, because sexual selection—the female's preference for a mate who will protect her—has shaped the male's best strategy to include concern for his mate and their offspring. The male needs to know which offspring are his because he intends to stick by them, and his tendency to stick by them could not have evolved without a female tendency to desire that impulse in males.

Two less speculative points suggest the same conclusion. First, many animals pair off much as humans do. Animal pairing is unarguably instinctive, and to deny that human pairing is instinctive would violate Newton's rule of simplicity. Second, the institutional limits on female sexual behavior (like the limits on female behavior generally) are less stringent than those constraining males. Males are expected to put women and children first and to control all violent impulses toward women. Rape is a capital offense in many societies. Until quite recently in Western society, heavy financial penalties were imposed on men who left their wives. The pressures to keep marriages together are pressures constraining men, since it is notoriously men who desire sexual novelty (a difference explained by parental investment theory). Men are penalized less severely for infidelity than women because of the male's needs to know that the children he is raising are his, but also because the male's promiscuous impulses are very powerful; society cannot in practice heavily penalize behavior that most of its male members are prone to.

Only complete ignorance of male emotions can account for the belief that men invented marriage to force the sexual compliance of women or that men must have invented marriage for some other reason because they can force the sexual compliance of women without it. For most men, sexual arousal vanishes without reciprocation. Even prostitutes find it useful to feign involvement. It would be psychologically impossible for the average man to meet his sexual needs by regularly forcing himself on an unwilling woman. The prevalence of the breeding territory theory suggests that a great many feminists have never met a normal man.

The idea that men could mother children as diligently as women if suitably socialized does not withstand empirical data. Apart from the parental investment theory, which makes their existence prima facie likely, there is abundant direct evidence of mechanisms that bond mothers to newborns during the first hours after birth. Breast feeding induces tranquilizing hormonal changes. Women, but not men, instinctively rotate their heads to make coplanar eye contact with infants.[17] Linguists have found baby talk to be an unlearned, female-specific cultural universal. When addressing a baby, female speakers of Greek, Arabic, Berber, Comanche, Japanese, Latvian, Rumanian, and Spanish all raise the pitch of their voices, stress vowels ("What a b-i-i-i-g boy"), repeat syllables ("Say bye-bye"), and add "ie" ("a horsie and a duckie").[18] Women instinctively cradle newborns so that their heads are on the left side of the torso—probably to allow the infant to hear the tranquilizing sound of the heart beat.

Young children react differently to their mothers and fathers. A great deal has been written about the anxiety experienced by children when separated from their mothers, but a review of the literature reveals no observation of infantile separation anxiety directed toward the father. Nor are there studies of the differential tendencies of children in pain to seek out their mothers and fathers, probably because the difference is so obvious it has never occurred to anyone to verify it. Children would not let their parents take interchangeable roles no matter how badly the parents might want to. (All these points are in addition to the universally observed, and thus very probably innate, differences in the ways mothers and fathers treat male and female infants.)

The causal significance of these innate programs is lost when the question of child rearing is phrased as who *ought* to care for children, a formulation which assumes that child care is a burden equally (un)appealing to both sexes.[19] The more fundamental question, once again, is *why* parenting has the structure it has, and the answer would seem to be that women prefer to care for children more than men do. It would be astonishing if maternal mechanisms suitable for rearing children evolved in women without an accompanying enjoyment of the use of those mechanisms, just as it would be astonishing to encounter a creature in nature whose digestive system were adapted to meat, but who disliked it. Evolution is too efficient for that.

Women's innate desire to care for their children is the simplest explanation of the universal expectation that women will be the ones to do it. If every child ends up in day-care, for instance, they will almost certainly be cared for by mostly female day-care workers—and it almost certainly will be their mothers who make the detailed arrangements for day care, pick-up times, and the like. Obviously, not every nuance of the intrafamilial division of labor is genetically programmed; at the same time, it is probable that society will evolve those arrangements which permit women easy access to their children. Women in a fishing village will weave the nets while the men sail the boats. In consequence, ancillary tasks which must be done close to home—care of clothing, preparation of food, cleaning—will also fall to women. The female advantage in fine motor coordination and tolerance for repetitive tasks may help to sustain this arrangement. It might seem "fairer" to assign women new roles at menopause, but no society has evolved such an arrangement; the permanence of task assignments which are most adaptive during the child-rearing years seems to be necessary for social stability. Fishing lore cannot be acquired overnight, and a society which decided that women "deserved" to do the fishing after their children were grown would soon starve. A forty-year-old woman with one child is going to have a lot of time on her hands in contemporary industrial society, and perhaps the race will someday evolve drives more adaptive to her situation, but industrial society is quite new by evolutionary standards and for the moment human society is still shaped by drives that were adaptive when infant mortality was high and a woman's chief energies had to be focussed on child care if her genes (or anyone else's) were to survive.

As for sex itself, women certainly *seem* to enjoy vaginal penetration, and there is an obvious evolutionary advantage to enjoying the mechanics of insemination. Females who prefer clitorial massage or "penis substitutes"[20] to penetration produce fewer descendants, and must have long since been displaced by females who find the mechanics of insemination more reinforcing. Those who claim that the clitoris must be the seat of female sexuality because "there are no nerve endings in the vagina" seem to be suggesting that the vagina is *numb,* that women *cannot feel* a penis reaching to the cervix. I do not see how this suggestion can be taken seriously. I would add, however, that while enjoyment of vaginal penetration strongly enhances inclusive fitness, it is not clear what adaptive function would be served by a female orgasm. (Conceivably, it gives the goal-oriented male a goal in intercourse beyond his own orgasm, thereby increasing the pleasures of intercourse and cementing the male-female bond.) Until telepathic communication is established between the sexes, the experiences of sexual satisfaction for men and women must most reasonably be regarded as incomparable.

Feminist Family Policy

Feminist criticisms of the family rest on the assumption that women have as great a need as men for extrafamilial esteem, achievement, and power, and that frustration of this need by confinement to child rearing deforms women and the children they rear. This theory was expounded in *The*

Feminine Mystique and repeated in *The Second Stage,* in which Betty Friedan emphasizes

> the needs of women, equally real and basic to the human condition, for mastery, power, assertiveness, security and control. . . . When woman was denied access to satisfaction of those needs in society as a person in her own right, she made home and the family into a vehicle for her power, control, status, and self-realization. . . . The family, which in a certain sense *was* woman's power base then became her Frankenstein's monster.[21]

This tenet has in turn generated the assumption that paid employment outside the home is as important for women as for men. This rather prosaic idea is the practical residue of feminist ideas about family sex roles: Society must see to it that women bear less of the responsibility for child care so they can hold jobs. Thus arises the feminist family agenda:

> Maternity and paternity benefits and leaves as well as accessible and subsidized parent- and community-controlled day care, innovative work-time arrangements, shared parenting, and other non-traditional child-rearing and household arrangements.[22]

The problems of mothers who work out of perceived economic necessity has lately come to be cited as further justifying these innovations, but those problems have *nothing whatever* to do with the feminist argument, which runs that paid employment is *good* for women. (The stated policy of the Federal Republic of Germany is that every woman should have employment outside the home because it is "mentally stimulating."[23]) Feminists, whatever they may say for tactical reasons, cannot regard the entry of women into the workforce as a regrettable necessity; rather, in Letty Pogrebin's clear words, "job training and career commitment are equally important and necessary for both . . . your daughter and your son."[24] If feminists have lately been decrying the strains experienced by woman who work, their explanation of these strains is the failure of society to foist sufficient child-care obligations on men, thus unfairly preventing the overworked mother from enjoying the developmental benefits of employment.

Is There a Moderate Feminist Agenda for the Family?

Despite the alleged emergence of a "profamily" feminist agenda, there is no logical room in feminism for a "moderate" program. One may if one wishes so define "feminism" as to have nothing to do with family sex roles (thus, a man who cooks dinner when his wife works late is a "feminist"), but as soon as one begins to discuss family sex roles one must decide whether they can be changed and whether they are the way they are exclusively because of socialization. The attempt to define a new ideal for the family which is noncommittal on this question leads only to muddle, as when Benjamin Barber describes his new ideal for the family:

> . . . the attenuation of rigid stereotypical roles in favor of a sharing of tasks and activities that calls on both partners to perform in their own distinctively archetypal ways jobs that are presently allotted by stereotypical features of femininity and masculinity, but neither fixed schedules nor universal labor allotments.[25]

Let us look more closely at *The Second Stage,* whose perceived moderation earned its author considerable animosity from other feminists. Friedan's pronouncement that "feminism must, in fact, confront the family" sounds conciliatory, as does her admission ("which those feminists still locked in their own extreme reaction deny") that women need "love and identity, status, security, and generation through marriage, children, home, the family."[26] This change of heart is entirely superficial. In full, Friedan's invitation to confront the family reads: "I believe that feminism must, in fact, confront the family, albeit in new terms, if the movement is to fulfill its own revolutionary potential."[27] Friedan has certainly not changed her mind about the political character of personal relations:

> The feminist insight that the personal is political remains. In fact, personal, family life in the idealized past has become more political than men like to believe, precisely because of the inequality, the imbalance of power between men and women.[28]

The political character of the family Friedan is referring to is, precisely, its crippling denial of women's right to extrafamilial status and authority.[29] Friedan charges:

> The real power, the rewarded power, was in her [Friedan's mother's] society outside, from which our mothers were barred and from which we retreated, not understanding the reality of their discontent.[30]

In addition to recognizing women's needs for children, "personal choices and political strategies" must be based on "woman's need for power, identity, status, and security through her own work or action in society. . . . *Both sets of needs are essential to women, and to the evolving human condition.*"[31]

Overlooking Friedan's curious assumption that the concentration of power in extrafamilial pursuits was unique to 1920s America, we may note that she nowhere denies that women need power as much as men, and never allows that sex differences in dominance-aggression might explain the broad characteristics of family life she finds "political." Friedan's writing is not distinguished by its clarity, but her talk of differences in power as inequities and imbalances suggests she thinks that innate differences do not exist. Her considered view is that

> the price of motherhood is still too high for most women; the stunting of abilities and earning power is a real fear, because professions and careers are still structured in terms of the lives of men whose wives took care of the parenting and other details of life.[32]

To "affirm their own personhood" women will need "child-care options and restructured jobs, flexible working hours and maternity and paternity leaves."[33] Friedan's recommendations continue:

> "the development of alternative forms of quality child care, both center and home based," and "creative development" (by business, labor, and government) of "policies that enable persons to hold jobs while maintaining strong family life," including "such work arrangements as flex-time, flexible leave policies for both sexes, job-sharing programs, dependent-care options, and part-time jobs with pro-rated pay and benefits." . . . Equal job opportunities for women "will turn out to be a recipe for overwork" unless "the sharing of unpaid household labor between men and women becomes a reality." . . . In "as yet unrealized ideal," the family will again become symmetrical, when "both the financial support and the physical maintenance of the family are equally shared between men and women."[34]

These changes will be speeded by a "quiet revolution" among men, who will demand "new choices"—"not to 'help' women, but because of their own new problems and needs and choices, as fathers and for themselves as men."[35] Society has moved so far in these directions that "we are now on the cusp of breaking through the obsolete image of the family [as] Papa-the-breadwinner, Mama-the-housewife," said to apply to only 11 percent of American households:

> And did we not, once and for all, have to acknowledge the diversity of the families' lives and get rid of the obsolete definition so it could no longer be a weapon in the hands of those trying to block the new programs today's families really need? . . . [The] new, broader, political family [includes] unmarried adults with or without children, single-parent families, multigenerational communes, various new groupings of the elderly, [any] two or more persons who share resources, share responsibility for decisions, share values and goals, and have commitments to one another over time.[36]

Friedan seems untroubled that her definition counts the U.S. Senate and the Mafia as families.

Anyone who thinks that the proposals in *The Second Stage* are anything but radical has simply not read the book. The rage directed at Friedan by other feminists who agree with her on all matters of substance was almost certainly provoked by her concession that women do derive some satisfaction from motherhood. "Profamily" in any feminist context means approval of the "as-yet-unrealized ideal" family in which mothers and fathers are fungible with regard to child care and extrafamilial pursuits.[37]

Friedan's funeral oration for the traditional family requires three caveats. First, it is based on a momentary statistical cross-section of the population. At any one time only 11 percent of the population belongs to a traditional family, but this is not to say that only 11 percent of the population passes through a traditional family. (Only 1 percent of the population is six years old, but everyone has been six at some point.) Second, these statistics count as nontraditional any family in which the wife devotes as little as one hour weekly to paid employment. Third, Friedan's willingness to take as unalterable what she sees as the end of the traditional family should be compared to her preparedness to regard much more deeply entrenched social realities as alterable by political will. This selective resignation is a recurrent theme of feminist family policy.

Feminist proposals about work may seem more down-to-earth than the feminist critique of sexual emotions, but both flow from one idea: the destructiveness of society's failure to allow the sexes to be fungible in family roles. Feminists have drawn a number of specific practical conclusions from this idea, to which we now turn.

Social Security

Concern for economic justice joins concern about the status of the homemaker in the demand for changes in the current Social Security system. Feminists claim that the current system fails to "recognize the housewife's contribution"; their positive proposals demonstrate their own idea of proper recognition.

Using as their base the salary a housekeeper would demand for the same work,[38] feminists commonly cite the figure of $12,000 per year in 1979 dollars as the monetary value of the housework exchanged by wives for security. (Feminists have yet to convert her sexual services into a yearly monetary equivalent; it would presumably be what a prostitute would charge for the yearly number of acts of intercourse the wife permits her husband.) The issue is whether the Social Security system treats the housewife as if she were contributing $12,000 per year worth of labor. Under the current system, the wife gets a "dependent benefit" equal to 50 percent of her husband's benefits upon his retirement, if this sum exceeds her own accumulated benefits. (The dependent benefit also covers those few men whose wives significantly outearn them.) On its face, this benefit seems to be precisely the recognition and compensation that feminists say homemakers deserve.

Feminists argue, on the contrary, that the dependent benefit is a paternalistic holdover from a time when fewer women worked and Social Security "took care" of older women. The first of the three main alternatives that feminists have proposed is a tax on the salary of a homemaker's husband computed as if he earned an extra $12,000 per year.[39] Sylvia Porter calls such a tax "fair and equitable," since the husband would have had to pay a payroll tax on a housekeeper's salary. (Miss Porter does not suggest a payroll tax equivalent based on sexual services, possibly because prostitutes are not currently covered by Social Security.) The principal effect of such a tax would clearly be to reduce the homemaker's net benefit. The family to which she belongs would lose $12,000 × (the number of years her husband works) × (the husband's average marginal tax rate) in lifetime income, fully extracted before the payment of any Social Security benefits.

A second proposal is elimination of the dependent benefit, with the wife's equal contribution to the marriage incorporated by averaging the salaries of husband and wife. For instance, a husband who averaged $30,000 per year for forty years and whose wife did not work would receive the same benefits as a couple who both averaged $15,000 per year for forty years. This proposal would also reduce the benefits paid to the family with the nonworking wife (and ultimately to the nonworking wife herself), since the single-earner family now gets roughly the benefits paid to the two $15,000 per year earners plus the dependent benefit. Families with working wives would be unaffected. The net effect of this second proposal is thus to make not working less attractive for the wife.

The third reform involves paying everyone a minimum benefit below the current dependent benefit, augmented by benefits proportional to wages earned outside the home. The net effect of this final proposal is also to lower what is received by the family in which the wife does not work.

All three proposals penalize the wife for not working, while the current system alone rewards her. As things are, the woman who spends not a day of her life in the workforce is subsidized for having aided her family. This if *not* sexually discriminatory to the working woman who, unmarried or more industrious than her husband, gets the standard return on her Social Security taxes, since a man who pays the identical taxes receives identical benefits (unless his wife significantly outearns him). Nor is the working woman getting something for something while the homemaker gets something for nothing—which would perhaps discriminate against working women—*unless it is assumed that housework contributes nothing of value to the family or society.* The current system considers the housewife to be as productive as the working woman. It sees the working woman as splitting her compensable efforts between two sites, while the homemaker confines her equal effort to one.

In pointing out this characteristic of the current Social Security system I do not mean to endorse its implicit assignment of "comparable worth" to housework. As I argued in chapter 6, such assignments are meaningless.[40] I am primarily concerned to point out that feminists wish to recognize the economic value of housework by taxing it. Looked at as a direct tax on the wife, feminist proposals create disincentives to performing housework. Taxing housework can perhaps be regarded as a (somewhat vindictive) assessment on the husband, but it still effectively penalizes the housewife by reducing the net family income, and discourages the wife from staying home. Feminists have been frank about their motives. Barbara Bregman told the Task Force on Social Security and Women that the law should not make it psychologically comfortable to be a housewife because this would interfere with feminist goals.[41]

Divorce and the Working Woman

After increasing for twenty years, the divorce rate has stabilized at the high rate of nearly 5 per 1,000 people in the U.S. One out of two new marriages ends in divorce. This phenomenon has many causes, of which feminism may itself be a further effect, but feminism's ongoing diabolization of marriage is almost certainly a factor. Divorce has been made socially and psychologically more acceptable by the idea that it is a reasonable response to a defective and dying institution. Increased rates of divorce create a feedback loop in which many divorced women embrace a theory which absolves them of blame for an emotional shambles. There are bound to be people for whom the normal frictions of marriage are made unendurable by the message that marriage is oppression. Finally, while I do not see how this could be verified statistically, it seems to me beyond doubt that many thousands of marriages and affairs vectoring toward marriage have been ruined as couples have tried to conform their sex lives to feminist imperatives. A man who regards himself as obligated to bring his partner to climax, particularly to massage his partner's clitoris after he himself has climaxed, will soon regard sex with his partner as work, and rapidly lose his sexual appetite for her. And, dare I suggest, a woman will not find sexual satisfaction with a man who has internalized the belief that he must *not* be dominant, that he must *not* take his female but treat her as an "equal."

Feminist ideology encourages a variety of other pressures against marriage. Rates of childlessness, divorce and failure to marry rise steeply for women in careers; to the extent that women are encouraged to pursue careers and defer children, they are being encouraged to be single. There is the related message that women ought to learn to be independent of men. A prominent theme in rationales for nontraditional vocational training for girls is that women will be alone for a good part of their lives, that "millions of women are a divorce away from destitution,"[42] and that men are unreliable:

> Ms. Foxx. I teach marriage and the family and most of my students are very traditional. You say there has been a revolution in this area and I talk to the women and the men in those classes. They have not yet internalized the revolution. Most of them think that they are going to work a few years and stay at home and take care of their children. Their husbands are going to make enough money to take care of them and they are not going to have to work. . . . But the statistics that show that they are going to work a long time, this is not internalized. Mr. Erdahl. . . . [T]he person who had the idea of settling down with the cottage, the kids, and the husband, and the whole bit, and all of a sudden things change.[43]

It may be replied that such programs do not endorse the instability of modern marriage, merely help girls prepare for it, but one must wonder why, if this instability is not something to cheer, one hears so little about the need to stabilize marriage.

Why are egalitarians so quick to regard the present divorce rate as unalterable? Some advocates of realism can certainly be taken as speaking more in anger than in sorrow:

> Ms. Jabonaski. [We] are trying to bring to their [secondary students'] attention that the world is changing . . . that only 7 percent of the families in this country do have that lifestyle where the mother stays home full time and the father works full time. . . . We are beginning to see that younger female students are recognizing the fact that they do have to work and they are beginning to plan for those careers. . . . The young males, however, are still seeing themselves as the sole breadwinner. This presents a conflict. . . . We think that this is one of the major reasons that so many young people are not marrying as early or are divorcing at a higher rate.[44]

A more tangible contributor to the divorce rate has been the embodiment in divorce law of the assumption that women are as independent as men and no more bound to their children.[45] *Orr* abolished alimony only for women, and, either because of court action or their state ERAs, most states have rejected the doctrine that mothers are better parents than fathers during their children's "tender years." The idea of marriage as an "equal economic partnership" has led to the replacement of alimony by grants to wives of part ownership in their husbands' pensions, medical licenses, and other assets. As fewer men have vested senoirity than can pay alimony, an important disincentive for men leaving has been removed. Divorce has also been facilitated by no-fault proceedings.

These changes have ensured that divorce will be an economic disaster for women. Heavy material burdens fall on the mothers and children of divorce, for obvious reasons. A single mother must devote more of her energy to her children than does a married working parent. The single mother will often have been out of the labor market while raising her children and lack the human capital of her competitors. The median income for female-headed families falls far below that for husband-wife families. It also falls far (although not as far) below the median income for male-headed families, possibly in part because a divorced man with custody is psychologically more able than a woman to hire a caretaker, put his children out of his mind, and go back to his job. The widely-publicized "feminization of poverty" has nothing to do with discrimination, everything to do with male abandonment of traditional responsibilities. Gordon Green and Edward Welniak have estimated that if family composition had remained constant through the decade 1970–80, White median family income would have risen 3 percent instead of the actual figure of .8 percent, and Black median family income would have risen 5 percent instead of *falling* 11 percent as it did.[46] They claim that had the rate of family break-up not increased, there would have been 4,200,000 families below the poverty line in 1980 instead of 6,217,000—and of that 2,017,000 surplus, 1,377,000 are female-headed. At the margin, in other words, over 68 percent of those becoming poor are single mothers and their children. The finding that female-headed households account for half the families below the poverty line and more than half at the margin, has been replicated in a study of public assistance in Canberra, Australia.[47]

Since feminists have never ceased to regard wage labor for women as a positive good, their response to the "feminization of poverty" has been to urge programs designed to ease the reenty into the workforce of the abandoned mother. The arguments for comparable worth and institutionalized childcare are recast to address the "necessity" of accommodating abandoned women, with the task of keeping men at home treated as beyond human power. Taking herself to speak for all feminists, Betty Friedan writes:

> We will accept the inevitability of continuing future changes in the relationships and roles of men, women, and children within families—unmarried adults with or without children, single-parent families, multi-generational communes. And we will seek new responses to the conditions that are cause and effect of such change.[48]

The married mother who must work is treated with equal fatalism. Eagerness to help the working mother with subsidized day care and tinkering with the structure of work is not matched by discussion of approaches to her problems that treat her working as avoidable. There is hostility to the policy of pursing government programs to reduce inflation, so that a single wage is sufficient to support a family and mothers retain the "option" of remaining in the home.[49] I have yet to find in the feminist literature any support for increasing the dependent deduction for minors on the federal income tax. Attempts to solve "the problem of the working woman" by reducing the number of women who have to work are, as Janet Richards frankly explains, too "conservative." The case she makes specifically against direct government payments to families with children is intended generally: "Except for making people who worked in the home financially independent, it would leave everything very much as it is now."[50]

The impression that feminists regard the unwilling entry of women into the workforce as at bottom desirable is reinforced by their route back to government-subsidized day care. Day care was originally needed because staying in the home was said to damage women. But when work turned out to be a strain which women endured for purely instrumental reasons, day care became necessary lest *work* damage women. Eloquence about the glories of paid labor gave way to eloquence about its miseries, both to the same end:

> If the predominantly male political establishment in Washington was left to juggle family child-care chores for a few hectic months, perhaps then the lawmakers would . . . finally create varied and broadly available child-care programs.[51]

The separation of mothers from children has served as the solution for diametrically opposed problems; one must assume it is the solution that is found desirable. Concern with the woman who must work inevitably gives way to talk of "a fundamental right of both women and men . . . to work at a job that offers some measure of dignity, security, and respect—with rewardable recompense" as "the foundation of a meaningful family policy."[52]

Work and Fulfillment

Let us consider in its undisguised form the idea that work can be so arranged that any woman, any mother, can claim her "right" to work at a dignified and well-paid job. The principal critics of this idea are children, who are uninterested in Mommy's personal growth, are not shy about demanding attention at inconvenient times, and will not take a half-hour of concentrated love or "quality time" as compensation for a day's absence. Further problems are created by arithmetic. Anne Oakley argues in *Sex, Gender, and Society* that a woman need devote only 3 percent of her lifetime to child rearing and devote the rest to a career. She calculates that a woman will wish to take it easy during the final months of pregnancy and care for her child through infancy, for a total of about two and one-half years out of a lifetime of seventy-five. This estimate assumes that a woman will have only one child, who dematerializes at the age of two. More realistic assumptions involve a woman who has two or three children. She will normally wish to spend at least three years with each one, and it is considered advisable to space pregnancies by no less. She will thus spend a decade in maternal pursuits during the years crucial for career development, making it impossible for her to "realize herself" in the world of work to the same extent men do (assuming that men work for expressive reasons rather than because they feel they "have to"). Conversely, as is conceded by officials of the West German government charged with "national family policy," the absolute practical limit on the number of children that can be borne by a woman interested in a full-time career is two.

The assumption that the average woman will have at least two children follows from the basic demographic principle that the replacement rate for humans is 2.1; a society whose females average fewer than two babies will disappear. This is not to say that women *ought* to have babies; perhaps in a showdown between self-realization for women and the survival of society, society should go. The fertility rate in most Western nations is now below 2.1[53] and perhaps that is the way it ought to be. It nonetheless remains biologically necessary that *if* a society is to continue, most women will devote the best energies of their early adulthoods to childrearing rather than extrafamilial, vocational pursuits. And if a society disappears, it is certainly pointless to wonder how the women within it may best realize their potential.

Janet Richards holds the feminist

> committed to leaving no stone unturned in a search for a way to rearrange the organization of society so that a woman can do her duty as a mother without neglecting other work she could do for the good of everyone. It is not in the least obvious how this is to be done, but that is a reason for devoting the full energy and imagination of everyone.[54]

Even if we share Richards's assumption that women spend time with their children only out of duty, it remains difficult to see how arithmetic might be outwitted. In addition to flex-time and communes, she adds the separation of promotion from experience, "since fitness for promotion is hardly ever a function of the number of hours spent on a job,"[55] but rejects day care (like a family income) as *"not radical enough,"* since it leaves the basic organization of work unchanged. She recognizes the inadequacy of her positive proposals and concludes "we have very little idea what arrangements will be best in the long run." She remains sure that a solution exists ("Make it essential that these things come about, and people will devise a way of doing them") and attributes the difficulty of seeing it to the male exclusion of women when work was created. Anyone who doubts that a solution is possible betrays "a preoccupation with women's remaining servants."

Proposals for the radical rearrangement of work evidence a failure to appreciate that solutions to problems of job designs may be entirely independent of human preferences. The only way to make an automobile that most people can afford is to gather a great many people and machines in a single place and mass-produce it. The treatment of cancer by radiation requires the medical facilities modern Western man is accustomed to. These are objective facts having nothing to do with anybody's desire to exclude anybody else. ⸍

Day Care, Maternal Care, and the Social Order

Once fantasies about rearranging work are put aside, what remains is publicly subsidized day care. When made on behalf of women who wish to work, as we are now supposing it to be, this demand usually employs the language of freedom. In Jill Norgren's words, "democratic governments should not dictate decisions but provide options." Now, to argue that not funding day care keeps women in the home, while funding it frees them to stay or leave, inverts the meaning of words. Publicly funded child care achieves no net gain in free choice, since those forced to foot the bill lose the option of doing what they wish with their money. Since the transfer of funds is not frictionless—the government officials supervising the transfer must be paid, and there are inevitable leaks in the pipeline—subsidies always *reduce* overall freedom in society, even when they can be justified on other grounds.

The issue of coercion does not arise for the woman willing to assume the consequences of the decision to work. If there is no law against her making that decision, and private discrimination is illegal, she already has the option to work. Egalitarians are entitled to urge her to work and her employer to provide on-site day care. But government support is appropriate for her only if it is also appropriate for males torn between work and competing desires. Those who value exercise and wish to see a healthier populace might wish employers would establish on-site running tracks, but government subsidies for daily jogging would normally be considered inappropriate. The choice between working and training for a marathon *is* a choice, perhaps a hard one in some cases, and the man who chooses jogging does not expect public help. The government has no reason to favor other kinds of personal growth.

It is also argued, especially by people who take the raising of children to be intrinsically valueless, that society will continue to lose the talents of half its citizens unless the government provides day care. This argument ignores the efficiency with which the market extracts productivity from a population. To the extent that mothers form a neglected pool of talent, employers will find a female-employee-plus-day-care package more profitable than the no-day-care-no-female-employee package, and subsidies will be unnecessary. And if instituting day care is unprofitable, that is because it is wasteful. Suppose the ablest male widget-maker can turn $100 worth of resources into ten widgets in a day while his wife can turn $50 of resources into ten widgets in a day, but suppose too that the husband will not just stay home with the kids if she is hired and the widget manufacturer does not hire her because to do so he would have to invest $60 per day in on-site care for her children. The profit motive prevents the manufacturer from hiring the woman because doing so would increase the cost of ten widgets to $110, which is also a socially undesirable outcome. Government intervention is required not because collective action is more rational, but, as usual, because egalitarian norms are so irrational that nobody acts on them voluntarily.

Much as I would prefer to leave the emotional topic of child care at the inconsistency of feminist arguments and individual liberty, the idea that "daycare is a permanent necessity for modern mothers"[56] persists, raising the question of the long-run consequences of institutionalized child care and other nontraditional arrangements for the liberal order. Reliable data does not yet exist about the developmental effects of the extensive creche systems in Sweden and the Soviet Union, but common sense suggests a few tentative conclusions.

First, since the large-scale rearing of children by strangers is new to human history, it is most prudent to place on its advocates the onus of proving, overwhelmingly and in detail, that it does no harm. So long as a child and its mother have the normal complement of playmates and friends, maternal care is more likely to produce happy, autonomous adults than care by paid surrogates. Clinicians are unanimous that a child needs the complete attention of his mother for at least his first year, and continuity in his personal caretaker for at least his first three years, if he is to have the best chance for satisfactory personal relations later in life. It is true (by definition) that sufficiently well staffed and loving day care is as good as maternal care, but the very question at issue is whether children *can* get sufficient attention anywhere but home. Accepting Alison Stewart-Clarke's figure of 8 million children with full-time working mothers, and her maximum children/staff ration of 5 to 1 (and forgetting her requirement that every day-care center have at least one man), this means that 1.6 million involved, affectionate surrogate parents must be found. (Others put the figure higher.[57]) Pay for day-care employment must remain low if work plus day care is to be more financially attractive than staying home, and cannot attract the cream of the workforce.

Human beings have always been reared within "traditional" families. It is true that in many cultures children are raised after infancy by communal groups, but these groups are generally composed of mothers who know each other. Not only has there never been an open, democratic society not based on the family, there has never been any society of any sort not based on the family. In every society a child's upbringing has been the responsibility of close blood relations, with his daily care a female task and his protection a male task. Some societies have favored polygamy, a very few polyandry; in some societies a number of married couples live together under a communal roof, while in others each of the basic units live separately. But no society has tolerated reproductive units with more than one member of both sexes, a temporary bond, or sex outside the reproductive unit. Still, since only a few societies have evolved into democracies, there remains the question of what sort of intrafamilial socialization conduces to the liberal order.

Extensive personal liberty requires, particularly of the male, the capacity to control impulses without external threat. It also requires the conviction that effort is rewarded, and faith in oneself as deserving such reward and capable of getting it. All social organizations assume some ego strength on the part of their members, and not everyone has to be Teddy Roosevelt for democracy to work, but the constant occasions for choice presented by liberal democracy put unusual demands on autonomy. According to the standard theory of personality, autonomy is best fostered by a strong male figure and a nurturant female figure.[58] The child originally learns to control his impulses as a means of gaining his parents' love. His mother's unconditional love teaches him that he is basically good; His father's respect instills a sense that he is competent. The respect a boy feels for his father causes him to internalize what he believes his father expects from him. His father's internalized voice, the superego, enables the boy to restrain himself in the absence of threats of punishment. (God, the good but stern judge, is always male.) Later in life, a boy will have to win the love of a woman and the respect of other men, and happy experiences with his parents serve to convince him that he will succeed.

On this theory, a surrogate mother can be found only with the greatest difficulty, and the male role—whether occupied by the biological father or some other strong male figure—is irreplaceable. This theory predicts that males not raised by fathers will not learn to control their impulsivity and will in later life display an abnormal readiness for aggression. These predictions have recently been tested. In the slums of the major American cities, most Black males are now being raised in the absence of male figures. (75 percent of all Black births in Harlem are currently illegitimate.[59]) As predicted, there is a disproportionate incidence of crime against persons, random violence, and drug use among young Black males. Black males between the ages of fourteen and nineteen commit 51 percent of all felonies in New York; the chief cause of death in this cohort is homicide. It has not proved possible to explain this destructive behavior in terms of racial discrimination or poverty. When social scientists first called attention to the breakdown of the Black family two decades ago, they were met with the assurance that all was well because the Black family is matriarchal. Subsequent events have verified that an entire society whose males are raised without male authority figures would, for its short existence, more closely resemble a Hobbesian state of nature than an egalitarian paradise.

In a larger sense it is pointless to get involved with just how much Mama a child needs to develop properly, or just what the proper pay should be for surrogates of mothers. The more important point is that feminism has caused a major shift in focus in all discussions of childrearing, from what is good for children during the years that their personalities are most influenced by their parents, to how soon this period can be gotten over so that mothers may get back to the important business of working.

Abortion, Homosexuality, and Feminism

A movement for legal reform and broadened attitudes toward women would not be expected to say very much about abortion or homosexuality. The equitable distribution of resources to men and women for abortion is nonsense. And, while "justice for women" might include the identical treatment of lesbians and male homosexuals as a minor component, it cannot be stretched to include anything about the joint treatment of male and female homosexuals in contrast to that accorded heterosexuals. "Justice for women" would certainly appear to have no bearing whatever on male homosexuality.

Yet abortion and homosexuality are central feminist concerns. *Ms* magazine lists "the freedom to decide whether and when to have children" as one of the four "real issues facing women today." For Betty Friedan "the right to choose [an abortion] is crucial to the personhood of woman."[60] The 1982 National Convention of NOW adopted "Lesbian Rights Resolutions" warning of the "destructiveness of heterosexism" and promising legal action to "overturn discriminatory statutes," including limits on custody and adoption rights for homosexuals.[61] Feminist activist Frances Lear cautions that

> our fundamental need is for a collective feminist persona that radiates good will. Some feminists attack "special interest groups," primarily the lesbians, because their movement co-opts feminist resources. Although gay rights may belong on the humanist agenda, gay political activities need to be separate. Admittedly, such a division could prove a hardship on the movement, since lesbians make up a large portion of the volunteer work force.[62]

Other feminists heatedly deny that feminism has anything essential to do with homosexuality (they are less inclined to make this claim about abortion) and contend that statements such as these represent the fringe. But apart from the fact that NOW and *The Nation* are not fringe phenomena, the positions of organizations representing feminist legal interests reveal deep commitment to these causes. When the Wisconsin State Assembly Judiciary Committee was considering a state ERA in 1983, it reasoned that, since ERA supporters reject as canards the claim that an ERA would mandate state funding for abortion and protection of homosexuals, the ERA could be amended to leave the Wisconsin legislature free not to fund abortions and to limit the rights of homosexuals. The committee was only proposing to exclude from the ERA what its proponents had said were irrelevancies, yet the Wisconsin Civil Liberties Union, NOW, the League of Women Voters, and Wisconsin Women's Network testified against the amendments, with the WCLU promising to oppose it until it was freed of "anti–civil libertarian language." Feminist organizations have uniformly resisted similar clarifying amendments for other state ERAs and the proposed federal ERA. As legislation may be presumed to intend what it easily could but does not exclude, these organizations may be presumed to intend the ERA to protect homosexuals and require public funding of abortion.

These seemingly arbitrary positions become quite natural once the denial of innate sex differences is taken to heart. If sex differences do not exist, or can and should be indefinitely minimized, same-sex pairings very probably are not, and certainly should not be treated as, significantly different from heterosexual pairings. The best analogue to homosexuality is miscegnation, against which no reasonable objections can be raised. To deny a man a marriage license because the person he wants to marry is also a man, while granting a license to a similarly situated man who wants to marry a female, is to stigmatize the homosexual's intended just because he is a man, and that is discrimination on the basis of sex. Furthermore, if women are to conduct their lives with the same freedom from the consequences of sex that men do, abortion becomes a vital desideratum. In Janet Richards's words, "from the point of view of freedom, the mother's claims are paramount."[63] Justice Harry Blackmun made substantially the same point in characterizing the legalization of abortion as a blow for the "independence" of women. The full emancipation of women requires the universal acceptance of all forms of sexual behavior and, as a subsidiary goal, the universal subsidized availability of contraceptives to minors. According to Thorne and Yalom,

> The contemporary women's movement has worked to give women a choice *not* to mother—hence, struggles for birth control and abortion rights and for legitimization of all forms of sexuality, including lesbianism, separated from reproduction.[64]

Judith Lorber writes yet more sweepingly: "A feminist goal is total freedom of choice in sex partners throughout one's life."

These ideas resemble feminist proposals about day care in two important respects. First, they use "choice" in the sense in which government subsidies confer the "choice" to work. Since a woman can choose not to become a mother by refraining from sex, the "choice" conferred by abortion and universally available contraceptives is the ability to choose barrenness without having to accept its disagreeable consequences. Second, insofar as the demand that contraceptives be freely available covers minors, the argument displays the by-now familiar selective resignation to which feminists seem vulnerable. Feminists profess concern about the high illegitimacy rate among teenage girls, and propose free contraceptives along with sex education to stem it, two measures which treat it as unalterable that teenage girls will have sexual intercourse outside marriage. Why do proposals for curbing teenage illegitimacy make this assumption when, to judge by the far lower illegitimacy rates experienced by societies in which reliable contraception was unavailable, the current incidence of sex among teenage girls is unique in human history?

Abortion

Abortion is a hard question, and I have no easy answers. It is all the more important, then, that discussions of abortion be conducted in good faith, with a clear focus on the relevant issues. Whatever the ultimate disposition of the abortion issue, this is an obligation that feminists have not met.

The pivotal question about abortion is whether the fetus is a human life; most other issues are distractions. If the fetus is human, killing it is murder. It is irrelevant whether abortion reduces welfare and crime, since murder is an impermissible means of social control. Abortion may guarantee that every child is wanted, but murder is impermissible even when everybody, including the prospective victim, would be better off with him dead.[65] Rape and incest do not justify abortion if the fetus is human, since the avoidance of shame and heavy financial obligations do not justify murder. Abortion might be safer if it were legal, but, if the fetus is human, this is only to say that certain kinds of murder would be safer if they were legal. Mafia killings would be safer for triggerman if gang wars were legal, but that is no reason to decriminalize gang wars. If the fetus is human it need not be a "person," in the sense of having neural organization sufficient for its being a continuing self-conscious being, to have a right against abortion. Neonates are not persons in this sense either, but few people recognize a right to commit infanticide.[66]

There are two arguments for abortion that grant that the fetus is a human life. The first is that abortion is permissible self-defense on the part of a pregnant woman or her medical surrogate if her pregnancy threatens her life. Many jurists have recognized a "right of necessity," but it is by no means clearly applicable to the case of life-threatening pregnancy. The right to kill innocents in self-defense justifies the killing of innocents in warfare as a means of preventing further attacks by a noninnocent aggressor. The right of self-defense likewise justifies attacks against hostages of terrorists (or attacks against terrorists in the certain knowledge that they will kill their hostages) as a means of preventing further attacks by noninnocent aggressors. The fetus, on the other hand, is an innocent nonaggressor who did not intitiate the life-threatening situation. He did not ask to be conceived. Attacks against him cannot be justified in the way that attacks against the innocent in warfare can be justified.

Francis Bacon took the "right of necessity" to justify a drowning man's pushing another man off a floating plank at sea, even if the original possessor of the plank was not responsible for the drowning man's plight. This wide reading of the right of necessity would indeed justify medically necessary abortions, but it conflicts with the even more fundamental Kantian rule against initiating aggression. If you find yourself adrift with only a nearby plank in someone else's possession to save you, you are obliged to let yourself drown. I claim no certainty for my own moral intuitions in these difficult cases, but from a practical point of view the wide Baconian right has little bearing on the abortion controversy. Fewer than 1 percent of the 1.5 million abortions performed annually in the United States are done to save the life of the mother, and advocates of decriminalizing abortions do not regard the right to abortion as ending when threats to the life of the mother do.

A second defense of abortion consistent with the humanity of the fetus maintains that abortion is not murder because it is not killing.[67] A woman who aborts a fetus is simply *refusing to continue to help keep it alive,* just as a host who ejects an unwanted guest into a blizzard is simply refusing to extend his hospitality, and just as a woman who awakens one morning to find herself attached to a violinist dependent on the use of her kidneys (Judith Thomson's example) is simply refusing to let him use her body if she rips out the tubes. Proper discussion of this argument requires a digression into metaphysics,[68] but the essential disanalogy between abortion and the other host cases is that in these other cases the person who withdraws his assistance is not completely responsible for the dependency on him of the person who is about to die, while the mother *is* completely responsible for the dependency of her fetus on her. When one is completely responsible for dependence, refusal to continue to aid is indeed killing. If a woman brings a newborn home from the hospital, puts it in its crib and refuses to feed it until it has starved to death, it would be absurd to say that she had simply refused to assist it and had done nothing for which she should be criminally liable.

So the question returns to the humanity of the fetus, and what else can the fetus be, if not human? If fetuses are not human, dog embryos are not canine, and cow embryos are not bovine, the entire taxonomy of nature would have to be duplicated pointlessly. There is a universally recognized continuity to fetal development which requires that a fetus be thought of as an early stage of a human being conceived as a four-dimensional entity, in much the way a thirty-year-old man is a later stage of that same four-dimensional entity.

We must tread carefully here, since many advocates of legal abortion appeal to this same continuity of fetal development. In reconstructing their argument, it is important to distinguish the *metaphysical* claim that there *is* no line to be drawn between fetus, neonate, and adult, from the *epistemological* claim that *nobody (now) knows how to draw the line*. The metaphysical claim cannot be used to defend the decriminalization of abortion and in fact undercuts it, by blurring any distinction between fetus and neonate which might be cited to justify radically different treatment of the two. Take, for instance, viability outside the womb as a trait fetuses lack but neonates and adults possess. In fact, viability is relative to environment: Adults are unviable at the bottom of the sea without proper life support equipment, while with proper life support equipment a late-term fetus can survive. Newborns are somewhere in between. Perhaps then a newborn deserves special protection and an insufficiently developed fetus does not because there is *some* extrauterine environment in which the newborn can survive and *no* extrauterine environment in which the undeveloped fetus can survive. But the point at which a fetus can survive in some extrauterine environment is retreating before technology. Within a century there may be artificial wombs capable of receiving embryos from the moment of conception. At that point the distinction in viability between fetus and neonate will have vanished, and the *only* difference between a fetus unviable *now* and an equally undeveloped fetus *then* is that nobody has actually gotten around to inventing an artificial womb. Surely, however, a distinction in moral status as profound as that between beings that it is permissible to kill and beings that it should be legally impermissible to kill cannot depend on circumstances completely external to those beings, such as what happens to have been perfected in a medical laboratory thousands of miles (or dozens of years) away.

So the appeal of abortion advocates to the continuity of fetal development must be epistemological. It is not best formulated as the claim that it is in principle impossible for anyone ever to draw the necessary line, for that would be to bet against science, which in the past has proven able to mark principled distinctions amid seeming flux. (Think of the classification of minerals.)[69] The argument, rather, must be that since no one can *now* tell when human life begins, the matter should (now) be left to private conscience. Proponents of this argument are often unclear as to whether they are making a claim about what is possible relative to our present knowledge or a claim about what is possible relative to all possible states of knowledge, but a great many defenders of decriminalized abortion clearly have some such argument in mind:

> As the Supreme Court recognized in *Roe v. Wade* . . . the concept of "fetal personhood" raises moral and philosophical problems that go beyond the capacity of legislative or judicial mechanisms to solve.[70]

I am confident that those who propose this argument would not apply it elsewhere. They would not approve of leaving the killing of Eskimos to private conscience on the grounds that no one can say when human life begins. But there is a deeper problem that has nothing to do with epistemology, and that is the *impossibility* of government neutrality about the status of the fetus. A fundamental function of government is to protect its citizens from aggression. Essential to this function is a decision as to which beings within its territory are to count as the citizens it will protect. Since a government monopolizes the legitimate use of force within its territory, it must also forbid the forcible protection by private parties of any being it itself does not actively protect. You are allowed to attack somebody attacking an adult human being, but you are not allowed to attack somebody stepping on an ant, since at the moment ants have no legal rights. The government protects attacks on anything it does not positively protect. In choosing not to decide whether to protect some vulnerable being, therefore, the government chooses not to protect it. Its function forces the state to decide about every being. In urging the government to "stay out of" decisions about the fetus, abortion advocates are asking the government to decide not to protect fetuses.

In strictness, "government neutrality" is very far from the standard feminist position. Probably the majority of feminists hold that abortion should be publicly funded, which would not leave the matter to private conscience at all, since it would force taxpayers who do not approve of abortion to support it. Public subsidies are not necessary to secure a "woman's right to her body," even if that could be shown to be an adequate justification for legalizing abortion, since a right to the use of one's body is a right against the invasion of one's body by other people, not a right to the means to do with one's body what one wants to. My "right to my body" does not create a right to public funds for an airline ticket with which to fly my body to the Caribbean for a vacation.

But forgetting this breach of neutrality, one is again struck by the selectivity of feminist bafflement. The difficulties in determining the status of the fetus are supposed to place action based upon its status in the realm of private conscience. Yet the difficulties in detecting discrimination are said to require hiring quotas. The difficulties—impossibilities, really—of determining comparable worth are said to require state cancellation of "residues." Proper pedagogy, so notoriously a matter of dispute, is said to require the censorship of texts and the enforced sex integration of small children. The danger that landlords, bankers, insurers, teachers, and male coworkers will discriminate is said to be too great, and the harm of discrimination too great, for the government to tolerate conscientious error. The only matter feminists are willing to entrust to private conscience—a matter in which, one assumes, they find the harm done by conscientious error tolerable—is the killing of fetuses.

Civil Rights for Homosexuals

Pleas for the sovereignty of individual conscience become yet more puzzling when entered by supporters of laws banning private discrimination against homosexuals. The laws in question have nothing to do with guaranteeing homosexuals the right to do as they please in private; these laws, rather, would forbid the private use of "sexual preference" as a criterion for employment and housing decisions.[71] These laws forbid third parties to refuse to associate with homosexuals on the basis of beliefs about and possible aversion to homosexual practices. It is unnecessary here to decide whether homosexuality is "unnatural"[72] or whether distaste for homosexuals is "prejudice." The fact is that many people dislike homosexuals. They think homosexuality is intrinsically abhorrent, a violation of divine commands, a threat to their children. How is one to justify denying to such people the freedom to avoid homosexuals if they conscientiously feel that avoidance of homosexuality is desirable? Surely one's willingness to hire or rent to homosexuals can be seen as a matter of private conscience, one's "right to one's own body" (a landlord may not wish to rent rooms to a homosexual in the same building his own body is situated in), one's "right to choose."

The analogy often drawn between homosexuals, Blacks, and Jews is obviously less than perfect. A Black man cannot hide his race but a homosexual can hide his sexual impulses. True, a Jew can also remove his head cover if he is indoors with an anti-Semitic hiring officer, and perhaps has only himself to blame if he does not get the job—but if the Jew does choose to lose the job in preference to (as he sees it) offending God, that is a matter of religious conviction. It is hard to think of a comparable motive that could induce a homosexual to refuse to disguise his homosexuality from a prospective employer. The point is that the analogy impresses some people but not others. Blacks and Jews no doubt have their own opinion of it. Genuine respect for freedom of conscience would allow each person to make up his own mind about it, and about whether to ignore "sexual preference" in those situations in which he is required by law to ignore race and religion. Perhaps permitting freedom of conscience will permit mistakes; perhaps some people will choose (wrongly, in some eyes) to consider sexual preference important. Perhaps as a result of such choices, many homosexuals will be worse off than they would have been had freedom of conscience been forbidden. Anyone whose considers this possibility too awful for the state to countenance, but also supports decriminalizing abortion, must consider the happiness of homosexuals more important than the lives of fetuses.

Notes

1. Benjamin Barber, "Beyond the Feminist Mystique," *New Republic* (July 11, 1983): 26.
2. Jane Flax, "Women Do Theory," in *Women and Values,* ed. Marilyn Pearsall (Belmont, Ca.: Wadsworth, 1986), p. 7.
3. Phyllis Chessler, *Women and Madness* (New York: Avon, 1972), p. 47ff. Chessler's fulsome account of her pregnancy in her subsequent *With Child* marks at most a personal defection from ideas that continue to enjoy currency. In Janet Richard's words, "One way of creating an absolutely fair arrangement between men and women [is to] break down the social stigma suffered by fatherless children." *The Sceptical Feminist* (Boston: Routledge & Kegan Paul, 1980), p. 253.
4. For Andrea Dworkin, male sex is "antagonism and violence, mixed in varying degrees . . . There is no male conception of sex without force as the essential dynamic." *Pornography: Men Possessing Women,* cited in David Bryden, "Between Two Constitutions: Feminism and Pornography," *Constitutional Commentary* 2 (Winter 1985): 154.
5. Alix Shulman, "Organs and Orgasms," in *Woman in Sexist Society,* ed. Vivian Gornick and Betty Moran (New York: Mentor, 1971), p. 205.
6. Barbara Seaman, *Free and Female* (New York: Fawcett World, 1972), p. 69.
7. Ruth Bleier, *Science and Gender* (New York: Pergamon, 1984), p. 171. Also see Sylvia Hewlett, *A Lesser Life* (New York, Morrow, 1986), p. 328.
8. Rosalind Petchesky, *Abortion and Woman's Choice* (New York: Longmans, 1984), p. 6.
9. Letty Pogrebin, *Growing Up Free* (New York: McGraw-Hill, 1980), p. 500.
10. Nancy Chodorow and Susan Contratto, "The Myth of the Perfect Mother," in *Rethinking the Family,* ed. Barrie Thorne and Marilyn Yalom (New York: Longmans, 1982), pp. 57–75.
11. P. 205.
12. Dorothy Dinnerstein, *The Mermaid and the Minotaur* (New York: Harper & Row, 1979), p. 28.

13. Riane Eisler, *The Equal Rights Handbook* (New York: Avon, 1978), p. 61. Miss Eisler approvingly cites John Kenneth Galbraith's characterization of housewives as "crypto-servants."

14. Renate Bridenthal, "The Family: A View from a Room of Her Own," in Thorne and Yalom, p. 234.

15. Beverly Jones, "The Dynamics of Marriage and Motherhood," in *Sisterhood is Powerful,* ed. Robin Morgan (New York: Vintage, 1970), p. 46ff.

16. *The Sceptical Feminist,* pp. 138–43. This theory is also expounded in Mary O'Brien, "Feminist Theory and Dialectical Logic," *Signs* 7 (1981): 144–57.

17. Alice Rossi ("A Biosocial Perspective on Parenting," *Daedelus* 106 (1977): 1–32) discusses this and many other innate mechanisms.

18. See Beth Birdsong, "Motherese," *Parents* (March 1983): 54–61.

19. "Perhaps most feminists would agree that the child should come first, and that the mother should sacrifice both her own interests and whatever good she could do elsewhere. . . . Although she may have chosen the best alternative, it is clear that the situation is still not ideal. Her child cannot possibly make full use of her abilities, and the consequence is that something is still being wasted" (Richards, p. 170).

20. Bleier, p. 172.

21. Pp. 92–93.

22. Chodorow and Contratto, p. 54.

23. Interview with official of the Foreign Ministry, July 21, 1985. "The same obstacles that stand in the way of a professional career usually hold true for a political career, i.e. household and family." *Women in Society.*

24. Pogrebin, p. 537.

25. Benjamin Barber, *Liberating Feminism* (New York: Delta, 1976), pp. 141–42.

26. Betty Friedan, *The Second Stage* (New York: Simon & Schuster, 1981), p. 95.

27. Ibid., p. 84.

28. Ibid., p. 90.

29. See n. 21 above.

30. Ibid., p. 94.

31. Ibid., p. 95.

32. Ibid., p. 87.

33. Ibid., p. 108.

34. Ibid., pp. 108–12. The phrases cited are from resolutions of the 1980 White House Conference on Families and a report by the World Watch Institute.

35. Ibid., p. 121.

36. Ibid., p. 109.

37. "A working environment worthy of the designation 'pro-family' must also take into account the interests of those mothers who interrupt their gainful activities for the purpose of child-rearing. On the basis of past experience, it is known that their former vocational skills very quickly go out of date and, moreover, that these mothers soon become alienated from working life. With this in mind, the Federal Minister for Youth, Family Affairs, and Health has been promoting a study since the beginning of 1983 on 'links with the world of work during the family phase.' This study is intended to indicate opportunities for remaining in touch with one's occupation during the child-rearing phase, too" (*Women in the Federal Republic of Germany,* p. 29). In support of a federal law requiring maternity leave: "A legislative effort that helps to promote family stability deserves the most serious consideration." "New Parents' Needs and Rights," *New York Times* (January 1, 1986): p. A22.

38. Evelyn Kayes puts the figure at $35,000 per year, to be paid by husbands, or the government if husbands cannot afford it.

39. These proposals are detailed in *Social Security and the Changing Role of Women* (Washington, D.C.: Department of Health, Education, and Welfare [now Health and Human Services], 1979). See also Judith Finn, *The Treatment of Women under Social Security* (Washington, D.C.: Free Congress Research Foundation, 1981) for detailed analyses of these proposals.

40. Paying a wife for housework is not the same as paying a housekeeper for the identical chores; a housekeeper would charge more if she were expected to sleep with the master of the house after tidying up.

41. Cited in Finn, p. 46.

42. Ruth Sidel, *Women and Children First* (New York: Viking, 1986), p. 190.

43. *Hearings on Reauthorization of the Vocational Education Act of 1963, Part 11: Sex Equity in Vocational Education,* House Hearings, December 16, 17, 1981 (Washington, D.C.: U.S. Government Printing Office, 1982), p. 113.

44. Ibid., p. 115.

45. For an overview of recent changes in divorce law, see "Divorce American Style," *Newsweek* (January 10, 1983): 42–48.

46. Gordon Green and Edward Welniak, "Measuring the Effects of Changing Family Composition during the 1970's in Black-White Differences in Income," manuscript (Washington, D.C.: Bureau of the Census, Department of Commerce, 1982).

47. "How the Intact Family Is a Buffer against Poverty," *News Weekly* (August 18, 1982): 7–8. Single mothers form 7.6 percent of Canberra households, but make up 27 percent of the households whose incomes fall below the Australian poverty level (somewhat lower than that of the United States).

48. Cited in Friedan, *The Second Stage,* p. 102. The same passage appears in somewhat different form in "The Family Needs to Be Changed," in *Male/Female Roles,* ed. Bruno Leone and M. Teresa O'Neill (St. Paul, Minn.: Greenhaven, 1983), pp. 122–23.

49. See Michael Levin, "Feminism: Stage Three," *Commentary* (August 1986): 27–31, for further discussion and references.

50. *The Sceptical Feminist,* p. 242.

51. Jill Norgren, "Child-Care Nonpolicy," *New York Times* (January 1, 1983): p. 19.

52. Sidel, p. 192.

53. Ben Wattenberg has kindly shown me preliminary data for a work in progress to be called *The Birth Dearth*. He estimates that at present rates of replacement, the fraction of the world's population represented by the Western community will drop from its current 15 percent to 4.5 percent by 2075.

54. *The Sceptical Feminist,* p. 171.

55. Ibid., p. 256.

56. Allison Stewart-Clarke, "The Day-Care Child," *Parents* (September 1982): p. 72.

57. In "Feminism: Stage Three" I gave the figure of 1.8 million; Selma Fraiberg puts the figure at 2 million in *Every Child's Birthright* (New York: Basic Books, 1977).

58. See Fraiberg. Also Robert Stoller, *Sex and Gender: On the Development of Masculinity and Femininity* (New York: Science House, 1968); Margaret Mahler, Fred Pine and Annie Bergmann, *The Psychological Birth of the Human Infant* (New York: Basic Books, 1975); Anna Freud, *The Ego and the Mechan-*

isms of Defense (New York: International Universities Press, 1966); Edward Levine and Charles Saiova, "Biology, Personality, and Culture," *The Israel Annals of Psychiatry and Related Disciplines* 12, 1 (March 1975): 10–28.

59. See Charles Murray, *Losing Ground* (New York: Basic Books, 1984) for further data, esp. chapter 9.
60. *The Second Stage*, p. 86.
61. *Resolutions of the National Organization for Women (NOW)*, Indianapolis, Indiana, October 9, 1982.
62. Frances Lear, "Now Is the Time to Get Organized," *The Nation* (December 12, 1980): 635–36.
63. *The Sceptical Feminist*, p. 215. Richards lists freedom and the prevention of suffering as the two supreme values. She finds the possible suffering of the aborted fetus "intolerable," which she seems to take to require that the fetus be aborted painlessly. She believes the principle that life outweighs both functions solely to rationalize "a deeply entrenched wish to control and oppress women" (p. 218), and she does not consider the right of the fetus to be free from aggression.
64. Thorne and Yalom, "Introduction."
65. Betty Friedan generously extends to the unwanted child the right to be aborted: "The value is life . . . the life of the women and the right of the child to be wanted in life." "Twenty Years After the Feminine Mystique," *New York Times Magazine* (February 22, 1983): 42–54. Not wanting a child before it is born is unrelated to postnatal bonding, see T. Berry Brazelton, "Effect of Maternal Expectation on Early Infant Development," *Early Child Development Care* 2 (1973): 250–73. For evidence that abortion facilitates rage against dependents, disinhibits aggressing the defenseless, and impairs the ability to mother future children, see A.D. and L.L. Colman, *Pregnancy: The Psychological Experience* (New York: Herder & Herder, 1971); R. Kuman and Kay Robson, "Previous Induced Abortion and Ante-Natal Depression in Primiparae: A Preliminary Report of a Survey of Mental Health in Pregnancy," *Psychological Medicine* 8 (1978): 711–15; W.G. Whittlestone, "The Physiology of Bonding," *Child and Family* 5 (1976): 36–42; M.H. Liebman and J.S. Zimmer, "Abortion Sequelae: Fact and Fallacy," in *Psychological Aspects of Abortion*, ed. D. Mall and W.F. Watts (Chattanooga, Tex.: University Publications of American, 1979); S. Lipper and W.M. Feigenbaum, "Obsessive-Compulsive Neurosis after Viewing the Fetus during Therapeutic Abortion," *American Journal of Psychotherapy* 30 (1977): 666–74; Phillip Ney, "Relationship between Abortion and Child Abuse," *Canadian Journal of Psychiatry* 24 (1979): 610–20.
66. Michael Tooley defends both abortion and infanticide in "Abortion and Infanticide," *Philosophy and Public Affairs* 2 (1972): 37–65. He argues that a person can only have a right to something he wants; since children and babies do not realize they have futures they cannot want to have futures and thus have no right to have them. Tooley's premise implies, implausibly, that a person has no rights to undiscovered minerals on his property.
67. See Judith Thomson, "A Defense of Abortion," In Pearsall, pp. 368–79; Walt Block "Woman and Fetus: Rights in Conflict?" *Reason* (April 1978): 18–25; Robert N. Wennberg, *Life in the Balance* (Grand Rapids, Mich.: Eerdmans, 1985).
68. See Michael Levin, review of Robert N. Wennberg, *Life in the Balance: Constitutional Commentary* (forthcoming).
69. But do we not know *now* what we mean by "human," or at least what criteria

we use for determining humanness? Not necessarily; people used water for a long time before discovering that water is hydrogen and oxygen, before being able to distinguish water from extremely diluted wine, and so on.

70. Petchesky, p. 331.
71. Among the measures to this effect introduced in recent sessions of Congress were H.R. 166, H.R. 13019, H.R. 451, and S. 2081. See Enrique Rueda, *The Homosexual Matrix* (Greenwich, Conn.: Devin Adair, 1981), chs. 5, 8 for connections between homosexual and feminist political organizations.
72. On this question see Michael Levin "Why Homosexuality Is Abnormal," *The Monist* 67 (April 1984): 251–83.

14

Feminism and the Future

Feminism and Democracy

For Plato, democracy was "an agreeable form of anarchy, in which equal and unequal are treated as if they were the same." He believed that, in a democracy, equality of rights and opportunity inevitably gives way to demands for absolute sameness of treatment: Democrats ignore the most obvious distinctions, democracy degenerates into anarchy, and anarchy is replaced by tyranny. Plato's understanding of the dynamics of this process was too narrow. He attributed the instability of democracy to envy, failing to understand the deeper sources of dissatisfaction with human differences and the gradual loss of individual liberty to an encroaching bureaucracy.

The United States resisted egalitarianism for two centuries. Its Constitution guaranteed certain procedural rights, such as freedom of speech, without presuming that everyone would use these rights in the same way or with the same effectiveness. Any two groups with similar endowments and aspirations might be expected to occupy similar positions after a few generations, but democracy never assumed any specific intergroup similarities. Recognition of differences is essential to the very contrast between procedural equality and equality of outcome. In particular, it went without saying that men and women would occupy different positions in a democracy or any other sociopolitical system responsive to basic individual preferences. The democratic machine might need occasional tinkering (such as the enfranchisement of women), and the activities of men and women would be bound to overlap somewhat, but male and female spheres would never coincide.

Feminism denies this, maintaining instead that no distinction between the sexes in any institution will emerge in a society respecting basic individual preferences. This book has traced the consequences of this denial. Feminism may no longer command the emotional loyalty it once did, but that has not weakened its entrenchment. Indeed, the "postfeminist" woman is portrayed as a young ingrate with all the advantages—principally a career and the right to be sexually aggressive—who, in her self-absorption, has forgotten that feminism won her her exciting life. Its critics assume that feminism was right about everything and that its problems are the problems of victory. Cultural commentators, having pronounced the 1950s an era of conformity and the 1960s an era of rebellion, have professed puzzlement at the character of what has come since. Since has come—and this may explain what many critics consider its emotional flatness—the era of bureaucratic feminism. Feminism has become more entrenched as it has become less emotionally compelling because legal rights tend to last as long as the society which undergirds them. Constitutional and common law expand because their basic legal protections are perceived as enshrining prior natural rights. New legal rights are therefore perceived as protecting further newly discovered natural rights, and these are not surrendered lightly. The presumption that a legal right is based on a moral imperative grows stronger the longer it goes unchallenged, that is, the more opportunities the state waives to challenge this presumption by seeking to repeal the law.

A major obstacle to appreciating the extent to which liberty has been curtailed in the name of sexual equality is the search for a key event, a turning point. Pessimists from Plato to Orwell have thought too much in terms of collapse, too little in terms of erosion. Contrary to Orwell, the best picture of the future may not be a boot stamping on a human face, but a bureaucratic black hole drawing one matter after another out of the sphere of individual discretion and into itself.

It is tempting to argue that America is a democracy, and that the ascendancy of feminism in public policy manifests the popular will. There are curbs, however difficult to apply, on unelected officials. Judges can be impeached, appointees removed, the elected officials who installed them voted out. A majority of Iowans must be at least willing to tolerate public indoctrination of their children, it could be argued, or they would stop it. Perhaps—or perhaps people simply ignore rules in conflict with human nature—but this would in no way reconcile individual liberty and feminism. A democracy can annul itself. People can voluntarily surrender their liberty, all at once or piecemeal. However representative a government may be, the more powers are lodged with public officials, the fewer prerogatives remain for private individuals. And as the majority cedes ever more of the liberty of all to the government, the minority that wishes to retain its liberty loses it just as surely as if it were snatched by a tyrant.

I leave the reader to decide between majoritarianism and individual liberty. However, without for one moment agreeing that feminism represents majority opinion in the United States, I note that the potential conflict between these two values has long been recognized, and that the fundamental principle of constitutional democracy is not majority rule. It is, rather, the existence of domains over which the government—in whatever way it draws its legitimacy—has no say. As Justice Jackson wrote in *Barnette,*

The very purpose of a Bill of Rights was to withdraw certain subjects from the vicissitudes of political controversy, to place them beyond the reach of majorities and officials and to establish them as legal principles [that] depend on the outcome of no election.

It is this purpose, whatever its ultimate validity, that feminism must override.

Glimpses Beneath

The foregoing discussion inevitably raises broad sociological issues: Where did feminism come from, why was it accepted, where is it going, and what sort of influence is it likely to have in the future? Any answers to these questions are necessarily speculative, and I intend mine in a highly tentative spirit. The reader should not view what I have to say here as meant as categorically as what I have said on the more concrete topics already treated. Nor should single causes of these phenomena be expected. What produced feminism need not be what prepared its eager reception, and different groups may have received it for different reasons.

It is best to begin with feminists themselves, since the psychological roots of feminism, as with any belief, bear indirectly on its truth, for the following reason. Most beliefs are held because they are true. Anybody who believes that a pink convertible just went by probably did see a pink convertible go by; beliefs like that are not held for just any reason. Any rejection of any belief should, therefore, be fortified by some account of why the belief is held that involves no reference to the putative fact believed. Rejection of feminist beliefs should ideally be fortified by an account not involving victimization of why a number of often highly intelligent women believe with great intensity that all women have been victimized.

Questions of psychological genesis also bear on the moral assessment of revolutionary ideologies. A new cure-all for the human condition has no past successes to advertise and can hardly solicit testimonials from the old standards it repudiates. The only evidence it can offer of the fullness of life lived in accordance with its precepts are the lives of its adherents. (If feminists themselves cannot live by their principles because they too have been corrupted by a sexist upbringing, feminism cannot even be tried and further discussion of its merits is pointless.) Do feminists exhibit traits that most people admire and want in themselves? Are feminists flexible and capable of laughing at themselves? Are they in control of their lives? Is anger, the characteristic state of mind of feminists, likely to produce insight or distortion? Is a readiness to collect grievances produced by the sort of childhood generally found in the lives of well-adjusted adults, or the sort of childhood found in the lives of adults apt to blame others for their own troubles? Feminists have sensed the pertinence of these questions, for from the beginning they have offered their own emotions as central to their case. Something must be wrong, they argued in effect, or we would not be this angry.

Unappeasable fury is almost always a response to a perceived wrong, but society and men are too nebulous to be the focus of indignation as sharp as feminists feel. Nor is feminist anger the result of the unhappy affairs and divorces that litter feminist memoirs, for feminist rage rises from a layer of the personality deposited before adulthood. Many people endure worse than seduction or divorce without turning on the human race. I would suggest that feminist rage is directed at the father, a figure of sufficient emotional significance to explain the depth and intensity of feminist rage. This hypothesis would also explain feminist dislike of womanhood. It was not a point stressed in chapter 2, but the briefest glimpse at the feminist classics, the works of de Beauvoir, Millett, and Juliett Mitchell, will uncover descriptions of women as small-minded, jealous, irrational, dependent, selfish, possessive, and passive. Feminists invariably add the caveat that they like women per se, and are only describing what has become of women under patriarchy, but this distinction is unreal. Women as they have always been is what they are. To dislike what something has always been is to dislike the thing itself. Someone who says he enjoys baseball, but is bored by baseball as it has actually been played since the time of Abner Doubleday, is fooling others (and perhaps himself) about his true feelings. Second-stage feminists who claim to have rediscovered femininity and in the next breath demand the complete redesign of society to accommodate it, are no more able to put femininity in emotional perspective.

The intensity of feminist rage at femininity should not be allowed to obscure the universality of feminist anger. It is difficult to call to mind another social movement in which feelings of displeasure and belligerence play so prominent a role. Now, the only thing so ubiquitous in the feminist's field of vision that she finds it everywhere she looks is herself. It is not femininity in the abstract that feminists hate, but their own femininity.

Nothing could have produced this degree of anger at men and hatred of self but a childhood in which femaleness went unconfirmed by an ineffectual father, together perhaps with a dominant mother. Neglect and uncertainty produced profound feelings of disappointment that festered into resentment and a desire for revenge against the man who failed the feminist-to-be. Committed feminists have indeed been cheated—of a father's love.

Few data exist on the personal background of feminists, but this conjecture is consistent with the social background of the most prominent of the first generation of feminists and those of their followers apt to be met in the universities (where feminism got started). These women were raised in first- or second-generation families in large American cities between, say, 1930 and 1960. Many of their fathers worked at hard, often unprestigious jobs, and were emotionally withdrawn in the home. Religion in these homes was often replaced by secular ideologies stressing class antagonism, factors which would have further disrupted the process by which girls resolve their relation with their fathers and identify with their mothers. Some psychiatrists see the emotional tone of feminism as adolescent fear of the transition to womanhood.[1] Certainly preoccupation with realizing one's full human potential, together with shock at life's failure to be consistently exciting—one thinks of Jill Johnston's lament in *Lesbian Nation* that "none of us were told what a drastic drag it was to become a mother"—are reminiscent of the "what shall I be?" fantasies of adolescence. Distrust of ordinary heterosexual intercourse, counterpointed by celebration of homosexuality, abortion, and the general absence of sexual restraints is also reminiscent of the adolescent girl's fear of the sexual consequences of growing up. Perhaps the feminist obsession with rape and male sexual brutality is a grotesque distortion of the impulse behind adolescent girl's fascination with horses, another symbol of the power she knows she must someday learn to tame.

Feelings of self-hate must eventually be acknowledged. The embattled ego resolves the tensions created by unacceptable emotions by projecting them onto someone else. By attributing the hatred she feels for herself to society—"Society hates women"—and confirming this attribution by endlessly reviling imagined enemies, the feminist gives her ego an organizing principle. She is an "authoritarian personality" in the sense used in Adorno's famous study,[2] namely one characterized by an obsession with powerlessness and a constant sense of threat. Authoritarian women are reported to harbor deeply seated hostility for their dominant mothers,[3] and authoritarian men and women both exhibit "underlying ego-alien identification with opposite sex parent's role."[4] It hardly needs further saying that feminists are obsessed with powerlessness and are on constant guard, and I am not the first commentator to have remarked on their implicit assumption that only what males do and prize has any value. The authoritarian women in the Adorno study were unlike feminists in being conventionally feminine, but to so exaggerated an extent that Adorno saw in this a reaction to "an exploitative and hostile attitude toward men, expressed only indirectly in the interviews and shown quite directly in the stories of the Thematic Apperception Test."[5] Perhaps the second-stage apotheosis of femininity as all that is decent, together with anger at society's supposed disregard of feminine values throughout all of history, is the beginning of the reactive exaggerated femininity predicted by Adorno's analysis.

Glimpses Beyond

The chasm between the paternal love they really want and what they think they want means that feminists will never be satisfied by anything they get. Accommodation to any particular demand will always be found unsatisfying and merely trigger further demands. Negotiations with feminists cannot terminate in compromise. Because she needs to believe that she is fighting a universal conspiracy, a feminist will tolerate any claim on behalf of "women." She may draw back from claims that are simply too bizarre, but always while extending sympathetic understanding to the sisters who make them.

The first feminist device for abolishing femininity and masculinity was direct wish fulfillment: denial that they exist. This escapist daydream has fared ill in the face of reality, so there will be changes in the ways in which feminists try to obviate sex differences. Instead of arguing that sex stereotypes are bad because false, feminist will argue that, although true, they should go unheeded, and feminists will continue to demand laws against the use of stereotypes. It is in this spirit that Mary Gray, speaking for WEAL, has maintained that pricing life insurance by sex is "discriminatory even though these stereotypic calculations [that women outlive men] might be true."[6] The admission of any sex differences will be accompanied by demands that their social expression be minimized. Admissions of sex differences themselves will remain guarded and always hedged with warnings against the encouragement of sexism. Having surrendered the argument that stereotypes are impermissible because they are social artifacts only to seize the argument that stereotypes are not true *enough* to be allowed to have effect, feminists will continue to support the invasive measures already deployed to disrupt the formation of individual judgement.

Finally, there will be continued pressure to change society so that the newly discovered cooperativeness of women can be harnessed *to enable women to continue to achieve "equality" with men at male tasks*. The admission that children are important to women will, as we have already begun to see, be taken to show that work must be redesigned so that a woman can have children and a career just like a man's. The calls for the state to make it happen will continue. A new ideological biology will replace the picture of women as indistinguishable from men with a picture of women as possessing all the virtues of womanhood superimposed on the strengths of manhood. This new picture will make even less ethological sense than its predecessor.

Why Feminism?

Feminism gained influence in the general culture, in part, from its natural alliance with the Left, broadly understood as that body of opinion which attributes a great and hitherto unrecognized measure of human woe to the dominance of the weak by the strong under "bourgeois liberty," woe preventable only by state intervention. Feminism shared with the Left a readiness to see oppression where others see liberty and injustice where others see free bargaining. The Left, in turn, would have risked embarrassment by asking close questions about "sexist oppression," because scepticism about this new form of oppression would have invited reappraisal of the Left's more hallowed forms. Then, too, the classical ideas of the Left—unionism, the nationalization of industry, the heroism of the Soviet experiment—were growing moribund by the middle of the present century, leaving the Left in need of new sources of vitality. Feminists were nothing if not energetic.

Public officials acceded to feminism for reasons which were in the main verbal. One such reason was the identification of feminism as the *women's* movement, achieved by feminists calling themselves "the women's movement" sufficiently often. Elected officials had no desire to oppose what they saw as the wishes of half their constituency, and most elected officials do want to do right by women; they simply took feminists at their word that encouraging women to compete against men in extrafamilial pursuits while implicitly downgrading motherhood would "improve the status of women." What is more, feminist slogans were shielded from examination by the equation of race with sex built into the terms of the debate, as "sexism" followed "racism" and "sex stereotype" followed "racial stereotype."

The tactical success of equating women with Blacks still leaves unanswered the fundamental question of why so many thoughtful people accepted the equation. Why did Blacks not bridle when privileged middle-class women with university degrees called themselves "niggers?" Why were Jews not outraged when Betty Friedan called the suburbs "a comfortable concentration camp?" The rhetorical success of these deranged analogies suggests a breakdown of critical thought, and without doubt the public paid little attention to what feminists were actually saying. The *Minneapolis Star* praised Woman in Sexist Society for being "free from rancor," yet the very first selection of this anthology ends: "Listen to my life and see that it has been intolerable and leave me the fuck alone." Probably the feminist message and the language in which it was conveyed were so unpleasant that ordinary people were reluctant to discuss them, and this reluctance in turn created the illusion that feminism had survived critical scrutiny.

Still, enough people heard the message for other factors to have been at work. The most obvious are the many features of modern society which erode a sense of sexual identity. With the passing of the environment in which a biological drive evolves, and with it the necessity of that drive for survival, there is a tendency to deny that the drive exists at all. As modern medicine made it unnecessary for a woman to devote her life to having babies in the hope that some would live to adulthood, women began doing other things, particularly getting educated. Since so much female energy was now being devoted to pursuits irrelevant to the maternal role, there came a tendency to think of these pursuits as very important and of the maternal function as unimportant. One wants to protect one's investment of energy by thinking that it has been invested wisely.

Meanwhile, task rationalization had deprived many activities of their masculine component. A woman can drive a car with power steering just as easily as, and what may be more important, in just the same way as, a man. Modern mass production requires objects designed to translate wide differences in the input of different users into identical outputs. Men, having lost contact with their masculinity, were tongue-tied when told that there is no such thing.

The entry of women into the workforce also contributed to the rise of feminism, but not because women decided to rebel at the blatant discrimination they discovered there. Rather, the entry of women into the labor force in large cities, where they lived away from parental supervision, together with the invention of the automobile, and, later, the contraceptive pill, made casual sex more feasible than at any previous time. The relaxation of sexual mores did not, as the standard story has it, given women a taste of the sexual freedom men enjoy, which prompted demands for that and every other kind of freedom for themselves. The female's genetic program for seeking commitment from males was not cancelled by the contraceptive pill. Rather, the feasibility of unceremonious sex created the expectation that women would consent to it, a circumstance that became known as the sexual revolution. This imperative to have casual sex created an immense reservoir of resentment against men on the part of young, unmarried women. Torn between the new rules of sexual compliance and her age-old impulse to hold back, angry at the men she felt duty bound to sleep with, the contemporary woman responded to the hatred of men and talk of victimhood in the feminist message.

Men cannot be blamed for the result, which even some feminists now recognize has been a catastrophe for women. Men acted in character throughout the sexual revolution, seeking as always to strew their seed as widely as possible. What changed was that for the first time in human history there were no incentives in the form of female noncompliance for men to learn to control their promiscuous impulses and ready themselves for romantic love. Having been instructed that the distinction between madonnas and whores was hopelessly outmoded, men naturally began to treat all women as whores. It is no use blaming *Playboy* magazine and "capitalism," as Barbara Ehrenreich does, for the perpetual adolescence of the contemporary male. Sexual mores were very strict during the nineteenth century heyday of free enterprise in the United States. It would be more appropriate to blame those who urged the relaxation of the social norms which make men grow up by instilling masculine pride, and singularly appropriate to blame whoever told women that they would enjoy casual sex. Feminists in search of culprits might begin by looking in the mirror.

It is also quite possible that men have begun shirking their responsibilities toward women because of their expectation that women will be competing against them. Restoration of the male's sense of responsibility may require a withdrawal of women from male areas, and on the part of women a renewal of the sort of femininity that feminists have taught everyone to despise. The hypothesis that men dislike females who adopt masculine modes of behavior deserves to be considered seriously, and not judged by ideological standards.

The World After Feminism

As the future unfolds, relations between the sexes will be determined by technological innovations and ancient drives. At least in the Western world, women have generally begun to take part in activities as they become widespread, and a great many activities have opened up as standards of living have climbed. Coeducation has greatly increased female participation in the growing number of areas in which information is processed. For instance, 36 percent of the current enrollment in law schools is female.

This does not mean that women will ever creep incrementally to a position of anything like equality with men, nor even that female participation in nontraditional activities will remain at current levels. Success in extrafamilial pursuits goes against deep-seated female impulses. Women are hypergamous. They seek men of higher status than themselves, for substantially the same reason that females have always sought to mate with the alpha male; he has proven his ability to protect her and her offspring. The higher a woman climbs in hierarchies, the fewer men she will find appealing—and, since males prefer to dominate sexual bonding pairs, the fewer men she will appeal to. It is silly to berate men for not being able to get interested in women who are their equals. On matters closely linked to reproductive success, people feel the way their genes tell them to feel. Perhaps as women notice that aping the success of men denies them husbands and children and stable families, they will lose interest in extrafamilial success. They will for a time feel guilty about this loss of interest—thanks to current norms—but genes are more persuasive than feminist proclamations. I have no idea what in particular women will decide to do when they find that they cannot have the family life they want when they try to compete with their husbands, even with all the day care, communal cooking, and affirmative action in the world, but in one way or another they will choose family.

As the number of female lawyers increases but the most powerful lawyers remain men, as childrearing remains fixed as a female concern—as men and women choose different adaptations to modernity—feminists will continue to offer what they have offered so far: grievance about sex differences. So long as feminism remains institutionalized it will purvey coercion. Feminists may be beyond rational persuasion, and will continue to proclaim their errors with complete assurance. But they are, in the end, asking women to make themselves unattractive to men and to forego love and children. Feminism will be forgotten, commanding only the loyalty of barren women whose genetic lines are running to extinction.

Notes

1. See Iradji Siassi and David O. Wesner, "Women's Liberation and Two Adolescent Movements," *International Journal of Social Psychology* 20, 1/2 (n.d): n.p.
2. T.W. Adorno, Else Frenkel-Brunswick, Daniel J. Levinson, and R. Nevitt Sanford, *The Authoritarian Personality* (New York: Norton, 1969).
3. Ibid., p. 368.
4. Ibid., p. 444.
5. Ibid., p. 477.
6. *MacNeil/Lehrer Report,* PBS, March 1983.

Bibliography

Books

Adorno, T.W., Frenkel-Brunswick, E., Levinson, D.J., and Sanford, R.N. *The Authoritarian Personality*. New York: Norton, 1969.

Barash, David. *The Whisperings Within*. New York: Penguin, 1981.

Barber, Benjamin. *Liberating Feminism*. New York: Delta, 1976.

Beauvoir, Simone de. *The Second Sex*. Trans. H.M. Parshley. New York: Knopf, 1953.

Berryman, Sue. *The Social Composition of American Enlisted Forces*. New York: Ford Foundation, 1983.

Bettelheim, Bruno. *The Uses of Enchantment*. New York: Vintage, 1977.

Biehler, Robert. *Psychology Applied to Children*. New York: Houghton-Mifflin, 1978.

Biryukova, Alexandra. *Soviet Women: Their Role in Society, the Economy, the Trade Unions*. Moscow: Profizdat Publishers, 1981.

Bleier, Ruth. *Science and Gender*. New York: Pergamon, 1984.

Brownmiller, Susan. *Against Our Will*. New York: Simon & Schuster, 1975.

Bruner, J., et al. *Studies in Cognitive Growth*. New York: Wiley, 1966.

Byrne, Eileen. *Women and Social Reconstruction, the Twenty-Ninth Tate Memorial Lecture*. Brisbane: University of Queensland Press, 1982.

Carden, Muriel. *The New Feminist Movement*. New York: Russell Sage Foundation, 1974.

Chesler, Phyllis. *Women and Madness*. New York: Avon, 1972.

Chodorow, Nancy. *The Reproduction of Mothering*. Berkeley: University of California, 1978.

Cohen, Dorothy, and Rudolph, Marguerita. *Kindergarten and Elementary Schooling*. Englewood Cliffs, N.J.: Prentice-Hall, 1977.

Colman, A.D., and Colman, L.L. *Pregnancy: The Psychological Experience*. New York: Herder & Herder, 1971.

Cooke, Cynthia, and Dworkin, Susan. *The Ms Guide to a Woman's Health*. New York: Doubleday, 1979.

Daniels, W.L., et al. *The Effects of Two Years Training in Aerobic Power and Muscle Strength*. U.S. Army Institute of Environmental Medicine, Report no. M-12/80, 1980.

Dawkins, Richard. *The Selfish Gene*. Oxford: Oxford University Press, 1978.

Deckard, Ruth. *The Women's Movement*. New York: Harper & Row, 1979.

Dinnerstein, Dorothy. *The Mermaid and the Minotaur*. New York: Harper & Row, 1979.

Dowling, Colette. *The Cinderella Complex*. New York: Summit, 1981.

Dworkin, Andrea. *Men Possessing Women*. New York: Putnam, 1981.

Eastman, Carol. *Aspects of Language and Culture*. San Francisco: Chandler & Sharp, 1975.

Ehrenreich, Barbara. *The Hearts of Men*. New York: Doubleday, 1983.

Eisler, Riane. *The Equal Rights Handbook.* New York: Avon, 1978.

Fausto-Sterling, Anne. *Myths of Gender.* New York: Basic Books, 1986.

Finn, Judith. *The Treatment of Women under Social Security.* Washington, D.C.: Free Congress Research Foundation, 1981.

Firestone, Shulamith. *The Dialectic of Sex.* New York: Morrow, 1970.

Fowler, William. *Battle for the Falklands (1): Land Forces.* London: Osprey,1 981.

Fraiberg, Selma. *Every Child's Birthright.* New York: Basic Books, 1977.

Freud, Anna. *The Ego and the Mechanisms of Defense.* New York: International Universities Press, 1966.

Friedan, Betty. *The Feminine Mystique.* New York: W.W. Norton, 1963.

_____. *The Second Stage.* New York: Simon & Schuster, 1981.

Fulenwider, Claire. *Feminism in American Politics.* New York: Praeger, 1980.

Gelb, Joyce, and Paley, Marion. *Women and Public Policy.* Princeton, N.J.: Princeton University Press, 1982.

Gesell, A., et al. *The First Five Years of Life.* New York: Harper & Row, 1940.

Gilligan, Carol. *In A Different Voice.* Cambridge, Mass.: Harvard University Press, 1983.

Golberg, Steven. *The Inevitability of Patriarchy.* Second edition. London: Temple-Smith, 1977.

Goodman, Richard A. *U.S. Productivity.* New York: W.R. Grace, 1982.

Gornick, Vivian, and Moran, Betty. *Woman in Sexist Society.* New York: Mentor, 1971.

Gould, James. *Ethology.* New York: Harper & Row, 1982.

Graham, Kennon. *My Little Book about Flying.* Racine, Wisconsin: Whitman, 1978.

Greenawalt, Kent. *Discrimination and Reverse Discrimination.* New York: Borzoi, 1983.

Greer, Germaine. *The Female Eunuch.* New York: McGraw-Hill, 1970.

Hall, Roberta M., and Sandler, Bernice. *Out of the Classroom: A Chilly Campus Climate for Women?* Washington, D.C.: PSEW AAC, 1984.

_____. *The Classroom Climate: A Chilly One for Women?* Washington, D.C.: PSEW, AAC, 1982.

Harding, Sandra, and Hintikka, Merrill, eds. *Discovering Reality: Feminist Perspectives on Epistemology.* Boston: D. Reidel, 1983.

Harris, Marvin. *Cannibals and Kings.* New York: Random House, 1977.

Hempel, Carl G. *Fundamentals of Concept Formation in Empirical Science.* Chicago: University of Chicago Press, 1950.

Hewlett, Sylvia. *A Lesser Life.* New York: Morrow, 1986.

Hocutt, Max. *The Elements of Logical Analysis and Inference.* Cambridge, Mass.: Winthrop, 1979.

Holme, Bryan. *Advertising: Reflections of a Century.* New York: Viking, 1982.

Howe, Florence. *Seven Years Later: Women's Studies Programs in 1976.* Washington, D.C.: Department of Education, 1977.

Hrdy, Sarah. *The Woman That Never Evolved.* Cambridge, Mass.: Harvard University Press, 1981.

Hutner, Frances. *Facts and Figures: Wage Discrimination and Job Segregation.* Washington, D.C.: Women's Legal Defense Fund, n.d.

Janeway, Elizabeth. *Man's World, Woman's Place.* New York: Morrow, 1971.

Jenkins, Lulu. *A Comparative Study of Motor Achievement of Children of Five, Six, and Seven Years of Age.* New York: Teacher's College, 1930.

Konner, Melvin. *The Tangled Wing.* New York: Harper, 1982.

Kowal, D., Voegl, J., Sharp D., and Knapnik, J. *Analysis of Attrition, Retention, and Criterion Task Performance of Recruits during Training.* I.S. Army Medical Research and Development Command Technical Report T2/82, 1982.

Kuhn, T.S. *The Structure of Scientific Revolutions.* Second edition. Chicago: University of Chicago Press, 1970.

Lakoff, Robin. *Language and Women's Place.* New York: Harper & Row, 1975.

Lapidus, Gail. *Women in Soviet Society.* Berkeley: University of California Press, 1975.

Laws, Judith Long. *The Second X.* New York: Elsevier, 1979.

Levin, Michael. *Metaphysics and the Mind-Body Problem.* Oxford: Oxford University Press, 1979.

Lewontin, Richard, Rose, Steven, and Kamin, Leon. *Not in Our Genes.* New York: Pantheon, 1984.

Lindsay, Cotton. *Equal Pay for Equal Worth.* Miami: Law and Economics Center, University of Miami, 1980.

Lippman, Peter. *Busy Trains.* New York: Random House, 1978.

Locke, John. *Essay Concerning Human Understanding.*

Lowe, Marion and Hubbard, Ruth, eds., *Women's Nature,* New York: Pergamon, 1983.

Luce, R. Duncan, and Raiffa, H. *Games and Decisions.* New York: Wiley, 1957.

Maccoby, Eleanor, and Jacklin, Carol. *The Psychology of Sex Differences.* Stanford: Stanford University Press, 1974.

MacKenzie, A.C.C. *The Major Achievements of Science.* New York: Simon & Schuster, 1973.

MacMillan, Susan. *Women, Reason, and Nature.* Princeton, N.J.: Princeton University Press, 1983.

Mahler, Margaret, Pine, Fred, and Bergmann, Annie. *The Psychological Birth of the Human Infant.* New York: Basic Books, 1975.

Menzies, Heather. *Women and the Chip.* Montreal: Institute on Public Policy, 1981.

Merton, Robert K. *Sociological Ambivalence and Other Essays.* New York: Free Press, 1976.

Midgley, Mary. *Beast and Man.* New York: Meridian, 1978.

Mill, J.S. *The Subjection of Women,* 1869.

Millet, Kate. *Sexual Politics.* New York: Doubleday, 1970.

Mitchell, Juliet. *Psychoanalysis and Feminism.* New York: Pantheon, 1974.

Moché, Dinah. *We're Taking an Airplane Trip.* New York: Golden Book, 1982.

Möens, Gabriel. *Affirmative Action: Concepts, Justifications, and Practice.* Report prepared for the Australian Human Rights Commission. Sydney: Center for Independent Studies, 1985.

Money, John. *Sex Errors of the Body.* Baltimore: Johns Hopkins University Press, 1968.

Money, John, and Erhardt, Anke. *Man and Woman, Boy and Girl.* Baltimore: Johns Hopkins University Press, 1972.

Morgan, Robin, ed. *Sisterhood is Powerful.* New York: Vintage, 1970.

Morgan, Robin. *Going Too Far.* New York: Random House, 1977.

Murray, Charles. *Losing Ground.* New York: Basic Books, 1984.

Oakley, Anne. *Sex, Gender, and Society.* New York: Harper & Row, 1972.

O'Neill, June. *The Determinants and Wage Effects of Occupational Segregation.* Washington, D.C.: The Urban Institute, 1983.

O'Neill, June, and Braun, Rachel. *Women and the Labor Market: A Survey of Issues and Policies in the United States*. Washington, D.C.: The Urban Institute, 1981.

Papalia, Sharon, and Olds, Sally. *A Child's World*. New York: McGraw-Hill, 1979.

Pearsall, Marilyn, ed. *Women and Values*. Belmont, Ca.: Wadsworth, 1986.

Petchesky, Rosalind. *Abortion and Woman's Choice*. New York: Longmans, 1984.

Player, Mack. *Federal Law of Employment Discrimination*. St. Paul: West, 1981.

Pogrebin, Letty. *Growing Up Free*. New York: McGraw-Hill, 1980.

Pomeroy, Sharon. *Goddesses, Whores, Wives, and Slaves*. New York: Shocken, 1975.

Reskin, Barbara, and Hartmann, Heidi, eds. *Women's Work, Men's Work: Sex Segregation on the Jobs*. Washington, D.C.: National Academy Press, 1985.

Richards, Janet. *The Sceptical Feminist*. Boston: Routledge & Kegan Paul, 1980.

Rueda, Enrique. *The Homosexual Matrix*. Greenwich, Conn.: Devin Adair, 1981.

Saad, L.G., and Storer, W.O. *Understanding in Mathematics*. Edinburgh: Oliver & Boyd, 1960.

Sadker, David, and Sadker, Myra. *Microteaching Skills for INTERSECT*. Washington, D.C.: U.S. Department of Education, n.d.

_____. *Sex Equity Handbook for Schools*. New York: Longmans, 1980.

Saxon, John. *Honesty Is One of the Better Policies*. New York: Viking, 1984.

Sayers, Janet. *Biological Politics,* New York: Methuen, 1982.

Seaman, Barbara. *Free and Female*. New York: Fawcett World, 1972.

Sidel, Ruth. *Women and Children Last*. New York: Viking, 1986.

Simon, Herbert. *The Sciences of the Artificial*. Second Edition. Cambridge, Mass.: MIT Press, 1981.

Smith, I. *Spatial Ability*. San Diego: R.R. Knopp, 1964.

Smith, John Maynard. *The Evolution of Sex*. Cambridge, Mass.: Cambridge University Press, 1978.

_____. *The Theory of Evolution*. Third edition. New York: Penguin, 1975.

Sommerhof, G. *Analytical Biology*. London: Oxford University Press, 1950.

Stewart-Clarke, Alison. *Day-Care*. Cambridge, Mass.: Harvard University Press, 1982.

Stoller, Robert. *Sex and Gender: On the Development of Masculinity and Femininity*. New York: Science House, 1968.

Stratton, Joanna. *Pioneer Women*. New York: Simon & Schuster, 1981.

Symons, Donald. *The Evolution of Human Sexuality*. New York: Oxford University Press, 1979.

Tiger, Lionel, and Sheper, Joseph. *Women in the Kibbutz*. New York: Harcourt, Brace, Jovanovich, 1975.

Thomas, Claire Sherman. *Sex Discrimination*. St. Paul: West, 1982.

Treiman, Donald J. *Job Evaluation: An Analytic Review*. Washington, D.C.: National Academy of Sciences, 1979.

Tuchman, Barbara. *A Distant Mirror*. New York: Ballantine, 1980.

Vandenberg, Steven, ed. *Progress in Genetics*. Baltimore, Md.: Johns Hopkins University Press, 1968.

Wattenberg, Ben. *The Birth Dearth*. Forthcoming.

Weidenbaum, Murray. *The Future of Business Regulation*. New York: American Management Association, 1979.

Wennberg, Robert N. *Life in the Balance*. Grand Rapids, Mich.: Eerdmans, 1985.

Whorf, Benjamin. *Language, Thought, and Reality*. Edited by J.B. Caroll. Cambridge, Mass.: MIT Press, 1956.

Wilson, E.O. *On Human Nature.* Cambridge, Mass.: Harvard University Press, 1978.

———. *Sociobiology.* Cambridge, Mass.: Harvard University Press, 1975.

Wirtemberg, J. *Expanding Girls' Occupational Potential: A Case Study of the Implementation of Title IX's Anti-Sex-Discrimination Provision in Seventh Grade Practical Arts.* Ann Arbor: University Microfilm, 1979.

Witt, Mary, and Nahmey, Patricia. *Women's Work: Up From 878: Report of the DOT* [Dictionary of Occupational Titles] *Research Project.* Madison: Women's Educational Resources, University of Wisconsin—Extension, 1975.

Wolchik, Sharon. *Women and Politics: The Eastern European Experience.* Institute for Sino-Soviet Studies, 1982.

Wolgast, Elizabeth. *Equality and the Rights of Women.* Ithaca: Cornell University Press, 1981.

Articles

Adelson, Joseph. "Living with Quotas." *Commentary* (May 1978).

Andrews, Lori. "Learning the Rules of the Game." *Parents* (January 1982).

Baker, Robert. " 'Pricks' and 'Chicks': A Plea for Persons." In Mary Vetterling-Braggin, ed., *Sexist Language.* Totowa, N.J.: Littlefield, Adams, 1981.

Bant, Bruce N. "Working Together: The Army's Assault on Sexism." *Soldier* (October 1980).

Barakat, M.K. "A Factorial Study of Mathematical Ability." *British Journal of Psychology, Statistical Section* 4 (1951).

Barber, Benjamin. "Beyond the Feminist Mystique." *New Republic* (July 11, 1983).

Barrett, Nancy. "Obstacles to Economic Parity for Women." *American Economic Review* (May 1982).

Bau, Carlene, et al. "Drug Use and Expenditures in 1982." *Journal of the American Medical Association* 253 (January 18, 1985).

Benbow, Camilla, and Stanley, Julian. "Consequences in High School and College of Sex Differences in Mathematical Reasoning: A Longitudinal Perspective." *American Education Research* 19 (Winter 1982).

———. "Gender and the Science Major: A Study of Mathematically Precocious Youth." *Advances in Motivation and Achievement* 2 (1984).

———. "Sex Differences in Mathematical Ability: Fact or Artifact?" *Science* 210 (December 1980).

———. "Sex Differences in Mathematical Reasoning Ability: More Facts." *Science* 222 (December, 1983).

Bernard, Jessie. "The Paradox of the Happy Marriage." In Vivian Gornick and Barbara Moran, eds., *Women in Sexist Society* (New York: Mentor, 1971).

Berryman-Fink, Cynthia. "Male-Female Interaction Patterns." Summary of "Communication Training as a Prevention of Sexual Harassment," Fifth Annual Communication, Language and Gender Conference, Athens, Ohio, October 16, 1982.

Birdsong, Beth. "Motherese." *Parents* (March 1983).

Block, Ned, and Dworkin, Gerald. "Heritability and Inequality." In Ned Block and Gerald Dworkin, eds., *The IQ Controversy.* New York: Pantheon, 1976.

Block, Walter. "Economic Intervention, Discrimination, and Unforeseen Consequences." In Walter Block and Michael Walker, eds., *Discrimination, Affirmative Action, and Equal Opportunity.* Vancouver: Fraser Institute, 1982.

———. "Woman and Fetus: Rights in Conflict?" *Reason* (April 1978).

Bock, Darrell, and Vandenberg, Steven. "Components of Heritable Variation in Mental Test Scores." In Steven Vandenberg, ed., *Progress in Genetics.* Baltimore: Johns Hopkins University Press, 1968.

Bock, R.D., and Kolakowski, D. "Further Evidence of Sex-Linked Major-Gene Influence on Human Spatial Visualizing Ability." *American Journal of Genetics* 25 (January 1973).

Bowles, Gloria, and Klein, Renate. "Introduction." In Gloria Bowles and Renate Klein, eds., *Theories of Women's Studies.* New York: Routledge & Kegan Paul, 1983.

Brazelton, T. Berry. "Effect of Maternal Expectation on Early Infant Development." *Early Child Development Care* 2 (1973).

Bridenthal, Renate. "The Family: A View From a Room of Her Own." In Barrie Thorne and M. Yalom, eds., *Rethinking the Family.* New York: Longmans, 1982.

Broverman, Donald, et al. "Sex Role Stereotypes: A Current Appraisal." *Journal of Social Issues* 28 (1972).

Brunch, Charlotte. "Lesbians in Revolt," In Marilyn Pearsall, ed., *Women and Values.* Belmont, Ca.: Wadsworth, 1986.

Bryden, David. "Between Two Constitutions: Feminism and Pornography." *Constitutional Commentary* 2 (Winter 1985).

Bunzel, John. "To Each According to Her Worth?" *Public Interest* 63 (Spring 1982).

———. "Rescuing Equality." In Paul Kurtz, ed., *Sidney Hook.* Buffalo, N.Y.: Prometheus, 1983.

Burns, Edward. "Math Games." *Graduate Woman* (January 1982).

Burns, Heywood. "The Bakke Case and Affirmative Action: Some Implications for the Future." *Freedomways* (First Quarter, 1978).

Carney, Larry. "Recruit Strength." *Army Times* (April 11, 1983).

Carroll, J.B., and Casagrande, J.B. "The Function of Language Classifications in Behavior." In A.G. Smith, ed., *Communication and Culture.* New York: Hold, Rinehart, & Winston, 1966.

Chodorow, Nancy, and Contratto, Susan. "The Myth of the Perfect Mother." In Barrie Thorne and M. Yalom, eds., *Rethinking the Family.* New York: Longmans, 1982.

Corah, N.L. "Differentiation in Children and Their Parents." *Journal of Perception* 33 (1965).

Cook, Beverly. "Evaluation of Textbooks for Sex Bias." *News for Teachers of Political Science* 30 (Summer 1981).

Corcoran, Mary, and Duncan, Gregory, J. "Work History, Labor Force Attachment, and Earnings Differences between the Races and the Sexes." *Journal of Human Resources* 14 (Winter 1979): 3–20.

Daly, Mary. "The Qualitative Leap beyond Patriarchal Religion." In Marilyn Pearsall, ed., *Women and Values.* Belmont, Ca.: Wadsworth, 1986.

Daly, Michael. "Firewomen." *New York* (January 10, 1983).

DeCrow, Karen. "Hardlining Title IX." *Perspectives* (Summer 1980).

Devilbiss, M.C. "Women and the Draft." In Martin Anderson, ed., *The Military Draft.* Stanford: Hoover Institution Press, 1982.

de Waal, Frans. Interview. *Success* (January 1985).

Du Bois, Barbara. "Passionate Scholarship." In Gloria Bowles and Renate Klein, eds., *Theories of Women's Studies.* New York: Routledge & Kegan Paul, 1983.

Eccles, Jacqueline. "Bringing Women to Science." *The Research News* (September 1982).

Elshtain, Jean Bethke. "Feminism, Family, and Community." *Dissent* (November 1982).

Emerson, Thomas, et al. "The Equal Rights Amendment: A Constitutional Basis for Equal Rights." *Yale Law Review* 80, 5 (April 1971).

Erhardt, Anke, and Baker, Susan. "Fetal Androgens, Human Central Nervous System Differentiation, and Behavior Sex Differences." In R.C. Friedman et al., eds., *Sex Differences in Behavior.* New York: John Wiley, 1974.

Erhardt, Anke, and Meyer-Blauberg, Heino. "Effects of Prenatal Hormones on Gender-Related Behavior." *Sciences* 211 (March 1984).

Etaugh, C., and Hughes, V. "Teachers' Evaluations of Sex-Typed Behaviors in Children: the Role of Teacher, Sex, and School Setting." *Developmental Psychology* 11 (1974).

Fausto-Sterling, Anne. "The Myth of Neutrality: Race, Sex, and Class in Science." *The Radical Teacher* 19 (1981).

Federbush, Marcia. "The Sex Problems of School Math Books." In Judith Stacey, Susan Bereaud, and Joan Daniels, eds., *And Jill Came Tumbling After: Sexism in American Education.* New York: Dell, 1974.

Fee, Elizabeth. "Women's Nature and Scientific Objectivity." In Marian Lowe and Ruth Hubbard, eds., *Women's Nature.* New York: Pergamon, 1983.

Feigen-Fasteau, Brenda. "Giving Women a Sporting Chance." *Ms* (July 1973).

Felsenthal, Carol. "How Feminists Failed." *Chicago* (June 1982).

Ferran, Dale. "Now for the Bad News." *Parents* (September 1982).

Flax, Jane. "Women Do Theory." In Marilyn Pearsall, ed., *Women and Values.* Belmont, Ca: Wadsworth, 1986.

Freed, Mayer, and Polsby, Daniel. "Comparable Worth in the Equal Pay Act," *University of Chicago Law Review* 51, 4 (Fall 1984).

Friedan, Betty. Review of Steven Goldberg, *The Inevitability of Patriarchy. New Statesman* (September 23, 1977).

_____. "The Family Needs to Be Changed." In Bruno Leone and M. Teresa O'Neill, eds., *Male/Female Roles.* St. Paul: Greenhaven, 1983.

_____. "Twenty Years After the Feminine Mystique." *New York Times Magazine* (February 22, 1983).

Frye, Marilyn. "Some Reflections on Separatism and Power." In Marilyn Pearsall, ed., *Women and Values.* Belmont, Ca: Wadsworth, 1986.

Gold, Doris. "Women and Voluntarism." In Vivian Gornick and Barbara Moran, eds., *Woman in Sexist Society.* New York: Mentor, 1971.

Goldberg, S., and Lewis, M. "Play Behavior in the Year Old Infant: Early Sex Differences." *Child Development* 40 (1969).

Gordon, Robert. "Taboo or Not Taboo: Research in IQ, Race, and Delinquency." In Edward Sagarin, ed., *Taboos in Criminology.* Beverly Hills: Sage, 1980.

Gordon, Suzanne. "The New Corporate Feminism." *The Nation* (February 5, 1983).

Gornick, Vivian, and Moran, Barbara. "Introduction." In Vivian Gornick and Barbara Moran, eds., *Woman in Sexist Society.* New York: Mentor, 1971.

Gottfredson, Linda. "Circumscription and Compromise: A Developmental Theory of Occupational Aspiration." *The Journal of Counseling Psychology* Monograph 28, 6 (November 1981).

Gray, Mary, and Schaefer, Alice. "Guidelines for Equality: A Proposal." *Academe* (December 1981).

_____. "Sex and Mathematics." *Science* 211 (January 16, 1981).

Green, Gordon, and Welnick Edward. "Measuring the Effects of Changing Family Composition during the 1970's in Black-White Differences in Income." Washington, D.C.: Bureau of the Census, Department of Commerce, 1982.

Grune, Joy Ann. "Pay Equity is a Necessary Remedy for Wage Discrimination." *Comparable Worth: Issue for the 80's.* Washington, D.C.: U.S. Civil Rights Commission, 1984.

Gwartney, James, and Stroup, Richard. "Measurement of Employment Discrimination According to Sex." *Southern Economic Journal* 39, 4 (April 1973).

Hacker, Andrew. "Why Women Still Earn Less Than Men." *Working Mother* (October 1983).

Hacker, Helen. "Women as a Minority Group." In Florence Denmark ed., *Who Discriminates against Women?* Beverly Hills: Sage, 1974.

Hamilton, William. "The Genetical Theory of Social Behavior: I and II." *Journal of Theoretical Biology* 7, 1 (1964).

Harris, Harold J. "How Women's Studies Came to Kalamazoo." Manuscript. Department of English, Kalamazoo College, Kalamazoo, Mich.

Harris, L.J. "Sex Differences in Spatial Ability: Possible Environmental, Genetic, and Neurological Factors." In M. Kinsbourne, ed., *Asymmetrical Functions of the Brain.* Cambridge: Cambridge University Press, 1978.

Hartlage, L.C. "Sex-Linked Inheritance of Spatial Ability." *Perceptual and Motor Skills* 31 (October 1970).

Hatch, Orrin. "Loading the Economy." *Policy Review* (Spring 1980).

Hier, D.B., and Crowley, W.F. "Spatial Ability in Androgen-Deficient Men." *New England Journal of Medicine* 306, 20 (May 20, 1982).

Hilbert, David. "Mathematical Problems." Address delivered to the Second International Congress of Mathematicians, Paris, 1900.

Hoffman, Carl, and Reed, John. "When Is Imbalance Not Discrimination?" In Walter Block and Michael Walker, eds., *Discrimination, Affirmative Action, and Equal Opportunity.* Vancouver: Fraser Institute, 1982.

Howe, Florence. "Feminist Scholarship, the Extent of the Revolution." *Change* (April 1982).

Hunter, John, Schmidt, Frank, and Rauschenberger, John. "Fairness of Psychological Tests: Implications of Four Definitions for Selection Utility and Minority Hiring." *Journal of Applied Psychology* 62, 3 (1977).

Hunter, John, Schmidt, Frank, and Mack, Murray. "Selection Utility in the Occupation of U.S. Park Ranger for Three Modes of Test Use." Manuscript. Washington, D.C.: Psychological Services, April 1983.

Imperato-McGinley, Julianne, Gaultier, Teofilo, and Strula, Erasmo. "Androgens and the Evolution of Male Gender Identity among Pseudohermaphrodites with 5α-Reductase Deficiency." *New England Journal of Medicine* 300, 22 (May 31, 1979).

Imperato, Julianne, Guerrero, Luis, Gaultier, Teofilo, and Peterson, R.E. "Steroid 5α-Reductase Deficiency in Man: An Inherited Form of Male Pseudohermaphroditism." *Science* 186 (December 27, 1974).

Imperato-McGinley, Julianne, and Peterson, R.E. "Male Pseudohermaphroditism: The Complexities of Male Phenotypic Development." *American Journal of Medicine* 61 (August 1976).

Jagger, Alison. "On Sexual Equality." *Ethics* 84 (July 1974).

Jenkins, L.M. "A Comparative Study of Motor Achievements of Children of Five, Six, and Seven Years of Age." *Teachers College Contributions to Education,* 414.

Jones, Beverly. "The Dynamics of Marriage and Motherhood." In Robin Morgan, ed., *Sisterhood Is Powerful*. New York: Vintage, 1970.

Kagan, Jerome. "The Idea of Spatial Ability." *New England Journal of Medicine* 306 (1982).

Keller, Evelyn Fox. "Feminism and Science." *Signs* 7, 3 (1982).

Kemble, Penn. "A New Direction for the Democrats?" *Commentary* (October 1982).

Kendrick, K.M., and Drewett, R.F. "Testosterone Reduces Refractory Period of Stria Terminalis Neurons in the Rat Brains." *Science* 204 (1979).

Klein, Renate. "Towards a Methodology for Feminist Research." In Gloria Bowles and Renate Klein, eds. *Theories of Women's Studies*. New York: Routledge & Kegan Paul, 1983.

Kohlberg, Lawrence. "A Cognitive-Developmental Analysis of Children's Sex-Role Concepts and Attitudes." In Eleanor Maccoby, ed., *The Development of Sex Differences*. Palo Alto: Standford University Press, 1966.

Kolata, G. "Math and Sex: Are Girls Born with Less Ability?" *Science* 210 (1980).

Kowal, D.M. "Nature and Causes of Injuries in Women Resulting from an Endurance Training Program." *The American Journal of Sports Medicine* (1980).

Kreitler, S., Kreitler, H., and Ziegler, E. "Cognitive Orientation and Curiosity." *British Journal of Psychology* 65 (1974).

Kuman, R. and Robson, Kay. "Previous Induced Abortion and Ante-Natal Depression in Primiparae: A Preliminary Report of a Survey of Mental Health in Pregnancy." *Psychological Medicine* 8 (1978).

Lacoste-Utamsing, Christine de, and Holloway, Ralph L. "Sexual Dimorphism in the Human Corpus Callosum." *Science* 216 (June 25, 1982).

Landsdell, Herbert. "A Sex Difference in Effect of Temporal Lobe Neurosurgery on Design Preference," *Nature* 1994 (1962).

Laws, Judith Long. Review of Eleanor Maccoby and Carol Jacklin, *The Psychology of Sex Differences*. *American Journal of Sociology* 83, 2 (September 1977).

Lawrence, Barbara. "Four-Letter Words *Can* Hurt You." In Robert Baker and Frederick Elliston, eds., *Philosophy and Sex*. Buffalo, New York: Prometheus, 1975.

Lear, Frances. "Now Is the Time to Get Organized." *The Nation* (December 12, 1980).

Leonard, Jonathan. "Anti-Discrimination or Reverse Discrimination: The Impact of Changing Demographics, Title VII and Affirmative Action on Productivity." Working Paper No. 1240, National Bureau of Economic Research, November 1983.

_____. "Splitting Blacks? Affirmative Action and Earnings Inequality Within and Across Races." Paper no. 1327, April 1984.

Levin, Michael. "Reluctant Heroes." *Policy Review* 26 (Fall 1983).

_____. Review of Robert N. Wennberg, *Life in the Balance*. *Constitutional Commentary* 3 (Summer 1986).

_____. "Reverse Discrimination, Shackled Runners, and Personal Identity." *Philosophical Studies* 37 (1980).

_____. "Theory Change and Meaning Change." *Philosophy of Science* 46, 3 (October 1979).

_____. "What Nairobi Wrought." *Commentary* (October 1985).

_____. "Why Homosexuality Is Abnormal." *The Monist* 67, 2 (April 1984).

_____. "Women as Soldiers—The Record So Far." *The Public Interest* 76 (Summer 1984).

_____. "Feminism: Stage Three." *Commentary* (August 1986).

Levine, Edward, and Saiova, Charles. "Biology, Personality, and Culture." *Israel Annals of Psychiatry and Related Disciplines* 12, 1 (March 1975).

Levy, Betty. "Do Schools Sell Girls Short?" In Judith Stacey, Susan Bereaud, and Joan Daniels, eds., *And Jill Came Tumbling After: Sexism in American Education*. New York: Dell, 1974.

Levy, Jerre. "Lateral Differences in the Human Brain in Cognition and Behavior Control." In P. Buser and Rougel-Buser, eds., *Cerebral Correlates of Conscious Experience*. New York: North-Holland, 1979.

_____. "Sex and the Brain." *The Sciences* (March 1981).

Liebman, M.H., and Zimmer, J.S. "Abortion Sequelae: Fact and Fallacy." In D. Mall and W.F. Watts, eds., *Psychological Aspects of Abortion*. Chattanooga, Tenn.: University Publications of America, 1979.

Lilla, Elizabeth. "Who's Afraid of Women's Studies?" *Commentary* (February 1986).

Lipper, S., and Feigenbaum, W.M. "Obsessive-Compulsive Neurosis after Viewing the Fetus during Therapeutic Abortion." *American Journal of Psychotherapy* 30 (1977).

Lowe, Marian. "The Dialectics of Biology and Culture." In Marian Lowe and Ruth Hubbard, eds., *Women's Nature*. New York: Pergamon, 1983.

Lynch, Frederick. "Affirmative Action, the Media, and the Public: A Look at a 'Look-Away' Issue." *American Behavioral Scientist* 28, 6 (July–August 1985).

_____. "Totem and Taboo in Sociology: The Politics of Affirmative Action Research." *Sociological Inquiry* 54 (Spring 1984).

Lyons, Phil. "An Agency with a Mind of Its Own: The EEOC's Guidelines on Employment Testing." *New Perspectives* 17 (Fall 1985).

Mascia, Daniel, Money, John, and Erhardt, Anke. "Fetal Femininization and Female Gender Identity in the Testicular Feminizing Syndrome." *Archives for Sexual Behavior* 1 (1971).

MacKinnon, Catherine. "Feminism, Marxism, Method, and the State: An Agenda for Theory." *Signs* 7 (1982).

MacLusky, N., and Naftolin, F. "Sexual Differentiation of the Central Nervous System." *Science* 211 (March 20, 1981).

McGuiness, Diane. "How Schools Discriminate against Boys." *Human Nature* 2 (February 1979).

McGuiness, Diane, and Pribram, Karl. "The Origins of Sensory Bias in the Development of Gender Differences in Perception and Cognition." In M. Bortner, ed., *Cognitive Growth and Development*. New York: Brunner/Mazel, 1978.

McGuiness, "An Analysis of the Cost of OFCCP's Compliance Activities and Its Impact, as Measured by National EEO-1 Forms." Washington, D.C.: Equal Employment Advisory Council, 1982.

Martin, Jane. Review of *New Essays in the Philosophy of Education*. *The Philosophical Review* 85 (October 1976).

Maxwell, Gerald, Rosenfeld, R., and Spilerman, S. "Geographical Constraints on Women's Careers in Academia." *Science* 205 (September 21, 1979).

Mead, Margaret. "A National Service System as a Solution to a Variety of National Problems." In Martin Anderson, ed., *The Military Draft*. Standford: Hoover Institution, 1982.

Metaxis, Theodore. "How Realistic Are Female PT Standards?" *Army Times* (March 21, 1977).

————. "WAC Training Needs Scientific Evaluation." *Army Times* (March 28, 1977).

Middleton, Thomas H. "Boys and Girls Together." *Saturday Review* (May 1980).

Minnich, Elizabeth. "A Devastating Conceptual Error: How Can We *Not* Be Feminist Scholars?" *Change* (April 1982).

Mintz, Ellen. "The Prejudice of Parents." In Florence Denmark, ed., *Who Discriminates against Women?* Beverly Hills: Sage, 1974.

Monagan, David. "The Failure of Coed Sports." *Psychology Today* (March 1983).

Money, John. "Origins and Options: Male Female Stereotypes." Presented to the American Association for the Advancement of Science Convention, 1975.

————. "Prenatal Hormones and Postnatal Sexualization in Gender Identity Differentiation." In J. Cole and R. Diensteiber, eds., *Nebraska Symposium on Motivation*. Lincoln: University of Nebrask Press, 1973.

————, Erhardt, Anke, and Mascia, D.N. "Fetal Feminization Induced by Androgen Insensitivity in the Testicular Feminizing Syndrome." *Johns Hopkins Medical Journal* 123 (1968).

Morris, Christopher. "Existential Limits to the Rectification of Past Wrongs." *American Philosophical Quarterly* 21 (April 1984).

Moskos, Charles. "Serving in the Ranks." In Martin Anderson, ed., *Registration and the Draft*. Stanford: Hoover Institution, 1982.

Moulton, Janice, Robinson, George M., and Elias, Cherin. "Sex Bias in Language Use." *American Psychologist* (November 1978).

Munich, Andrienne. "Seduction in Academe." *Psychology Today* (February 1978).

Nakatsuru, Ken, and Kramer, Donald L. "Is Sperm Cheap? Limited Male Fertility and Female Choice in Lemon Tetra (Pisces, Characidae)." *Science* 216 (May 14, 1982).

Ney, Phillip. "Relation between Abortion and Child Abuse." *Canadian Journal of Psychiatry* 24 (1979).

O'Brien, Mary. "Feminist Theory and Dialectical Logic." *Signs* 7 (1981).

Paley, Vivian Gussin. "Superheroes in the Doll Corner." *Natural History* (March 1985).

Partington, Geoffrey. "What History Should We Teach?" *Oxford Review of History* 6 (1980).

Perlman, Nancy, and Ennis, Bruce. "Preliminary Memorandum on Pay Equity: Achieving Equal Pay for Equal Work." Albany, N.Y.: Comparative Development Studies Center, Graduate School of Public Affairs, SUNY, 1980.

Perkins, Samuel, and Silverstein, Arthur. "The Legality of Homosexual Marriage." *Yale Law Review* 82 (1973).

Perskey, H. "Reproductive Hormones, Moods, and the Menstrual Cycle." In R.C. Friedman et al., eds., *Sex Differences in Behavior*. New York: John Wiley, 1974.

Pierce, Christine. "Natural Law, Language, and Women." In Vivian Gornick and Barbara Moran, eds., *Woman in Sexist Society*. New York: Mentor, 1971.

Platen, Owen. "Women in the Ranks." *Firehouse* (March 1983).

Raisman, G., and Field, P. "Sexual Dimorphism in the Neuropil of the Preoptic Area of the Rat and Its Dependence on Neonatal Androgen." *Brain Research* 54 (1973).

Rands, Marilyn. Summary of "Toward a Balanced Curriculum." Wheaton, Ill.: Wheaton College, 1981.

Reinisch, June, and Karow, William. "Prenatal Exposure to Synthetic Progestins and Estrogens: Effects on Human Development." *Archives for Sexual Behavior* 6 (1977).

Rosen, Sherwin. "Output, Income, and Rank in Hierarchical Firms." Stanford University, Working Papers in Economics no. E-81-10, August 1981.

Ross, Stephanie. "How Words Hurt: Attitudes, Metaphors, and Oppression." In Mary Vetterling-Braggin, ed., *Sexist Language*. Totowa, N.J.: Littlefield, Adams, 1981.

Rossi, Alice. "A Biosocial Perspective on Parenting." *Daedalus* 106 (Summer 1977).

_____. "Equality between the Sexes: An Immodest Proposal." *Daedalus* 93 (Spring 1964).

Sadker, David and Myra. "The One-Percent Solution? Sexism in Teacher Education Texts." *Phi Delta Kappan* (April 1980).

Salliday, Susan. Letter to the Editor. *Proceedings of the American Philosophical Association* 52, 6 (August 1979).

Sandler, Bernice. "A New Weapon in the Fight for Equal Pay." *Chronicle of Higher Education* (February 26, 1973).

Schilb, John. "Men's Studies and Women's Studies." *Change* (April 1982).

Schmidt, Frank. "Sex Differences in Some Occupationally Relevant Traits: The Viewpoint of an Applied Differential Psychologist." Washington, D.C.: Office of Personnel Management, 1972.

Seligman, Daniel. "Moving South on ERA." *Fortune* (January 11, 1982).

Shea, Steven, and Fullilove, Mindy Thompson. "Entry of Black and Other Minority Students into U.S. Medical Schools." *The New England Journal of Medicine* 313, 15 (October 10, 1985).

Shearer, Marie. "Solving the Great Pronoun Problem: Twelve Ways to Avoid the Sexist Singular." *Perspectives: The Civil Rights Quarterly* 13, 1 (Spring 1981).

Shepela, Sharon, and Viviano, Ann. "Some Psychological Factors Affecting Job Segregation and Wages." In Helen Remick, ed., *Comparable Worth and Wage Discrimination*. Philadelphia: Temple University Press, 1984.

Sher, George. "Justifying Reverse Discrimination in Employment." *Philosophy and Public Affairs* 4 (Winter 1975).

Shoemaker, Randall. "Women Officers Expected to Increase to 12%." *Army Times* (July 12, 1983).

Shulman, Alix. "Organs and Orgasms." In Vivian Gornick and Barbara Moran, eds., *Woman in Sexist Society*. New York: Mentor, 1971.

Siassi, Iradji, and Wesner, David O. "Women's Liberation and Two Adolescent Movements." *International Journal of Social Psychology* 20, 1/2 (n.d.)

Singer, Peter. "Ten Years of Animal Liberation." *New York Review of Books* (January 17, 1985).

Smith, I.M. "The Validity of Tests of Spatial Ability as Predictors of Success in Technical Courses." *British Journal of Educational Psychology* 30 (1969).

Smith, Lee. "The E.E.O.C.'s Bold Foray into Job Evaluation." *Fortune* (September 11, 1978).

Smith, Peter, and Connolly, Kevin. "Patterns of Play and Social Interaction in Pre-School Children." In N. Blurton-Jones, ed., *Ethological Studies in Child Behavior*. Cambridge: Cambridge University Press, 1972.

Snitow, Ann. ". . . And the Rest are Girls." *The Nation* (May 28, 1983).

Sowell, Thomas. " 'Affirmative Action' Reconsidered." *Public Interest* 42 (Winter 1975).

_____. "Weber, Bakke, and the Presuppositions of Affirmative Action." In Walter Block and Michael Walker, eds., *Discrimination, Affirmative Action, and Equal Opportunity*. Vancouver: Fraser Institute, 1982.

Stafford, R.E. "Sex Differences in Spatial Visualization as Evidence of Sex-Linked Inheritance." *Perceptual and Motor Skills* 13 (July–December 1961).

Steele, Diana. "Women in the Military: Substantial Barriers Remain." *Women's Rights Report of the American Civil Liberties Union* 3, 1 (Winter 1981).

Steinberg, Ronnie. "Identifying Wage Discrimination and Implementing Pay Equity Adjustments." In *Comparable Worth: Issue for the 80's.* Washington, D.C.: U.S. Civil Rights Commission, 1984.

Steinem, Gloria. "What Would It Be Like if Women Win?" In Wendy Martin, ed., *The American Sisterhood.* New York: Harper & Row, 1970.

Stewart-Clarke, Alison. "The Day-Care Child." *Parents* (September 1982).

Stiehm, Judith. "Women and the Combat Exemption." *Parameters* 10, 2 (June 1980).

Terman, L.M., and Tyler, Leona. "Psychological Sex Differences." In L. Carmichael ed., *Manual of Child Psychology.* Second edition. New York: John Wiley, 1954.

Thomson, Judith. "A Defense of Abortion." In Marilyn Pearsall, ed., *Women and Values.* Belmont, Ca.: Wadsworth 1986.

Tibbetts, L.S. "Sex Role Stereotyping in the Lower Grades: Part of the Solution." *Journal of Vocational Behavior* 6 (1975).

Tooley, Michael. "Abortion and Infanticide." *Philosophy and Public Affairs* 2 (1972).

Toran-Allerand, C. Dominique. "Sex Steroids and the Development of the Newborn Mouse Hypothalamus and Preoptic Area *in vitro:* Implications for Sexual Differentiation." *Brain Research* 106 (1976).

Trivers, R.L. "Parental Investment and Sexual Selection." In B. Campbell, ed., *Sexual Selection and the Descent of Man.* Chicago: Aldine, 1972.

Valian, Virginia. "Linguistics and Feminism." In Mary Vetterling-Braggin, ed., *Sexist Language.* Totowa, N.J.: Littlefield, Adams, 1981.

Vitz, Paul. "Religion and Traditional Values in Public School Textbooks: An Empirical Study." To appear as technical report NIE-G84-0012. Washington, D.C.: National Institute of Education, 1986.

———. "Textbook Bias Isn't of a Fundamentalist Nature." *Wall Street Journal* (December 26, 1985).

Walzer, Judith. "New Knowledge or a New Discipline?" *Change: The Magazine of Higher Education* (April 1982).

Wasserstrom, Richard. "On Racism and Sexism." In R. Wasserstrom, ed., *Today's Moral Problems.* Second edition. New York: Macmillan, 1981.

Webb, James. "Women Can't Fight." *Washingtonian* (November 1979).

Welch, Finis. "Affirmative Action and Its Enforcement." *American Economic Review* 71 (May 1981).

———. "Employment Quotas for Minorities." *Journal of Political Economy* 84, 4 (1976).

Whittlestone, W.G. "The Physiology of Bonding." *Child and Family* 5 (1976).

Wirtemberg, Judith, Klein, S., Richardson, B., and Thomas, V. "Sex Equity in American Education." *Educational Leadership* (January 1981).

Witelson, Sandra. "Sex and the Single Hemisphere: Specialization of the Right Hemisphere for Spatial Processing." *Science* 193 (1976).

Yarborough, Jean. "The Feminist Mistake." *Policy Review* 33 (Summer 1985).

Law Cases

AFSCME v. Washington. 578 FSupp 846 (1983).

Bakke v. University of California Regents. 438 US 265 (1978).

Berkman v. NYFD. 536 FSupp 177 (1982); 580 FSupp 226 (1983).
Brandenburg v. Ohio. 395 US 444 (1969).
Christiansen v. Iowa. 417 FSupp 423 (1976).
Continental Can Co. v. Minnesota, Minnesota S.C. (1980).
County of Washington v. Gunther. LW 2175, September 11, 1979.
Craig v. Boren. 429 US 190, 197 (1976).
DeFunis v. Odegaard. 416 US 312 (1974).
Dothard v. Rawlinson. 433 US 321 (1977).
Frontiero v. Richardson. 411 US 677, 684–86 (1973).
Fullilove v. Klutznick. No. 78-1007 (1980).
Griggs v. Duke Power Co. 401 US 424 (1971).
Grove City v. Bell. 459 US 1199 (1984).
Kyriazi v. Western Electric. 527 FSupp 18 (1982).
Lemons v. City and County of Denver. 620 F.2d. 228 (1980).
Lynn v. University of California. 656 F. 2d 1377 (1983).
Manhart v. Los Angeles. 403 US 702 (1978)>
Miller v. Bank of America. 20 FEP Cases 462 (9th Cir. 1974).
Mississippi v. Hogan. 458 US 718 (1982).
Norris v. Arizona. 671 F. 2d. 330 (1982).
Orr v. Orr. 440 US 268 (1979).
Owens v. Brown. 455 F Supp 291.
Pennsylvania v. Board of Trustees. 353 US 230 (1957).
Rostker v. Goldberg. 453 US 57 (1981).
Rios v. Enterprise Association Steamfitters Local 698. 501 F 2d. (2nd cir. 1974).
Schlesinger v. Ballard. 419 US 498 (1975).
United Steelworkers of America v. Weber. 443 US 193 (1979).

Newspaper Articles, Newsmagazines, Etc.

ACA News
      "Comparable Worth: A Few Thoughts on the Issue." February 1984.
Academe
      "Affirmative Action Plans." *January–February 1982.*
Boston Globe
      Knox, Richard. "Growing Pains for Women Cadets." June 19, 1978.
Chronicle of Higher Education
      "Scholars' Conflict in Sears Sex-Bias Case Sets Off War in Women's History." February 5, 1986.
Columbia Spectator
      "Panel Debates Women's Studies." January 31, 1986.
Daily News
      "Affirmative Action: Women Feel the Pinch." September 10, 1981.
      "Fem Cop Beaten on Subway." April 28, 1983.
      "Lawyer: Gender Cost Boy a Spot on HS Girls' Team." January 14, 1986.
Ford Foundation Newsletter
      15: February 1, 1984
      16: December 1, 1985.
Fortune
      Sharp, Susan. Letter. September 6, 1982.
MS
      "Gazette." May 1983.

Philadelphia Enquirer
   Mann, Judith. "Is It Really Discrimination, or Just Hazing?" June 3, 1982.
Newsday
   "State Panel Confirms Ruling: Girls Can Play on Boys' Teams." January 23, 1986.
Newsweek
   "Divorce American Style." January 10, 1983.
   "Victory for Quotas." July 9, 1979.
   "A Mother's Choice." March 31, 1986.
News Weekly (Australia)
   "How the Intact Family Is a Buffer against Poverty." August 18, 1982.
New York
   "Fire Retardant." February 7, 1983.
   Schaffran, Lynn Hecht. Letter. January 31, 1983.
   Stern, Ralph. Letter. January 31, 1983.
New York Times
   "Airline Must Pay Women $52 Million." December 1, 1982.
   "Child-Care Nonpolicy." January 1, 1983.
   "Comment on Passage of Equal Rights Constitutional Amendment." March 26, 1972.
   "Equal Rights Ruling for Auto Insurance Expected to Spread." October 23, 1984.
   "Group Examines Selection of Minority Judges." December 23, 1985.
   "Jersey Bars Schoolboys from Girls' Athletics." May 22, 1986.
   "Male Voice Carries Authority, Says Study." February 5, 1981.
   "New Parents Needs and Rights." January 1, 1986.
   "Old Images are Fading Rapidly." October 29, 1982.
   "Panel Reports Sex Disparity in Engineering." December 16, 1985.
   "Poll Says Most Women Perceive Job Sex Bias." August 15, 1982.
   "Regents to Let Girls Compete with Boys in the Contact Sports." January 14, 1986.
   "Scholars Face a Challenge by Feminists." November 23, 1981.
   "Single Mothers Join Suit to Enlist in the Military." December 25, 1984.
   "Study of Productivity Implies a Dim Future." May 31, 1981.
   "When the Boss Is a Woman." January 14, 1980.
People
   "What Does a Woman Need? Not to Depend on a Man." September 13, 1982.
Time
   "Every Man for Himself." September 7, 1981.
   "A Rousing *Oui* for Married Men." May 31, 1982.
Wall Street Journal
   "Sex-Discrimination Suit May Force Big Changes in Retirement Benefits." January 10, 1983.
   "Women Firefighters Still Spark Resentment in Strongly Macho Job." March 3, 1983.

Government Documents or Government-Funded Studies

A Comparable Worth Study of the State of Michigan Job Classifications: Executive Summary. Lansing, Mich.: Prepared by Arthur Young and Co. for the Office of Women and Work, Michigan Department of Labor, n.d.

Advance Report on Final Mortality Statistics. National Center for Health Statistics Report 33, 3, Supplement. June 22, 1984.

Affirmative Action in the 1980's: Dismantling the Process of Discrimination. U.S. Commission on Civil Rights, 1980.

"The Analysis, Design, and Installation of an Executive Compensation Program." Hay Associates, n.d.

Annual Report of the National Advisory Council on Women's Educational Programs. Washington D.C.: Department of Education, 1981.

Annual Report of the Women's Educational Equity Act Program 1980. Washington, D.C.: Department of Education, 1981.

Current Population Reports P-60, no. 129. Washington, D.C.: Bureau of the Census, Department of Commerce, 1980.

"The Economic Role of Women." In *Economic Report of the President.* Washington, D.C.: U.S. Government Printing Office, 1973.

Estimates of Worker Trait Requirements for 4000 Jobs. Washington, D.C.: U.S. Government Printing Office, 1957.

Federal Civil Rights: A Sourcebook. Subcommittee on the Constitution, Senate Judiciary Committee. November 1980.

Federal Employee Attitudes: Phase 2: Follow-Up Survey 1980. Washington, D.C.: Office of Personnel Management. Doc. no. 139-38-6. 1981.

FM-100-5. Revised August 20, 1982. U.S. Department of the Army.

Federal Register, 45, 219, sec. 1604.11. November 10, 1980.

Going Strong: Women in Defense. Washington, D.C.: Department of Defense, 1984.

Hearings before the Subcommittee on the Constitution of the Committee on the Judiciary on S.J. Res. 10. Part 1. Washington, D.C.: U.S. Government Printing Office, 1985.

Hearings on Reauthorization of the Vocational Education Act of 1963, Part 11: Sex Equity in Vocational Education. Washington, D.C.: U.S. Government Printing Office, 1982.

Job Opportunities for Women in the Military. GAO Report FPCD-76-26. Washington, D.C.: General Accounting Office, 1976.

Legislative History of Titles VII and XI of the Civil Rights Act of 1964. Washington, D.C.: Equal Employment Opportunity Commission, 1965.

News Release no. 522-83. Washington, D.C.: Office of the Assistant Secretary of Defense (Public Affairs), October 20, 1983.

Profile of American Youth: 1980 Nationwide Administration of the Armed Services Vocational Aptitude Battery. Washington, D.C.: Office of the Assistant Secretary of Defense (Manpower), March 1982.

Request for Proposal RFP-NIE-R-80-0018. Washington, D.C.: National Institute of Education, 1980.

Resources for Educational Equity, 1981–82. Newton, Mass.: Education Development Center, 1982.

Sadker, Myra, and Sadker, David. *Microskills Teaching for INTERSECT.* Washington, D.C.: National Institute for Education, 1983.

Social Indicators of Equality for Minorities and Women. Washington, D.C.: U.S. Commission on Civil Rights, 1978.

Social Security and the Changing Role of Women. Washington, D.C.: Department of Health, Education, and Welfare [now Health and Human Services], 1979.

Statement on Affirmative Action for Women and Minorities. Washington, D.C.: Equal Employment Opportunity Commission, October, 1977.

Title IX: The Half Full, Half Empty Glass. Washington, D.C.: Department of Education, 1981.

Voices of Women. Washington, D.C.: U.S. Government Printing Office, 1980.

Voting Rights Act: *Hearings before the Subcommittee on the Constitution of the Senate Judiciary Committee.* Washington, D.C.: U.S. Government Printing Office, 1983.

Welcome to Federal U., Campus #1037: Regulations and Academic Freedom. Washington, D.C.: House Republican Research Committee, April 22, 1980.

Women in the Federal Republic of Germany. Bonn: Federal Minister for Youth, Family Affairs, and Health, 1984.

Women in Society. Bonn: Press and Information Office of the Government of the Federal Republic of Germany, n.d.

"Women in Soviet Forces." *Air University Quarterly.* (January–February 1983).

Women in the Military: Hearings before the Military Personnel Subcommittee on the House Armed Services Committee. Washington, D.C.: U.S. Government Printing Office, 1981.

Women in the Army Policy Review. Washington, D.C.: Department of the Army, November 12, 1981.

Women in Traditional Male Jobs: The Experience of Ten Public Utility Companies. Washington, D.C.: U.S. Government Printing Office, 1978.

The Women's Rights Issues of the 1980's. Washington, D.C.: National Academy Press, 1985.

Women, Work and Wages. Washington, D.C.: National Academy Press, 1981.

Miscellaneous

"Multiple Productivity Indexes," 2, 3. Houston: American Productivity Center, February 1982.

Resolutions of the National Organization for Women. Indianapolis, Indiana: NOW, October 9, 1982.

Sports Participation Surveys. National Federation of State High School Associations.

"Statement on Educational Diversity, Equality, and Quality." Washington, D.C.: Office of Women in Higher Education, American Council on Education, June 1984.

"Women in Combat." Washington, D.C.: Women's Equity Action League, 1981.

Women on Patrol: A Pilot Study of Police Performance in New York City. New York: VERA Institute, 1978.

Index

Abortion, 285–91, 292; as self-defense, 287–8; subsidized, 294
Academic freedom, 199; its curtailment by feminism, 199–203
Adelson, Joseph, 200, 206
Adorno, T.W., 301, 306
Affirmative action, 102; compliance costs of, 121–2; in universities, 200 (*see* Quotas)
AFSCME v. Washington State, 132, 150f., 153
Aggression, 81; political implications of male advantage in, 90–2; sex differences in, 55, 74, 89ff.
Alaska, 192
Alcoholism, 7
Alexander, Clifford, 225, 227
All-female armies, their impossibility, 247
Allott, Gordon, 109
American Anthropological Association, 173
American Association of University Professors, its support of quotas, 201, 202
American Civil Liberties Union, 225, 240
American Compensation Association, 152
American Council on Education, 121
American Historical Association, 197
American Philosophical Association, 173
American Political Science Association, 173–4
American Psychological Association, 173
Analogy between minorities and women, 46; in civil rights law, 100–1
Andrews, Lori, 13
Androgen insensitivity, 80
Androgenization of fetal brain, 79ff.
Animal mating, 269
Arenson, Karen, 129
Assimilationist ideal, 17 (*see* Wasserstrom, Richard)
ASVAB tests, 99, 126–7
ATHENE Series, 21

Austin, J. L., 263
Autonomy, 165–8
Awakening, The te Chopin), 177

Babytalk, 270
Bacon, Francis, 288
Baker, Robert, 263
Baker, Susan, 95
Bakke v. University of California Regents, 115, 128
Bant, Bruce, 225, 248
Barakat, M. K., 96
Barash, David, 67, 77–8, 93
Barber, Benjamin, 6–7, 13, 40, 43, 52, 272, 292
Barrett, Nancy, 153
Basic Training, 227
Bau, Carlene et al, 14
Behavioral genetics, 164–73; and evolution of sex differences, 75–78 (*see* Sociobiology)
Benbow, Camilla, 96
Benbow, Camilla and Stanley, Julian, their study of mathematically precocious youth, 83–4; replies to, 84, 85, 86; on the soul, 72
Bennett, Johnathan, 263
Benston, Margaret, 26
Bergman, Barbara, 277
Berkman v. NYFD, 1–2, 3, 4, 6, 9, 13, 30
Bernard, Jessie, 18, 32, 49
Berry, Mary, 53
Berryman, Sue, 244, 246, 247
Berryman-Fink, Cynthia, 190
Bettleheim, Bruno, 172
Biehler, Robert, 171
Birdsong, Beth, 293
Biryukova, Alexandra, 50
Black crime and family disintegration, 284–5
Black Studies, 175, 176
Blackmun, Harry, 286

Bleier, Rith, 20, 26, 27, 32, 49, 61, 62, 69, 93, 96, 188, 191, 292; on Benbow-Stanley study, 84–5; on innateness, 61, 68
Block, Ned, 93
Block, Walter, 144, 154, 295
Blumrosen, Sheila, 133, 153
Bock, R.D., 68, 82, 95
Bowles, Gloria, 180, 190
Boys, excluded from girls' athletic teams, 215
Brainwashing, 28–9, 50
Braithewaite, R.B., 69
Brandenburg v. Ohio, 263
Braun, Rachel, 126
Brazelton, T. Berry, 295
Breeding territory theory, 268–9
Bridenthal, Renate, 293
Brooklyn College, 176
Broverman, Donald et al, 14
Brown University, 176, 202–3
Brownmiller, Susan, 6, 13
Brunch, Charlotte, 52
Bruner, Jerome et al, 255
Bryden, David, 13
Bunzel, John, 130, 144
Burns, Edward, 96
Burns, Heywood, 128
Byrne, Eileen, 10, 14

California, 192–3
Capital investment, effect of quotas on, 122 (*see* Quotas, their cost)
Carden, Muriel, 22, 49
Carnegie Corporation, 9
Carney, Larry, 248
Carpenter, Kathleen, 237, 248
Carrier, Allen, 248
Carrol, J.B., 263
Carter, Jimmy, 107, 227
Casagrande, J.B., 263
Cassedy, Ellen, 133f.
Central Committee of the Communist Party of the USSR, 91 (*see* Soviet Union)
Cerebral lateralization, 87 (*see* Sex differences, in cerebral morphology)
Change, 176
Chase Manhattan Bank, its sexual harassment policy, 262

Chayes, Antonia, 53, 208, 223, 224, 233, 237, 240, 248
Chessler, Phyllis, 292
Children, 168–71, 266, 270, 284 *et passim;* as equivalent to scholarly articles, 203; psychological health of, 8
Chivalry, 186, 246
Chodorow, Nancy, 25, 26, 37, 50, 90, 292
Choice, individual vs. collective, 36
Christiansen v. Iowa, 155
City University of New York, 200
Civil Rights Act, 100, 110 (*see* Title VII)
Civil Service Reform Act, 118f., 123f.
Clausewitz, 81, 238
Club Maria, 6
Coalition of Women's Art Organizations, 189
Coefficient of discrimination, 138
Cohen, Dorothy, 156, 171
Colgate University, 198
Colman, L.L., 295
Colt .45, 235
Columbia College, 173, 174
Combat, 224, 238–42; as a right, 240–1, 242; exclusion from, 226, *et passim*
Commission on Civil Rights, on statistical evidence, 43, 44
Comparable worth theory, 131–7; and back pay; for comparable effort, 133; for comparable social value, 133; compared to other economic regulations, 149–50; its costs, 150–1; and economic liberty, 150; its incentive structure, 151–2; and single mothers, 133; in the university, 200–1
Comparative superiority of the sexes, repudiated, 12
Compensatory justice, 112–3; feasability constraints on, 116f.
Competition, and sports, 219–220
Competition for women in the military, 243–4
Competitive ability, 115–6; and personal identity, 115–6
Congenital adrenal hyperplasia, 80
Connolly, Kevin, 95
Continental Can Co. v. Minnesota, 204
Contraceptives for minors, 287
Contratto, Susan, 292

Contribution to profit, as measure of economic value, 146-7 (*see* Comparable Worth)

Cook, Beverly, 189

Cooke, Cynthia, 221

Coordinating Committee of Women in History, 205-6

Coordination problems, 29

Corah, N.L., 82, 95

Corcoran, Mary, 154

Corpus callosum, 87 (*see* Cerebral lateralization *and* Sex differences, in cerebral morphology)

Council on Interracial Books for Children, 196

Craig v. Boren, 45, 53

Creationism, 66-7

Crime, 7, 284-5

Critical Period, 63 (see Sensitive Period)

Criticism, its objectivity, 186

Crowley, W.F., 96

Currency, constructed from barter, 154-5

Curriculum, its sex-neutrality in the university, 180

Czech national assembly, its composition by sex, 91

Daly, Mary, 14

Daly, Michael, 248

Daniels, W.L. et al, 221

Davis, Angela, 26

Dawkins, R., 93

Daycare, 282-5; subsidized, 282-3

de Beauvoir, Simone, 18, 25, 26, 49, 50

De Crow, Karen, 171

de Waal, Frans, 97

Deckard, Ruth, 190

Defense Advisory Committee on Women in the Services, 226, 231-2, 239

Defunis v. Odegaard, 215, 221

Democratic Party, 133, 153; its internal quotas, 92; its 1984 National Convention (*see* Comparable worth, for comparable social value)

Demographics, and military manpower, 229

Denison University, 175

Department of Labor, 200, 250 (*see* Office of Contract Compliance Programs)

Descartes, 191

Deterrence, 245-6

Devilbiss, M.C., 240-1, 249

Dewey, John, 201

Dialectic of Sex, The (Shulamith Firestone), 177

Dinnan, James, his incarceration, 202

Dinnerstein, Dorothy, 266, 292

Discrimination, 1-156; conceived as sin, 117, detected in classrooms, 163; institutional, its non-existence, 101 (*see* Merton, Robert); measured by effect, 141; its ontology, 117, perceptions of, 123-4; understood statistically, 100ff., 198; in workplace, 100 (*see* Oppression *and* Quotas)

Disdain for Women, society's alleged, 136-7

Dispositions, 58ff.; their time-dependence, 68

Divorce, 278-80

Dominance-aggression, 81 (*see* Aggression)

Dominican Republic, 80-1

Dothard v. Rawlinson, 47, 53, 100

Dowling, C., 38, 51

Dress codes, 198

Drives, 65; their context-sensitivity, 66

Drewett, R.F., 94

Drug abuse, 7

du Bois, Ellen, 207

du Bois, Susan, 186, 191

du Plessis, Rachel, 166

Duncan, Gregory, 154

Dworkin, Andrea, 13, 292

Dworkin, Gerald, 93

East Germany, 229

Eastern Bloc, 6 (*see* Wolchik, Sharon)

Eastman, Carol, 255, 263

Eccles, Jacqueline, 96

Effort, 148-9

Egalitarianism, 35, 297

Ehrenreich, Barbara, 38, 39, 51

Eisler, Riane, 54, 199, 293

Elementary and Secondary Education Act, 195

Emerson, Thomas, 53

Engels, Friedrich, 26-7

English Equal Opportunity Commission, 192

Ennis, Bruce, 152, 155
Enrollment in night school courses, female increase in, 7
Environmentalism, 20ff.; and statistics, 43–5; and the burden of proof, 74–5; as a form of Creationism, 66–7 (*see* Creationism); as the product of intimidation, 73; in S. Goldberg and M. Lewis, 72; in military personnel policy, 222ff.; its failure to ask "why," 73–4; its place in feminism, 31–32; scientific caveats emphasizing, 72–3
Environmentalist evasion of innate sex differences, 32–40, 67–87
Environmentalists, their attitude toward violence, 73
Equal Employment Advisory Committee, 121, 123
Equal Employment Opportunity Commission, 1, 109f., 121, 122, 127, 201; guidelines, 2; on statistical proportionality, 43, 44
Equal Employment Rights Act, 100
Equal Pay Act, 131, 152, 201
Equal Rights Amendment (ERA), 53, 226; and abortion, 47; and analogy between race and sex, 47; and "benign" discrimination, 47; and conscription, 47; and Fourteenth Amendment, 48; and homosexual marriage, 47; Betty Friedan on, 40
Equal Rights Amendment, Wisconsin State, 286
Equality, 35
Equality of opportunity, 3; and role models, 105; attitude towards as part of military training, 228; its relation to equality of outcome, 45 (*see* Equality of outcome)
Equality of outcome ("disparate impact"), 47–8
Equipment redesign, 120
Erhardt, Anke, 94, 95
Eskimo, 254
Etaugh, C., 171
Evidence, its transmission via theory, 77
Evolution, 75ff.; applied to man, 66; feminist misunderstanding of, 37; of function, 64–5; Goldberg and Levin on, 56

Executive Order 11246, 111
Exogenous progestogens, 80

Fact-value gap, 33–7
Failury to ask "why," 93; about mathematics, 86 (*see* Goldberg, Steven)
Fairy tales, 168
Falklands campaign, 242
Family, The, 25ff., 283–4; feminism on the, 267–8 *et passim;* and liberal democracy, 284–5; and policy, 271–2
Fausto-Sterling, Anne, 14, 49, 93, 176, 190
Federal Republic of Germany, 272
Federbush, Marcia, 171
Fee, Elizabeth, 187, 188, 191
Feedback, 100; in socialization, 56–7
Federal Property and Administrative Services Act, 110f.
Feigen-Fasteau, Brenda, 208, 213, 218–9, 221
Felsenthal, Carol, 49, 54
Female nurturance, its inclusive fitness, 75–6
Female-headed households, 278–9
Feminism, 16–49; attitude toward free market, 98ff.; and children's books, 160–3 (*see* Publishers' guidelines); and classroom protocols, 163–5; conditions on the definition of, 16–17; and coordination problems, 29–30; currency of, 8–11; defined, 43; defined abstractly, 20–1; defined operationally, 23–4; and divorce, 277–8; on the family, 267–8; as ideological belief system, 22–3; and the Left, 302–3; as a form of liberalism, 272–5; and Marxism, 26–7; "moderate," its non-existence, 41–3; Nineteenth-century, 4; possible pedagogical effects of, 168–71; possibility of moderate family agenda of, 272–5; and propaganda, 30–1; psychological origins, speculations concerning, 299–301; its scientific sterility, 74; "second stage," 38, 39–40; its success, speculations concerning, 302–5
Feminist guidelines (*see* Publishers' guidelines); mandatory in public schools, 192–5
Feminist Press, 10

Fennema, Elizabeth, 85
Fetal development, its continuity, 289–90
Fetus, its humanity, 287–290
Field, P., 79, 94
Firestone, Shulamith, 18, 26, 49, 266
Flax, Jane, 292
Ford Foundation, 9, 10, 21–2
Ft. Benning, 228
Ft. Jackson, 235
Ft. Monroe, 227
Fortune 500, 121
Fourteenth Amendment, 48
Fowler, William, 259
Fraiberg, Selma, 294
France, feminist legislation in, 10, 92
Free market, 135ff.; and economic value,
    145–6 (*see* Comparable Worth)
Freed, Mayer, 152
Freedom, 27–9
Freud, 38
Friedan, Betty, 7–8, 14, 37–8, 39, 40, 51,
    224, 247, 268, 271–5, 285, 293, 295
Frontiero v. Richardson, 24, 45, 49
Frye, Marilyn, 52
Fulenwider, Claire, 29, 52–3, 182
Fulilove v. Klutznick, 128
Fulilove, Mindy Thompson, 129
Function, 64–5
Fund for modern courts, their advocacy of
    quotas, 92

Garner, Judith, 267
Garrity, Mary Ellen, 211
Gaultier, Teofilo, 95
Gelb, Joyce, 52
General Accounting Office, 226
General Education Provision Act, 197
Generate-and-test strategy, 60, 68
Georgia, 4
Gibson, Charles Dana, 259
Gilberg, Sandra, 267
Gilligan, Carol, 38–9, 51, 89, 185
Girls on football teams, 215
Goal-directedness, 65, 69
Goals and timetables, 102–3 (*see* Quotas
    and Affirmative Action)
Gold, Doris, 15
Goldberg, Steven, ix–x, 51, 55–7, 81, 93,
    97, 217, 249

Goldberg, S. and M. Lewis, their environ-
    mentalism, 72
Goldberg v. Rostker, 105
Gombrich, Ernest, 189
Goodman, Nelson, 186
Goodman, Richard, 129
Gordon, Robert, 93
Gordon, Suzanne, 52
Gornick, Vivian, 13, 26, 128
Gorsky, Roger, 79
Gottfredson, Linda, 137, 153
Gould, James, 63, 68, 93
Gould, Stephen Jay, 66
Government, 29–30, 289 (*see* Coordination
    Problems)
Graham, Kennon, 171
Gray, Mary W., 96, 207
Greek, 257
Green, Gordon, 279
Greenawalt, Kent, 130
Greer, Germain, 26, 39, 50, 51
Grice, H.P., 263
Griggs v. Duke Power Co., 47, 54, 100
Grove City v. Bell, 128, 206
Grune, Joy Ann, 152
Guerrero, Luis, 95
Gunther v. County of Washington, 153, 155
Gwartney, James, 154

Hacker, Andrew, 155
Hacker, Helen, 49
Hall, Roberta, 189
Hamilton, William, 93
Hardin, Sandra, 191
Harris, Harold, 190
Harris, L.J., 95
Harris, Marvin, 93
Hartlage, L.C., 82, 95
Hartmann, Heidi, 126
Hatch, Orrin, 117, 121, 128
Hay Associates, 138–9
Height, 209
Hempel, Carl, 153
Herritability, relativized to environments,
    68
Hermaphroditism, 80–1
Hewlett, Sylvia, 292
Hidden-variable hypotheses, 85–6
Hier, D.B., 96

Hier-Crowley study, 83, 85
Hilbert, David, 86–7, 96
Hintikka, Merrill, 191
Historical objectivity, 182–4
History, 182–4
Hobbes, 17, 250
Hocutt, Max, 173, 189
Hodgskin, Thomas, 147
Hoffman, Carl, 142–3, 144, 154
Holloway, Ralph, 87f., 97
Home, Bryan, 221
Homomorphism condition, 153
Homosexual rights, 291–2
Homosexuality, 285–7, 291–2; and miscegnation, 286
Homosexuals compared to Jews and Blacks, 291–2
Hopi, 254
Hormones, 79–82
Housework, feminists on, 268
Howe, Florence, 26, 176, 179, 180, 181, 190
Hrdy, Sarah, 94
Hughes, V., 171
Hunter, John, 119, 129
Hunter-gatherer existence, 76
Hutner, Frances, 152, 153
Hypothalamus, 79
Hysteresis, 61

IBM, its discrimination against men, 102
Ice Cream Boy, 11
Ideology, 22; and propaganda, 30–1
Idiopathic hypogonadism, 83
Imperato-McGinley, Julianne, 80–1, 95
Impossibility, defined, 35
Inclusive fitness, 65; defined, 69
Individual liberty, 78
Innate drives as obstacles, 38, 100
Innate Sex differences, 55–92; and justice, 128; and wage disparities, 144–5; as "small," 32–3
Innateness, 55–67; defined in terms of learning, 57–9; dispositionality of, 57–8 (see *Dispositions*); relativity to stimuli, 59; reinforcement of, 59–60; relation to environmental triggers, 61–4; relation to learning, 60–1; of structure, 64–5; tests for, 61–2

Insanity, 7
Instinct, 64
Institute for Research on Public Policy (Canada), 10
Instruction, its non-political character, 181
Insults, 257–8
Intention and meaning, 258, 263
Intrinsic economic value, its non-existence, 146–9
Iowa, section 257.25 of its code, 193–5
Israel, 89; women in its military, 228–9
Issues in Feminism (Sheila Ruth), 177

Jacklin, Carol, 36, 37, 51, 74, 81, 88, 95, 97
Jagger, Alison, 19, 49
Janeway, Elizabeth, 50, 68; on children's greed, 266
Jealousy, 268–9
Jenkins, Lulu, 221
Job surveys, 137–41; their reliability, 138–9
Johnson, Lyndon, 107, 111
Jones, Beverly, 293
Justice, 16–7

K-selected species, 76–7
Kagan, J., 85, 96
Kaiser Aluminum, 108
Kalamazoo College, 176
Kamin, Leon, 62, 68
Karow, William, 80, 95
Karplus, Robert, 96
Kayers, Evelyn, 294
Keller, Evenly Fox, 188, 191
Kelley, Joan, 26
Kemble, Penn, 155
Kendrick, K.M., 94
Kessler-Harris, Alice, 207
KGB, 228
Kibbutzim, 57
Killing/letting die distinction, 288–9
Klein, Renate, 180, 186, 190, 191
Knox, Richard, 247
Kohlberg, Lawrence, 14
Kolakowski, D., 82, 95
Kolata, G., 96
Konner, Melvin, 78, 89, 94
Korb, Lawrence, 232

Kowal, D. et al, 221, 248
Kramer, Donald, 94
Kreitler, H., 97
Kreitler, S., 97
Kuhn, T.S., 93
Kuman, R., 295
Kung, 90; homicide among, 97
Kyriazi v. Western Electric, 128

Labor Department, 117, 120; Office of
    Contract Compliance Programs of, 108,
    110-2 (*see* Quotas)
Labor productivity by race and sex, 120
Lacoste-Utamsing, Christine, 87f., 97
Lakoff, Robin, 263; on sewing, 255-6
Landsdell, Herbert, 96
Language and thought, 252-7; and forms
    of life, 255
Lapidus, Gail, 97
Lawrence, Barbara, 263
Laws, Judith Long, 19, 49; on scientific
    method, 74
Leacock, Eleanor, 26
League of Women Voters, 286
Lear, Frances, 285
Learning, 59 (*see* Innateness); not involved
    in love at first sight, 63; as presuppos-
    ing innate mechanisms, 63-64; pro-
    grammed, 63-4
Legal rights, their tenacity, 298
Lemons v. City and County of Denver, 155
Leonard, Jonathan, 117, 118, 120, 121,
    123, 129
Lesbianism, its place in feminist scholar-
    ship, 185
Levin, Michael, 14, 50, 93, 127, 128, 248,
    263, 294, 295, 296
Levine, Edward, 295
Levy, Betty, 171
Levy, Jerre, 96
Lewis, 263
Lewis, M., 97
Lewontin, Richard, 62, 66, 68, 84; the
    abysmal level of his argumentation, 69
Libertarian feminism, 30
Lilla, Elizabeth, 190
Lindsay, Cotton, 144
Linguistic change, 259-60
Linguistic reform, 252
Lippman, Peter, 171

Locke, 68; his obfuscations, 62
Loco parentis doctrine, 204
Lopiano, Linda, 221
Lorber, Judith, 287
Lord, Sharon, 232, 233
Lovejoy, Arthur P., 201
Lowe, Marian, 19, 32, 49, 209, 221
Luce, R. Duncan, 50
Lynch, Frederick, 93, 128
Lynn v. University of California, 199, 206
Lyons, Phil, 127

Maccoby, Eleanor, 34, 36, 37, 51, 74, 82,
    88, 95, 97
Mack, Murray, 119, 129
MacKenzie, A.C.C., 173, 189
MacKinnon, Catherine, 6, 8, 23, 26, 187
MacLusky, N., 94
MacMillan, Susan, 51
Mahler, Margaret, 294
Maintenance of order, 11-12
Majority rule, 298-9
Male bonding, 244-5
Male conspiracies, 24-5; and women's
    wages, 133-5
Male dominance and military discipline,
    243 (*see* Sex differences)
Management, effect of quotas on, 123
Manhart v. Los Angeles, 14, 45
Mann, Judith, 249
Marriage, feminists on, 268
Martin, Jane, 172
Marxism and feminism, 26-7 (*see* Femin-
    ism, and Marxism); and relativism, 189
Mascia, Daniel, 80, 95
Massachusetts, Chapter 622 of its code,
    192
Maternity leave, mandatory, 30
Maxwell, Gerald, 154
McCloskey, Pete, 230
McCormick, Michele, 248
McGuiness, Diane, 67, 88, 89, 95, 97, 172
McGuiness, Kevin, 117
Mead, Margaret, 90, 230, 248
Medical College Admissions Test, 119
Memoirs of An Ex-Prom Queen (Alix Kate
    Shulman), 177
Menstruation, 235
Menzies, Heather, 14
Merit and quotas, 102-3

Merton, Robert K., 101, 127
Metaxis, Theodore, 248
Meyer-Blauberg, Heino, 95
Middleton, Thomas, 220
Midgley, Mary, 93
Military, Friedan on female presence in,
39–40
Military Entrance Physical Strength Capa-
city Test (MEPSCAT), 231, 233
Mill, John Stuart, 17, 25, 34, 49, 52
Miller v. Bank of America, 204, 207, 261
Millett, Kate, 4, 13, 18, 26, 32, 49, 50, 51
Mincer, Jacob, 142
Minnich, Andrienne, 204
Minnich, Elizabeth, 179–180, 187, 190
Mintz, Ellen, 28–9, 50
Miscegnation compared to homosexual
marriage, 286
Missiles, ground launched cruise and MX,
229
Mississippi v. Hogan, 45, 53
Mitchell, Juliet, 25, 26, 50
Moché, Dinah, 171
"Moderate" Feminism, 3
Moens, Gabriel, 127
Monagan, David, 220
Mondale, Walter, 153
Money, John, 80–2, 94, 95; his sympathy
for feminism, 81–2
Morale, effect of quotas on, 123f.; mili-
tary, 242ff.
Moran, Barbara, 13
Morgan, Robin, 13
Morris, Christopher, 49
Moskos, Charles, 238, 249
Motherhood, feminists on, 266–7
Moulton, Janice et al, 263
"Ms.", 256–7
Ms Foundation for Women, 10
Munich, Andrienne, 207
Murray, Charles, 295

National Advisory Council on Women's
Educational Programs, 203–5
Naftolin, F., 94
Nagel, Ernest, 69
Nahmey, Patricia, 153
Nairobi Conference, 10, 14
Kakatsuru, Ken, 94
Nation, The, 286

National Academy of Science, 137
National Committee on Pay Equity, 10,
132f.
National Educational Association, 9
National Endowment for the Humanities,
110, 197
National Institute for Education, 196–7
National Opinion Research Center, 99
National Organization for Women (NOW),
10, 18, 208, 222, 225; its Lesbian
Rights Resolution, 285
National Organization of Office Workers,
131f.
National Park Ranger Service, 119f.
National Science Foundation, 98
National Weather Service, 250
Nativism, burden of proof on, 74–5; nature
of debate concerning, 55
Nelson, Jeanne-Andree, 202
Norris v. Arizona, 45, 46
New Jersey Highway Patrol, 236
New York Board of Education, 237
New York Department of Sanitation, 238
New York Life Insurance Co., 9
New York Marathon, its prize structure,
214
New York Police Department, 235–6, 237;
its Sargeant's test, 129
Newmann, Winn, 135
Newsweek, 108, 127
Newton on induction, 74
Newton's principle, 67
Ney, Phillip, 295
Norgren, Jill, 294
Northwest Airlines, 151
Norton, Eleanor Holmes, 110
Null results, 71–2

Oakley, Anne, 50, 280
Objectivity, its rejection by feminist scho-
lars, 186–9
O'Brien, Mary, 293
Office on Contract Compliance Programs,
121 (*see* Labor Department)
Office of Personnel Management, 121,
123f.
Olds, Sally, 171
O'Neill, June, 126, 141–2
Operational doctrine of US Army, 239
Operationalization, 71–2

Oppen, Mary, 267
Oppression, 31-3, 66-7
Organizational objectives, 147-8 (see Comparable Worth)
Orgasm, 271 (see Penile penetration)
Orr v. Orr, 45, 53, 278
Orwell, George, 253, 298
Ostriker, Alicia, 267
Our Bodies, Ourselves, 177
Owens v. Brown, 248
Oxytocin, 79

Paley, Marion, 52
Paley, Vivian Gussin, 67
Papalia, Sharon, 171
Parental Investment theory, 75ff., 269 (see Sociobiology)
Parents, 10
Partington, Geoffrey, 183, 190
Peguy, Charles, 11
Penile Penetration, 265, 271 (see Orgasm)
Pennsylvania State Equal Rights Amendment, its effect on insurance, 46
Pennsylvania v. Board of Trustees, 48
Pensions, 45-6
People, 9-10
Perkins, Samuel, 53
Perlman, Nancy, 152, 155
Perskey, J., 94
Petchesky, Rosalin, 20, 49, 292
Peterson, R.E., 95
Philosophy and Sex (Jane English), 178
Pierce, Christine, 34
Pirie, Robert, 248
Platen, Owen, 248
Plato, 297, 298
Player, Mack, 119, 127
Pogrebin, Letty, 25, 50, 172, 209, 221, 266, 272, 292
Policy-capturing scales, 139-40
Polsby, Daniel, 152
Pomeroy, 191
Population, 281
Pornography, 5-6
Porter, Sylvia, 276
Positive feedback, 57 (see Feedback)
Preferences, x
Pregnancy, 265-6; in the military, 235
President's Advisory Committee for Women, 197

Preventive measures, 106
Pribram, 88, 89, 95, 97
Primatology, 12
Probability, 74-5; assessments of, as crystallized in stereotypes, 42
Productivity, 122-3
Project on the Status and Education of Women, 9, 174-5
Pseudohermaphroditism, 80-1
Public education, 194-5
Public funds as inducements to discrimination, 111f.
Public Works Act, 110
Publishers' guidelines, 157-60, 173

Quality time, 280
Quine, W.V.O., 255
Quotas, 98-126, et passim; arguments for, 104-7; costs, 117-24; defined, 101; in electoral politics, 92; in France, 10, 92; as indemnification, 106-7, 112-7; and justice, 105; and merit, 102-3, 119-20; in the military academies, 226-7; as preventive measures; 105-6; racial distinguished from gender, 104, 112f.; and rights, 124-5; and role models, 104-5; and sports, 215-7; and Title IX, 198 (see Title IX)

Racial minorities used in definition of "feminism," 23-4
Racial minorities, their well-being, 7
Raiffa, Howard, 50
Raisman, 79, 94
Ramey, Estelle, 50-1
Rands, Marilyn, 190
Rape, 6
Rapp, Rayna, 26
Rauschenberger, John, 129
Reagan, 4, 11, 232
Reagan Administration and women in the military, 227-8
Reed, Evelyn, 26
Reed, John, 154
Reference, 251, 259-60
REFORGER War games, 228
Regression, mathematical meaning of, 137-8
Reinforcement, 59; self-, 65-6
Reinisch, June, 80, 95

Relativism, philosophical, 187–8
Reskin, Barbara, 126
Retrodiction, 77
Reverse discrimination, 102–3
Rehnquist, William, 128
Rhodes scholarships, 213
Rich, Andrienne, 266
Richards, Janet, 19, 32, 34, 48, 104–5,
    128, 268, 281, 292, 295
Rights of the unusual, their non-existence,
    42–3
*Rios v. Enterprise Ass'n Steamfietters Local
    698,* 108, 128
Rogan, Helen, 238
Role models, and quotas, 104–5
Rose, Steven, 62, 68
Rosen, Max, 247
Rosen, Sherwin, 123, 130
Rosenfeld, Rachel, 154
Rosenthal, Michael, 189
Ross, Stephanie, 263
Rossi, Alice, 21–2, 30–1, 49, 93, 293
Rostker v. Goldberg, 127
Rothman, Stanley, 93
Rowbottam, Sheila, 26
Rudolph, Marguerita, 156, 171
Rueda, Enrique, 296

Saad, L.G., 96
Sacremento Unified School District, 193
Sadker, David and Myra, 171, 172, 206;
    on First Amendment, 199; their
    protocols, 163–5
Salliday, Susan, 263
San José, 151
Sandler, Bernice, 14, 190, 207
Saxon, John, 169–70, 172
Sayers, Janet, 51
Scaling, 139
Schafer, Alice T., 207
Schafran, Lynn Hecht, 13
Schemta, 62–4 (*see* Innateness)
Schiffer, Stephen, 263
Schilb, John, 190
Schlesinger v. Ballard, 45, 53
Schmidt, Frank, 119, 127, 129
Science as viewed by feminists, 188–9
Science, its consistency with observation,
    71
Scientific Revolutions, 71

Seaman, Barbara, 292
Searle, John, 263
Sears, Roebuck & Company, 207
Seattle Firefighters' Union, 236, 237–8
Section 1604.11 of Federal Register, 260ff.
Self-defense, 288
Sensitive periods (*see* Critical Periods), 64
Separation anxiety, 270
Sex, 264–6, 269, 271 (*see* Orgasm *and*
    Penile penetration)
Sex Desegregation Centers, 197
Sex differences, 70–92; and homeostasis,
    34–5; and vocational behavior, 99–100;
    and compensation, 144–5; in aerobic
    capacity, 210; in aggression, 39, 55,
    89ff.; in aggression, as a female handi-
    cap, 37–8, 39, 100; in cerebral mor-
    phology, 87–8; in fat/muscle ratio, 210;
    in hearing 82; in interhemispheric com-
    munication, 87; in mathematics, 82–7;
    in morality, 38–9; in orientation to
    objects, 88–9; in sociality, 88–9; in
    spatial-visualizing ability, 82–3; in
    throwing, 210–1; in upper body
    strength, 210; in verbal skills, 82, 88–
    9; in vocalization, 82; relevant to ath-
    letic performance, 209–12; relevant to
    combat, 23ff.; statistical nature of, 12–
    3; their marginal effects, 216–7; their
    reinforcement by society, 59–60, 68
Sex equality in sports, 208–9, 212–14; and
    justice, 213–4, 217; as psychic
    fulfillment, 218–20
Sexual harassment, 243
Sex integration of the military, its costs,
    234–5
Sex linkage, 82–3, 95
Sex roles, their origin, 24–5
Sex stereotypes, 5, 70; their acceptance by
    children, 8; as compensible injuries,
    113
Sex-typing of jobs, 137
Sexual division of labor, 24, 270–1
Sexual harassment, 260ff.; and power,
    204–5
Sexual receptivity in human females, 94
Sexual selection, 76 (*see* Sociobiology *and*
    Parental investment theory)
Sexual slang, feminist displeasure with,
    256

Shackled runner analogy, 107, 111, 115–6
Shaefer, Alice, 96
Shalala, Donna, 126
Shea, Steven, 129
Shearer, Marie, 263
Sher, George, 127, 128
Sherman, Julia, 85
Shepala, Sharon, 136
Sheper, Joseph, 67
Shoemaker, Randall, 248
Shulman, Alix Kates, 265, 292
Siassi, Iradji, 306
Sidell, Ruth, 294
Sifton, Charles, 2
Silverstein, Arthur, 53
Simplicity, 67
Singer, Peter, 49
Small Business Administration Act, 110
Smith, I.M., 96, 127
Smith, John Maynard, 93
Smith, Lee, 154
Smith, Peter, 95
Snitow, Ann, 171
Social Security System, 275–7
Social value, 146 (*see* Comparable worth)
Society, its flexibility, 61
Sociobiology, 62–3, 69; its ad hocness
    denied, 76–7
Sommerhof, G., 69
Southern Alambama University, 200
Soviet Union, 26, 50, 89, 91–2; women in
    the military forces of, 228, 229
Sowell, Thomas, 118, 154
Spilerman, Seymour, 154
Sports and Quotas, 215–7 (*see* Quotas)
Stafford, R.E., 82, 96
Stage, Elizabeth, 96
Standards, military, 223–4 (*see* 235–8)
Standards, in the protective services, 235–8
Stanley, Julian, 96
State action, and race and sex differences,
    125
Statistics and environmentalism, 43–5 (*see*
    Environmentalism)
Steele, Diana, 247
Steinberg, Ronnie, 150, 151, 155
Steinem, Gloria, 18, 26, 49, 51
Stephen, Beverly, 129
Stereotypes, as expressing spontaneity,
    42–3

Stern, Ralph, 49
Stewart-Clarke, Alison, 283, 294
Stiehm, Judith, 238, 249
Stockton State College, 202
Stoller, Robert, 294
Stony Brook College Society for Women in
    Philosophy, 185 Storer, W.O., 96
Stratton Bill, 226
Stratton, Joanna, 190
Strawson, P.F., 263
Strict liability, 261–2
Stroup, Richard, 154
Structure, innateness of, 64–5
Strula, Erasmo, 95
Suicide, 57
Supreme Court, its environmentalism, 45;
    on pensions, 8–9
Surfacing (Margaret Atwood), 177
Sweden, 89
Symons, Donald, 93

Tanner, Jack, 153
Television, 9
Tenure, 201–3
Terman, L.M., 127
Theory and observation, 77
Third Latin American and Caribbean
    Feminist Encounter, 10
Thomas, Claire Sterling, 127
Thomson, Judith, 295
Tibbetts, L.S., 14
Tiger, Lionel, 67
Time, 118, 123, 127; its discrimination
    against white males, 103
Title VII of the Civil Rights Act, 104, 132,
    237, 260; secs. 703(a)(2) and 703(j) of,
    108–9; and military manpower, 233
    (see *Discrimination*)
Title IX of the Educational Amendments to
    the Civil Rights Act, 195, 197–9, 214,
    260; and the First Amendment, 198–9;
    and quotas, 198; and athletics, 198–9,
    214–5ff.; effects on boys' teams, 217
Title X of US Code, 226
Tobias, Sheila, 86, 96
Tomizuka, Carl, 86, 96
Tooley, Michael, 295
Top-down hiring, 119–120
Toran-Allerand, Dominique, 79, 94
Toys, as explanatory factors, 85–6

Training, 148
Tranquilizers, 7
Translation, 254–5
Tree, Marietta, 247
Treiman, Donald, 153
Trivers, R.L., 93
Tsongas, Paul, 53 (*see* Equal Rights
    Amendment)
Tuchman, Barbara, 184, 190
Turner's Syndrome, 96
Tyler, Leona, 127

Uniform Guidelines on Employee Selec-
    tion, 44
United Nations Convention on the Elimina-
    tion of All Forms of Discrimination
    Against Women, 19
US Employment Service, 99
US Navy, its retention of present cockpit
    design, 9
United Steelworkers v. Weber, 108, 128
Universal National Service, 230
University of California at Berkeley, 200
University of California at Irvine, 199
University of Indiana, 178–9
U'ren, Majorie, 166, 172
Use of Statistics in determining
    discrimination, 1 (*see* Discrimination)

Valian, Virginia, 263
Vandenberg, Steven, 68
VERA Institute of Justice, 104, 237
Viability of fetus, 289 (*see* Abortion)
Victims, their identification, 113ff.
Victorians, compared to feminists with
    regard to attitudes about sex, 260
Vitz, Paul, 162, 171
Viviano, Ann, 136
Vocational Training, 277–8

Wage gap, 131; factors determining, 138–
    9, 141–5; and innate sex differences,
    144–5; and marriage, 141ff.; and
    motivation, 142–3; as a residual, 140–
    1; for single Canadian women, 141 (*see*
    Comparable Worth)
Waltzer, Judity, 175, 190
Washington v. Gunther, 132
Wasserstrom, Richard, 17, 49 (*see* Assimi-
    lationist ideal)

Wattenberg, Gen, 294
Webb, James, 249
Weber, Brian, 108
Wegner, Judity, 47–8
Weidenbaum, Murray, 129; his rule, 1212
Welch, Finis, 117, 129
Welniak, Gordon, 279
Wennberg, Robert, 295
Wesner, David O., 306
West Point, discrimination against men at,
    233
White, Richard, 223
Whittlestone, W.G., 295
Whorf, Benjamin, 263; his hypothesis,
    253ff.
Williams, Harrison, 109
Williams College, 178
Wilson, E.O., 78, 93
Wirtemberg, Judy, 163, 171
Wisconsin Civil Liberties Union, 286
Wisconsin Women's Network, 286
Witelson, Sandra, 69, 87
Witt, Mary, 153
Wittgenstein, Ludwig, 255
Wolchik, 97
Wolgast, Elizabeth, 40, 51; on innate sex
    differences, 40; on affirmative action,
    40
Wolof, 255
Women, 1–306; in All Volunteer Force,
    226 *et seq;* and combat, 238–242; not a
    historical group, 182; and sexual revo-
    lution, 304–5; and work, 272, 280–2
Women in the Military (WITA), 231–3, 235
Women's Educational Equity Act Program,
    195–7
Women's Equity Action League, 10, 222,
    231–2, 233
Women's Movement, The (Ruth Deckard),
    178
Women's Studies, 175–82; their
    justification, 179–82
Women's wages; and herding, 135–6; and
    workforce participation, 141 *et passim*
    (*see* Comparable Worth)
Working mothers, 282–3

XYZ affair, 142–3

Yarborough, Jean, 249

Youth Sports Institute of Michigan State
    University, 210

Zaretski, Eli, 26

Zelizer, Viviana, 154
Ziegler, E., 97